Transatlantic Connections

THE IOWA WHITMAN SERIES | Ed Folsom, series editor

Transatlantic Connections

Whitman U.S., Whitman U.K.

M. Wynn Thomas

UNIVERSITY OF IOWA PRESS | IOWA CITY

University of Iowa Press, Iowa City 52242

Printed in the United States of America

Design by April Leidig-Higgins

http://www.uiowa.edu/uiowapress

The University of Iowa Press is a member of Green Press Initiative and is committed to preserving natural resources.

Printed on acid-free paper

Library of Congress Cataloging-in-Publication Data
Thomas, M. Wynn.
Transatlantic connections: Whitman U.S., Whitman U.K. / by M. Wynn Thomas.
p. cm.
Includes bibliographical references and index.
ISBN 0-87745-925-8 (cloth)
1. Whitman, Walt, 1819–1892—Appreciation—England. 2. Whitman, Walt, 1819–1892—Criticism and interpretation—History. 3. Whitman, Walt, 1819–1892—Appreciation—United States. 4. National characteristics, American, in literature. 5. American poetry—Appreciation—England. 6. English literature—American influences. 7. Whitman, Walt, 1819–1892—Influence. I. Title.
PS3237.4.G7.T47 2005
811'.3—dc22 2004058850

05 06 07 08 09 C 5 4 3 2 1

To Dan Aaron and Helen Vendler

"That they are there!"—George Oppen

Contents

A Note on the Text

All quotations from Whitman's work are taken, unless otherwise indicated, from Justin Kaplan, ed., *Walt Whitman: Poetry and Prose* (Library of America; New York: Viking Press, 1982).

Acknowledgments

My debts are as sincerely acknowledged as they are many. I am particularly grateful to the following for advice, information, and assistance: Peter Black, Tony Brown, Larry Buell, Edward Cadava, Jasmine Donahaye, Caroline Franklin, Ed Folsom, Ezra Greenspan, George Hutchinson, Dan Lewis, Liu Shusen, Frank Murphy, Rob Penhallurick, Claire Powell, Glyn Pursglove, John Turner, Huw Walters, Daniel Williams, and John Worthen. As for the dedicatees, Dan Aaron and Helen Vendler, I owe them the inestimable gift of friendship, of support, and of scholarly guidance.

Some sections of this study have appeared in a different form elsewhere. I am grateful to those associated with the following for permission to mine those sources here: *American Literary History*, the *Anglo-Welsh Review*, *The Cambridge Companion to Walt Whitman*, the *Walt Whitman Quarterly Review*, *Walt Whitman: The Centennial Essays*, and *Whitman East and West: New Contexts for Reading Walt Whitman*.

Invited lectures at several conferences and institutions encouraged and enabled me to complete this work. I should particularly like to thank Peking University, Indiana State University (Terre Haute), the University of Iowa, and the University of Saint John in New Brunswick.

And it is with this as it has been with all my books: but for my wife and daughter (with help from the cat) it would not have been possible. Diolch o'r galon, unwaith yn rhagor.

Preface

In February 1889, Walt Whitman was sent a letter by his friend Ernest Rhys, describing his "stay in a cottage . . . overlooking the pleasant sweep of Swansea Bay." He was, he informed Whitman, about to set off "for a two or three days tramp through the remote sea-slopes of Gower. The coast scenery is said to be very fine. We expect to reach the lonely headland of Worm's Head some time tomorrow."[1] This book has been written on those very Gower cliffs and is in some ways a sequel to a previous study, *The Lunar Light of Whitman's Poetry*, published over fifteen years ago.[2] When completing that book, I stumbled on a letter Whitman had sent, along with a copy of *Leaves of Grass*, to the manager of a tin-plate works on the banks of the River Loughor; the study where I wrote *Lunar Light* overlooked that very river and the site of the old works.

Such coincidences serve to emphasize the carry of Whitman and his poetry; his uncanny ability to appear in distant places and cultures; his powers of transit. That, then, is one implication of the title of this volume. It first instances, and then attempts to explore, the paradox that the work of one who was a mid-nineteenth-century New Yorker, through and through, has somehow been able not only to pronounce itself indefatigably to be international in outlook but also to be accepted as such by non-American cultures. This is the first reason for the peculiar dual structure of this book.

The second reason is related but somewhat different. Much of the best work on Whitman over the last three decades has been informed by a sense of his historical cultural situation, and my own publications have been a minor contribution to this approach. Fertile though it has undoubtedly proved, however, there are now signs that the law of diminishing returns may be beginning to take inexorable effect. In structure, therefore, this book is intended to suggest, if not to trigger, a transition in Whitman studies from the historical to new approaches. The aim of the second section of this study is to exemplify a less localized, implicitly exceptionalist, reading of Whitman in this age of globalization, when scholarship has taken to speaking of a postnationalist stage in American studies. It attempts to consider him instead in a wider perspective of comparison and response, and may therefore be understood in the context of transatlantic studies.[3] Insofar as the last three chapters are concerned with the reception of Whitman by foreign cultures, they seek to build on the important work already accomplished by such scholars as Betsy Erkkila and Walter Grünzweig and in such composite volumes as *Walt Whitman and the World*.[4] To examine Whitman in a British context is scarcely, of course, to undertake a radically innovative approach; nor does this study set an obvious example for the kind of wide-ranging scholarly work that now needs to be undertaken—there would seem to be a clear case, for instance, for setting Whitman's American nationalism against the extensive background of the nation-building programs of nineteenth-century Europe and Latin America.[5] But culturally limited and conservative though the second section may be when viewed in this context, it does attempt an innovative approach to the reception of Whitman in Britain by raising issues of intercultural transfer that hopefully have a wide cultural resonance.

Being personal, the third reason for this book's structure is less interesting but needs to be admitted. A section of chapters dealing with the response of U.K. writers to Whitman's work allows me, in the end, to satisfy a personal need to bring together the two halves of my divided world, to find a point of convergence between my extensive studies in the Welsh-language and English-language literatures of Wales and my longstanding work as a Whitman scholar. My first language is Welsh, and it remains the language of my most intimate and formative life experiences. I was five when I began learning (or rather assimilating) English at school, and thereafter it became the first language of my maturing mind, even as Anglophone culture threatened to dominate the very different Welsh-language culture of my home upbringing. Cut, then, to my later schooling; for it was then that I began to form a companionable image of American culture, although it is intriguing now to remember that two GIs bound for the Normandy beaches and God knows what sort of fate were billeted on my parents in the Rhondda when my mother was expecting me. Who knows what effect the rhythms and tones of their voices may have had on my prenatal, embryonic self? Certainly, it was the distinctive foreign music of American speech that later opened my mind, as well as my imagination, to the phenomenon of America during my university years.

But it was with my secondary schooling that I gained an unlikely sense of solidarity—of common cause—between my Wales and America. This began to form when certain of my teachers who were English, and had relatively recently returned from the war, regaled the class with tales of how the Yanks were only Johnny-come-latelies who had contributed little to Allied victory. Since the contempt made evident in these stories seemed similar to the disdain those same teachers displayed toward the Welsh-language culture of many of their pupils, a connection was made in my young mind between Wales and America; and that instinctive sense of alliance between the two countries has persisted in me to this day, despite all the decisive evidence my mature mind is now capable of mustering to disprove it.

I also felt that in the Leavisite anti-Americanism of the English studies culture to which I was exposed at my supposedly Welsh university I could recognize the condescending tones of my grammar school teachers who, I had become convinced, spoke from an Anglocentric imperial Britain's resentment at total eclipse by this new world power on the block. Another feature of the postwar British higher education system, however, was the introduction of American literature, and particularly American studies—courtesy, in many instances, of (politically motivated) financial assistance from the U.S. government. And in following a special seminar course in American literature, I felt strangely at home as I did not when studying the mainstream "English" syllabus. With an American (George Dekker) as my initial inspirational teacher, there was, of course, no way in which the irreducible foreignness of the material could escape me. And yet, I related to it with a strange degree of intimacy, discerning in it—no doubt distortingly—many features corresponding to those in my Welsh-language literary culture. In the long, enveloping sentences of Faulkner's prose, enacting the way in which the southern present was, to adopt Henri Bergson's celebrated remark, nothing but the past gnawing into the future, I recognized my own literary culture's constant, ambivalent awareness of almost two thousand years of history; in Allen Tate's characterization of Emily Dickinson as the product of a transition from a socio-intellectual world saturated with religious belief to a new, skeptical secularism I recognized the condition of the poet in post-Nonconformist Wales; in the powerful social fictions of the prose realists, I recognized some of the political concerns of that "heroic" industrial culture of the south Wales coalfield valleys of which I was myself a product; in the open, abiding concern of American literature (and literary criticism) with the issue of national identity I recognized the very symptom of what was later to be called the postcolonial condition that similarly afflicted modern Welsh society; the beleaguered cultural politics of the southern fugitives was, for me, all too recognizable, and tempting, an option; in Ellison's *Invisible Man* and all the other cultural products of black America I (most presumptuously) sensed a subaltern experience passingly akin to my own; and, in a final act of significant self-recognition, I warmed to Whitman's exhilarating myth of social egalitarianism. It is scarcely necessary to add that all these instances of recognition were, I now realize, based on naive, highly selective, and glamorizingly distorted views of both the United States and Wales. Indeed, the reading of America favored by Welsh-language culture (of which I am a product) has overwhelmingly concentrated on its role as cultural imperialist. It is, for instance, no wonder that Philip Jones Griffiths (the longest serving president of the Magnum Photo Agency) became a great world-renowned photographer of the Vietnam War. As Murray Sayle has noted, Griffiths's famously lacerating images derived from his passionate identification, as a Welsh-speaking artist, with the hideously suffering people of a small culture being pulverized into extinction by an Anglophone superpower. He was faced with "a daily visual reminder that a big, powerful country had come to make war in (or, as Philip said, on) a small, insignificant one."[6]

Nevertheless, my adolescent impressions went deep, proved resiliently formative, and continue(d) to shape my responses to American literary culture. Indeed, many of those impressions remained unconsciously operative when I came to write *The Lunar Light of Whitman's Poetry*. The book's attempt to place Whitman in his sociopolitical context would not have been possible had it not been for my interest in, and respect for, the long proud history of socialism in Wales, dating back to the times of Robert Owen—Welsh but so often mistakenly styled Scottish: Whitman himself wrote of "his shrewd Scotch face, but benevolent look."[7] It is a history, particularly as enacted in the remarkable proletarian "civilization" of industrial south Wales, that also secretly informed the influential theorizing of my fellow Welshman, Raymond Williams, upon whose work I drew at several key points in that study. In retrospect, I am fully aware that the viewing of Whitman and his America through such a lens—an act made seductively easy by the fact that, at the time of writing, I had not actually visited the United States—proved, from the scholarly point of view, to be an experience at least as disabling as it was enabling.

In its first section, this present study returns to the kind of issues that concerned me in that earlier volume: Whitman's poetry is successively read as the peculiar product of new urban experience, a kind of unique inscription of New York politics, a textual attempt to unify national consciousness, a poetic exercise in building labor relations, and a singular record of intimate war experience. The second section, however, attempts to open up a different line of inquiry, into the phenomenon of cultural translation. I feel licensed to use such a term, even when (save in the case of Welsh-language culture, to which I pay some attention) the acts of cultural transfer that are considered do not, in fact, involve a transfer between two different languages. My authority for this practice is George Steiner, whose *After Babel: Aspects of Language and Translation* is surely one of the twentieth century's most brilliant and seminal works on those subjects.[8] In registering his concern with interpretation ("as that which gives language life beyond the moment and place of immediate utterance or transcription"), Steiner suggestively observes that "the process of diachronic translation inside one's own native tongue is so constant, we perform it so unawares that we rarely pause . . . to note its formal intricacy" (29). He also recognizes that "literature, whose genius stems from what Éluard called *le dur désir de durer*, has no chance of life outside constant translation within its own language" (30). In the second section of this study I therefore record, and attempt to explain, salient examples of the transfer (or intercultural, but intralingual, translation) of texts, and the examples I consider range from poetic imitations of Whitman's poetry to critical interpretations of it, not least by creative writers.

Whitman U.S.

One. A Tale of Two Cities

"I was born," wrote Dylan Thomas, "in a large Welsh town at the beginning of the Great War—an ugly, lovely town, or so it was and is to me."[1] To come from Thomas's city of Swansea is to know what wonderfully creative liars poets can be about their hometowns, and so to be naturally inclined to wonder how reliable a guide Whitman would have been to the place whose spirit he addressed in *Leaves of Grass* as "you lady of ships, you Mannahatta, / Old matron of this proud, friendly, turbulent city" (418). In his Manhattan could be found, he added, "[a] million people—manners free and superb—open voices—hospitality—the most courageous and friendly young men" (586). Visitors to mid-nineteenth-century New York would, surely, have done far better to listen to the "Advice to Strangers" offered in the journal *Life Illustrated.* "Every great city," they would have learned, "is a sort of countryman-trap . . . [Avoid] wandering about the streets or parks unnecessarily in the evening. The degrading confession and warning is necessary, that New York is one of the most crime-haunted and dangerous cities in Christendom."[2] This streetwise writer has got the very literal measure of his New York—shrewdly estimating, for instance, the distances between various streets so that a traveler could calculate how much a hackman should charge. The reliable, hardheaded guide turns out, of course, to be none other than Walt Whitman himself, in another of his bewilderingly frequent "changes of garment." "Don't be in haste," this wily Walt continues, "to make city street acquaintances. Any affable stranger who makes friendly offers is very likely to attempt to swindle you as soon as he can get into your confidence. Mind your own business, as we said before, and let other people mind theirs" (141). How different this recommended conduct is from the trustful tryst of glances that he celebrates in his poetry: "as I pass O Manhattan, your frequent and swift flash of eyes offering me love, / Offering response to my own—these repay me, / Lovers, continual lovers, only repay me" (279).

Faced with such barefaced and unmitigated contradictions, some readers have concluded there was not one Walt Whitman, but two. On the one hand, the time-bound figure of the hack journalist from New York, more or less routinely reflecting the political prejudices and reporting the social ephemera of his own particular period; on the other, the suprahistorical poet of an imaginary Mannahatta who addressed not so much his own age as all American (and all-American) time and whose best work was inspired by private, rather than public, affairs. Yet in those sections of *Specimen Days* in which Whitman outlines his anti-Wordsworthian version of the growth of a poet's mind, he pointedly insists that not only the plays and operas he saw but also "those Broadway omnibus jaunts and drivers and declamations and escapades undoubtedly enter'd into the gestation of *Leaves of Grass*" (703). Equally entranced by both plays and omnibuses, Whitman was doubly stagestruck, and an understanding of the mixed historical sources of his mongrel talent informs and invigorates the best recent biographical and cultural studies of his work. Other more specialized studies have concentrated on demonstrating how contemporary fads and interests from phrenology to photography and from hydrotherapy to linguistic theory are inscribed in his poetry.[3] Implicit in these forms of study is the belief that his journalistic prose and his poetry are two fundamentally different but essentially complementary ways of mediating the modern, of articulating by means either direct or symbolic the character of life in his time. Whitman's poetic Mannahatta is, then, the Siamese twin of his journalistic New York: the one image is linked internally and inseparably to the other, and the point at which they are joined is the point at which they jointly connect with history. Or, to change the image, Whitman may be thought of as building his New York up, through his different kinds of writing, on several different levels. This was a strategy appropriate to a New York that, as it increasingly assumed its distinctive modern shape as a vertical city, gave rise to the Otis elevator at the very same time that it produced the dumbwaiter, a device that emphasized anew, in the context of this ostensibly democratic city, the distance between life above and life below stairs.

In recent times, Peter Conrad has been an incomparable cartographer of Whitman's Mannahatta. He notes how walking the streets is for Whitman a way of "dispensing sociability," how "the commonality of experience" in his city "makes all parts of one another."[4] In one place Whitman find his own electric body the very image of the galvanic body politic; in another he "establishes an official religion for New York: a metropolitan pantheism . . . [refusing] to distinguish between the city's vital plenum and the profusion of nature" (12). Possessed by the spirit of the collective, Whitman "writes chorally, not lyrically" (15). Concerned for the city's good name, he rebaptized it "Mannahatta," the original Algonquin term for "the place encircled by many swift tides and sparkling waters," and in 1860 he wrote a poem to explore "what there is in [that] name" (585).

As an account of the poetry with the history left out, Conrad's corruscating commentary on this "urban ode," or "prayer to a place," could hardly be bettered. But "Mannahatta" also resounds with the name that *is not* spoken—the prohibited term "New York" that bespeaks the actual proscribed historical identity of Whitman's city. By midcentury that identity was troubling many inhabitants who were seeing the population grow over eightfold in forty years, from 120,000 in 1820 to not far off a million people by 1860. Between 1840 and 1859, immigration into the United States rose to a total of 4,242,000, and 428,000 of these newcomers entered New York in 1848.[5] By 1858, two-thirds of the male population was foreign-born, a development that provoked violent reactions from nativists and others who resented the disappearance of an America they took to be more socially stable, economically equitable, and ethnically homogeneous. The remarkable, if gross, vitality of midcentury New York was the product of socioeconomic upheavals that had split the old order apart, on the one hand producing an increasingly dominant class of capitalists, plutocrats, and political bosses, while on the other bringing into being a vast new world of subordinated, degraded labor that extended from boardinghouses and sweatshops to the teeming tenements of the slums and the ragpickers' shacks on the fringes of a city with the highest death rate in the civilized world.[6]

By 1850, New York was the undisputed "commercial emporium" for the whole of the United States.[7] It was uniquely situated to benefit both from the large and growing market for goods throughout the populous Northeast and from its role as exporter of the South's cotton. As trade expanded, downtown New York was virtually emptied of inhabitants and given entirely over to business. The city indulged in an orgy of tearing down and building up. Lower Broadway ceased to be a place for "solid residences" and became "the great stage for the display of metropolitan wealth and success, a great 'agglomeration of trade and fashion, business and amusement, public and private abode, churches and theatres, barrooms, and exhibitions, all concentrated into one promiscuous channel of activity and dissipation'" (*New Metropolis*, 95). Memorable monuments to luxury included the new hotels, with their gaslights, plumbing, and steam heat, and the giant stores of which A. T. Stewart's was unquestionably the most imposing. Besotted with Broadway, Whitman boasted that "it is never still" but also noted that the only person to be seen there after midnight was a "lonely man with an enormous birch broom" who slowly worked his way from side to side as he cleared away the accumulated muck and filth of the day (*New York Dissected*, 122). Here can be glimpsed the dark underside of all that glitter.

Even as the residences of New York, removed from the downtown area, raced up the island, 58 percent of the inhabitants remained penned into the fifteen downtown wards. For a long period, the bulk of the working population couldn't afford to ride on the omnibuses that linked downtown to the much more salubrious new regions; but it was those very horse-drawn omnibuses that were to serve Whitman as a kind of modern urban equivalent to Pegasus. Writing in 1881, he was to indulge in a litany of nostalgic praise to the vanished omnibus companies—"The Yellow-birds, the Red-birds, the original Broadway, the Fourth Avenue, the Knickerbocker"—of long ago (702). And as he recounted the names and exploits of the drivers—"Broadway Jack, Dressmaker, Balky Bill, George Storms, Old Elephant, his brother Young Elephant (who came afterward), Tippy, Pop Rice, Big Frank, Yellow Joe, Peter Callahan, Patsy Dee, and dozens more" (703)[8]—he was consciously proclaiming himself to be the Homer, the aboriginal epic poet, of his city.

Although these downtown areas occupied less than 9 percent of Manhattan, they were twice as densely populated as London's notorious East End. Only a tiny fraction of the population earned an adequate living wage. By 1855, 30 percent of the workforce were little better than laborers or clerks, while another 30 percent worked as menials in the new factory system. Whitman's reaction to these consequences of the shift to a market economy was a creatively ambivalent one—a doubleness of response that partly reflected his divided social allegiance. He came originally from an artisanal background and so had firsthand experience of the workingmen's futile collective effort, particularly during the 1830s, to prevent the incoming phase of capitalism from disabling them socially, economically, and politically. However, he went on to become a journalist and was therefore professionally attuned to progress even as he vigorously campaigned for reforms. His class position was correspondingly ambiguous, a fact of considerable importance for one's understanding of every aspect of his writing.

Reporters are, after all, nothing if not connoisseurs of the contemporary, and New York newspapermen of the 1850s relished the challenge to make sense of a kaleidoscopically changing social scene. That by midcentury New Yorkers needed new guides to their city is evident from the enthusiasm with which in the summer of 1846 they flocked to view a carved wooden model of New York. Executed by E. Porter Belden and 150 assistants, it was a monumental thirty feet square, cost $120,000, and was adorned with a magnificent ornamental Gothic canopy decorated with oil paintings of the leading business establishments of the city. The painted model included perfect facsimiles of every building, down to the smallest detail of window frame and fence color.[9] Since the model was advertised complete with testimonials to its accuracy from the Common Council of New York, editors of city newspapers, an assortment of the clergy, and thousands of the principal citizens, it was clearly the business establishment's effort to ensure that their city incarnated them as they had incarnated it. This Whitmanesque way of putting it is quite appropriate. The New York City of that time was a contested space, both literally and symbolically, and through his poetry Whitman participated in the contest. "Were I to you as the boss employing and paying you, would that satisfy you?" (355), Whitman inquires in "A Song for Occupations," in a sentence part of whose significance derives from the fact that the very word "boss" came into English in the New York of the 1820s and was coined (from the Dutch "*baas*") to reflect a key aspect of the new class relationships that a new capitalism was introducing into the world of work (*Gotham*, 516). "The learn'd, virtuous, benevolent, and the usual terms, / A man like me and never the usual terms," Whitman continues. "Terms" here equals salary, equals legal contract between employer and employee, equals social relations, and of course equals style of spoken and written discourse. In his poetry Whitman was out to change the terms *on* which contemporary New York conducted its affairs by changing the terms *in* which it spoke, and thus thought, of life.

The new phase of capitalism that had transformed the modest town of Whitman's childhood into a gigantic city was blatantly powered by money. In his 1869 study, *The Great Metropolis*, Junius Henri Browne irritably complained that "[t]he first impression one gets of . . . New York, is, that everything in [it] is for sale. . . . All signs, all faces, all advertisements, all voices, all outward aspects of things, urge you to buy."[10] It was i-dollar-try agreed Whitman as he tried, in "Song of Myself," to rewrite contemporary life in the hieroglyphics of the soul. Words themselves seemed in his city to be coined only for commercial use. One enterprising business, he noted, avoided the prohibition on advertising in Broadway by printing its slogans on a perambulated red umbrella (*New York Dissected*, 120). Whitman's own restless patrolling of the streets of Mannahatta in "Song of Myself" and countless other poems can be partly construed as his attempt to challenge the sovereignty of that umbrella; to cover its print with his own different imprint; to redistribute the type, in his printer's fashion, in order to retextualize his city. No wonder that printing had become New York's fastest growing industry. In a city where some 90 percent of the population was literate, signs proliferated everywhere, constituting what has been described as a "pageant of text" (*Gotham*, 679). Appropriately enough, an 1862 cartoon, "The Bill-Poster's Dream," featured a huge billboard plastered with messages that, "creating a patchwork of odd and quintessentially urban juxtapositions," read like a parody of Whitman's famous paratactical lists: "People's Candidate for Mayor . . . The Hippopotamus." "Miss Cushman will . . . take Brandreth's Pills." "The American Bible Society will meet at the . . . Gaieties Concert Saloon." "$100 Bounty Wanted . . . A Jewess for one Night Only" (*Gotham*, 680).

It was the age of advertising—the first advertising agencies opened in the 1840s—and Whitman as poet was quick to practice this key art form of the new urban capitalism. But his advertising of self and publications was for the sake of a poetry that undermined the commercial order rather than reinforcing it. Every word of *Leaves of Grass* 1855 testifies to the truth of that definition of the English language Whitman offered in its preface: "It is the powerful language of resistance" (25). And in an adjacent passage he included "the treatment of the bosses of employed people" in the list of practices and products that could not "long elude the jealous and passionate instinct of American standards. Whether or no the sign appears from the mouths of the people, it throbs a live interrogation in every freeman's and freewoman's heart after that which passes by or this built to remain. Is it uniform with my country? Are its disposals without ignominious distinction? Is it for the evergrowing communes of brothers and lovers?" (25). In this passage, Whitman commits himself to the work of opposing the ubiquitous "signs" of the inequitable commercial society of his day and of realizing instead the unspoken "sign" that throbs in the hearts of a people yearning for a society governed by "democratic" forms of relationship. It is in order to advance "the evergrowing communes of brothers and lovers" that "I give the sign of democracy" (50).

But Whitman remained as loath simply to condemn the new capitalism as he was uncertain of how to reform it, and so he strove to redeem it in terms that ran the risk of seeming simply to condone it. Many of his greatest poems were the outworking of these tensions, but by 1860 the strain had almost got beyond him. To see Whitman the poet as contesting the very streets of New York with the business establishment is to discern deeper levels of meaning in the poem "Mannahatta." Conrad shows how Whitman finds in the aboriginal name a new founding myth for the city, but he does not mention the reigning myth that this was designed to displace. For instance, according to the anonymous author of a *Sketch of the Resources of the City of New York* (1827), "the city of New York had its origin in commercial interests," since it was established in 1609 as a trading post for the Dutch West India Company.[11] Other early American settlements were established as asylums for political and religious refugees and "could be considered as consecrated by the presence of a great moral principle," but "the first settlement of New York was without the benefit of any moral impulse of this nature" (9–10). It has been said that folklore starts with the fact and ends with the symbol. The fact of New York's commercial origins passed into folklore through the story that Manhattan Island had been purchased from the Indians by Peter Minuit for trinkets worth sixty guilders or twenty-four dollars. The Dutch governor had intended to take only "as much land as could be contained by a bull's hide and then proceeded to shave the hide into a razor-thin thong that enclosed several score acres."[12] In "Mannahatta," Whitman attempts to take the island away from the heirs of Minuit and to restore it, spiritually speaking, to its aboriginal owners without evicting the present occupants. He repossesses it, as it stands, with all its "[n]umberless crowded streets, high growths of iron, slender, strong, light, splendidly uprising toward clear skies" (585). Buildings are here not made; they grow spontaneously toward the sun. Every cunning word in this verbal diorama is designed to supply commercial New York with a moral impulse straight from nature: no wonder Stephen Spender teasingly accused Whitman of wanting to "spiritualize real estate."[13]

Underlying all these rival attempts at possessing New York through authoritative representation of it was the problem of how to image this new New York at all.[14] So radically had the physical and social topography of the city been altered that this precipitated what a historian of urban culture calls "a crisis of perception." He goes on to note that "particular writers . . . establish[ed] new genres and tropes" in order to "reformulate . . . the cultural understandings that gave meaning to individual and collective life in the metropolis." These new literary formations emerged, he adds, as "new . . . visual and social experience were textualized by writers."[15] And for years before Whitman reconstituted poetry partly by reconstituting his city in poetry, he worked in the new media of urban representation.

Popular newspapers were in several senses the order of the day.[16] Literally the product of that new piece of urban technology, the steam printing press, they not only provided the age, as it demanded, with a glimpse of its own accelerated grimace but also reflected in the very layout of their pages the intelligible pattern, as well as the content, of contemporary social life. Whitman was particularly interested in this new order. To his eye, a newspaper seemed the typographic equivalent of that other notable invention of his time, the department store. "The great daily journals," he writes, "have a department for all. The business man glances anxiously at his own corner of the sheet to mark the quotations of stock or the fluctuations of trade; the . . . [litterateur] turns to his own particular column for reviews or announcements of new books; . . . the unemployed, to the columns of wants," and so on.[17] It is a fascinating image that reveals Whitman's obsession with the problem of how to bring the whole of his increasingly stratified society together into a single space so as to give the illusion, at least, of a common life. Typography was used to rearrange the topography of a socially segregated city in which industrious German immigrants settled in the *Kleindeutschland* of the northeastern wards, the rich lived in a few streets surrounding Washington Square, and the destitute were packed into the noxious Five Points district. That was the only region of the city where races mingled: otherwise, blacks were confined to separate ghettos. But there is hint of the constraints upon their freedom—they were, for instance, excluded from even those blue-collar occupations, such as those of cartmen, that required a municipal license (*Gotham*, 546ff.)—in Whitman's hymn to a black man's physique in "Song of Myself": "The negro holds firmly the reins of his four horses . . . / His blue shirt exposes his ample neck and breast and loosens over his hipband" (37).

Between 1834 and 1840, no fewer than thirty-five penny dailies made their appearance in New York and revolutionized the style of reporting the city. As editor of such penny press publications as the *New York Aurora*, Whitman took great pride in the mass readership they were able to reach and scoffed at the pretensions of the up-market sixpenny papers:

> Had we in America a monarchical or an aristocratical form of government, it is very probable that the sixpenny papers might exercise a greater sway than the small ones. As things are, however, the converse of this supposition is really the case. Here, the mass of men comprise the governing classes, "the people." And while the cheap papers have influence with this mass, they can well afford to let their inflated neighbors parade their (somewhat laughable) claims to exclusiveness and the top of the ladder. (*Journalism*, 124)

The new discourses the popular papers developed amounted to new images of urban life, and this service of self recognition, offered to the masses for the first time in something like their own language, was symbolized by the *New York Sun*'s gesture of collecting money from readers to set the Statue of Liberty literally on its feet by providing it with a pedestal. Insufficient attention has, unfortunately, been paid to the sheer range of popular discourses Whitman quite consciously employed during his long career in prose and poetry. A fellow journalist of the period commented on the variety of journalistic styles:

> Talk of the power of abstraction and individualization in Shakespeare—what is it, compared with the same power as manifested by the accomplished New York journalists? . . . [S]uppose your Shakespeare had been called upon to hammer out a leader for the *Courier* and *Enquirer* on Monday; condense an almanac for the *Journal of Commerce* on Tuesday; revolutionize Cuba for the *Sun* on Wednesday; prove in the *True Sun* of Thursday that Martin Van Buren was no Democrat; conduct the country through a "tremendous crisis" in the *Herald* on Friday, and correct all the blunders of the *Express* for *The Tribune* on Saturday. . . . [W]hat think you the world would ever have heard of the Bard of Avon?[18]

In addition to the styles of Whitman's journalism—in the plural because they were several, depending on the character both of the paper and of the subject—there is the fascinating variety of styles in his letters, each chosen to match the correspondent. Out of his journalistic experience came also his experiments with popular literary conventions of the day. His sensationalist bestseller of 1842, the temperance novel *Franklin Evans*, belonged to what has been called "a new literary genre of urban commentary."[19] Three hundred forty urban novels were published between 1840 and 1860, compared to thirty-eight in the previous sixty years, and around midcentury, authors vied with one another to show which was the wickedest American city. Whitman interestingly balances the lurid depictions of low life, from dreary boardinghouse to squalid brothel, with Franklin Evans's dream of "one of the greatest cities" in an oneiric America. Entering the city during a great festival ("business seemed to be suspended—and each one given up to the spirit of the time"[20]), he discovers that the populace is celebrating its newly won freedom from vassalage to "The Snake-Tempter": "[N]ow man is free! He walks upon the earth, worthy the name of one whose prototype is God! We hear the mighty chorus sounding loud and long. Regenerated! Regenerated!" (*Uncollected*, 202). Whitman was a connoisseur of urban spectacle, the street theater of the city's pageant of life, but he was also disturbed by the way New York festival was being manipulated, and corrupted, by the new world of financial and political management, as will be seen in chapter 2.

One of the favorite figures used to describe the city in the new urban novels was that of deception or concealment, which came with the warning, as Franklin Evans puts it, "to question the reality of many things I afterward saw" (*Uncollected*,

136). Mystery and misery, secrecy and iniquity—these were the terms commonly twinned in urban description, and Whitman the journalist himself resorted frequently to such rhetorical strategies.[21] In "Faces," however, the poet Whitman inverts this value of concealment so that the trope comes instead to signify the mystery of hidden worth that he, unlike William Blake, marks in every disfigured face he meets. The city's tricksiness consists of its efforts to entice him to despair rather than any attempt it makes to flatter and deceive. This aspect of his work has sometimes been desocialized by being attributed to the influence of transcendentalism, but it reads differently if we study it next to George G. Foster's 1850 novel *Celio: Or, New York Above Ground and Under-ground.* The hero of that novel is Captain Earnest, a philanthropic reformer who disguises himself as the leader of a band of thieves. Eventually he unmasks himself to reveal that he has used all the stolen money to buy the gang an idyllic house in the country, complete with workshops, where they can turn over a new leaf. His men are overwhelmed by his revelation, not least because they feel that he has saved them from "utter self-contempt" and recognized their secret inner worth. When Captain Earnest breaks the news to his band of thieves, "their countenance underwent a kind of change, as if a dead odious mask were to become by degrees a living, placid, agreeable, and loving face."[22] "Why," asks Whitman, "what have you thought of yourself? / Is it you then that thought yourself less? / . . . / (Because you are greasy or pimpled, or were once drunk, or a thief, / . . . / Do you give in that you are any less immortal?)" (356). What Foster's novel allows us to see is the social grammar of this rhetorical move. So intractable a problem did the new vast urban society of crime and squalor represent that writers could only manage it by resorting to the reassuring, simplifying myth that these brutalized masses were inwardly craving to be transformed and reclaimed. Unlike Captain Earnest, however, Whitman did not trust to dramatic short-term ameliorative measures.

The regions of vice and squalor, as depicted by the new school of New York writers, amounted to more than a murky urban underworld: they were secret social coordinates that could provide the initiated with a wholly new map of the supposedly respectable life of the city. For instance, all roads, even Broadway, secretly led to the fashionable door of "The Wickedest Woman in the City, Madame Restell the Abortionist"—a fascinating subject because of "Her Long and Shuddering Career, Her Notorious Trial and Acquittal, Her Dreadful Secrets and Practices, and Her Palace in Fifth Avenue."[23] As Graham Clarke has persuasively demonstrated, Whitman wrote some disturbingly Poesque poems about a "city of dreadful night."[24] Clarke reads "The Sleepers" as a surrealistic urban text, present in even the first edition of *Leaves of Grass* as the darkly perverse antitext of "Song of Myself." "The Sleepers" treats psychological disturbance and social decay as versions of each other as Whitman wanders all night not *with* his vision (as in "Song of Myself") but *in* his vision: "I turn but do not extricate myself, / Confused, a past-reading, another, but with darkness yet" (546). Clarke talks about Whitman's anguished exploration of a compulsively imagined landscape where there is a disturbing fit between his own psychic obsessions, his private fetishes, and "the urban *lumpen* of a diseased and decaying body politic" (105). Here the metropolis is recreated as a necropolis—"The wretched features of ennuyés, the white features of corpses, the livid faces of drunkards, the sick-gray faces of onanists" (542)—and Whitman's own great cosmos-creating voice is reduced to a stammer.

Some small part, at least, of this dark complex of feelings found more conventional and rational expression in Whitman's editorial attack on social reformers in 1858:

> If there be balm in Gilead for the correction of abuses and the healing of moral and physical evil, it can be found in no such little doses as you make specialties and hobbies withal. The origin of evil is a question that has puzzled all developed thoughtful minds through all the ages, and it is so deep and dark and mystic a problem that not the wisest of them has ever been able to peer behind one fold of the thick veil. (*I Sit*, 44–45)

In a rhetorical move that is surely closely paralleled in some of his poems, he advises reformers to place their faith not in social reconstruction but in the serenity and grandeur of nature. On the face of it he is simply preaching the anti-urban pastoralism typical of his time.[25] One of the favorite midcentury haunts of New Yorkers of refined sensibility was Greenwood Cemetery, beyond Brooklyn, which was regarded as a rural retreat where the "high pulsations, . . . progressive throes and onward movements" of modern city life could be forgotten and where "the dead may welcome the living to their homes with the smiles of nature."[26] Contrary to restless New York, Greenwood Cemetery was, after all, a place where people never moved house and could always be found at home. It was, in its way, the very image of a bygone settled community. It was also the final resting place of tragic souls such as "the Mad Poet, the unfortunate McDonald Clarke," whose work Whitman championed in his early journalism with a passion that suggests he saw in Clarke an alter ego. In retrospect, the elegy for Clarke he included in one of his Greenwood Cemetery pieces reads like a portent of his own poetic career:

> From his peculiarities, he was exposed to the ridicule of vulgar men, who seldom go beyond externals; yet Clarke possessed some of the requisites of the true poet. Whoever has power, in his writings, to draw bold, startling images, and strange pictures—the power to embody in language, original, and beautiful, and quaint ideas—is a true son of song. Clarke was such an one; not polished, perhaps, but yet one in whose faculties that all important vital spirit of poetry burnt with a fierce brightness. From his being so out of the common channel; from his abruptness, and if we may so call it, jaggedness, of style—many persons have not taken the trouble to read the fugitive effusions which he gave to the world. But they are mostly all imbued with the spiritual flame. (*Journalism*, 422–423)

The passage seems to anticipate the aging Whitman's moving tribute to Edgar Allan Poe—another of his unlikely alter egos.

In his love of creeping "up the knolls, and into the more retired groves" of Greenwood, and of contrasting that "Beautiful Place of Graves" with the crassly commercial spirit of the neighboring city, Whitman typified the refined middle-class taste of his day. But at his best, he took a much more unconventional view of the relation of city to country, and the structure of his feelings is perfectly embodied in the formal structure of "Give Me the Splendid Silent Sun." The poem appears to consist of two opposing halves, the first a yearning celebration of rural life and the second, following a violent change of mind, fiercely embracing the wartime city's ways. But although the emphasis clearly falls on this heavily marked antithesis, an important contrary dimension of the poem's meaning is inscribed in the parallelism of syntactical structure between the two contrasted parts. The implication is that although the city is obviously and significantly different from the country, it is nevertheless the continuation of nature by other means. And this naturalization of city life, this conceiving of it as organic process, was for Whitman more than a novel figure of speech: it was his creative answer to the newly pressing urban problem of pervasive evil that haunts both the editorial quoted earlier and "The Sleepers." The metaphor of nature allowed him to take a benignly holistic view of New York life, to see both good and evil as part of the natural ecosystem of the urban habitat and to believe that even the worst aspects of city life would be duly accounted for in the teleology of nature.

But within the constraints imposed by this concept of symmetry between city and country, "Give Me the Splendid Silent Sun" successfully distinguishes between their two ways of life. It brings out the felicitous serendipity of the life of the streets; registers the way in which both the calendar and the clock change from one environment to the other; even notices that the very grammar of sense experience seems altered by the move from "nights perfectly quiet as on high plateaus west of the Mississippi" (446) to "[p]eople, endless, streaming, with strong voices, passions, pageants" (447). The history of the growth of the new metropolis was more than the history of streets and buildings and water pipes; it was the history of the alteration of consciousness, as some of Whitman's contemporaries realized in a dazed kind of way. Lydia Maria Child noted that

> there is something impressive, even to painfulness, in this dense crowdings of human existence, this mercantile familiarity with death. It has sometimes forced upon me, for a few moments, an appalling nightmare sensation of vanishing identity; as if I were but the unknown, unnoticed, and unseparated drop in the great ocean of human existence; as if the uncomfortable old theory were true, and we were but portions of a Great Mundane Soul, to which we ultimately return, to be swallowed up in its infinity.[27]

These comments throw intriguing light on Whitman's own habitual transcendentalizing of urban experience and suggest that some aspects of transcendentalism were uncannily well suited to express aspects of modern crowd psychology. Of course, Whitman ostensibly reversed the whole sinister thrust of Child's experience by alternately identifying with and personifying the very flux that in her case gave rise to moments of existential anxiety. But there are also examples where his poetry is exquisitely balanced between her negative reading of urban experience and his own impulse to affirm, an impulse that found precociously early, if unformed, expression, in an editorial he wrote when only twenty-one, for the *New York Aurora* on April 20, 1842. Beginning by evoking a miserable day on the streets of New York—"drizzle, drizzle, drizzle—drop, drop, drop—hour after hour, and no cessation. The omnibusses [*sic*] roll along, dragged by their melancholy horses; shivering pedestrians pass with a kind of dog trot on the side walks" (*Journalism*, 132)—the piece concludes by quoting lines from Coleridge about the "ministers of love" and adding:

> So let us be more just to our own nature, and to the gifts which the Almighty has made ineradicable within us. Casting our eyes over this beautiful earth, where so much joy and sunshine exist—looking on the human race with the gentle orbs of kindness and philosophy—sending our glance through the cool and verdant lanes, by the sides of the blue rivers, over the crowded city, or among those who dwell on the prairies, or along the green savannahs of the south—and we shall see that every

> where are the seeds of *happiness* and *love.* Yet unless they are fostered, they will lie entombed forever in the darkness—and their possessors may die and be buried; and never think of them but as baubles and worth no care. (133)

Here his expression of his vision remains jejeune for want of the forms of thought and expression appropriate to its fullest, most subtle, and mature articulation. Only poetry could supply such forms, and in some of his best poetry Whitman is able to convey not only this child-like vision but also all of the Childe-like uncertainties and misgivings that, in shadowing it, provide it with poignant substance. A notable instance is "Sparkles from the Wheel." The whole poem positively aches with the unstated questions: What is the relationship between foreground and background, between the old man and the ceaseless crowd, between the quiet children and the loud streets, between the sparkles from the wheel and the float of urban life? Are these two different planes of the same existence, or are they related only as warm dream is to cold reality? In some respects perhaps this poem is to Whitman what the "The Lady of Shalott" is for Alfred, Lord Tennyson: a coded interrogation of the assumptions and indeed of the very substance of his own art. It may not be altogether wrong to see Whitman the poet in that old man, and to see glittering in those sparkles (golden, prolific, yet ephemeral) the visionary terms into which he attempted to translate his city.

"Sparkles from the Wheel" could be read as an equivocating meditation on the following proposition: "The deeper problems of modern life derive from the claim of the individual to preserve the autonomy and individuality of his existence in the face of overwhelming social forces." This is the opening sentence of Georg Simmel's classic nineteenth-century essay on "The Metropolis and Mental Life," which remains one of the best studies of the urban character of Whitman's poetry, although it never mentions him.[28] Simmel's essay is important not because it offers a definitive account of urban consciousness but because, being itself, broadly speaking, a product of Whitman's period, it can be regarded as the rational, systematic, sociological counterpart to Whitman's own instinctual act of registering in poetry the mentality of the city. The distinctive psychology of metropolitan life resulted, according to Simmel, from the internalization of the new money economy that actually produced and sustained the modern city. This changeover to a thoroughgoing money economy—with results that included the division of labor, the impersonalization of social relations, and the quantification of previously fluid experiences such as the experience of time—was the change Whitman had himself lived through as he was growing up. Indeed, the class from which he originally came, the artisanal class, fell victim to that socioeconomic transformation, and, whereas his father's response to this had been political (he was a supporter of the radical workingmen's movements), Whitman—once he had become disillusioned with Democratic politics—used his poetry to engage with the shifts in consciousness that had accompanied the advance to a new phase of capitalism.[29]

From beginning to end, the first edition of *Leaves of Grass* involves in substantial part a critical probing of the mental conditions of contemporary metropolitan existence. In the preface, "the prudence of the greater poet" is contrasted to the "lesser prudence" of those concerned with "mere wealth and respectability" (20–23). In "A Song for Occupations," Whitman sets out to restore the self-respect of the myriads who have been devalued, demoted, and mentally deformed by the new social, economic, and political order: "The sum of all known value and respect I add up in you whoever you are" (93). In "I Sing the Body Electric" he brings two images into socially significant juxtaposition. "The swimmer naked in the swimmingbath . . . seen as he swims through the salt transparent greenshine, or lies on his back and rolls silently with the heave of the water" is followed by "Framers bare-armed framing a house . . . hoisting the beams in their places . . . or using the mallet and mortising-chisel" (118–119). Such a witty conjunction daringly turns the world of economic productivity into a world of sensuous physical satisfactions. In fact, in his catalogs Whitman frequently produces these telling social, as opposed to metaphysical, conceits, although critics have been slow to recognize them.

As for "Song of Myself," from the opening moment when Whitman provocatively describes himself as an economically nonproductive loafer the poem sets out to upset the mindset of the day. Even the brag and swagger is interestingly related to what Simmel identified as a typical reaction to the strain of life in the depersonalizing environment of the modern metropolis: "[A man] has to exaggerate [the] personal element in order to remain audible even to himself" (59). It is what Whitman literally did, when he roared his lines from Shakespeare's plays out over the din of the unheeding streets as he rode New York's omnibuses. "[Y]ou could roar as loudly as you chose in that heavy, dense, uninterrupted street-bass," (703) he recalled, thereby inadvertently registering the dubious power of his own poetry to make itself heard above the raucous din of "his" city, however loudly, thanks to his rhetoric, it raised his voice. But it was by promoting, and indeed provoking, such acts and gestures of self-assertion that, Simmel claimed, the nineteenth-century city gave birth, despite its impersonal self, to a new form of individualism based on the idea of each "man's qualitative uniqueness and irreplaceability" (60). Whitman helped bring this individualism into healthy being and struggled to distinguish it from the mere economic individualism that competitive capitalism promoted. Owing to the sense of solidarity he had inherited from his early artisanal background, he continued to bear in mind a different, earlier version of individualism that, Simmel argued, had first appeared in the eighteenth century, namely the notion of "'the general human being' in every individual" (60). "One's-Self I sing, a simple separate person," writes Whitman, "[y]et utter the word Democratic, the word En Masse" (165). And in his singing, his utterance, his words, Whitman could give reality to what Simmel later dreamed of: to the belief that "the metropolis presents the peculiar conditions which are revealed to us as the opportunities . . . for the development of both these ways of allocating roles to men" (60), that is, to both the individualist and the collective forms of modern social identity.

Simmel's urban sociology combined nostalgia with progressivism, thus reproducing the very doubleness of perspective that one finds in many of Whitman's social descriptions. New Yorkers, disoriented by the new capitalist revolution, were prone to look back, at midcentury, to an earlier period of supposedly greater social equality, when the people were, said George Ellington in 1869, "slow and Democratic" (18). "In those days . . . there were no fashionable restaurants like Delmonico's; there were no great hotels filled with hundreds of boarders; there were no club-houses, yacht clubs, jockey clubs, sorosis clubs . . . no dry goods palaces for shopping excursions; no castle-like country-seats on the Hudson" (19). Nevertheless, some observers managed, like Whitman, to invest the dynamically new socioeconomic scene with some of the imagined virtues of the previous period. Thus John C. Gobright, describing in 1859 the ultramodern machine shops of the Singer Company, where a labor force of six hundred produced over five hundred sewing machines a week, makes the new socially revolutionary system of division of labor, where "each workman [is] continually engaged upon one particular part of the machine," seem like the republican society of an old-style craftsman's workshop. Whereas in actual socioeconomic reality this new system was radically rearranging society and introducing a new class structure, Gobright sees only that "throughout the building perfect harmony and system are uniformly manifested."[30]

A like harmony is produced not only in, but specifically through, Whitman's catalog poetry, as the rhythms of parataxis supply the heartbeat of an increasingly heartless world: "Shipcarpentering, flagging of sidewalks by flaggers . . . dockbuilding, fishcuring, ferrying; / The pump, the piledriver, the great derrick . . . the coalkiln and brickkiln, / Ironworks or whiteleadworks . . . the sugarhouse, steam-saws, and the great mills and factories" (96). One later detail from this list is particularly worth noting: "The cylinder press . . . the handpress . . . the frisket and tympan . . . the compositor's stick and rule" (96).[31] Here the old print technology and the new happily coincide, implicitly complementing each other precisely as they did in the printing trade at that time. Whereas the lightning presses had made possible the mass production of newspapers by the 1840s, compositors continued to set type by hand in the old, skilled, artisanal style until 1886 (Barth, 90–93). In other words, in the very industry that Whitman himself knew best, it seemed as if technological advance need not entail social disruption, a hopeful assumption that may partly explain the wishful social thinking behind his catalogs.

However, in historical fact, mid-nineteenth-century New York was a city divided several ways along new lines of economic interest, social class, and race. Even Broadway, that avenue of wealth, had its cheaper shilling side and its chic expensive dollar side, for financial considerations were built into the very layout of the city. Through the gridiron plan devised by the commissioners in 1811 partly to satisfy commercial interests, land was everywhere divided into rectangles of real estate of obligingly uniform dimensions. This made for an urban landscape that was easy for business to play with, though Whitman in his poetry never mentions this rigidly geo-metric design. Instead he uses a holistic descriptive language of riverine flow, of oceanic tides, or of electric currents—totalizing images that resist the very idea of subdivision and create the illusion of a single, unsegregated urban scene.

The gridiron system facilitated the breakdown of New York into areas of starkly contrasting social character, and as contemporary writers attempted to map the increasingly congested social space of the city, they devised their own simplified, stylized points of reference. Elegant Broadway, "the centre of fashion and republican aristocracy" (Foster, *New York in Slices*, 8), was paired with the racy, raffish "entertainment strip" (*Gotham*) of the Bowery, and both were routinely contrasted to the pestilential slum district of the Five Points, which supplied "every heart-throb of metropolitan life with a pulse of despair" (*New York in Slices*, 22). A promenade at the Battery could be followed by a pleasantly shuddery visit to the prison known as the Tombs—that "grim mausoleum of hope! Foul lazar-house of polluted and festering Humanity"—or perhaps a somber peep into the City Dead House (*New York in Slices*, 18).[32] By such selective exercises as these in the urban picturesque writers attempted to construct an intelligible social geography of the city. Yet even though, or perhaps precisely because, the social life of New York had become so markedly divided, new cultural forms proliferated that in some ways were class specific but in others involved "an intermingling of audiences and tastes," as Peter Buckley has put it (27). The working classes were catered to not only by the penny press but also by a colorful range of commercial entertainments, including popular forms of theater such as melodrama, burlesque, and minstrelsy. The elite had their opera, symphonic music, and performances of Shakespeare.

Whitman, who loved to boast of the ease with which he passed from Broadway to the Bowery and back, acted in some respects like a broker between the two cultures, the popular and the modestly cultivated. For instance, once he had overcome his mistrust of the patently elitist form of opera, he tried to sell it to the masses for all he was worth. Then he wrote nervously approving pieces of journalism about emerging popular forms of mass entertainment, such as the prizefight (*I Sit*, 106) and the circus *(New York Dissected*, 193–196). Although he rather primly deplored the raw violence of the former and the risqué banter in the latter, he acknowledged both to be lively products of what we might nowadays call working-class culture. To see Whitman as a mediator between two urban cultures (although operating in his journalism only at a point where the respectable working class merged imperceptibly with the lower middle class) is to gain an interesting new perspective on his poetry. Behind his startling innovations in style, form, and subject there lay in part a social imperative—a deep but unacknowledged need to deny the disturbing divisions that were evident in the world around him. There was in Whitman a wild, transgressive, and creative impulse to mix, to "intermingle," to blend—this, after all, was the age when the cocktail was "discovered," supposedly by one Jerry Thomas, renowned barman at the Metropolitan Hotel (Botkin, 109). In its violation of inherited kinds and genres, Whitman's poetry may therefore be compared with the new hybrid art forms produced by the emergent working-class culture of the period. One example of this is the blackface minstrelsy created by Thomas Dartmouth "Daddy" Rice in the 1830s. Through the characters of "Jim Crow" and "Zip Coon"—white parodies of the southern rural black and the new northern urban black, respectively—this burlesque theater featured "an exercise in creative cultural amalgamation." "It blended black lore with white humor, black banjo with Irish fiddle, African-based dance with British reels" (*Gotham*, 691). Even more significantly, it enabled the coherent expression of new forms of ambivalent feeling, generated by the class and racial tensions endemic in the new urban environment:

> Crow and Coon were paradoxical creations. Their primary import was racist ridicule. Slavery was presented as right and natural; slaves as contented, lazy and stupid; northern blacks as larcenous, immoral, and ludicrous. At the same time, Rice's

act (like that of his colleagues) was laced with envy. At a time when employers, ministers, and civic authorities were demanding productivity, frugality, and self-discipline, Crow and Coon shamelessly indulged in sensual pleasures. Minstrelsy projected unbuttoned modes of behavior onto "blacks," allowing spectators to simultaneously condemn and relish them. (*Gotham*, 491)

In its hybrid character and its ambivalent message, "Song of Myself" could be thought of as having certain affinities with new art forms such as this. It is, after all, the unlikely combination of Brahman transcendentalist and Bowery B'hoy—with each persona mocking as much as complementing the other—that makes "Song of Myself" such a heady poem. As for the actual "Bowery B'hoy," that colorful instance of the new youth and gangland culture of the streets, he (like blackface minstrelsy) was a cultural conglomerate, "a multiethnic construction, part native American rowdy, part Irish 'jackeen,' part German 'younker'" (*Gotham*, 753).

Like the B'hoy himself, "Song of Myself" is notable for the provocative air of swagger that surrounds it, the glee with which it defies the established order of things. Bodily self-display is here raised to the level of an art form, so that it amounts to a sort of dandyism of nudity. Then there is the colorful pride, the assertive egalitarianism, combined with good-natured expansiveness and an unfailing generosity of spirit. The exuberant language of extravagance is periodically laced with the slang of street wisdom. "Magnifying and applying come I, / Outbidding at the start the old cautious hucksters" (233), boasts Whitman, contemptuously making the great cultural prophets of the past seem like mere second-rate versions of the modern, advanced sharpers who ran the mock auctions and the notorious clothes shops on contemporary Chatham Street. "You there, impotent, loose in the knees," he insolently harangues us elsewhere, "[o]pen your scarf'd chops till I blow grit within you" (232). Here the crude accents of a blackguardly holdup can still be heard reverberating within the promise of spiritual reinvigoration.

The famous lines of self-identification in "Song of Myself" are of course spoken very much in the boasting tones and terms of a New York rowdy of the time: "Walt Whitman, a kosmos, of Manhattan the son, / Turbulent, fleshy, sensual, eating, drinking and breeding" (210). Critics have (correctly) detected in such passages the lineaments of the Bowery B'hoy—"one of the roughs, large, proud, affectionate, eating, drinking and breeding"[33]—but have not gone on to consider the social reasons why the B'hoy was such a cult figure in 1855.[34] Whatever the real B'hoy may have been—and his violent, thuggish tendencies were part of the violent turf wars of the city streets luridly recreated for our time in Martin Scorsese's powerful film *Gangs of New York* (a twenty-first-century instance of artists' continuing fascination with the figure) — in the hands of writers (and Whitman was far from the first to be fascinated by him) the B'hoy became typically a working-class swell and volunteer fire-laddie, noted for his sartorial style:

> [T]hat's him, in the very last agony of the "ton" — black silk hat, smoothly brushed, sitting precisely upon top of the head, hair well-oiled, and lying closely to the skin, long in front, short behind, cravat a-la-sailor, with the shirt-collar turned over it, vest of fancy silk, large flowers, black frock coat, his jewelry, except in a few instances, where the insignia of the [fire] engine-company to which the wearer belongs, breastpin, black pants, one or two years behind the fashion, heavy boots, and a cigar about half-smoked, in the left corner of the mouth, as nearly perpendicular as it is possible to be got. He has got a peculiar swing, not exactly a swagger, to his walk, but a swing, which nobody but a Bowery boy can imitate, and is always upon the *qui vive* — never caught napping. (Bobo, 164)

But he "renders himself essentially useful as well as ornamental," is always ready to attend a fire or perform a kind, generous act, and is invariably straight and true, unlike your devious, foppish Broadway dandy (Bobo, 164).

The essentials of the B'hoy's public character were derived from the legendary East Side character of Mose, a Popeye or Superman of the mid-nineteenth-century working class and in part a genuine figure from urban folklore. Mose was reputed to be at least eight feet tall with hands as big as hams and flaming red hair surmounted by a two-foot-tall beaver hat. "In his lighter moments," as the folklorist B. A. Botkin recalls, "it was the custom of this great god of the gangs to lift a horse car off the tracks and carry it a few blocks on his shoulders, laughing uproariously at the bumping the passengers received when he set it down. And so gusty was his laugh that the car trembled on its wheels, the trees swayed as though in a storm and the Bowery was filled with a rushing roar like the thunder of Niagara" (217). He once saved a becalmed ship in the East River from drifting helplessly toward dangerous rocks by rowing out to it, calmly lighting his two-foot-long cigar, and blowing such clouds of smoke against its sails that the ship was sped all the way to the other side of Staten Island. "Unscrew the locks from the doors!" cries Whitman in the terribleness of his extravagant strength, "Unscrew the doors themselves from their jambs!" (210); "I skirt sierras, my palms cover continents, / I am afoot with my vision" (219).

In 1848, Mose was put on the Broadway stage in a part the actor Frank Chanfrau immediately made his own, and over the next ten years the Bowery fireboy became a national favorite. The pattern was invariably the same: plenty of dance hall brawls and street fisticuffs culminating triumphantly in the thrilling rescue by Mose of a swooning maiden from a fire-engulfed building. And his daring was always set off by the insouciance of his slangy, catchy comments.[35] Mose's popularity faded after 1860, like Whitman's poetry one might add, because he had outlived his social usefulness. What his function had been over the previous dozen years or so can be clearly understood from the account of the Bowery B'hoy offered by Foster in *New York in Slices* (1849) and *New York by Gas-Light* (1850).[36]

To Foster, the B'hoy is the quintessential democratic American, a free spirit who is the urban counterpart of the Indiana Hoosier and the trapper of the Rocky Mountains.[37] While professing to deplore the reckless B'hoy's occasional high-spirited lapses into thuggery, Foster praises his honesty, courage, and goodheartedness: these, he insists, "bespeak for him and his future destiny our warmest sympathies and our highest hopes" *(New York by Gas-Light*, 102). The B'hoy hates the nonproductive classes with an honest hatred, firmly believes in the socioeconomic egalitarianism preached by Whitman's great hero William Leggett, and is the very soul of American independence. The B'hoys, as a brotherhood, "are brave, easily led astray, but not naturally wicked. They are good, unselfish, and frolicsome creatures" *(New York by Gas-Light*, 44), and Foster dreams of a time when they will redeem America by building a new society in the West. This romanticized version of the Bowery B'hoy was a nostalgic dream of free labor and yeoman farms that Whitman also found irresistibly attractive.[38]

Perhaps the most revealing phrase used by Foster is that in which he describes the B'hoy and his G'hal as constituting "the great middle class of free life under a republic of which they are the types and representatives" (*New York by Gas-Light*, 109). Here the phrase "the middle class" means Foster's hopefully imagined, and desperately idealized, middle way between the two antirepublican extremes of new aristocratic wealth and new slum poverty. The real character of a new capitalism that promoted the socioeconomic distinctions and divisions it needed in order to thrive was in fact starkly evident in those extremes. But Foster and Whitman were deeply disturbed by what they saw, and both sought and found in their different versions of the Bowery B'hoy the nodal point of alternative social development. So Foster pithily writes in *New York in Slices* that when the B'hoy and his G'hal drive along Broadway "social inequalities are, like the avenue itself, Macadamized" (i.e., leveled and smoothed [46]). In "Song of Myself," Whitman produced a remarkable mythic version of the B'hoy that, through the range of social experience it encompassed and the variety of social discourses it employed, turned the figure of the B'hoy into an incarnation of social harmony. Ranging as it does, in subject, style, and register, from high life to low and integrating them all into a single normative discourse (or megadiscourse) that is the verbal equivalent of the Bowery B'hoy's swagger, "Song of Myself" is partly Whitman's attempt to produce a "great middle class of free life," in Foster's sense of the phrase: "Sure as the most certain sure, plumb in the uprights, well entretied, braced in the beams, / Stout as a horse, affectionate, haughty, electrical, / I and this mystery here we stand" (190).

Already a superannuated figure by 1860, the Bowery B'hoy, alias Mose, was dead as a doornail by 1865. The Civil War did not kill him; it was the social and economic transformations that were associated with the war. As the age of giant corporations and organized labor dawned, the ideal of little-man freedom and independence embodied in the cult of the B'hoy became hopelessly anachronistic. This is one reason why "Song of Myself" could not have been written much later than it was. Of course, there were many diverse factors responsible for Whitman's decline as a poet, some of them emotional, psychic, and psychological, others simply physical. But in stressing these, the social factors (which are interwoven with the other factors) should not be overlooked. After 1865 (at the latest), New York and America simply could not be handled any longer by those inspired strategies of symbolic re-presentation that Whitman had devised in the 1850s.

Indeed, by the late 1850s, Whitman himself had become almost disablingly aware of the strain of sustaining the enabling social fiction in which he had invested when it was still soundly underwritten by the then-existing social facts. The war came just in time to save this vision—now clearly suffering from runaway inflation—from drastic devaluation. The strain was evident in Whitman's relations with New York. Troubled at the very best of times, these relations almost reached breaking point when Whitman realized that the city's commitment to maintaining the Union was suspect. Then came euphoria, as New Yorkers rallied to the cause following the attack on Fort Sumter, only to have disillusionment honeycomb Whitman's faith thereafter, as the city made clear that its first commitment was to commercial prosperity.

In "City of Ships" Whitman tries to repossess wartime New York in the name of the democratic imagination, virtually viewing the city through the beautifying compositional frame of ships' rigging: just as fifty years later the photographer Alfred Stieglitz and the painter Joseph Stella were to net chaotic New York for the imagination by viewing it through the cables of the Brooklyn Bridge.

A September 1864 letter—typical of several—written when he had returned from Washington to Brooklyn to recover from exhaustion, tells a very different story:

> I don't know what move I shall make, but something soon, as it is not satisfactory any more in New York & Brooklyn—I should think nine tenths, of all classes, are copperheads here, I never heard before such things as I hear now wherever I go out—then it seems tame and indeed unreal here, life as carried on and as I come in contact with it & receive its influences.[39]

His Bowery B'hoy had gone, having volunteered, or so no doubt Whitman liked to believe, for the Union army. As he writes in the Washington notes later published in *Specimen Days*, "Even the typical soldiers I have been personally intimate with,—it seems to me if I were to make a list of them it would be like a city directory" (774). The hospitals then became Whitman's New Jerusalem, the heavenly city of comrades that he continued to hope postwar New York would come to resemble.

Of course, it was not to be, and Whitman was never again to make New York his permanent home. He lived the life of an internal émigré after 1865, first staying on in Washington to be near what remained of the hospitals and then settling in Camden once his health had finally broken down. No wonder that, in the second half of *Specimen Days*, Whitman's postwar return to the New York so vibrantly invoked in the work's opening pages as the wonderful scene of his youth and the nursery of his talent seems endlessly deferred. "Returned to New York last night," Whitman eventually records, describing the inspiring vista as he approached the city after a sail "in the wide bay, southeast of Staten Island" (822).

Perhaps, one symptom of the problem he had in experiencing postwar New York in terms suitable for his poetic imagination is a section of the passage recording his visit to Washington that he included in *Specimen Days*:

> I took a walk there [Chestnut Street] between one and two. Doubtless, there were plenty of hard-up folks along the pavements, but nine-tenths of the myriad-moving human panorama to all appearance seem'd flush, well-fed, and fully-provided. . . . The peddlers on the sidewalk—("sleeve-buttons, three for five cents")—the handsome little fellow with canary-bird whistles—the cane men, toy men, toothpick men—the old woman squatted in a heap on the cold stone flags, with her basket of matches, pins, and tape—the young negro mother, sitting, begging, with her two little coffee-color'd twins on her lap—the beauty of the cramm'd conservatory of

rare flowers, flaunting reds, yellows, snowy lilies, incredible orchids, at the Baldwin mansion near Twelfth street—the show of fine poultry, beef, fish, at the restaurants . . . (837)

And so the list continues, through a series of the kinds of vivid vignettes so familiar from Whitman's prewar poetry. Except that in this case there are significant differences. First, there is the uneasy admission, and immediate downplaying, of the poverty to be seen jostling with plenty on the streets. Second, there is the lack of the exuberant motion, and onward propulsion, characteristic of Whitman's great poetic listings. Third—and it would seem to be an inevitable corollary of the first and second points—this passage is, after all, written not in poetry but in prose. The effect of the whole is, surely, to suggest that Whitman's prewar urban vision has been bled dry of all its essential, animating energy. His writing has consequently become "glib with prose" (to borrow a phrase from the great Welsh poet R. S. Thomas), since his vision is now unequal to "the poem's harsher conditions." And after the war, a lot of Whitman's writing of this inferior kind and reduced quality was to be nothing but "prose" masquerading as "poetry."

In fact, when in *Specimen Days* Whitman eventually records a visit to New York, he proceeds to dramatize the encounter by stressing that he had never been back to stay since the "Secession War" and representing this return as the ultimate test both of the postwar city and of his own faith in America. He even implies that the improvement in health he had precariously made at Timber Creek was here being consciously put at risk, as he claims that the visit in the end proved to be "the best, most effective medicine my soul has yet partaken" (824). His conclusion is that New York is certainly "the city of superb democracy, amid superb surroundings" (824). Yet the language in which he tries to render the thronging life of the streets is stiff with cliché.

Whitman's great early poetry was, in substantial part, a successful instrument for the management of history, an effective means of bringing fact into tolerable alignment with dream. But the resourceful discourse his poetry allowed him to devise was itself, in certain crucial respects, internally linked to the very period it was designed to address. Therein lay both its power and its weakness. As a functional device it could not survive the age from which it had, after all, been triumphantly made. His historical situation as poet is imaged compellingly in an early draft for one of his Broadway poems:

As seen in the windows of the shops as I turn from the crowded street and peer
through the plate glass at the pictures or rich goods.
In Broadway, the reflections, moving, glistening, silent.
Turn from the heavy bass, the great hum and harshness
The faces and figures, old and young all so various, all so phantasmic—
The omnibus passing and then another and another—the clear clear sky up . . .

(*New York Dissected*, 222)

Plate glass was one of the inventions of the time with which Whitman's imagination seemed understandably affined. Here it becomes a magical medium, transforming that which is otherwise unmanageable and unbearable—the "hum and harshness" of Broadway—into enchanting "reflections, moving, glistening, silent." Yet beyond the glass and still visible through it are "the pictures [and] rich goods" of the shop. So materials from the two worlds of the aristocratic store and of populous Broadway meet and mingle, images brought together through the medium of the plate glass that in one way transfigures them both and yet fails to alter or mitigate their contrasting realities at all.

The plate glass can stand for Whitman's medium of poetry, historically circumstanced in ways that made it both potent and impotent, powerful and vulnerable, magically true yet illusory. It was in this glass that his socially divided, money-driven city appeared to Whitman in its redeemed form, lovely Mannahatta. But for the magic glass to work, Whitman had first to gather and record the real raw materials of his time—he was the kind of poet who always needed fact to supply the collateral of vision—and the specificity of contemporary historical reference in his poetry is one of its most striking features. So when in "Song of Myself" (1855) he speaks of "[t]he heavy omnibus, the driver with his interrogating thumb, the clank of the shod horses on the granite floor" (33), he has vividly in mind the very recent improvements made to the roads through the use of Belgian granite blocks that allowed the horses greater purchase and thus protected against the accidents caused by slipping. In the same section he singles out "[t]he excited crowd—the policeman with his star quickly working his passage to the centre of the crowd" (34), and thus highlights the recent creation (1843) of the "copper," the policeman recognizable by, and eventually synonymous with, his new badge of office. And the butcher boy, who "puts off his killing-clothes, or sharpens his knife at the stall in the market, / I loiter enjoying his repartee and his shuffle and breakdown" (36), is evidently an astute reference to the brand new cultural phenomenon, unique to New York, of new working-class art forms spontaneously produced out of, in this instance, an amalgam of the black and Irish dances of the day.

Wherever one looks, it is specifically the New York of the 1850s upon which Whitman so powerfully draws, in graphic detail, in the first version of "Song of Myself" to vivify his vision. So even when he identifies with the concealer and protector of the escaped slave ("The runaway slave came to my house and stopped outside" [35]) and seemingly evokes a rural, or semirural environment ("I heard his motions crackling the twigs of the woodpile / . . . And went where he sat on a log, and led him in and assured him . . ."), it is important to remember that the Underground Railway which is being defiantly advertised here was created in New York in 1835 by David Ruggles, founder of the New York Committee of Vigilance (*Gotham*, 560ff). And Whitman's details are usually as faithful to actual contemporary reality as his vision is transfigurative of the character of that reality. Thus, in that tour de force of transfigurative poetry, "Crossing Brooklyn Ferry," Whitman carefully and accurately records the following:

> On the river the shadowy group, the big steam-tug closely flank'd on each side by
> the barges, the hay-boat, the belated lighter,
> On the neighboring shore the fires from the foundry chimneys burning high and
> glaringly into the night
> Casting their flicker of black contrasted with wild red and yellow light over the
> tops of houses, and down into the clefts of streets. (310)

Picturesquely rendered though these forges may be, they are also there as an acknowledgment of the real sources of power—not only economic power, but also the other related forms of power, including steam—of midcentury New York City. The ferry itself is the product and servant of such power. The East River featured huge riverside ironworks evidencing the fact that the city was actually one of the fastest growing industrial centers in the world. It was necessary for Whitman—given his instinctive understanding that his vision must always, for its own good, remain on first-name terms with social reality—to ensure that the glow of the benignly equalizing sun that eventually works its transcendentalizing magic in his poem is, in its way, credible as a reflection of the glare of the raw, savage power of New York as made evident by those fiery furnaces.

When Whitman crows in "Song of Myself" that his feet are "mortis'd and tenon'd in granite," he could well be thinking in part of the Belgian granite of the new paving stones of his city. His greatest poetry does indeed offer confirmation that, as poet as much as person, he was inescapably "of Manhattan the son," and that his is a poetry in which existent facts are constantly being laid down, solid as

Belgian granite blocks, to produce "riprap" (to borrow Gary Snyder's metaphor) for his vision. The poetry convinces only to the extent that it seems to have the measure of its actual world, and Whitman repeatedly noted, and rejoiced, that his was an age in which human advance in measuring had helped make possible advance in material understanding and control of the human environment. How, otherwise, could the new Croton Reservoir have been constructed, or the Erie Canal built, or the railroad to Albany completed? And wasn't modern New York itself the ultimate product of those feats of modern measurement that had first reduced a hilly terrain to a flat expanse and had then produced the city's gridiron pattern of streets?

But "we level that lift to pass and continue beyond" (82) and "Count ever so much . . . there is limitless time around that" (81). If one feature of Whitman's poetry is the respect it constantly shows for measurement, its other, complementary feature is the understanding it manifests that the actual terms of such physical measurement may be as restricting of human beings as they are instrumental in improving the human condition: "I know I have the best of time and space—and that I was never measured and never will be measured" (82). Hence, Whitman seems repeatedly in his early poetry to be placing himself in a liminal position—at a point that baffles precise measurement because not only does it exist simultaneously inside and outside established boundaries, it thereby constitutes a "place" of an altogether different order. So, for instance, in "Who learns my lesson complete?" at the very same moment he wonders "that I grew six feet high . . . and that I have become a man thirty-six years old in 1855," thus presenting himself as the sum total of height and age, he also adds "And that my soul embraces you this hour, and we affect each other without ever seeing each other, and never perhaps to see each other, is every bit as wonderful" (141). He thus emphasizes the paradox that, while he can apparently be "fixed" in place and time, he simultaneously exists outside of both. Read in the light of this paradox, his earlier statement that he "was born on the last day of May 1819" (141) takes on a new significance; the threshold date seems to signify his liminal identity as a human being—no more to be exactly contained by a month than by an era. And take his splendid, characteristically outrageous, boastful announcement of "entrance" in "Song of Myself": "Unscrew the locks from the doors!" (50). Whitman came from a house-building family, and thus knew from firsthand experience that the building industry had been central to the growth of New York into the world's first modern commercial metropolis. He also knew how vitally important measuring was in this line of work: "the square and mitre and jointer and smoothingplane; / The plumbob and trowel and level . . . the wall-scaffold, and the work of walls and ceilings . . . or any mason-work" (95). The early editions of *Leaves of Grass* are replete with images drawn from building. Indeed, there is an important sense in which Whitman thus closely associates himself, as poet as well as person, with the building industry—"A framer framing a house" is more than the equal of all the old-world gods he defiantly proclaims (74). Hence the dramatic significance of his insistence ("Unscrew the doors from their jambs!") that he is nevertheless not to be identified with building; instead, he gives the family business the heave, in an act of rebellious renunciation suggestive of a young Samson breaking impatiently free of all such constraints on his identity. He bursts out of the frame. Similarly, "Song of Myself" proceeds by instantly deconstructing every construction it places on reality and replacing it with another in that infinite process of self-revision which is, for Whitman, the very libertarian essence of self-identity.

And then there is the matter of the image he famously chose as frontispiece to the first edition of *Leaves of Grass*, the image by which he chose first to become known to the world as a poet. As is well known, that image is an engraving based on a daguerreotype, a fact that may be as symbolically appropriate as it was doubtless actually dictated by practical considerations. It is perhaps appropriate that it is not a photograph, that new form of "definitive" image making that seemed to possess the miraculous reproductive power of taking the very measure of a subject's actual appearance. Rather, in being an engraving, it is an image of the old-fashioned kind, which seems always to make implicit allowance for the need for other images, of other representations, of the very same phenomenon. And in that frontispiece portrait, Whitman famously boasts a beard of a luxuriance burgeoning beyond that hinted at in the photographs of his earlier self. Indeed, in a *New York Aurora* editorial of April 13, 1842, he had made fun of hirsute gentlemen:

> Near the City Hotel we passed a man with the face of a goat; his upper lip was completely covered with black bushy hair, as were also his jaws and under his chin. People turned round in their walk to look at the creature. It is an abominable practice, this, of converting a human countenance into a locomotive map! Wasn't it Paulding, when he was navy secretary, who issued the order for a general shearing and cropping of these diabolical appendages? (*Journalism*, 116)

Beards had come into fashion in the New York of the fifties, and as such Whitman's sproutings may be read as yet another sign of his sensitivity to changing tastes and to contemporary mores. But as his poetry makes abundantly clear, a beard had already quickly become a signifier for him of much greater and deeper portent. In the 1855 preface, he exults in "the roughs and beards and space and ruggedness and nonchalance that the soul loves" (5), while in "Song of Myself" he assigns "washes and razors [to] foofoos . . . for me freckles and a bristling beard" (48). The beard is for Whitman expressive of many things precisely because it is inherently unmanageable and not reducible to neat and tidy formulation. As such, it signifies that concept of free, untrammelled, multifaceted, and multileveled personality that Whitman dramatizes in his signature poem, that grand luxuriant tangle of personal expression which is "Song of Myself."

Whereas Whitman is careful in one sense to build his poetry out of the very materials of contemporary New York experience, that experience is never allowed to become the measure of a poetry that is firmly "placed" instead in a liminal relation to the actual historic New York of Whitman's prewar prime. And it is perhaps this vital defining feature of the poetry that has enabled it to effect its remarkable feats of "travel," as for a century and a half readers and writers from cultures physically and existentially remote from 1850s America have been so evidently transported by it. When Yeats died, Auden wrote a powerful elegy to him in which he memorably observed that "[n]ow he is scattered among a hundred cities, / And wholly given over to unfamiliar affections."[40] The same could be written of Whitman. By composing his tale of New York as a tale of two cities—the actual historic city and the city of democratic vision—he made a poetry of local, American provenance available and accessible to "a hundred cities" worldwide. And it is the remarkable nature of that achievement that will be under consideration throughout this study.

Two. The New Urban Politics

He came into his own in 1855, although his thinking remained rooted in the Locofoco brand of Jacksonianism that had awakened his political imagination two decades earlier. A tireless champion of the working class and protector of the rights of immigrants, he was also a skillful self-publicist who succeeded in writing, incognito, such flattering accounts of his life and work as appeared in print.

Thus described, Fernando Wood could easily be mistaken for the Walt Whitman who was, in fact, one of his harshest critics. And there is another intriguing coincidence. The first edition of *Leaves of Grass* was published by Fowler and Wells in July 1855. That very same month they also published the most recent number of the *American Phrenological Journal*, a journal keen to promote the self-help philosophy that aided social mobility, and a journal with which Whitman—an ardent aficionado of phrenological publications—was undoubtedly familiar.[1] And who is the prominent figure whose "phrenological character" is outlined over three pages (each of three columns) in that journal but Fernando Wood, who "one year ago . . . was little known. . . . But all at once, he strikes out a new line of action. He fills the mayoralty as no other man has ever filled it, either in New York or in any other city." There then follows a gushing analysis of this powerful mayor's remarkable qualities—an analysis that is graciously confirmed by Wood himself as entirely accurate. As the journal diplomatically concludes: "In summing up, his developments every way fit him for his present position. Better it would be difficult to find."

The journal also pronounced Wood to be endowed with "an extreme of Combativeness," and this is certainly relevant to understanding Whitman's relationship to his strange alter ego. Not only were he and Wood at the height of their very different powers between 1855 and 1860, but there is a significant sense in which the wily Wood, grandmaster of the new urban order, pioneer of machine politics, the prototypical city boss whose power base was the ethnic, immigrant vote, epitomized for Whitman so much that had gone wrong in antebellum America.[2] Wood, as a popularly elected mayor, incarnated the real New York—the new city that was being brought into being in the 1850s through the turbulent convergence of a new capitalism and a new (largely immigrant) workforce—just as, or so his campaign rhetoric skillfully suggested, New York incarnated him. That his rhetoric was specious and his political persona in some ways an inspired sham had been conclusively demonstrated by his opponents even before Wood was first elected mayor: this ardent champion of immigrant labor had been exposed in 1854 as a secret member of the virulently anti-immigrant Nativist (American, or Know-Nothing) Party. But Wood survived to be officially acknowledged, through his election as mayor of New York a mere matter of months later, as the public voice of that working class whose unofficial (but would-be authentic) representative Whitman chose to image himself as being in the 1855 edition of *Leaves of Grass.*

To hear the "voice" of that poetry as pitched in part to challenge that of Wood, and to see its persona as attempting to outface the two-faced politician, may be a historically valid way of reading not only the first, but also the second and third editions of *Leaves of Grass.* Hidden from our modern sight in some of Whitman's most powerful writings is an argument with Fernando Wood and his kind about what sort of society America should develop. Unearthing this is a way of realizing anew that Whitman's response to national politics had always been influenced by local conditions, by the exact form politics took not only across America but specifically in New York City itself. And so the 1850s presented him with a particular problem, because, as Amy Bridges has pointed out, "It was in the antebellum years that city politics came to have an independent existence, turning on its own issues rather than on national events."[3] Wood's genius was to realize this and to capitalize on it: his success as a politician was the result of his inspired ability to speak to working-class New Yorkers in their own language, in terms of those matters that most urgently concerned them—not "free soil" (the great subject of Whitman's political pamphleteering in 1856) but employment (which meant political support of the southern slavery upon which the economy of New York was dependent); not the consensus politics preached by

Whitman through his poetry but the pragmatic "new" factional politics of class and ethnicity, albeit under cover of a rhetoric of consensus that Whitman must have read as a virtual parody of his own discourse.

By the 1850s, a modern, capitalist, cosmopolitan America totally different from that in which Wood and Whitman had grown up was appearing in New York.[4] And it was part of Wood's genius to realize that this new America was divided into new social and economic groups that needed to be managed by new forms of political organization. During the 1840s, New York was a city caught in the throes of a socioeconomic revolution that turned it into the prototype of a throbbingly modern metropolis. Its population exploded from 123,706 in 1820 to 813,669 in 1860; and almost half of that population was immigrant—with particularly large groups crowding in from Ireland, Germany, and Italy. The new underclass of poor immigrant workers tended to live in ethnic enclaves such as the German district of *Kleindeutschland.* And thousands of the poorest immigrants were crammed into the new slum districts of the city, most particularly the infamous Five Points district, where conditions, stinking of vice and crime, were appreciably worse even than in the notorious East End of Dickens's London. This huge pool of immigrant labor was brought into being and maintained by a new kind of capitalist economy, which broke down the social structure Whitman had been used to as a young man. A new class distinction emerged between the owners of businesses, who were employers, and the workforce who worked for them and were simply their employees. It was a social division both Wood and Whitman deeply disliked; but their reactions were different—where Whitman used his poetry to imagine a more equal society, Wood set out to offer a political voice to this new working class; and in particular to that huge part of it that was most oppressed and disadvantaged—this was the poor underclass of immigrants, to whom some New Yorkers were very hostile because they seemed to represent an endless supply of cheap labor that enabled employers to keep working-class wages damagingly low.

What Wood did, in effect, was target the new ethnic, immigrant vote that was being ignored by the existing political groups in New York. In 1854, Wood ran for mayor of New York as a maverick, radical Democrat. He appealed to the new oppressed urban working class in general, but appealed most particularly and directly to the despised immigrant groups. He spoke a new language of class struggle, of ethnic power, and of economic reform. Not only did he win the election, but in the process he created for himself a new power base that enabled him to create a wholly new system of political control and management that typifies American urban politics even today.

With all its evident moral drawbacks (Wood soon became mired in the sleaze of a corrupt culture of patronage, involving the sale of public offices), this new politics answered the needs of the present, by nurturing the (shady) management skills needed to bring a chaotically diverse city under central executive control, and shaped things to come. Wood's recent biographer has persuasively given us Wood the artist, as innovative in his field of politics as Whitman was in his of poetry:

> [H]e created several unique advances in the art of governing cities. He was New York's first modern mayor, a prescient city builder whose proposed improvements in the quality of urban life anticipated several of the divergent strands that formed the later and often contradictory Progressive Movement. He championed the interest of the working class and immigrants, and sought to avoid incipient class conflict by urging businessmen to develop a social conscience that placed human rights over property rights. At the same time, Wood was a prototypical professional politician, replacing the older elite that had considered public service a temporary civic duty. As a political organizer, he laid the basis constructing a political machine, headed by a fresh type of centralized leader; the city boss.[5]

Considered as prophet and as answering to the new needs of his period, a politician like Wood may fruitfully be regarded as the negative source of that portrait of the poet Whitman fashioned in the 1855 poem later entitled "Song of the Answerer." Wood's concentration of executive power into his own hands is countered by the poet whose "word is decisive and final," while the mayor's conspicuous promotion of his city's economic welfare is offset by Whitman's vision of the poet as enlightened city boss: "The noblest and costliest cities . . . others grading and building, and he domiciles there; / Nothing for any one but what is for him . . . near and far are for him" (129). Above all, the egalitarian poet outdoes the populist artist-politician in his chameleonlike power to change according to the social context: "Then the mechanics take him for a mechanic, / And the soldiers suppose him to be a captain . . . and the sailors that he has followed the sea" (131). And, again like the political spellbinder, the poet is a great orator, except that his words have not a seductive but a pentecostal power:

> Every existence has its idiom . . . every thing has an idiom and tongue;
> He resolves all tongues into his own, and bestows it upon men . . . and any man translates . . . and any man translates himself also:
> One part does not counteract another part . . . He is the joiner . . . he sees how they join. (130)

There is, of course, no proof that Whitman was thinking of Fernando Wood when he wrote those lines. But it seems clear that behind this poetry is deep concern about those discourses, the linguistic determinants of the powers of meaning, that were controlling America in 1855; and Wood and his kind were masters of such discourse. Indeed, maybe the opening lines of "Song of the Answerer" are ambivalent in meaning partly because they register Whitman's initially uncertain search for a radically alternative discourse, one empowered to address current conditions on its own dissenting, recreative terms. What is clear, however, is that here, as repeatedly in the early editions of *Leaves of Grass*, Whitman turns to the Bible as an important source of alternative discourse, alternative value inscribed in an alternative language:

> A young man came to me with a message from his brother,
> How should the young man know the whether and when of his brother?
> Tell him to send me the signs. (129)

What is also clear is that—perhaps in order to break decisively with the Christian churches and sects who "owned" this discourse, and whose social power he deeply resented—Whitman here conflates material from several different Biblical sources. There is the echo of the occasion when a young man came to Christ inquiring about what he needed to do to be saved, only to be given the unpalatable answer that he should sell all that he had, give it to the poor, and follow him; there may also be, in the implied claim to be able to read the "signs," an allusion to the mystery of the "Last Things" mentioned in Revelation—that handbook of apocalypse that Whitman repeatedly used in his writings at this time; and there seems certainly to be an implied reference in this passage to that famous question asked of Christ, "And who is my brother?" In other words, obscurely inscribed as parable in the opening lines of "Song of the Answerer" are the anxieties buried deep in Whitman's reluctant consciousness about the state of America in 1855—damnably materialistic (Whitman's response to the new capitalism), savagely divided (not only between North and South but also between classes and ethnic groups), and able to be saved from apocalyptic disaster only through the intervention of a redeemer (answerer-poet). This, then, is one of the poetic models of opposition to Wood that he adopts.

That Whitman regarded Wood as a powerful adversary, as the kind of false redeemer that Revelation warns will abound in the last days, is clear from some of his prose writings of this period. One that best reveals the light in which Whitman regarded him concerns the grand parade to celebrate the Fourth of July 1856, an event historians of the period associate with the Democratic Wood's triumphant thwarting of the Republican state government's attempt to implement a prohibition law. The question of how precisely America should celebrate the glorious Fourth was one that had much exercised Whitman for over a decade. In 1846, when he was editor of the *Brooklyn Daily Eagle*, he devoted four whole editorials to the subject, beginning by scolding his city for having failed "for several years"[6] to celebrate the Declaration of Independence which, a subsequent editorial emphasized, "[has] led already to such great results, and opened for the future such glorious prospects, that the return of it should be hailed with the liveliest emotion." But the Common Council preferred to hang on to its dollars, a gesture that could be seen as anticipating the withering away of the old republican spirit in the face of the challenge of the new capitalism that so disturbed Whitman in 1856.

Reporting for *Life Illustrated* the grand parade with which New York marked the Fourth of July that year, Whitman began by listing the groups taking part.[7] Heading the parade were "two platoons of police—to indicate that, after all, the civil power is first," closely followed by marching ranks of soldiers ("Light infantry, hussars, dragoons, riflemen, Highlanders, lancers"), each regiment led by "pioneers," "who wear enormous caps of bearskin and broad aprons of buckskin, and who carry fancy pickaxes and exaggerated tomahawks, polished like silver." This spirit of burlesque (as the jaundiced Whitman saw it) afflicted even the honest cart-men, symbols of the honest labor he so admired and saw as embodying all the physical and spiritual virtues of the American republic. These followed on their own strong, heavy horses, and from the saddlecloth of each animal there dangled "a gay, red tassel, which swings to and fro, and plays tickle, tickle, tickle, under the bellies of the horses, who don't know that under all the grandeur, both human and equine, there is always something tickling, and who squirm and fret about it." So the pageant kept on unrolling, before Whitman's disapproving eye, for another two miles, as it headed for Union Square "to be reviewed by Mayor Wood." This was a procession not to celebrate what was best about American life but to emphasize the power of one person. For Whitman, it was a betrayal of everything he believed American democracy stood for, because it elevated one individual above the whole people; and turned the people into a subordinate, subservient mass, meekly marching in that one man's direction and to that one man's tune. It stood for little less than the betrayal of America itself.

For Whitman, the whole affair was the sorriest of spectacles, absurd and degrading—a vulgar show that turned what should have been a dignified ceremony into a mere carnival—as he explained in no uncertain terms at the end of his report of the day's proceedings. "The most noticeable fact," he began by pronouncing, "is that *everybody is sober*," a caustic comment surely on Mayor Wood's (triumphantly successful) efforts to ensure, through the circumventing of the Prohibition Laws, that everybody might, if they chose, be drunk. But by describing the citizens as sober Whitman primarily meant, as he proceeded to explain, that they had been subdued, almost cowed, into merely mechanical compliance. This was a population merely going through the motions on a day that no longer possessed "any conscious reference to the significance of the time," a day that "seems only the listless vacation of laborers overworked—not the joyous exultation of a free people." And Whitman had no doubt who was to blame for this sullen state of affairs. He identified the culprits, in the course of proposing the steps that needed to be taken to remedy the situation:

> What reform to recommend is not difficult to say. Discontinue all the "sound and fury, signifying nothing," from the cannon's mouth, or the juvenile oratoricalist's; stop the noise and the evil smell. Let there be fireworks, perhaps, for there is much beauty in them. But let the features of the day be addressed by the best speakers—not the poorest, as now—for those that want them, and let the remainder of the community "celebrate" for themselves, as on a great day of hereditary national thanksgiving and pride, with rustic festivals and friendly hospitality, with public triumphs, *if spontaneous*, but not by chilly management of squabbling civic authorities; with visitings and gifts, with song and mirth; in short, with spontaneous social and affectional display of joy, in civil and decorous forms; not with brutal noise and sulphury streams, aimless lounging, and empty fatiguing processions made to order. (Holloway and Adimari, 84)

The passage alerts us to the broad political overtones of several of the apparently innocent key terms in Whitman's poetry. "Spontaneous me" (to give the poem the title it acquired only in 1871) takes on an altogether different complexion when read in conjunction with the above, as does "Song of Joys" and the many great "gift" poems Whitman wrote, starting with "Song of Myself." Indeed, poetry was Whitman's primary means of subverting the very terms, the very language, by which Wood and his allies practiced their "chilly management," and brought their city into regimented order. It seems likely that behind Whitman's urgings that "the best speakers not the poorest" be licensed to address the masses was his wish that his poetic voice might triumph over orator Wood's demagoguery. What a world of contempt is compressed into "oratoricalist," that grotesque term Whitman seems to have minted especially for the populist rhetoricians of the new urban politics. Certainly the picture of a two-mile procession all obediently headed in Wood's direction powerfully evokes the dictatorial power that

Wood was, in the eyes of his enemies, in process of amassing. It is a picture to set against some of Whitman's demonstrations of his own powers and functions in his poetry, as in section 15 of the 1855 "Song of Myself":

> The crew of the fish-smack pack repeated layers of halibut in the hold,
> The Missourian crosses the plains toting his wares and his cattle,
> The fare-collector goes through the train—he gives notice by the jingling of loose change,
> The floormen are laying the floor—the tinners are tinning the roof—the masons are calling for mortar,
> In single file each shouldering his hod pass onward the laborers;
> Seasons pursuing each other the indescribable crowd is gathered . . . it is the Fourth of July . . . what salutes of cannon and small arms!
> Seasons pursuing each other the plougher ploughs and the mower mows and the wintergrain falls in the ground;
> Off on the lakes the pikefisher watches and waits by the hole in the frozen surface. (41)

By inserting the Fourth of July celebrations into the ongoing activities of ordinary life, Whitman turns it into an authentic national holiday; an affirmation, and confirmation, of a democratic America, thus restoring it to the people and to its true significance. Also, by associating it with "seasons pursuing each other," he naturalizes this festival, removing it from the social and political order, representing it instead as an activity as seasonal as the ploughing of the ploughman. Thereby he makes American society itself seem not a historically specific human social and political device but a natural product of the American landscape. The conclusion of the passage from "Song of Myself" underlines the difference between the position of those such as Mayor Wood, who (in Whitman's opinion) stood above and apart from the people whom he "represented" only by virtue of his power to command their obedience, and the situation of the poet who was the very embodiment of the people among whom he lived and worked. "And these one and all tend inward to me," Whitman writes of the individuals he has identified in his all-embracing list, but then he underlines the striking contrast between himself and the very differently pivotal Wood by adding, "and I tend outward to them, / And such as it is to be of these more or less I am" (42).

In this section from "Song of Myself," Whitman notes how "[t]he cleanhaired Yankee girl works with her sewing-machine or in the factory or mill, / . . . The pavingman leans on his twohanded rammer—the reporter's lead flies swiftly over the notebook—the signpainter is lettering with red and gold, / The canal-boy trots on the towpath—the bookkeeper counts at his desk—the shoemaker waxes his thread" (40). Loosely speaking, these emblematic images identify the person with an activity signified iconically by the tools of his/her trade, and there may be interesting clues here about the politics of Whitman's practice of listing in the early editions of *Leaves of Grass*; there seem to be highly suggestive connections between these lists of descriptors (that may be seen as constituting an "alternative" version of the Fourth of July processions) and the long-established artisan pageants organized to mark public holidays (including the Fourth of July) and prominently featuring banners and floats carrying the emblems of the participating trades.

Sean Wilentz has demonstrated how the history of the fateful, turbulent change from a "world of [artisanal republicanism], petty production, and early commercial capitalism" to that of industrial capitalism and entrepreneurial republicanism may be vividly read in the apparently minor record of "public trade rituals and political festivals of the artisans in early national and Jacksonian New York City."[8] Whitman's experience of living through this change, and indeed of working his way through it in more senses than one, was one of the formative experiences of his life, and it entered intimately into his writing of *Leaves of Grass*. During the early 1830s, the young Whitman was drawn into the politics of a working world convulsed by drastic changes that were reflected in workers' pageantry.[9] Radical Jacksonians, including Whitman, saw themselves as the heirs of a Jefferson who had believed true Americanism to be founded on the rock not only of the rural yeomanry whom Jefferson had so adored but also of the urban yeomanry represented by the "ideally interdependent workshop roles of master, journeyman, and apprentice" of the artisanal system (46). It is no accident that the mature Whitman declares, "I believe a leaf of grass is no less than the journeywork of the stars." Right up to the 1830s, artisanal pageants, pointedly made central to the celebrations of American red-letter days, proclaimed through the icons on banners and the tableaux on floats that the values and practices of the traditional trades were at the very heart of American society. Typical of what Wilentz calls "the richness of New York artisan ceremony" (45) were the arm and hammer of the General Society, the schooner of the Society of Shipwrights and Caulkers, the St. Clement of the hatters, the chairmakers' chair, all of them designs accompanied by appropriate mottos and slogans and frequently incorporating the American eagle. The point was clear: artisanal ideology was at the very core of American life, and central to the republicanism of the artisan community was a commitment to social service, to "what one master called '. . . common bonds and mutual sympathy'" (48). But already by the 1830s, the development of an entrepreneurial capitalism was threatening the break up of the artisanal system, as the more successful masters turned to merchants and financiers for the kind of backing necessary for setting up in business to cater for a new consumer market.[10] The consequent replacement of the master-journeyman relationship with that of employer to employee was the beginning of a process leading to sweatshops and to the degradation of artisan labor that helped create a new, proletarianized workforce. Wilentz has pointed out that "[t]he transformation of the rituals of mutuality into declarations of class began in the late 1820s and early 1830s with the activities of the American Institute" (56), whose trade fairs became "new forms of public ceremony . . . [that] expanded upon the entrepreneurial messages delivered by the masters after 1815 and recombined them with the older images of the trades" (57). In reply, an artisanal movement that had been politicized, and radicalized, by the threat from the new capitalism supported "[q]uite different festivities [begun] in 1833 under the aegis of the General Trades Union," a union of wage-earning journeymen and one from which all masters were excluded (57). The union was committed to the militant defense of the old artisanal republicanism that was based on the labor theory of value: "To save the republic, the journeymen organized across trade lines to oppose the defenders of egoistic competition, resurrect the cooperative spirit, and insist that they be paid the full value of their labor" (59). And the GTU's commitment to the traditions of labor was emphasized by the use of the old craft emblems to advertise its claims to represent " 'a complete counter-system' to industrial capitalism, one that would honor labor rather than property, useful work rather than social privilege, fraternity rather than selfish competition" (64).

There was, indeed, a long and colorful history of street processions and pageants in New York, and they persisted well into the second half of the century. In *American Notes*, Dickens appreciatively recorded seeing a company of firemen marching back from target practice: "[T]hese street processions are incessant in New York, and contribute much to the gayness of the streets."[11] The golden age of such events was the antebellum era, and every parade necessarily passed through the Bowery district.[12] The volunteer firemen had begun their parades in 1824, and the annual Evacuation Day procession (November 25) was second only to that of the Fourth of July. Public events were promoted in particularly spectacular fashion—the completion of the Erie Canal in 1825 was an excuse for a pageant about which a whole book was written; the completion of the Croton Aqueduct in 1842 also occasioned a prominent display, as did the laying of the first transatlantic cable in 1858. It was only natural, therefore, that political parties should capitalize on the public appetite for such fetes by staging pageants of their own.

So the Jackson Democrats had in 1830 staged a "celebration of the downfall of absolute monarchy in the person of Charles X of France"; and the pageant in 1851 to welcome Kossuth, the great Hungarian revolutionary, was similarly politically inspired. The deaths of presidents were marked by particularly imposing mock funeral processions. A riderless warhorse was led behind the hearse at one such "funeral" for President Harrison in 1841, because the Whigs were anxious to commemorate his military service. New York Democrats responded four years later, with the "trades" much in evidence in the mighty cortege, featuring "a great gilded urn on wheels" (to represent Jackson's body), "drawn by four richly plumed and caparisoned black horses, which were led by Negroes, turbaned and dressed in oriental style." But in 1850, the Whigs trumped even that effort for Zachary Taylor's funeral. They turned out more than 30,000 men to march in a seven-mile long procession "which had to counter-march because the customary route was not long enough for it." And this time the centerpiece was

> a $1,000 hearse fifteen feet long, specially built for the occasion and drawn by eight white horses, each led by a richly dressed Negro. The hearse was crowned by a golden eagle and covered with a rich canopy lined with white and red. On the sides of the vehicle were the names of Taylor's battles . . . and his supposed last words. . . . The old white horse led behind the hearse was presumed by the mob to be the original "Whitey," General Taylor's charger, and so many people pulled hairs out of his tail for souvenirs that the poor beast had little tail left. (283)

Whitman's response to the Wood-organized Fourth of July procession needs, then, to be set in the context of this elaborate, politically complex history of street theater. And to read the great passage in "When Lilacs" about the somber, unifying progression of Lincoln's funeral train across so many of the Union's states in light of this tradition is to see it in a different, deeply political light.

The decline of the street pageant was again read by Whitman as a symptom of the political state of New York City in a newspaper article of February 22, 1858. This time it was Washington's birthday that seemed to him to be inadequately celebrated. He thundered against the "class in our midst—who would measure everything by the rule of dollars and cents [and would] affect to despise the celebration of the 'glorious Fourth' and the like occasions." He went on to urge, "Let these days be as widely commemorated as possible—they keep alive by their unusual recurrence the flickering flames of patriotism. . . . When a nation's Holy-days are treated with indifference and neglect, it should be considered a sign of national degeneracy and decay"[13] (*I Sit*, 59). No wonder that in "Thou mother with thy equal brood," Whitman would carol, "Thee in thy democratic fêtes en-masse, thy high original festivals, operas, lecturers, preachers" (572). So many of the lists of his own compilation may usefully be regarded as processional; as celebratory street theater; as textual fetes. No wonder either that the artisanal pageants of his younger years had left such a permanent mark on his imagination, for their spirit of mutuality, their songs, their emblems, their affirmation of the labor theory of value, and their vision of America. This is most evident in the 1855 poem later entitled "A Song for Occupations." Indeed, whole passages read like the textual equivalent of an artisanal pageant, as Whitman celebrates "[t]he anvil and tongs and hammer . . . the axe and wedge . . . the square and mitre and jointer and smoothingplane," and all the other innumerable emblems of the artisans' world (95). But alongside "the implements of every trade," Whitman deliberately includes "[m]anufactures . . . commerce . . . engineering," as if wanting to suggest, by association, that these engines of industrial capitalism also contributed to what Wilentz has called "the harmony of the free-labor republic" (64). It was a reading of contemporary New York that the remnants of an artisanal order, devastated by the advance of industrial capitalism, would not have agreed with. The historian Amy Bridges has calculated that by 1855 the artisan class had dwindled to a mere 12.2 percent of the New York population: 28.3 percent were employed as wageworkers in occupations formerly reserved for artisans; 39.2 percent belonged to the huge new pool of labor in which immigrants figured very large (46). In fact, so dated was Whitman's picture from the beginning, that he soon substituted a "more formal" title, reflective of class, "A Song for Occupations," for the 1856 "Poem of the Daily Work of the Workmen and Workwomen of These States" (1856). And in 1867, he also excluded from his original text a passage that had "conveyed the living sense of a way of life now lost."[14]

By understanding certain aspects of the political dynamics of this change in New York's class structure, we may best understand the power base of Fernando Wood, the basis of Whitman's hostility toward him, and certain overlooked features of Whitman's poetry. One of the several ways in which artisans responded to their social, economic, and political degradation was by blaming it on the immigrants who, by 1855, constituted over half the population of New York City. Partly as a result, the secretive Nativist Party, with its aggressively anti-immigrant platform, briefly became a very considerable force, and that at a time when what was widely seen as a "crisis of community" was causing the utter collapse of the old two-party (Whig/Democrat) system.[15] Wood, a maverick Democrat—who was even to split from Tammany and establish his own headquarters at Mozart Hall—realized that the immigrant communities, threatened by Nativism and ignored by both old Democrats and new Republicans, represented a huge new political constituency. His own remarkable career was to be built on the exploitation of this insight.

And insight it was—indeed it deserves to be recognized as involving a genuinely empathic act of imagination (however mixed, or even plain dubious, the motives), the very identification with the condition of others that Whitman prided himself on possessing. With particular reference to the Germans and Irish, Wood understood how the immigrant communities, and the working class they joined, constituted an underclass for whom living in the new world of industrial, entrepreneurial, and financial capitalism meant sporadic employment, low wages, bitter competition for jobs, squalid living conditions, and class and ethnic tensions. What he instinctively realized was that these new socioeconomic conditions were the breeding ground of a new politics. And he accordingly attempted to adapt his "durable Democratic principles rooted in Locofocoism" (Mushkat, 244) to these new circumstances, so as to realize "a Jacksonian commitment to be a tribune of the people" (244). Whitman, also a lifelong Locofoco at heart, broadly shared Wood's ends but differed profoundly from him in his means, as quickly becomes apparent when one examines Whitman's response to immigrants.

He had always been opposed to the insolently self-named "American Party," regarding it as anti-American in spirit since it failed to accept that the United States was not just a new nation but a "teeming nation of nations," the highest stage so far reached in human progress, and as such the natural goal, or home, of all mankind. The corollary of such a belief was Whitman's natural sympathy with the masses who remained in thrall to the reactionary political order of "feudal" regimes—hence his editorial, in the later 1840s, on "Poor Poland!"[16] and his championing of the cause of the refugees from the Irish famine. His attack on the Native American Party, in an editorial on June 22, 1846, was based on a melodramatic contrast between "The New World and the Old": "On the shores of Europe are panting multitudes, who sicken with nakedness and starvation. . . . How, then, can any man with a heart in his breast, begrudge the coming of Europe's needy ones, to the plentiful storehouse of the New World?"[17]

But given that by 1855 more than half the population of New York was foreign born, and that the existence of a huge immigrant underclass was the most prominent sign (if not, as Nativists supposed, the actual cause) of a revolutionary change in the character of urban experience, what strikes one about the first edition of *Leaves of Grass* is how very few references there are in the poetry to this highly contentious phenomenon, and how very bland are the rare descriptions of immigrant life. Witness how smoothly immigration is glossed over in "A Song for Occupations": "Mechanics, southerners, new arrivals, sailors, mano'warsmen, merchantmen, coasters, / All these I see" (91). Or consider the sentimental attention paid, in "The Sleepers," to the dreams born of nostalgia and homesickness:

> The fugitive returns unharmed . . . the immigrant is back beyond months and years;
> The poor Irishman lives in the simple house of his childhood, with the well-known neighbors and faces,
> They warmly welcome him . . . he is barefoot again . . . he forgets he is well off;
> The Dutchman voyages home, and the Scotchman and Welchman voyage home . . . and the native of the Mediterranean voyages home . . . (114)

Or notice the routine inclusion of immigrants in the lengthy list of American incidents in "Song of Myself": "The groups of newly-come immigrants cover the wharf or levee" (39). The phrasing is so laconic, it borders on disingenuousness.

Implicit in these treatments of immigrants is, however, Whitman's dislike of Nativist xenophobia—by seeing newcomers as reluctant refugees still innocently homesick for their native countries, he counters the propaganda representing them as opportunistic interlopers; by casually integrating immigrants into his poetic rhetoric, he minimizes the devastating socioeconomic impact immigration had on the host culture, and makes it seem as if, far from radically altering the distinctive character of American life (as Nativists heatedly argued), foreigners were being smoothly assimilated by it. Not that Whitman's response to immigrants was wholly and unequivocally affirmative. During his period as editor of the *New York Aurora* Whitman campaigned vigorously—and indeed virulently—against Bishop John Hughes's introduction of a "sectarian" divide into the public school system by seeking legislation to allow separate Catholic schools to be established. The campaign opened Whitman's eyes to the potential political power of the immigrant communities as, attending a meeting outside City Hall, he heard a number of politicians, anticipating the tactics of Fernando Wood by more than a decade, shamelessly "soft-soap[ing] the foreigners present":

> Such low, vulgar scurrility—such beastly coarseness—such claptrap, stale trash—such gross egotism, and such pandering to the worst prejudices of the Irish, whom it seemed his peculiar design to make his hail fellows well met—our ears were never before disgusted with; and we cannot but be solemnly impressed with

> the idea that Fortune has made a great mistake in placing this overgrown lubber among the society of decent men. He said he was "half an Irishman" himself. We presume respectable Americans would not grieve were the "whole hog" Irish. (*Journalism*, 111)

The immigrant Irish community was, of course, also the spiritual constituency Hughes effectively represented, and in attacking the bishop's proposals as dangerously un-American, Whitman repeatedly railed against "foreign" usurpation and distortion of the American constitution. While vehemently protesting that "[w]e look upon emigrants to our republic with friendly and generous eye," Whitman added, "but many things they bring with them might far better be left at home," since they are "brought up to believe in the doctrine of loyalty, and the superstitions of every kind that mark all the countries of Europe" (66). So intemperate did his objections to foreign infiltration of American society seem that he was accused of being a Nativist himself, and had to hasten to distance himself from that emergent party's policy of denying immigrants the vote (84ff): "We have no antipathy or bigoted ill-will to *foreigners*. God forbid! . . . Our mind is not one of that narrow description which confines its good will by a shore or a boundary line; we look upon all human beings as brethren, entitled all to our regard, our good offices, the protection of government, and the enjoyment of freedom" (85).[18] But he also reiterated his belief that foreigners had to be Americanized as soon as possible, in the sense of abandoning their European feudal prejudices, superstitions, and loyalties, and of adopting "American" values. This is, in a sense, the transformation, or transmutation, his own poetry silently and implicitly achieves by integrating immigrants seamlessly into the general, racially and culturally undifferentiated, panorama of contemporary American life.

Such an impression is, of course, very much at odds with historical reality as politicians like Wood knew and understood it; and to realize this is to appreciate the relevance to Whitman's case of John Berger's observation that "all art is an attempt to make unnatural the distinction between the actual and the desired." Whitman (who was that most improbable of creatures, a libertarian communitarian) desired an America of spontaneous communality generated by harmonious individualism, and poetry was his means of actualizing and naturalizing that desire. Whereas Wood's genius lay in his ability to recognize, at an early stage, the way political power was being reconfigured by the embryonic collectives (ethnic groupings and class solidarities) formed by the socioeconomic processes of a new commercial capitalism, Whitman's genius was dedicated to the breaking up of these collectives and the redesignation of their members as free individual agents.

It was, however, only as a poet that he possessed this power to re-form America by actualizing and naturalizing his desires; as a hack journalist, he was forced to operate in the unaccommodating historical world of whose conditions and circumstances Wood was master, and where Whitman's desires could only assume the ineffectual form of conventional political protest. It is therefore to the journalism we must turn to discover the deep anxieties aroused in him by his times, including the immigrant experience so confidently embraced in his poetry: in a *Brooklyn Daily Times* editorial of April 1858, we find mention of the corrupt Democratic Party's dependence, in Mayor Wood's New York, on "the blind following obedience of large masses of adopted citizens" (*I Sit*, 95). Following Jerome Loving's important discussion of this issue in his recent biography of Whitman, we must be wary of assuming that Whitman acted as editor of the *Times* from 1857 to 1859, but it remains clear that he did contribute to the paper's editorial columns, and several of the pieces traditionally attributed to him seem consistent in political outlook with the previously mentioned, and well-authenticated, *Life Illustrated* article.[19]

Whitman's bitter mistrust of these "masses" derived, in no small part, from the notorious riots of the previous year's Fourth of July, on which Whitman had commented in "The Dead Rabbit Democracy," a scathing editorial printed a few days after the event. The allusion was to the brutal street gang ("The Dead Rabbits"), largely composed of fighting Irish, whose vicious brawling with their rivals, the "Bowery Boys," brought near anarchy to New York's streets on July 4, 1857.[20] Clubs, iron bars, stones, and eventually guns were used as weapons in a riot engulfing almost a thousand people. Background to the fighting was the power struggle between Wood, the Democratic city mayor, and the Republican state legislature in Albany, several bills enacted by the latter during 1857 having savagely reduced Wood's political powers. Particularly damaging were the Municipal Charter (ostensibly strengthening the mayor's position but in fact denying him control of the key Department of Finance), the Excise Law (aimed pointedly at the bibulous working-class immigrant culture that was Wood's urban power base), and the Metropolitan Police Act (replacing the city-controlled force with a completely new unit answerable to a state-appointed board). In response to this last move, Wood formed his own Municipal Police Force (defiantly alternative to the new Metropolitan Force) and dug in, refusing to hand the state's station houses over to the new body, all the while escalating the rhetoric in which he represented himself as the people's champion against Albany (and upper-class) tyranny.

In his "Dead Rabbit Democracy" editorial, Whitman fulminated against "the most unscrupulous schemers [who] have so far managed as not to give up possession of the party 'station-houses,'" and a year later still saw the future of the Democratic Party (and of the United States) as to be decided by the internal struggle between corrupt fixers like Wood and the respectable, progressive element represented by Douglas, Wise, and Walker (*I Sit*, 96). And this struggle Whitman also saw as centrally involving a contest for the hearts and souls of the masses. Whereas Wood and company exploited the ignorance of the massive new immigrant population ("the blind following obedience of large masses of adopted citizens"), their opponents ("warned," as Whitman tellingly noted, "by the stern attitude of the best classes of the American people") relied on "greater enlightenment, and a steady advance of political knowledge among the masses. All this is as a death-knell to sneaking politicians" (96).

Such comments are valuable to us primarily for the sharp light they throw on Whitman's writings, silhouetting his obsession with offering the "people" an image of their true (if potential) selves against his fear of the alternative (and much more immediately persuasive) images peddled by Wood and his kind. And the tone of Whitman's remarks are as prophetic of his poetry as is their content. It hovers uneasily between the confident (based on a gradualist, evolutionist reading of the situation) and the urgently anxious (based on an intense awareness of the fatefulness of present choices, decisions, and outcomes). It is this rich mix of feelings that helps his imagination ignite in *Leaves of Grass*; it is also what fills those early editions with unpredictable switches of mood, sudden changes of direction, and related somersaults of opinion. As will become evident in a later chapter, when the long-term, gradualist approach is in the ascendancy (as it tends to be, for example, when Whitman reflects on the southern slavery question) he favors a rhetoric of consensus. On the other hand, when his mind is in crisis mode (as it is, for instance, when engaging with the Kansas, and Free-Soil, issue), then he is inclined to go ballistic (in today's colorful parlance), and to employ a rhetoric of apocalypse.

The most crudely striking examples of this latter rhetoric are to be found, of course, in *The Eighteenth Presidency!* the political pamphlet he angrily wrote (but never distributed) as his highly personal contribution to the presidential race of 1856. This scurrilous squib has long been regarded as a key source for understanding Whitman's political opinions, but has never been read for what it has to tell us about the complex relationship that, for Whitman, existed between the politics of New York City and the national political scene. It needs therefore to be pointed out that Whitman's opposition to Buchanan is voiced partly in terms of his fear and hatred of Wood's Democratic regime in New York—Wood having been one of the first to support Buchanan's candidacy. If this address to "each Young Man in the Nation, North, South, East and West" is seen in the light of Wood's control of the working class in New York, it becomes clear that Whitman's pointed extension of his appeal to workingmen in every state of his continental nation was an attempt to get the politically corralled and imaginatively blinkered to see themselves as part of a bigger, wider picture. This was necessary because Wood played on the urgent concerns of the urban proletariat with jobs and wages in order to advocate a pro-southern policy of appeasement over Kansas and other territorial issues. But Whitman was, of course, convinced that on the outcome of the Free-Soil issue depended the whole future of democracy in America, and with it the future of the working people. Therefore, his pamphlet (like his poetry) includes an attempt to get the workers to think more "globally," to see their place within an enlarged geography of space and time, to identify their long-term interests and thereby to identify with the Kansas-Nebraska struggle. If the new politics invented by Wood was the sectional politics of place—Wood had unquestionably made the city of New York his own—then Whitman countered by creating a geopolitics of space. The two presidential candidates, says Whitman, "live in respectable little spots, with respectable little wants. Still their eyes stop at the edges of the tables of committees and cabinets, beholding not the great round world beyond. What has this age to do with them?" (1314). This should help us see that Whitman's poetic panoramas and listings can serve an important political purpose. They are mind-expanding devices, textual attempts to get New York workers who were being blinkered by Wood's parochial, factional politics to reorient themselves politically by viewing themselves in a much wider perspective. For Whitman, the new politics of Fernando Wood worked by restricting the people's field of vision, as a passage in *The Eighteenth Presidency!* makes clear: "Workmen! Workwomen! Those immense national American tracts belong to you; they are in trust with you; they are latent with the populous cities, numberless farms, herds, granaries, groves, golden gardens, and inalienable homesteads, of your successors. The base political blowers and kept-editors of the North are raising a fog of prevarications around you" (1316). As always, Whitman is oblivious to the Native Americans, the aboriginal inhabitants of these "tracts" he otherwise so generously wishes to open up to the "divine average."

While the intention to expand the reader's politico-geographic horizons remains implicit in many of his key poetic strategies, it is explicitly announced, and openly implemented, in *The Eighteenth Presidency!* The individualism he there advocates is related to this, since it involves a repudiation of the ethic of the collective that he associates with parties, always inclined to "make common cause just as soon in advocacy of the worst deeds . . . as the best" (1317). He equates party with faction, and hence with the elevation of the part (*part-y*) above the whole: "What impudence! for any platform, section, creed, no matter which, to expect to subordinate all the rest, and rule the immense diversity of These free and equal States!" (1317–1318). In nature, and in an apparently natural society, he therefore discovers a liberating antipolitical politics: "[W]hile all is drowned and desperate that the government has had to do with, all outside the influence of government, (for ever the largest part,) thrives and smiles. The sun shines, corn grows, men go merrily about their affairs, houses are built, ships arrive and depart" (1311–1312). Ten years later, in "When Lilacs," he was strikingly to reverse this vision, and explicitly to represent both the fertility of the American landscape and the prosperity of the citizens as the gift, and now the joyous-sad legacy, of a great martyred politician.

Fernando Wood's political genius was manifested in the management culture of the new machine politics he effectively invented to bring his explosively expanding, chaotically unruly metropolis under control. But Whitman raged against the fixers and creatures of this new representative politics—"not one in a thousand has been chosen by any spontaneous movement of the people; all have been nominated and put through by great or small caucuses of the politicians, or appointed as rewards for electioneering" (1309). By deliberate contrast, therefore, Whitman's writing is infused with the spirit of "spontaneity." As has already been noted, "spontaneous" is a prominent word in Whitman's lexicon, and a signature term in his poetics, yet the political implications of the spontaneity so deliberately inscribed in the very style of his writing have been overlooked. Even in his prose, he practices a rhetoric of exclamation, of outburst, of calculated indiscretion, in his attempt to enact the arrival of that for which he is pleading —what, in *The Eighteenth Presidency!* he suggestively calls "another power," profoundly different in origin and in kind from that "of the nominees that have arisen out of the power of the politicians" (1312). In social and political terms, he professed to place his trust in the "counteraction of a new race of young men" (1312), but for Whitman it was in truth poetic discourse that was the unique dwelling place of "another power"; poems were for him enabling instruments, means to the radical empowerment of the people through the potent textualizing of spontaneity. Poetry was the revolutionist's answer to the otherwise irresistible oratory of powerful new-style "representatives" such as Wood.

"Another power": what kind of power that was, and how poetry was uniquely equipped to serve it, is made apparent at the very end of *The Eighteenth Presidency!* "The times are full of great portents in These States and in the whole world," Whitman announces in prefacing this grand climactic passage:

> What whispers are these running through the eastern continents, and crossing the Atlantic and Pacific? What historic denouements are these we are approaching? On all sides tyrants tremble, crowns are unsteady, the human race restive, on the watch for some better era, some divine war. No man knows what will happen next, but all know that some such things are to happen as mark the greatest moral convulsions of the earth. (1324–1325)

This is eschatological writing; the language of revelation. The millenarian strain in Whitman's poetry of the mid-1850s remains to be fully explored, and is one of the profoundest manifestations of his stance as a "revolutionist," in contrast (and opposition) to Wood and other political "representatives." It is important to sensitize oneself to its presence in his poems, since poetry was for the early Whitman the native discourse of apocalyptic vision.

"On all sides tyrants tremble," Whitman wrote. A passage from the open letter he addressed to Emerson the very same year as he wrote *The Eighteenth Presidency!* is worth bringing to mind at this point:

> Just so long, in our country or any country, as no revolutionists advance, and are backed by the people, sweeping off the swarm of routine representatives, officers in power, book-makers, teachers, ecclesiastics, politicians, just so long, I perceive, do they that are in power fairly represent that country, and remain of use, probably of very great use. To supersede them, when it is the pleasure of These States, full provision is made; and I say the time has arrived to use it with a strong hand. (1331)

Obviously, the likes of Wood were in his mind when thus characterizing "representatives." As for describing himself as a "revolutionist," Whitman was identifying with those leaders of the 1848 revolutions in Europe whom he saw as providing further dramatic evidence that he was living in an apocalyptic age. The inclusion in the first edition of *Leaves of Grass* of the poem "Europe, the 72d and 73d year of These States" has therefore a multiple significance. A defiant boast that though liberty may have been checked (through the crushing of the European revolutionaries), it can never be defeated, the poem also furnishes

Whitman with the opportunity of giving indirect expression to his feelings about the threats to freedom in his own country of America from the new-style tyrants of democracy such as Fernando Wood. The conclusion of the poem is particularly suggestive:

> Is the house shut? Is the master away?
> Nevertheless be ready . . . be not weary of watching,
> He will soon return . . . his messengers come anon. (134)

This is, of course, an allusion to the parable of the wise and foolish virgins, which is the classic Biblical text of millenarian expectation of a redeemer figure—such as the Redeemer President that Whitman prophesied, in *The Eighteenth Presidency!* would inevitably appear in America. And "Song of Myself" is Whitman's ultimate redemption song, to borrow a phrase from the great reggae singer Bob Marley. It is a poem in which Whitman seeks to redeem his people by showing them how, in an egalitarian society, every man is his own redeemer, the only true begetter of his perfected self. As Emerson put it, "No man, in all the procession of famous men, is reason or illumination, or that essence we were looking for; but is an exhibition, in some quarter, of new possibilities."[21]

Whitman included in the 1855 edition of *Leaves of Grass* a companion piece to his poem about Europe, in the form of his Boston ballad. There he produced a savage piece of satire through a kind of reversed and parodic millenarianism. The dead are raised from their graves not for the Last Judgment, but to pass judgment themselves on the scene they see enacted before their incredulous eyes in the streets of Boston. And the poem ends not with the fufillment of time, as promised in the millennium, but with the reversal of time, as American history regresses, and the skeleton of George III is recrowned king. But at that point, this reversed millenarianism reverses itself, thus reverting to authentic apocalypse. Because is it not one of the signs of the coming millennium that king death shall be given dominion over all the earth during the dark premillennial period? It is this affirmative aspect of Whitman's otherwise dark vision that is highlighted in the 1855 edition by having "A Boston Ballad" followed by "There was a child went forth every day."

As "A Boston Ballad" reminds us, Whitman was periodically afflicted during the 1850s with deep crises of confidence in his America, and in such moods history seemed to him to reverse its flow, turning from progression into regression. Hence, in *The Eighteenth Presidency!* he pauses at one point to brood on what the future might yet hold:

> Shall the future mechanics be serfs? . . . If slaves are not prohibited from all national American territory by the law, as prohibited in the beginning, as the organic compacts authorize and require, and if, on the contrary, the entrance and establishment of slave labor through the continent is secured, there will steadily wheel into this Union, for centuries to come, slave state after slave state, the entire surface of the land owned by great proprietors, in plantations of thousands of acres, showing no more sight for free races of farmers and work-people than there is now in any European despotism or aristocracy. (1316)

No wonder he began one of the poems in the 1855 *Leaves of Grass* with the words "To Think of Time." Whitman did a lot of that sort of thinking in the 1850s, bringing into play several different models of the temporal order. Thus "Sun-Down Poem" (later "Crossing Brooklyn Ferry"), first appearing in the very same year as *The Eighteenth Presidency!* turns on the trope of continuity, invoking a future the character of which can be reliably extrapolated from the familiar features of the speaker's own time:

> It avails not, time nor place—distance avails not,
> I am with you, you men and women of a generation, or ever so many generations hence,
> Just as you feel when you look on the river and sky, so I felt.[22]

What is now secretly immanent, hidden except to those with redeemed, apocalyptic vision, will become manifest in the fullness of future time. Hence the poem's great concluding benediction on time's process: "Flow on, river! flow with the flood-tide—and ebb with the ebb-tide" (*Variorum*, 224).

Yet, when it is read in the light of the passage from *The Eighteenth Presidency!* this passage of consecration takes on a different complexion. The assured rhetoric of affirmation seems not so much an expression of confidence as an attempt to cast a spell; an attempt to magic the American future into assuming the very image of freedom that Whitman felt was so profoundly at risk in the year the poem was actually written. In the face of the great political events of his time—and, from the Fernando Wood problem to the Free-Soil issue, they represented for Whitman dangers to the political democracy of his America—he understood, with growing desperation, that the whole future of the United States turned on the *actions* taken in the present. That is why, like so many visionaries before him, Whitman paradoxically produced out of millenarianism a revolutionary rhetoric designed to promote actions to ensure that the millennium would actually happen; that Fernando Wood and everything he stood for would be defeated. In other words, Whitman effectively turned a determinist model of history into an optative and volitive one. In *The Eighteenth Presidency!* for example, he notes that "To-day, those who are free here, and free in the British islands and elsewhere, are free through deeds that were done, and men that lived, some of them an age or so ago and some of them many ages ago. The men and deeds of these days also decide for generations ahead, as past men and deeds decided for us" (1315). Consequently, while consoling himself in "Sun-Down Poem" with a vision of a future America in which the freedoms implicit in the New York of 1856 had become fully manifest, Whitman was at the same time marrying present to future in a beguiling way that would make the concept of freedom precious enough for his readers for them to want to *act* to safeguard it. It is thus worth noticing, for instance, the two lines that appear in the 1856 text but were dropped from later editions, because in these lines Whitman specifically underlines his status as a freedom-loving New Yorker, in defiance of Fernando Wood's political strategy of stressing New York's economic bondage to the slaveholding South. In the first of these lines Whitman announces, "But I was a Manhattanese, free, friendly, and proud!" while in the second he urges his city, and his land, to stand proud on its freedoms: "Stand up, tall masts of Manahatta!—Stand up, beautiful hills of Brooklyn! / Bully for you! you proud, friendly, free Manhattanese" (*Variorum* I, 224).

In the mid-1850s, Whitman therefore emerged as a "revolutionist" in his writings partly by defining himself against powerful new "representatives" like Fernando Wood. But Whitman may be followed one step further, to the point in *The Eighteenth Presidency!* where he suddenly, pointedly, and wittily collapses his customary distinction by turning "revolutionist" and "representative" from oppositional terms into cognates, if not equivalents:

> The times are full of great portents in These States and in the whole world. Freedom against slavery is not issuing here alone but is issuing everywhere . . . Never were such sharp questions asked as today. Never was there more eagerness to know. Never was the representative man more energetic, more like a god, than today. He urges on the myriads before him, he crowds them aside, his daring step approaches the arctic and antarctic poles, he colonizes the shores of the Pacific, the Asiatic Indias, the birthplace of languages and of races, the archipelagoes, Australia; he explores Africa, he unearths Assyria and Egypt, he re-states history, he enlarges morality, he speculates anew upon the soul. (1324)

This is Whitman the millenarian reading the signs of the times, and who should appear as an unlikely figure in this apocalyptic landscape, and as a portent of a dynamically emergent new order, but his old adversary "the representative man." Except, of course, that Whitman the revolutionist is here using the term not in its politically established but in its redeemed sense, the sense given it by Emerson in his book on *Representative Men*, when he remarked that "the constituency determines the vote of the representative. He is not only representative, but participant" (17). The true representative, therefore, is the quintessential type, or embodiment, of that which he represents, and as such he makes visible qualities in it that were previously invisible even to itself.[23] Whereas the "routine representatives," as Whitman put it in his open letter to Emerson, were so only in the narrow political sense that they had been elected by their "constituencies," the true representative is endowed with apocalyptic power, the power of privileged disclosure, and the power to act as a revolutionist. Whitman the revolutionist was, then, in his own eyes, also Whitman the truly representative American, authorized by time itself to read the secret signs of his times, and to "divine another's destiny better than the other can," as Emerson had put it. And had not Emerson furthermore asserted that "[t]he pleasure of full expression to that which, in their private experience is usually cramped and obstructed . . . is the secret of the reader's joy in literary genius" (20)? Whitman's writings in the mid-1850s, in response to the politics so balefully represented by Fernando Wood, were therefore imbued with the apocalyptic spirit Emerson had so eloquently celebrated in *Representative Men*:

> Justice has already been done to steam, to iron, to wood, to coal, to loadstone, to iodine, to corn and cotton; but how few materials are yet used by our arts! The mass of creatures and of qualities are still hid and expectant. It would seem as if each waited, like the enchanted princess in fairy tales, for a destined human deliverer. Each must be disenchanted, and walk forth to the day in human shape. (15)

But although in Whitman's American dream, "representatives" became indistinguishable from "revolutionists," he well knew that in fifties America those two terms, as he defined them, stood for characters as implacably hostile to each other as Fernando Wood and himself. And this is confirmed in a revealing—if fortuitous—juxtaposition of entries Whitman made in 1857 in an unpublished notebook:

> [*Entry One*]: [Mayor Wood] this forenoon issued an order to the various Captains, directing them to call in the men at 4 o'clock this afternoon and have them deliver

> up the city property. [The reference is to the aftermath of the Fourth of July riots.]
> [*Entry Two*]: Poem of (my brothers and sisters) artists, singers, musicians.[24]

The first entry records the factional actions of representatives; the second defiantly celebrates the visionary company of revolutionists.

Three. *Leaves of Grass* and *The Song of Hiawatha*

Emerson wrote two particularly interesting letters in 1855. One was to become famous as his unwisely generous, messianic welcome to Walt Whitman: "I greet you at the beginning of a great career."[1] The other remains comparatively unknown, and shows the writer in a markedly less attractive light:

> I find this Indian poem very proper and pertinent to us to read, and showing a kind of manly sense of duty in the poet to write. The dangers of the Indians, are that they are not really savage, have poor, small sterile heads, no thoughts, and you must deal very roundly with them, and find them in brains, and I blame your tenderness now and then, as I read, for accepting a legend or a song, when they had too little to give.[2]

Reflecting as it does the contemporary theories of "American ethnography" about the invincible racial inferiority of Native Americans compared with whites (a theory that in several influential cases was based on the racially extreme theory of polygenesis, or separate creation of races), Emerson's unpleasant remarks highlight by contrast the relatively sympathetic way in which Native Americans are portrayed in *The Song of Hiawatha*.[3] His comments thus help temper the understandable, if somewhat patronizing, inclinations of late twentieth-century scholars to dismiss Henry Wadsworth Longfellow as fundamentally unsound on the subject of American aborigines.[4] It is indeed as difficult as it would be morally inappropriate to overlook the shocking history of the treatment of Native Americans during the very period in which Longfellow was writing. And there can be no doubting the ultimate truth of the observation Leslie Fiedler made a long time ago "that the white Americans have, from the first, hopelessly confused the real Negroes and Indians, with whom they must for the sake of social survival and civil peace learn to live, with certain projections of their own deepest minds, aspects of their own psychic life with which precisely they find it impossible to live."[5] Much recent scholarship involving *Hiawatha* has been devoted to indicting the poem on these unanswerable grounds. But in the process, we may be overlooking the extraordinary power of the work in its time as a white man's poem—one that, in the twenty-first century, can still "like voices from afar off / Call to us to pause and listen," as Indian "ballads" did to Longfellow in his time.[6]

Such scoldings of Longfellow are nothing new. The phenomenal success of *Hiawatha* in its day, and for the best part of half a century thereafter, seems to have aroused strong passions in literary critics, cultural historians, and other scholars for most of the twentieth century, envy mingling prominently with contempt for its author's meretricious achievements. Their judgments seem to echo the Lear-like Whitman's excoriating verdict on a Longfellow whose apparently bland indifference to the Civil War had enraged him: "And who has projected beautiful words through the longest time? By God I will outvie him! I will say such words, they shall stretch through longer time!"[7] Over the last couple of decades corrective voices have begun to be heard, as Longfellow has been reviewed not least in the light of a new understanding of him as a complex product of the America of his period—which was also, of course, Whitman's America. But refined, hypereducated, Europhile Bostonian and abrasively egalitarian, self-educated, streetwise, and in-your-face New Yorker—could they actually be said to occupy the *same* America? In an obvious sense, no, and it was the instructive contrast between them—not least, that difference in social class made physically evident in the contrast between Longfellow's permanent residency in the majestically haute-bourgeois Craigie House in Cambridge, Massachusetts, and Whitman's restless peregrinations from one humble, unkempt, urban working-class property to another—that fascinated critics for much of the last century. Binaries consequently proliferated—genius versus talent; originality versus derivativeness; Europhile versus nativist (but never Nativist) American. These polarities are couched in the very terms so insistently favored by Whitman, as both propagandist and poet, but when one turns directly to him for confirmation that he did, indeed, read Longfellow in this way, one is refreshingly disappointed as, he records, were those of his own time who were predisposed to believe he could feel nothing but "contempt and scorn and intolerance" for his more renowned contemporaries. It is true that in the obituary for Longfellow included in *Specimen Days*, Whitman did slightingly mention "an idiosyncrasy, almost a sickness, of verbal melody" in the work of a "poet of the mellow twilight of the past in Italy, Germany, Spain, and in Northern Europe" (918). But he embedded these comments in an altogether more complex assessment of Longfellow's work. Indeed, as in so many of his obituaries for rival writers—his remarkable commemoration of Edgar Allan Poe is, perhaps, the most arresting example—Whitman movingly affirms an intimate kinship with his subject, even to the extent of representing him as a kind of alter ego:

> [Longfellow] is certainly the sort of bard and counteractant most needed for our materialistic, self-assertive, money-worshipping, Anglo-Saxon races, and especially for the present age in America—an age tyrannically regulated with reference to the manufacturer, the merchant, the financier, the politician, and the day workman—for whom and among whom he comes as the poet of melody, courtesy, deference. (917–918)

And if one returns from this passage to the opening sentences of the obituary—where Whitman mentions hearing of Longfellow's passing when spending a "clear forenoon" in "an old forest haunt" (the natural setting is tellingly appropriate)—it is possible to find a touching, Calamus-like token of intimate comradeship in his mourning gesture of commemoration: "let me lightly twine a sprig of the sweet ground-ivy trailing so plentifully through the dead leaves at my feet, with reflections of that half-hour alone, there in the silence, and lay it as my contribution on the dead bard's grave" (917).

Vigil strange, indeed, and sufficient surely to suggest complex bonds of attachment—bonds of fellow feeling that attach Whitman to Longfellow in recognition of their common chafing bondage to their time.

Whitman's figuring of Longfellow as a "counteractant" might seem odd, even perverse, given how very warmly the reading public had welcomed so many of the New Englander's poems, and how very lavishly it had financially and otherwise rewarded its pet writer, national poet laureate by popular acclaim. Thirty thousand copies of *Hiawatha* sold in the first six months after publication—what better evidence is there for the prosecution, those later critics who saw this "infamously popular"[8] poem as the nineteenth-century equivalent of a Walt Disney kiddies' classic, subpastoral pap for the emerging urban and suburban bourgeoisie, escapist fodder, a pop-up book of exotic verbal pictures; or as (to modify Philip Rahv's celebrated terms) the ultimate American "paleface" writer's travesty of genuine "redskin" experience? So successful had Longfellow been in 1855 in reaching the mass audience Whitman himself craved that David Reynolds has recently suggested the New Yorker may in 1856 have changed the format of *Leaves of Grass* in an attempt to learn from the Bostonian's example.[9] But look more closely into the reception afforded *Leaves of Grass* and *Hiawatha* in 1855, and the obvious dramatic contrast between their respective fates begins to be complicated by other factors. If Whitman's volume was frequently derided for "resemb[ling] nothing so much as the war-cry of the Red Indians . . . the vociferations of a few amiable savages" (Murphy, 60), then Longfellow's self-confessed "Indian Edda," with its tom-tom beat, was also "savaged" for its supposed plagiarism from the Finnish *Kalevala.* "Some of the newspapers howl like dogs, or demons at it; but it only sells the faster," Longfellow wrote with apparent satisfaction to James Russell Lowell on December 31, 1855 (*Letters*, 514), while elsewhere appearing both hurt and indignant at "the blatant absurdities that have been written on the subject here" (*Letters*, 518).

In his retrospective assessment of Longfellow, Whitman himself seems conspicuously, and self-servingly, disinclined to defend his subject against the charge of lacking the "racy nativity and special originality" that Whitman implicitly reserves as his own characteristics. Instead, he prefers diplomatically to take his cue from Longfellow himself by commenting that "ere the New World can be worthily original, and announce herself and her own heroes, she must be well saturated with the originality of others, and respectfully consider the heroes that lived before Agamemnon" (919). Whitman thereby cunningly echoes, but in a tactfully muted key, the famous fanfare with which he had announced the American funeral of European culture at the very beginning of the famous 1855 preface to *Leaves of Grass*: "America does not repel the past or what it has produced under its forms . . . perceives that the corpse is slowly borne from the eating and sleeping rooms of the house . . . perceives that it waits a little while in the door . . . that it was fittest for its days . . . that its action has descended to the stalwart and wellshaped heir who approaches . . . and that he shall be fittest for his days" (5). Whitman's understanding of "inheritance" in this connection was, self-evidently, very different from that of Longfellow's. While acknowledging, en passant, the "passing on," of culture from "feudal" Europe to America, Whitman's emphasis is primarily on the final "passing away" of European culture that makes possible the coming of an essentially new culture. And it is in keeping with this cultural stance that Whitman states in 1882 that Longfellow the poet is "not revolutionary, brings nothing offensive or new, does not deal hard blows" (918). Undeniable though Whitman's strongly drawn contrast between his own originality and Longfellow's "saturation in the originality of others" may at first seem, it will not survive closer investigation. If recent scholarship has persuasively demonstrated how indebted Whitman was in actual practice to European precursors,[10] it is correspondingly conceivable that Longfellow was not unoriginal but differently "original" from Whitman in experimentally modeling *Hiawatha* on the Finnish *Kalevala* and other European texts. Moreover, it is possible that he experimented in this fashion from motives strikingly similar to those that impelled Whitman to produce his astonishingly "revolutionary" 1855 work.

Longfellow's distinctive "orginality" has been well characterized by Virginia Jackson, in an outstanding recent article on picture-writing in *Hiawatha*, and in the process she brings out the notion of American "national character" that is "the liberal idiom" of the poem. Her discussion hinges on Longfellow's own journal comments in 1847, as he prepared to write *Evangeline*:

> much is said now-a-days of a national literature. Does it mean anything? Such a literature is the expression of a national character. We have, or shall have, a composite one, embracing French, Spanish, Irish, English, Scotch, and German particularities. Whoever has within himself most of these is our truly national writer. In other words, whoever is most universal is also the most national. (Jackson, 479)

Of this, Jackson perceptively remarks that "the concept of *Weltliteratur* that Longfellow took from Goethe turns in the American context to a personage of world letters, a miracle of trans-European breeding." And it takes little imagination to see strong affinities between this concept of Americanness and Whitman's celebration of the United States as a "teeming nation of nations," or his celebration of "the renovated English speech in America"[11] as being in its libertarian, "lawless" (*Primer*, 6) essence an oxymoron—a polyglot language:

> Never will I allude to the English Language or tongue without exultation. This is the tongue that spurns law, as the greatest tongue must. It is the most capacious vital tongue of all—full of ease, definiteness, and power—full of sustenance—An enormous treasure house, or range of treasure houses, arsenals, granary, chock full with so many contributions from the north and from the south, from Scandinavia, from Greece and Rome—from Spaniards, Italians, and the French,—that its own sturdy home-dated Angles-bred words have long been outnumbered by the foreigners whom they lead—which is all good enough, and indeed must be. (*Primer*, 30)

In turn, *Hiawatha* can be read, in Whitmanian terms, as a polyglot exercise—a poem that is not only in form a fusion of genres from the new and the old worlds but also in language evidence that, as Whitman wrote, "All aboriginal names sound good. I was asking for something savage and luxuriant, and behold here are the aboriginal names" (*Primer*, 18). Although Longfellow may have been startled by the raw appetitiveness of these comments had he been able to read them, he might well have warmed to Whitman's sighing remark recorded elsewhere in the same text—"What the strange charm [the word 'fitness' is cancelled] of aboriginal names—Monongahela—it rolls with venison richness upon the palate" (*Primer*, frontispiece)—and he might have been further intrigued by Whitman's intention, as recorded in a notebook from the late 1850s, to write a "poem of the aborigines."[12]

The similarity between Whitman and Longfellow in this and other significant respects is not, of course, mere coincidence.[13] Both were products of the literary nationalism movement that had begun in the United States in the 1820s and had thus appeared and grown in strength during the formative years of their youth and early manhood. Thus began a longstanding literary tradition for, as Philip Rahv noted, "it would seem that one of the principal functions of literature in America has been to serve as a vademecum of Americanness, if not of Americanism."[14] Scholars have long charted Whitman's early involvement with the *Democratic Review*, one of the most powerful promoters of the movement under the editorship of John L. O'Sullivan, and similar work has been done on Longfellow, tracing his cultural nationalism from its very early manifestation in the then-seventeen-year-old's precocious essay "The Literary Spirit of Our Country" to later comments such as those in 1840 about the "*National Ballad*" being "a virgin soil here in New England" (quoted in Jackson, 471). Taking its cue from that veritable slogan of the movement, "Westward the star of empire takes its way," the former piece waxes eloquent on the prospect of the gradual emergence of a "national literature," and Longfellow draws very close to Whitman in arguing that it is by "intercourse and long familiarity that our native scenery comes to exert so strong an influence upon the mind, and that the features of intellect are moulded after those of nature."[15] And it is in the context of this discussion that Longfellow first, some thirty years before *Hiawatha*, declares that it is through its Indian population that America will first qualify as "classic ground . . . rich in poetic associations":

> And when our native Indians, who are fast perishing from the earth, shall have left forever the borders of our wide lakes and rivers, and their villages have decayed within the bosoms of our western hills, the dim light of tradition will rest upon those places, which have seen the glory of their battles, and heard the voice of their eloquence:—and our land will become, indeed, a classic ground. (794)

This contributionist view of the Indian who, in disappearing, "charg[ed] the land with names," also formed a prominent part of the ambivalent reactions to Native Americans of Whitman, whose involvement with Native Americans ranged from "The Inca's Daughter" (one of his earliest published poems) through his brief postwar work in the Indian Bureau, to the late poems "Red Jacket (aloft)," "Yonnondio," and "Osceola."[16] Like many of their European contemporaries, who were also products of a Romantic culture and engaged in nation-building movements, both Longfellow and Whitman were fascinated by the vatic role of "bards" and artists in the classical and antique worlds. It was the scattered, disparate fragments of oral epic materials sung by Finnish bards, particularly of the Karelia region, that were collected together by the scholar Elias Lönnrot and shaped into the *Kalevala* (1849). Longfellow read this text primarily in a German translation, and not only did it provide materials and a broad structure for *Hiawatha* it also probably emboldened Longfellow to link together often unrelated Indian materials he obtained from the writings of contemporary American ethnographers, particularly Henry Schoolcraft. It has been well observed of Elias Lönnrot that he was much more than a mere humble collector of oral folk materials: "he was a great rhapsode, performing in print as Homer's interpreters had performed at festivals in the fifth century BC: as it happens, a rhapsode was literally a 'stitcher together' of (presumably) separate poems into a performance, a rhapsody."[17] There is surely a loose, but highly suggestive, sense in which the Longfellow of *Hiawatha* may be regarded as an American "rhapsode," stitching together materials that were not only disparate but derived from several very different cultures.

Thus, the prophetic aspects of the Bible, for example, so conveniently in tune with Manifest Destiny, spoke to both Longfellow and Whitman, setting the whole tone as well as influencing the style of the first edition of *Leaves of Grass* (as was noted in chapter 2) and determining the typological structure and messianic message of *Hiawatha*. In the late eighteenth century, Herder's influential theorizing of organic national community had underpinned antiquarian interest in collecting "traditional" folk materials, Bishop Percy's *Reliques of Ancient English Poetry* (1765–1794) and Scott's *Minstrelsy of the Scottish Borders* being only two of the best-known British products. One of the most curious by-products of this "volkish" cult was James Macpherson's hugely influential and pseudo-antique *Ossian* (published in the 1760s), a work that (along with the poetry of the proto-democratic "Heaven-sent ploughman" Burns) haunted Whitman's imagination almost as much as it had Napoleon's.[18] *Ossian* has recently been demonstrated to have contributed substantially to the development of a "folklore of democracy" in nineteenth-century America,[19] and Ossianism is alive and well in *Hiawatha*'s elegiac claims—emphasized by the employment of graveyard poetry's *siste viator* (stop, traveler) convention at the beginning—to derive from the "authentic" record of a vanished people. As has recently been remarked, "*Ossian* marks the beginning of what might be called the Romantic epic, though it was not always epic in form" (*Kalevala*, xv). The most important subgroup of this genre was the collection of "national" epics, sometimes claiming to be, or to be based on, ancient sources, that were produced by the emergent nation states of nineteenth-century Europe intent on national self-determination. These included "*Zalán futása* ('The Flight of Zalán,' 1825), by Vörösmarty the Hungarian and *Pan Tadeusz* ('Master Thaddaeus,' 1834) by Mickiewicz the Pole . . . ; to these might be added *Mirèio* ('Mireille,' 1859) by the Provençal poet Mistral" (*Kalevala*, xvi). The Finnish *Kalevala*, one of the most famous works of the genre, served as one source for Longfellow's own Romantic national epic of America.

When Longfellow therefore apostrophizes, "Ye who love a nation's legends, / Love the ballads of a people," he is thinking of Continental and British sources, as well as of the Indian materials made available (albeit in forms that travestied actual Native American cultures) by Henry Schoolcraft and others. Through Longfellow's extensive travels and periods of stay in Europe from his late teens onward, the Continent had, said his biographer Newton Arvin, entered "into the tissue of Longfellow's sensibility as it has entered into that of few Americans."[20] The familiarity he attained with many of Europe's major languages and literatures remains very impressive, although those he omits also have much implicitly to say about Longfellow's "construction" of Europe—a selective construction that may be said to have political as well as literary connotations. Something of Longfellow's range may be gauged from his mammoth 1845 anthology of *The Poets and Poetry of Europe* in English translation. A volume in double columns that runs to almost a thousand pages, it ranges from the Eddas, *Beowulf*, and *The Cid* to Longfellow's own time (Foscolo, Lamartine, and Heine), and from Italy to Sweden. As Longfellow explains, it includes work in "the six Gothic languages of the North of Europe" and "the four Latin languages of the South of Europe," each of the sections on these "national" languages being prefaced with a substantial, learned essay by Longfellow himself.[21] The whole volume is, in essence, a classic text of nineteenth-century literary nationalism and valuable evidence of the vital part literature played in the great nineteenth-century undertaking of nation building. A central plank of such an undertaking was the demonstration of the antiquity of the nation, and of the continuity of national character that could be traced through the "nation's literature." Hence, for example, the prominence given in the introduction to the German section to the "songs" of the Minnesinger, to "the noble old epic" (181) of the Niebelungenlied, and to the role of the guilds and their "master singers" in arousing "the genius of the German people" (184), thus helping to bring order, prosperity, and unity between previously feuding principalities. These proto-Wagnerian interpretations are culled by Longfellow from the work of a fellow scholar, who concludes with the observation that the society of the master singers "had the peculiar merit to become the guardian of [Germany's] native tongue, and transmit it pure through the deflux of barbarous languages" (186).

Aspiring to be the "master singers" of their own nation of America, both Longfellow and Whitman were naturally interested to the point of obsession in the concept of song. Of the twelve poems in the 1855 *Leaves of Grass*, three were later to be entitled songs, and virtually the whole of the preface to that first edition is devoted to amplifying the role of the American master singer. By claiming that, of all nations, the Americans "have probably the fullest poetical nature" and that "the United States themselves are essentially the greatest poem" (5), Whitman is able to claim for himself as poet the status of true Native American. And declaring that, in effect, he can hear America singing allows him further to assert that the poet alone is truly in tune with the United States, whereas the actual ongoing life of the country is full of false notes and discords: "To him [the poet] enter the essences of the real things and past and present events—of the enormous diversity of temperature and agriculture and mines—the tribes of red aborigines . . . the union always surrounded by blatherers and always calm and impregnable" (7–8). That last statement rings with the note of anxiety about the times, which is the real ground note not only of the preface but also of *Hiawatha*, another work of 1855, deeply concerned with the role of the poet and his song. And, again like Whitman, Longfellow is particularly concerned with exploring the *power* of the poet, in a poem that seems particularly intent on distinguishing between many different forms of power. A fantasy particularly close to Longfellow's heart surfaces in the dream of an alliance between the poet-musician Chibiabos and the "very strong man," Kwasind, respectively representing the power of the imagination and the power of action: "For they kept each other's counsel, / Spake with naked hearts together, / Pondering much, and much contriving / How the tribes of men might prosper" (43). But through the early death of both characters—a defeat for pacific goodness that anticipates the later death of Hiawatha, who in his youth defeated the tyrannical, bellicose, death-dealing Megissogwon—Longfellow seems to be articulating a fear that haunted all his work; a fear that poetry would after all prove powerless in the face of brute circumstance; a fear that politics would prove impervious to poetry. In the early collection *The Belfry of Bruges* (1845), for example, two beautiful lyrics form a diptych on this theme. In the first, "The Arrow and the Song," what is celebrated is the unpredictable vitality and durability of poems ("For who has sight so keen and strong, / That it can follow the flight of song?" 53); but in the second, "Curfew," books pass away like an author's mind: "Dim grow its fancies; / Forgotten they lie; / Like coals in the ashes, / They darken and die" (55). And it is this last feeling that is again in the ascendant in the powerfully somber Civil War poem "The Wind over the Chimney":

> And again the tongues of flame
> Start exulting and exclaim:
> "There are prophets, bards, and sects;
> In the horoscope of nations,
> Like ascendant constellations,
> They control the coming years."

This is a pentecostal image worthy of the Whitman who declared of the poet in the first edition of *Leaves of Grass* that "He resolves all tongues into his own, and bestows it upon men . . . and any man translates . . . and any man translates himself also" (130). But in Longfellow's poem the night-wind quenches those tongues of fire with a different, stark, message:

> Dust are all the hands that wrought;
> Books are sepulchres of thought;
> The dead laurels of the dead
> Rustle for a moment only,
> Like the withered leaves in lonely
> Churchyards at some passing tread. (477)

Nor is this simply conventionally lugubrious *ubi sunt* lamentation. Rather, these fears of the effective impotence of creative acts are the dark underside of the febrile affirmations of creative potency that echo through *Hiawatha* and the 1855 *Leaves of Grass*. They hint at the sinister contemporary agencies to which the poems are, in Whitman's terms, "counteractants."

It is perhaps no accident that 1855 saw both Whitman and Longfellow produce some of their most strikingly original and powerful work. The midpoint of a singularly turbulent decade leading to the Civil War, it was a year in which America was forced to undergo radical political realignment in the face of violent social and economic pressures threatening to tear the country apart. And it was those very same pressures that also produced radical realignments of creative imagination, most notably instanced in two controversial, experimentally hybrid texts, *Hiawatha* and *Leaves of Grass*. These were "counteractants" to extraordinary contemporary developments in the political, economic, and social sectors (already touched upon in chapter 2)—ominously growing tension between North and South, severe social dislocations caused by the rapid expansion of a rapacious new capitalist order, and an organized urban backlash against increasing immigration.

Gone are the days when Longfellow was supposed to be an unworldly dreamer, a poet wholly detached from politics. Any reading of the *Letters* or *Journals* would quickly dispel that impression, and in an excellent article Robert Ferguson has demonstrated how "properly understood, Longfellow's anxieties over the sectional strife leading to the Civil War cast a strong shadow over such works as *The Song of Hiawatha* in 1855 and *The Courtship of Miles Standish* in 1858."[22] His concerns had been earlier expressed in the memorable conclusion to "The Building of the Ship":

> Thou, too, sail on, O Ship of State!
> Sail on, O UNION, strong and great!
> Humanity with all its fears,
> With all the hopes of future years,
> Is hanging breathless on thy fate! (126)

But when pressed by Francis Lieber in 1850 to follow up this success with a volume of "patriotic tunes . . . Songs to the Country," Longfellow replied "One Song—one good Song would be enough. All could be said in one. I am a Unitarian" (*Letters*, 245). *The Song of Hiawatha* could be said to be that "one good Song," and Hiawatha himself the ultimate political, as well as religious, Unitarian. As early as 1850, Longfellow's correspondence shows him mentally contrasting the bellicosity of white Americans with the different spirit of Native Americans. A letter dated June 12, 1850, addressed to English lawyer Arthur Mills, opens by presenting to him

> a chief of the Ojibway nation, by name Kah-ge-ga-gah-Buwh; or, if you prefer the English name, George Copway.
>
> Do not be alarmed, and think that he will burst into your drawing-room with a war-whoop. On the contrary, he is a man of Peace, and "the things that make for

> Peace," and is on his way to the Peace Convention at Frankfurt. You will have much pleasure in knowing him, I am sure, and will take an interest in his conversation, and his plans for his race. (260)

And Longfellow ends by writing:

> I suppose you read in the papers about as much of American politics as you care to know. The great question is still the Slave Question. The South is angry, because it cannot work the mines of California with its slaves, and is making a rather noisy but, I hope, unsuccessful effort to extend slavery in the new territories, and to increase its power in the Senate, by making new Slave States. Webster's course on this last point, has grieved and disappointed many of his friends at the north; and Horace Mann . . . has taken the highest and only true ground, of opposition to Slavery wherever it can be reached. To this I say Amen. (260)

Always inclined to favor the more radical abolitionist line, Longfellow was a close friend of the fiery Charles Sumner, to whom he wrote no fewer than thirty letters from 1851–1853, "bolstering," as Longfellow's editor has put it, "Sumner's courage on the congressional battlefield" (286).[23] Longfellow's letters from the early fifties include one to Sumner congratulating him on his speech in support of the motion to repeal the 1850 Fugitive Slave Act (354) and another in 1853 to Harriet Beecher Stowe praising *Uncle Tom's Cabin* (371). He grew particularly heated over the Kansas-Nebraska issue,[24] bitterly opposing Stephen Douglas's "popular sovereignty" thesis (418) and praising Sumner's "very noble—very cogent—very eloquent—very complete" speech against the Nebraska bill that sought to overturn the Missouri Compromise and admit slavery into territories west of the Mississippi (408). And when the bill was nevertheless passed on the night of March 3–4, 1854, Longfellow wrote posthaste to Sumner mourning "that *noche triste* of our history" (425). Yet throughout this period, Longfellow persisted also in expressing his deep sympathy for a southern society he saw as being betrayed by its leaders. Writing to a southern acquaintance in 1853, he could declare "Ah! would that the North and South knew each other better! My heart has a southern side to it, and I am sure yours has a northern. We could speak of Slavery I am sure, *sans peur et sans reproche*" (378). And this turn to French—like the turn to Spanish in the previous use of *noche triste*—may usefully be seen as adumbrating the very linguistic and cultural strategies that characterize that bilingual, multicultural hybrid, *Hiawatha.* In order to allow full imaginative play for his confusion of feelings yet avoid being overwhelmed by contending passions, Longfellow needed to refract the bitter conflicts of contemporary American politics through a series of different lenses—enabling devices of language, style, and convention, that allowed him to gain a degree of mental control over materials that would otherwise be wholly intractable, dangerously inimical to imagination.

"All your strength is in your union, / All your danger is in discord; / Therefore be at peace henceforward, / And as brothers live together" (8). The chiding of "Gitche Manito, the mighty, / The Great Spirit, the creator" (9) makes it amply clear that *Hiawatha* is in part a fantasy of reconciliation—rapprochement between North and South; between the northern and the southern aspects of Longfellow's own heart. Equally clear, as Robert Ferguson has emphasized, is the fact that in the end the fantasy sadly confesses its own limits and limitations. And as many scholars have by now demonstrated, there is a like dynamic at work in Whitman's work of 1855, powered as it too is by a passionate old Free-Soiler's angry bewilderment at the turn of political events.[25] His extraordinary success in the 1855 edition at devising textual means of overcoming his own inner confusion and the murderous divisions within his country is suggestively prefigured in a passage from the preface. In one of its characteristically long sentences—themselves the stylistic evidence of Whitman's sociopolitical purpose—the bare bones of a key rhetorical strategy are exposed. Whitman here reduces his version of the historical development of the United States to a single sentence. It begins by invoking the coming of the white settlers to the shores of the "red aborigines"; moves on to "the haughty defiance of '76" and the formation of the Union on the basis of the Constitution; traces the growth of maritime America; notes the opening up of the West; and then dwells at length, through phrase piled upon euphoric phrase, on the new urban democratic America of "free . . . workmen and workwomen," a democratic society Whitman firmly associates with the New York and Yankee milieu of "factories and mercantile life and laborsaving machinery." This paean of praise to democratic America predictably culminates in the example of "the New-York firemen and the target excursion"; and it is right next to this image that Whitman tellingly places—in implied contrast to the whole irresistible "logic" of national development as conveyed by the growing momentum of his sentence—a studied neutral reference to "the southern plantation life." He then immediately highlights, as political corrective, "the character of the northeast and the northwest and southwest," before his sentence finally allows what has been stylistically repressed to surface at last as Whitman turns to confront what has now been implicitly defined as the un-American abomination of "slavery and the tremulous spreading of hands to protect it, and the stern opposition to it which shall never cease till it ceases or the speaking of tongues and the moving of lips cease" (7–8). As will have been noticed, he is careful here, even at the very end, not to allow slavery to stand grammatically apart, using the copula to bind slavery irrevocably to the true spirit of free, democratic America, which opposes it and which, by implication, will inevitably triumph over it. This long sentence is, therefore, a highly instructive study in the politics of grammar, and as such it alerts us to the subtle means by which political anxieties are inscribed in, and mastered by, the very rhetoric of convention, style, and structure in the 1855 work of both Whitman and Longfellow. To realize this is also to realize that *Leaves of Grass* is no less, and no more, a creative fantasy than *Hiawatha.* What is needed is not a simple, sterile contrast between the two works in terms of a distinction between the "escapist" and the "visionary"—between a writer evading the political "realities" of the day and a writer facing them—but a more generously inclusive, more flexible understanding of fantasy as a potently ambivalent mental (and political) activity, every bit as enabling as it may become disabling.

Viewed in the light of Native American studies, for instance, it is the seriously disabling aspects of Longfellow's fantasy of "Indian" life and lore that immediately loom overwhelmingly large. He is open to any number of charges on this score. His cavalier mixing and garbling of the cultural materials of several very different tribes now seem symptomatic of a deplorable tendency to see "Indians" as a single, undifferentiated racial phenomenon; his very sympathy with the "vanishing Americans" may be sensed as a readiness to hasten their passing; his implied message of "Christian" values shared by whites and American aboriginals can appear to prefigure the appalling late nineteenth-century policy of cultural "assimilation" of native peoples.[26] And there are plenty more charges that could be pressed—for example, his infatuation with an Indian language seems to bespeak a condescending primitivism and to lead to the kind of appropriation by English of a "foreign" tongue that is deplored in postcolonial theory.

But it is at least possible to view Longfellow's handling of Native American materials in a rather different light. By the time he came to write *Hiawatha* there was an established tradition in northern culture, particularly in abolitionist circles, of loosely but suggestively associating Indian experience with black experience. As Linda K. Kerber has noted, "The Florida War, even more than the First Seminole War and Cherokee removal, seemed to demonstrate America's failure as a republic and helped to establish in the minds of a number of abolitionists the conviction that the problem of the slave and the Indian were related."[27] One consequence, as Kerber further notes, was that some writers (including Thoreau) came to use "the Indian theme as a mode of criticizing the failings of white

America" (272); and *Hiawatha* may be said to be a somewhat unconventional instance of this practice. As with other examples of this "genre," the poem therefore uses Indians partly as a means of indirectly addressing the condition of a ruthlessly materialistic America that would allow no human sympathies or humane scruples to interfere with the business of generating profit. And there are examples in *Leaves of Grass*, too, of Whitman conflating blacks and Indians. In the 1855 version of "The Sleepers," the celebrated "Lucifer" passage—"Now Lucifer was not dead . . . or if he was I am his sorrowful terrible heir" (113)—in which Whitman identifies sympathetically with violently vengeful black slave reaction against white oppression, immediately follows the almost equally celebrated account of how his mother had once strangely befriended "a red squaw"—"The more she looked upon her she loved her, / Never before had she seen such wonderful beauty and purity" (112)—and had pined at her disappearance.

Whitman's juxtaposition of these two passages is an instance of what might loosely be termed the politics of parallelism—an ideologically charged structuring device that is fundamental to *Leaves of Grass*. It is an example of the way in which in literary texts social vision is as often present as a function of style as it is manifest as content. This is a truism that, until very recently, seems to have been better understood by Whitman scholars than by Longfellow scholars. In the mid-1850s, the imminent danger of the rupturing of the sociopolitical ties that bound the United States together lent urgency to both Whitman and Longfellow's search for a poetics of unification, one aspect of which was their attempt to establish, by textual means, an intimate relationship with their readers. Reading needed to be a bonding experience rather like pressing the flesh. Several of Whitman's texts notoriously attempted to radiate a kind of body heat, and the rhythms of his writing approximate to those primal rhythms of human bodily existence he associates, at different points in "Song of Myself," with "the procreant urge of the world," "My respiration and inspiration . . . the beating of my heart . . . the passing of blood and air through my lungs" (27). These "organic" features of the style have been documented and interpreted by scholars, whereas critics of Longfellow's verse confined themselves, for far too long, to noting (and frequently regretting) the supposedly monotonous, metronomic rhythm.

Critics would have been better advised to take their cue from an essay by Longfellow's distinguished contemporary and fellow Bostonian Oliver Wendell Holmes, entitled "The Physiology of Versification."[28] Respiration and the pulse "are the true timekeepers of the body," writes Holmes (315), and "the reason why eight syllable verse"—Holmes specifically instances *Hiawatha*—"is so singularly easy to read aloud is that it follows more exactly than any other the natural rhythm of respiration" (316). Holmes's theory is therefore evidently based on his understanding of the orality of the text, an essential feature *Hiawatha* of course shared with Whitman's *Leaves of Grass.*[29] For both poets, to "lend voice" to a text was to empower it with infinitely greater immediacy of "presence," an essential attribute if it was to operate as a socially binding act. When reading *Hiawatha* aloud, Holmes further observes, "the only effort required is that of vocalizing and articulating; the breathing takes care of itself, not even demanding a thought except where the sense may require a pause in the middle of a line. The very fault with these octosyllabic lines is that they slip away too fluently, and run easily in a monotonous sing-song" (317). And there we come to one of the most common complaints about *Hiawatha.*

But what if "monotonous sing-song" was, in a somewhat different sense from that intended by Holmes, precisely what Longfellow set out to achieve? Like Whitman, Longfellow seems to have been interested in devising a meter that would alter ordinary rational mental processes, transporting the listener to a very different state of consciousness. This feature of Whitman's writing has been suggestively dubbed "shamanistic" by George B. Hutchinson,[30] and David S. Reynolds has vividly documented his indebtedness to spiritualism, mesmerism, and the whole culture of "trance poetry and lecturing . . . [that] was very common in the fifties" (*Walt Whitman's America*, 267). In particular, Reynolds draws attention to the figure of Thomas Lake Harris, an unorthodox Swedenborgian whose church Whitman may have attended in the early 1850s. Guided by the spirit of Dante—whose *Divine Comedy* Longfellow was to translate—"Harris's soul sped to vast reaches of space, beyond distant stars and suns to the highest or 'seventh' sphere, where he saw a society of rapturously united conjugal lovers, a society of infinite love and brotherhood prefiguring a future Harmonic society on earth" (267). Reynolds's conclusion is that Whitman "was a cultural ventriloquist who gave expression to the mass interest in trances and spiritualism. The midfifties, when he produced his mystical poetry, was a kind of watershed moment for popular mysticism. Whitman participated in the popular trend" (271). And as Reynolds pertinently notices, these characteristics of the writing "explain the appeal of Whitman's verse for many of his contemporary admirers . . . by far the most common response to his poetry expressed in letters he received was that he was a healer and soul-rescuer" (277–278).

No doubt, all this would have been far too vulgar for the well-bred and intellectually refined Longfellow, but he, too, had aspirations to be "a healer and soul-rescuer." Unlike Whitman, he aimed to achieve this through en*chant*ment—by producing a poem that would be spellbinding. One of Longfellow's lifelong friends was Nathaniel Hawthorne, and he marked his passing by writing an elegy for "the wizard hand [that] lies cold . . . that hand of magic power" (474). A generic term that seems to illuminate *Hiawatha* very well, yet seems to have been rarely applied to it, is "fantasy."[31] Pupil to Washington Irving, steeped in the fantastical writings of E. T. A. Hoffmann, a contemporary of Hans Christian Andersen and—yes—a precursor of the much-maligned Walt Disney, Longfellow may be thought of as the J. R. R. Tolkien of his day, an apparently dry-as-dust scholar, linguist, and cultural antiquary who nevertheless managed to produce one of the most magical, best-loved books of his century. And just as *The Lord of the Rings*, originating as in part it did from Tolkien's personal experiences of the trenches during World War I, gives oblique expression to the nightmare world of the Europe of the 1930s, so *Hiawatha* is haunted by the specters that stalked white America in the 1850s.[32] Through fantasy Longfellow is able to create a wondrous parallel universe, in which the anxieties of the time undergo displacement, becoming metamorphosed into actions and beings rich and strange—metamorphosis being one of the fundamental animating principles of the whole text. *The Song of Hiawatha* is no more "escapist" than are *The Faerie Queene*, Kipling's *Jungle Book*, or, for that matter, the late plays of Shakespeare. Like all true fantasy, it is an enabling device: it allows the mind to "dwell in possibility," as Emily Dickinson put it, floating free from the gravity of established reality and thus making possible the kind of paradigm shift that can make an alternative social, political, and economic reality visible and viable. By some such indirections and sly obliquities does all art no doubt work, but fantasy makes the fictionality of art unapologetically egregious, refusing as it does to masquerade as servant of the currently regnant version of the reality principle. That *Hiathawa* functions in this way, in relation to white American culture, may need emphasizing as a corrective, since so much has understandably been made of the way in which Longfellow's fantasy served to obscure the grim reality of contemporary white American treatment of the very Native American culture that Longfellow himself "raided" for the raw materials of his narrative.

The virtual world of fantasy is necessarily an all-enveloping world that consumes the reader's attention, and hence the magical drumming of the rhythm in *Hiawatha*. The rhythm tells the truth about the poem—that it is its own place, with its own laws, its own structures, and, above all else perhaps, its own language. There is a sense in which the learned notes Longfellow provides as textual glossary are as irrelevant, as redundant, as Eliot's notorious annotations of *The Waste Land*. Reason's revenge on the imagination, they may be variously read as a sop to Longfellow's moralistic conscience—the author's nervous and necessarily futile attempt to anchor his free-floating, fathomless text in the safe and sound bottom of scholarship—or as a sop to the average, robustly commonsensical reader who requires imaginative texts always to come complete with a guarantee of their functional "reality." But if, as Noel Coward once memorably quipped, "having to read a footnote resembles having to go downstairs to answer the door while in the midst of making love,"[33] then having to read an endnote is even more of an impediment to the free abandonment of the reading self to an unabashed enjoyment of jouissance; of the erotics of a fantasy text. In the case of *Hiawatha*, it is therefore best rather to take one's cue from the language *within* the text, which is a kind of synecdoche for the language *of* the text. Longfellow's way with Native American words has received much attention in recent times, but much of it has—quite properly from the purely political point of view—concentrated on the cultural implications of such "theft," in the context of postcolonial concerns with the inevitable vicious double bind of any attempt by an imperial subject to voice "authentic" subaltern experience. However, Longfellow's use of these materials may be read in a different way, from the perspective of his textual construction of a fantastical world. As the text makes clear, the Native American words are the language of *Hiawatha*'s world (as distinct from the language of the world of a putatively "real" Indian called Hiawatha). In this respect, they relate to the poem rather as Elvish and the other imaginary languages (conjured from Welsh, Cornish, Old Irish, and other elements) relate to *The Lord of the Rings*. In this connection, what is worth noting is not the dutiful—and from present-day perspectives, suspect—glossary of terms Longfellow appends to the text, but rather the way in which the text itself teaches us to *speak* this/its language. And here the rhythm of the poem plays an indispensable role, since it is the very predictability of the distribution of the accent in a four stress line that allows us always, in *poetic* context, to tell how to pronounce words that would otherwise defeat us. We are thus initiated unawares into a different speech community:

> Heard the lapping of the water,
> Sounds of music, words of wonder;
> "Minne-wawa!" said the pine-trees,
> "Mudway-aushka!" said the water.
> Saw the firefly, Wah-wah-taysee,
> Flitting through the dusk of evening . . . (21)

We therefore find ourselves—particularly as we read aloud, as Holmes advised—enabled by the text to "speak" the language of this particular fantasy realm. The analogy would be with nonsense poetry—that poetry of pure fantasy—

except that Longfellow is, of course, always careful to gloss the "foreign" words within the confines of the text itself, in a linguistic gesture that implicitly recognizes that his poem is a single, closed system of meaning. And if "Indian" words are thus "translated" into English, so, too, is the English of *Hiawatha* implicitly "translated" into a language that, as the Indian words themselves suggest, is the discrete language of Longfellow's fantasy world. As between the Native American and the English languages of *Hiawatha* it is, at least in this connection, a case of cross-pollination, of mutual infection.

Insofar as it is palpable fiction brazenly staring down "reality," the tall tale may usefully be regarded as one of the more colorful minor branches of the literature of fantasy. In her incomparable study of American humor, Constance Rourke long ago demonstrated how Whitman's "large impetus seems to have come from popular sources, particularly in the West,"[34] noting how at times his poetry approximated to the exuberantly excessive narratives of "the wildest of western comic boastings [of] the rhapsodic, leaping, crowing backwoodsman" (173): "Unscrew the locks from the doors! / Unscrew the doors themselves from their jambs!" (50); "I dote on myself . . . there is that lot of me, and all so luscious, / Each moment and whatever happens thrills me with joy" (51); "My ties and ballasts leave me . . . I travel . . . I sail . . . my elbows rest in the sea-gaps, / I skirt the sierras . . . my palms cover continents, / I am afoot with my vision" (59). As Rourke notes, "To enter the world of Whitman is to touch the spirit of American popular comedy, with its local prejudices, its national prepossessions, its fantastic beliefs; many phases of comic reaction are unfolded there" (175). And she interestingly homes in not on "Song of Myself" but on "A Boston Ballad" as an instance of how "Whitman joined in the classic comic warfare between the backwoodsman and the Yankee. Half gravity, half burlesque, in its swift slipping from the foothold of reality the poem is not far from the pattern of the tall tales or from the familiar extravagant form of mock-oratory" (174).

But brilliant—if nowadays sadly overlooked—though Rourke's discussion is, she fails to take the hint afforded by her own example of "A Boston Ballad" to explore the cultural, and indeed the specifically political, wellspring of Whitman's outrageous rhetoric. The "Ballad" derived, of course, from his outrage at the Anthony Burns affair, the notorious legal case that resulted in the forcible return by federal marshalls, under the recently reinforced Fugitive Slave Act, of Burns from "free" Boston to enslavement in Virginia. Whitman placed his poem toward the end of the 1855 collection, but there is a sense in which it could well have served as prologue to the whole volume, as it offered explicit insight into those aspects of Whitman's America to which *Leaves of Grass* related as "counteractant." The Burns affair also deeply disturbed the Bostonian Longfellow, and in *Hiawatha* he, too, produced a poem that acted as "counteractant" to prevailing sociopolitical conditions by demonstrating, and thus defiantly asserting, the wild unsubduable power of the imagination. Unlike "Song of Myself," *Hiawatha* has, perhaps, been insufficiently valued for its extravagance. Yet included in the poem is "wonderful Iagoo," "the great boaster, / He the marvellous story-teller" (80), who entrances with "immeasurable falsehoods" to justify his own powers and to warn off jesters. He entertains the guests at Hiawatha's wedding with a tale that Longfellow prefaces with an extraordinary Iagoo-like excursion of his own imagination:

> Can it be the sun descending
> O'er the level plain of water?
> Or the Red Swan floating, flying,
> Wounded by the magic arrow,
> Staining all the waves with crimson,
> With the crimson of its lifeblood,
> Filling all the air with splendor,
> With the splendor of its plumage?
>   Yes; it is the sun descending,
> Sinking down into the water;
> All the sky is stained with purple,
> All the water flushed with crimson!
> No; it is the Red Swan floating,
> Diving down beneath the water;
> To the sky its wings are lifted,
> With its blood the waves are reddened! (83)

By maintaining a dual perspective, or offering a bifocal vision, in this extended passage which twins common sense with fantasy throughout, Longfellow advertises his own transformative powers—powers of the same order as those Iagoo is to celebrate in the tale of transfiguration that follows. In other words, Longfellow as poet implicitly identifies himself with Iagoo and his gargantuan powers of fantastical imagination. Intensely aware of the fateful power struggle that was going on within the United States, Longfellow was, as has been suggested earlier, understandably obsessed with power in *Hiawatha*, and many of the poem's figures and events allow him to distinguish between different kinds of power in society. One little incident can serve as a parable in this respect. On the one hand, in Book XIII, Hiawatha believes in his wife Minnehaha's power to "draw a magic circle" by walking naked around the cornfields at night to protect them from destruction. But when Hiawatha hears those cynical exponents of realpolitik, the black crows, mock Minnehaha's efforts, he—good Yankee that he is at heart—takes the expedient practical step of spreading snares over all the fields to catch and destroy them. The incident neatly encapsulates two competing, but also in some ways complementary, impulses in Longfellow—the impulse to trust to the magic counteractant spell of poetry and the impulse to recognize that it can exert little power in the political arena where the rapacious crows cockily, mockingly rule the roost.

Much of Whitman's boasting in "Song of Myself" is transgressive, in the sense that it overrules set limits and distinctions, between soul and body, for instance, but also between one region of America and another. Hence, when he so exhilaratingly asserts that "[m]y ties and ballasts leave me . . . I travel . . . I sail . . . my elbows rest in the sea-gaps, / I skirt the sierras . . . my palms cover continents, / I am afoot with my vision" he is, in fact, embracing the whole of America in a manner that specifically defies the divisive political arrangements of 1855. As will be emphasized in the next chapter, there is, after all, an important sense in which slavery had been turned into a geopolitical issue, first by the Missouri Compromise and then by the Kansas-Nebraska Act of 1854. Slavery was about winning territory—specifically the new territories that were up for grabs following the violent seizure of land from Mexico and the Midwest from Native Americans—and Whitman's Free-Soil principles were increasingly hard pressed to hold their ground. No wonder that the preface as well as much of the poetry of the first edition of *Leaves of Grass* 1855 is fixated on the natural landscape of the United States, and that Whitman militantly constructs "Nature" in the image of his ideology of a democratic America. The circularity of his argument is therefore perfect, and within that magic circle his visionary ideology is perfectly safe from destruction by social and political realities. It cannot be too often stressed that "Nature" in Whitman is *white American* nature, the very source and protector of *Americanness* as so conceived. And there was another, related reason for this obsessive turn to nature. The Fugitive Slave Act was but the latest of a number of legal measures taken that exposed potential weaknesses in a theory of American nationhood based on a legal, contractual agreement entered into by nominally free, independent states. It then followed that any of those states could withdraw from the contract virtually at will—hence the logical argument of the southern states that they were at liberty to secede from the Union. There is a perceptible mistrust of law expressed in Whitman's writings of the fifties, and by turning increasingly to arguments for nationhood not from law but from nature he was able to "ground" Americanness solidly on the very rock and soil, and in the flora and fauna, of a whole continent that was literally single and indivisible under God. This is one of the most significant of the political strategies enacted through the rhetoric of discourse in the preface and poetry of the 1855 *Leaves of Grass*.[35] Whitman's recurrent refrain is that "[t]he largeness of nature or the nation were monstrous without a corresponding largeness and generosity of the spirit of the citizens" (6), a theme that swells into magnificent diapason in one of the most remarkable paragraphs of the preface, which includes the following incomparable passage:

> When the long Atlantic coast stretches longer and the Pacific coast stretches longer he easily stretches between them north or south. He spans between them also from east to west and reflects what is between them. On him rise solid growths that offset the growths of pine and cedar and hemlock and liveoak and locust and chestnut and cypress and hickory and limetree and cottonwood and tuliptree and cactus and wildvine and tamarind and persimmon . . . and tangles as tangled as any canebrake or swamp . . . and forests coated with transparent ice and icicles hanging from the boughs and crackling in the wind . . . and sides and peaks of mountains . . . and pasturage sweet and free as savannah or upland or prairie . . . with flights and songs and screams that answer those of the wildpigeon and highold and orchard-oriole and coot and surf-duck and redshouldered-hawk and fish-hawk and white-ibis and indian-hen and cat-owl and water-pheasant and qua-bird and pied-sheldrake and blackbird and mockingbird and buzzard and condor and night-heron and eagle. (7)

Whitman here turns himself into the American equivalent of the Green Man; a fertility spirit of American politics. He demonstrates the mythopoeic cast of his imagination—having the germ of it in him, he can grow myth from seed, so to speak, whereas Longfellow deals only in transplanted myths and legends. It may be that Longfellow is acquainted with the *Kalevala*, but it is Whitman who is instinctively and wholly unconsciously to produce the American equivalent of an episode such as the following, where the Air-daughter, future mother of Väinämöinen "the eternal bard," sculpts earth:

> Where she turned her hand around
> there she arranged the headlands;
> where her foot touched the bottom
> there she dug out the fish troughs;

where else she bubbled
there she hollowed out the depths.
She turned her side to the land;
there she formed the salmon haunts;
with her head she reached the land:
there she shaped the bays. (*Kalevala,* 8)

But Whitman, of course, does not see himself as simply adding to the stock of existing mythic lore. The thrust of his whole passage is rather that America is the true native country of the human imagination, since it is in very fact more fantastical than fiction; brag is therefore the natural idiom of the country, and the democratic "experiment"—which might otherwise be mistaken for the tallest human story of all—is here the only, natural form of social and political arrangement. This is what Whitman means when he asserts that "[t]he Americans of all nations at any time upon the earth have probably the fullest poetical nature. The United States themselves are essentially the greatest poem. In the history of the earth hitherto the largest and most stirring appear tame and orderly to their ampler largeness and stir" (5).

Whereas this fundamental aspect of Whitman's 1855 writing has been tolerably well appreciated by critics, the corresponding aspects of *Hiawatha* have tended to be overlooked. Yet Longfellow's turn to nature is surely motivated, in part, by the same desperate political need as Whitman's to find safer, sounder "grounds" for a free, democratic Union than extant legal and political arrangements—so graphically exposed by the Burns affair—could possibly provide. And he too accordingly constructs nature in the very image of his own concept of authentic Americanness, thereby sanctioning it as the only form of Americanness that nature could allow.

That brings us, inevitably, to the search for the "authentic" in the poetry of both Longfellow and Whitman—their common search, aggravated by urgent contemporary political need, for a foundational Americanness. Postcolonial theory, particularly as practiced by Gayatri Spivak, has been understandably scathing about the bad faith of notions of this kind. As Eve Patten has recently written: "The concept of cultural authenticity has of course been heavily interrogated within postcolonial critique, leading to a range of questions concerning the validation, manipulation and fetishization of the subaltern voice by an imperial or a post-imperial authority."[36] And as Virginia Jackson has recently written: "*Hiawatha* not only actively joins the American campaign to 'disappear' native cultures by appearing to chronicle genocide passively as a fait accompli; it makes the passage of one American language into another—of the na-*tive* into the na-*tion*—the vehicle of that disappearance" (Jackson, 478). Nevertheless, when historically contextualized, the search by both American authors in 1855 for primal validation of their enlightened social and political vision is not without its power—nor without its poignancy, because neither of them can ignore the fact that, to alter Frost's famous expression, the land was theirs (the Indians) before we (the Americans) were the land's. In other words, both Whitman and Longfellow were faced with the indisputable fact of prior possession, of previous occupation of that very "Nature" to which they nevertheless felt they had "authentic" claim in the name of white democratic America. It was here, of course, that pre-Darwinian notions of cosmic evolution and human progress came very much into their own—American nature could only fully realize itself in human terms through, and as, the new "experiment" of democratic society. Nevertheless, both Whitman and Longfellow remained haunted by the conviction that the Indians had enjoyed a special, privileged relationship of intimacy with the land. It was a relationship of which they were, so to speak, jealous and which they wanted somehow to replicate in their own writing. And, in Longfellow's case (as, partly, in Whitman's), this led to a wish to write in the very language of the Indians—"language" here meaning not only the actual words but also the mythic and legendary modes of expression characteristic of aboriginal cultures.

Longfellow's account in *Hiawatha* of the supposed origins of Native American language in pictographs has been splendidly analyzed by Virginia Jackson. Attributing his interest to an expressed wish to touch the hearts of his readers—a wish she suggestively associates with that of Whitman, but without noting that for both writers it was in part a textual strategy for managing a political crisis—she shows how *Hiawatha* succeeds in making "not only classical literacy but vernacular literacy available at a discount" (Jackson, 476). She draws on Jacques Derrida's work to demonstrate the fallacy of the theory of "presence" that Longfellow advances in Book XIV ("Picture-Writing"), from which aspects of his own linguistic practice in the poem derived. (Like philosophical objections could, of course, be made from the modern perspective to much of Whitman's theory and practice of language.) And particularly interesting, from the point of view of the present discussion, are Jackson's remarks about the motives attributed to Hiawatha for devising pictographs:

> For these reasons Hiawatha invents picture-writing: to preserve the memorial trace, to create a history, to transmit a history, to claim an inheritance, to establish kin-

> ships, to disseminate presence across distance but also to keep communication private. (Jackson, 483)

In every particular, these reasons exactly conform to Longfellow's (and Whitman's) political reasons in 1855 for writing poetry such as they did at the time when they did. And one of the key, poignant aspects of their practice is captured in that mention of the apparent paradox of an utterance that, while intended to reach as wide a public as possible, nevertheless keeps "communication private." Both Whitman and Longfellow dreamed of producing, by poetic means, what Edward Thomas evocatively called "a language not to be betrayed"[37]—that is, a language that could not be politically hijacked, or otherwise falsified by being twisted from its truth; a language that could never be rendered inauthentic but would forever remain the sanctuary of the highest moral, social, spiritual, and political values; a language that would be the true tabernacle, or inner sanctum, of "authentic" Americanness; the language that was the authentic Edenic idiom of American nature. This language was paradoxically conceived of by both Whitman and Longfellow as the exclusive, elite vernacular of true mass, popular democracy. (In 1860, Whitman was to give expression in *Calamus* to a related dream, but now defensively couched in much more limited, intimately personal terms.) And for both Whitman and Longfellow, this language was the unique visionary gift of the poet-prophet to "his" people:

> Thus it was that Hiawatha,
> In his wisdom, taught the people
> All the mysteries of painting,
> All the art of Picture-Writing,
> On the smooth bark of the birch-tree,
> On the white skin of the reindeer,
> On the grave-posts of the village. (105–106)

But as Jackson points out, Hiawatha's is a disappeared language before the poem ever begins, a sad fate that, by implication and extension, Longfellow recognizes in the political gloom of 1855 America as very probably being his own. Triumphantly successful though he might be as poet laureate of white bourgeois America—such was his success in 1855 that he felt confident and financially secure enough to resign his Harvard post—Longfellow may nevertheless have sensed that the social vision with which he so passionately identified in *Hiathawa* was doomed to be rejected. Poet laureate he might be, but bardic prophet he was not.

Fundamental to Longfellow's, as to Whitman's, "political" dream of realizing authenticity, of planting true democracy, of producing social harmony is the unstinting, undifferentiating bounty of the American continent—its "free" giving of itself. This is a theme first explicitly sounded by Gitche Manito:

"I have given you lands to hunt in,
I have given you streams to fish in,
I have given you bear and bison,
I have given you roe and reindeer,
I have given you brant and beaver,
Filled the marshes full of wild-fowl,
Filled the rivers full of fishes;
Why then are you not contented?
Why then will you hunt each other?" (7–8)

In context, the word "hunt" here takes on a poignant ironic edge, highlighting as it does the sheer perversity of civil strife in such a setting. But the theme is most powerful in *Hiawatha* where it is left implicit, where Longfellow's political vision is transmuted into the very "landscape writing" and "picture-painting" modern critics have so often sniffed at. One attractive example is where nature readily offers up all its gifts to a young Hiawatha who has the tact and courtesy to ask:

"Give me of your quills, O Hedgehog!
All your quills, O Kagh, the Hedgehog!
I will make a necklace of them,
Make a girdle for my beauty,
And two stars to deck her bosom!"
From a hollow tree the Hedgehog
With his sleepy eyes looked at him,
Shot his shining quills like arrows,
Saying, with a drowsy murmur,
Through the tangles of his whiskers:
"Take my quills, O Hiawatha!" (50)

Charming bourgeois fantasy, à la Beatrix Potter or Kenneth Grahame, though this may seem, it features—as does so much of *Hiawatha*—the nineteenth-century reworking of a classical pastoral trope. For instance, it brings to mind Ben Jonson's celebrated praise-poem "To Penshurst," the home of the aristocratic Sidney family, apostrophized by Jonson as a noble model of bounty and featuring a rich tributary domain:

The painted partrich lyes in every field,
And, for thy messe, is willing to be kill'd.
And if the high swolne Medway faile thy dish,
Thou hast thy ponds, that pay thee tribute fish,
Fat, aged carps, that runne into thy net.
And pikes, now weary their owne kinde to eat,
As loth, the second draught, or cast to stay,
Officiously, at first, themselves betray.
Bright eeles, that emulate them, and leape on land,
Before the fisher, or into his hand.[38]

Despite its gorgeous, almost heraldic, affirmations, Jonson's poem is very much a "counteractant," literally designed to privilege the code of a decaying feudal order over the vulgar, brash emergent order of the noveaux riches that he scarifyingly depicted in his great plays. And Longfellow's *Hiawatha* is likewise designed to serve a not dissimilar purpose.

Detailed attention has been paid, both in the present volume and elsewhere, to the ways in which, despite his progressivist outlook, Whitman the poet in part clung retrospectively to his youthful ideology of artisanal republicanism in the face of the rapid, brutal transformation of midcentury New York by a rampagingly aggressive new capitalism.[39] *Leaves of Grass* 1855 is a critique from this and other standpoints of the resulting new *mentalité*. The preface is studded with the key terms of the new capitalism's vocabulary (riches, interest, thrift, prudence), all redefined by Whitman so that they embody meanings and values of a very different order. And from the moment that "Song of Myself" opens with "I lean and loafe at my ease . . . observing a spear of summer grass," it is set to critique the very pace of existence in this insatiable new society and the reductive manner in which it views life. It is indeed through the eyes, as well as through all the other senses, that Whitman proceeds to build up the very "body" of his argument in favor of a very different way of being in the world. So he scoffs at those who would haggle over the bounty that an intimately loving and neighborly God offers secretively, like "baskets covered with white towels bulging the house with their plenty":

Shall I postpone my acceptation and realization and scream at my eyes,
That they turn from gazing after and down the road,
And forthwith cipher and show me to a cent,
Exactly the contents of one, and exactly the contents of two, and which is ahead?
(29)

And he returns to the theme later, imagining his money-crazed contemporaries as ghoulish revenants:

> Here and there with dimes on the eyes walking,
> To feed the greed of the belly the brains liberally spooning,
> Tickets buying or taking or selling, but in to the feast never once going;
> Many sweating and ploughing and thrashing, and then the chaff for payment
> receiving,
> A few idly owning, and they the wheat continually claiming. (75–76)

Nor is it only at the superficial level of content that "Song of Myself" engages with such matters. As has been argued at length and in detail elsewhere, the very structures of the poem—its grammar, syntax, and rhythm—are such as enact modes of feeling, of relating, and above all of sheer simple *being* that ran directly counter to what prevailed in possession-orientated New York at the time Whitman was writing.[40]

But while these aspects of Whitman's poetry have been thoroughly explored, very little attention has been paid to the ways in which related socioeconomic transformations in the Boston area influenced Longfellow's writings. These transformations developed apace from 1845 onward and between then and the end of the century Boston "changed from a merchant city of two hundred thousand inhabitants to an industrial metropolis of over a million. In 1850, Boston was a tightly packed seaport; by 1900 it sprawled over a ten-mile radius and contained thirty-one cities and towns."[41] The wealth acquired by the upper-middle-class storekeepers, manufacturers, bankers, and lawyers raised grand town houses on the area of Boston—the Back Bay—that from 1857 was being reclaimed for that very purpose from the saltwater bay and tidal flats of the Charles River, matching a similar undertaking in the South End. Streets in the Back Bay were laid out on the model of the new boulevards of Paris.[42] As for members of the central middle class, they largely migrated to the newly built suburbs, leaving the lower middle class to move, as business dictated, around the growing city itself. But this new capitalist economy depended crucially on the inexhaustible supply of cheap working-class labor, very largely supplied from 1850 onward by the impecunious immigrant Irish, recruited to work in the sweatshops and other centers of mass production that were the powerhouses of the new economy. Marjorie Ross has written, "as the factory system developed the social order changed. Personal contact between the artisan and the apprentice was replaced by the more impersonal relationship of capital labor."[43] The better-off came increasingly to appreciate what has aptly been called the romance of the new capitalism, balancing hard work against speculation. By the Gilded Age of the late nineteenth century, Boston had been rebuilt on a "metropolitan, more plutocratic scale . . . and with plutocracy came vulgarity":

> [In 1869] the Anvil Chorus from *Il Trovatore* was performed by 10,000 singers, 1,000 musicians, 100 firemen beating anvils with sledge hammers, climaxed by cannons that were fired by electric control from the platform. John S. Dwight, Boston's Yankee music critic, left town for the occasion.[44]

In some senses, this was no place for a Boston Yankee of the old school and, as Green has pointed out, the last decades of the nineteenth century saw the remnants of aristocratic old Boston society retreating into ever more etiolated forms of high culture.

Longfellow's *Hiawatha* bears all the marks of the transitional period in Bostonian, and indeed American, cultural history during which it was written. Green has characterized the Boston of the first half of the nineteenth century as undertaking a noble sociocultural experiment, the adventure to refashion the town into "a model and ideal city," to quote Edward Everett Hale (42). "[W]hat was special about [early nineteenth-century] Boston within America," writes Green, "was that there the economic vitality and political pride co-operated with intellectual seriousness and moral hope" (43). That was the Boston to which Longfellow had originally come, and it was that Boston that spawned socially progressive reform movements, including the Abolitionist movement of which he was a fervent supporter.

The sociocultural changes produced by this new economy are inscribed in *Hiawatha* in any number of ways. For instance, "the impact of ever more intensive urbanization called forth the emotional reaction of the rural ideal" (Warner, 5) and Longfellow's poem catered to this. In some ways, *Hiawatha* is an expression, in exotic terms, of Longfellow's own idealized recollections of his early life in Portland, a small rural town in provincial Maine. "The Village Blacksmith," one of his earliest, and most celebrated, poems testifies to the nostalgic ideal of organic rural community that was probably a legacy of his upbringing. There are many traces of that ideal in *Hiawatha*, too, reinforced by the "counteractant" poem's attack on the grasping, competitive spirit of the new socioeconomic order. For instance, it is Pau-Puk-Keewis who first "vexed the village with disturbance" (113) by introducing gambling, in the form of "the game of Bowl and Counters" (114). Proving as predictably adroit at this as a Mississippi steamboat gambler, or perhaps a new Boston speculator, he quickly strips his fellow villagers of their precious belongings, playing

Till the cunning Pau-Puk-Keewis
Of their treasures had despoiled them,
Of the best of all their dresses,
Shirts of deer-skin, robes of ermine,
Belts of wampum, crests of feathers,
Warlike weapons, pipes and pouches.
Twenty eyes glared wildly at him,
Like the eyes of wolves glared at him. (116)

The episode culminates in the mischief maker embarking on an orgy of destruction, laying waste to all that Hiawatha has cherished and protected. His actions bespeak the antithesis of the values Longfellow has been implicitly recommending through the person of Hiawatha himself: community spirit, collective responsibility, and what nowadays would be called environmental management.

Longfellow's animus against the new acquisitiveness in *Hiawatha* is as great as is Whitman's in "Song of Myself." It is therefore worth remarking how, when the ghosts of the departed "From the kingdom of Ponemah, / From the land of the Hereafter" (141) visit Hiawatha they come to ask of him a favor:

"Do not lay such heavy burdens
In the graves of those you bury,
Not such weight of furs and wampum,
Not such weight of pots and kettles,
For the spirits faint beneath them,
Only give them food to carry,
Only give them fire to light them." (140)

The curse of an insatiable appetite for possessions is what much of *Hiawatha* is about. Just as Whitman's "Song of Myself" is a magnificat to being as distinct from having, so Longfellow's *Hiawatha* celebrates a life of cooperative harmony and of simple natural sufficiency. In places, this is reminiscent of Blake's idyllic pastoral vision in the suggestively entitled lyric "The Echoing Green" from *Songs of Innocence*:

All around the happy village
Stood the maize-fields, green and shining,
Waved the green plumes of Mondamin,
Waved his soft and sunny tresses,
Filling all the land with plenty . . .
Till the corn-fields rang with laughter,

Till from Hiawatha's wigwam
Kahgahgee, the King of Ravens,
Screamed and quivered in his anger,
And from all the neighboring tree-tops
Crowed and croaked the black marauders,
"Ugh!" the old men all responded,
From their seats beneath the pine-trees! (94 and 100)

The ravens are, of course, the dark, rapacious, malicious spirits prophetic of disorder that, save when they are subdued and captured by Hiawatha, menacingly haunt his cornfields and threaten the civility and civilization he has so carefully cultivated.

For someone of Longfellow's privileged social background and refined temperament, the ravening new economic order may well have been most alarmingly apparent in the form of the unruly immigrants crowding into the slums of Boston's North End. Cholera, smallpox, and tuberculosis were to plague an area that became notorious for its pauperism, drunkenness, prostitution, and crime. For fifty years after *Hiawatha* was written the North End was to continue to be home to successive waves of immigrants—there were ten thousand Italians and Jews living in the city by 1890, while by 1910 "there were 30,000 Italians jammed into the old North East, and more than 40,000 Jews packed into the West end" (Buni and Rogers, 91). But the first wave of immigrants was, of course, the Irish who flocked to Boston in the wake of the Great Famine. Proslavery, antitemperance, antiprison reform, and antiwomen's rights, these "bog Irish" were reactionary on a scale that shocked and disgusted progressive old Boston society, seeming to confirm the racial theories of the day that consigned the "Celts" to an earlier, much more primitive stage of racial development than the "Anglo Saxon." No wonder that, in the very year *Hiawatha* was published, Longfellow could write in a letter: "I am again in want of a man-servant. Can you help me? No Irish need apply. Much as I like Mrs. Moore's Melodies, and respect the Giant's Causeway, a wild Irishman in the kitchen cannot be tolerated" (468).

The speech prophetic of Manifest Destiny that Longfellow puts in Hiawatha's mouth at the end of the poem, so he in effect condemns himself and his people to a self-sacrificial act of extinction, is imbued with a sense of melancholic misgiving about the very process it predicts is inevitable, and celebrates as "progress." The misgiving concerns the dynamic of migration and immigration that powers this process:

I beheld, too, in that vision
All the secrets of the future,
Of the distant days that shall be.
I beheld the westward marches
Of the unknown, crowded nations.
All the land was full of people,
Restless, struggling, toiling, striving,
Speaking many tongues, yet feeling
But one heart-beat in their bosoms.
In the woodlands rang their axes,
Smoked their towns in all the valleys,
Over all the lakes and rivers,
Rushed their great canoes of thunder. (153)

If there is perhaps an ominous air of the later infamous *lebensraum* doctrine about this passage, it may well be because Longfellow was not entirely convinced that "progress" would take a form that would compensate for the disappearance of Indian culture as depicted in *Hiawatha*—a like feeling, of course, famously haunts Scott's depiction of the disappearing Highlanders in *Waverley.* Civilization and its discontents, as Freud was to style it, stalks the page, as the lines seem ghosted by feelings exacerbated by Longfellow's doubts about the way in which the coming America would be shaped by those coming to America.

Longfellow was no Nativist, but, like Whitman, he believed in the "nativizing," or "normalizing" of these newcomers—their conversion, as well as contribution, to Americanness. And both poets used their poetry of the fifties as a means to this end. How Whitman achieved this has been considered in chapter 2. As for Longfellow, *Hiawatha* was the first of a series of works designed, in part, to "educate" a society that was being rapidly transformed by immigration. Having in 1855 constructed the figure of Hiawatha as a kind of idealized incarnation of those native (white) American values Longfellow himself professed, he turned in 1856 to what was to be the first of his *New England Tragedies, John Endicott,* upon which he continued to work until 1868. The preface to the poem asks why the reader should be invited to read "This city, like an ancient palimpsest; / And bring to light, upon the blotted page, / The mournful record of an earlier age" (502). And in answering his own question, Longfellow makes clear how important it now seemed to him to found America not only on a vision of the future but upon an awareness of the past—upon a sense of tradition and continuity:

I answer: "For the lesson that they teach:
The tolerance of opinion and of speech.
Hope, Faith, and Charity remain—these three;
And greatest of them all is Charity." (503)

If there is, even in Longfellow's case, an element of paradox in thus basing a faith in progress on a return to the values of the past, then how much more ironic must the same paradox be when it appears in the work of that arch futurist, Whitman! But appear it does, although it has tended to be overlooked by scholars. One unexpected but important aspect of Whitman's performance in the apparently open-ended, blithely freewheeling, relentlessly progressive "Song of Myself" (1855) is his adoption of the role of national remembrancer, in such passages as those recalling the exploits of John Paul Jones, and the fall of the Alamo. And by this recalling of chosen heroic episodes in the past, Whitman, like Longfellow, is recalling his fellow countrymen to the colors—to the service of those values that have "traditionally" defined America. His, too, is a return to the past in order to find a way forward, through the crises of the time. And there is another paradox that, for the same sociocultural reasons, stubbornly haunts the work of both poets—the paradox of the belief that the future of a fully egalitarian democratic society may, after all, depend on the efforts of single heroic individuals; that the Whitmanesque society of the ordinary divine average may be founded only through the efforts of decidedly extraordinary leaders. True, Whitman blurs the issue in "Song of Myself" by making his hero an everyman and his everyman and everywoman a hero. But the preface rather gives the game away, making it clear that the poet needs to act the Hiawatha to the American people, showing them the way to realizing a better society through self-realization.

And if in both *Leaves of Grass* 1855 and *Hiawatha* the prophetic leader sometimes seems a forlorn figure, destined for defeat, then both Whitman and Longfellow might have drawn comfort—albeit cold comfort—from the fact that such was ever the fate of the poet-visionary, as the bards of the *Kalevala* had long ago foretold. At the conventional, formulaic ending of that Finnish heroic "epic" upon which *Hiawatha*, an American bourgeois "epic," was based, the bardic singer confesses that he—like Whitman and Longfellow—is condemned to be nature's child (just like Hiawatha, and just like the Whitman of "Song of Myself"), as human society has rejected him:

My mother is not alive
my own parent not awake
nor is my dear one listening
my own darling observing:
the spruces listen to me
    the pine boughs observe
the birch foliage fondles
    the rowans hold me.
Small I was left motherless
lowly without my mamma—
left like a lark on a rock
to be a thrush on a cairn
    as a lark to soar
    as a thrush to chirp
in a strange woman's keeping
    a stepmother's care.
    She turned poor me out
    drove the orphan child
to the cabin's windward side
    to the home's north side
to face the wind unsheltered
    and the home's north side
to face the wind unsheltered
    and the gale unloved.
I, a lark, began roaming
and, a wretched bird, walking
a weak one, strolling abroad
a woeful one, wandering
    knowing every wind
    suffering the roar
    shaking in the cold
    howling in the frost. (*Kalevala*, 664–665)

In this radical, and ancient, sense, the poet may be said to be doomed eternally to be an outcast, and his or her poem destined always to be a dubiously effective "counteractant" to the values and practices of established, mainstream society.

Four. The Dreams of Labor

Hidden in the title of this chapter is a phrase from Robert Frost's sonnet "Mowing": "The fact is the sweetest dream that labour knows. / My long scythe whispered and left the hay to make."[1] Typical of Frost's best work in being cunningly innocent of its potential for larger meanings, the poem is about making poetry precisely to the extent that the speaker insists it is simply about mowing grass to make hay. Take him at his word, though, and his sonnet becomes a twentieth-century example of what Irving Howe called "the literature of work."[2] This, he claimed, represents an interesting segment of American writing in the nineteenth century, and he acknowledged Whitman to be a major author in this minor genre. The aim of the present discussion will not, however, be to examine the ways in which Whitman actually depicts work in his writings; instead, it will be to consider just a few of the ways in which both the dreams and the realities of the nineteenth-century world of labor, as outlined in preceding chapters, crucially influenced, in different ways at different times, his reading of American political affairs.

Since the first two editions of *Leaves of Grass* have already been examined from this frankly limited point of view,[3] attention will here be paid instead to the 1860 edition. As Fredson Bowers painstakingly demonstrated, Whitman began to prepare material for this third edition as early as 1856—a conclusion Bowers safely based on the discovery of a notebook containing both an early draft of the 1860 poem "Proto-Leaf" (later "Starting from Paumanok," but originally—and suggestively—entitled "Premonition") and the following extract from the *New*

York Express, October 21, 1856, carefully copied out in Whitman's own hand: "But for the American party, the Northern, sectional, geographical party of Wm. H. Seward and Co. would, under Fremont, have swept the whole Northern country."[4] We may, then, note that politics is there at the very start of what became the 1860 edition of *Leaves of Grass*, sharing a notebook with the embryonic poetry.

Less than a year before the *Express* report appeared, Whitman had actually written to William Henry Seward, requesting such items as copies of "public documents, your speeches." He closed the letter by explaining: "I am a writer, for the press, and otherwise. I too have at heart Freedom, and the amelioration of the people."[5] Seward, of New York, had been an antislavery Whig, but in the run-up to the 1856 election he joined the newly established Republican Party and supported its candidate for the presidency, John C. Frémont. That party's campaign song was written to be sung to *La Marseillaise*: "Arise, arise ye brave / And let your war-cry be, / Free speech, free press, free soil, free men—Frémont and liberty."[6] This provides an interesting gloss on Whitman's fondness for his own political battle cry of "Allons" in the poetry of that period. As Whitman's letter implies, these were freedoms that mattered passionately to him also in 1855 and 1856, even if he was reluctant to couple the name of Frémont so glibly with that of liberty and correspondingly unwilling to declare himself an out-and-out Republican.

"Free soil, free men": this was close to what, for Whitman, the confirmed Free-Soiler, American democracy essentially stood for. It is worth noting exactly how the 1860 edition of *Leaves of Grass* actually opens: "Free, fresh, savage. . . ."[7] It is a very politically pointed beginning, and by the end of the first verse paragraph Whitman has made his political position even more uncompromisingly clear: "Solitary, singing in the west, I strike up for a new world." Slightly later he refers, with deceptive casualness, to his "program of chants" as "Inland chants—chants of Kanzas [*sic*]" (*Variorum* 2, 275). When it was first written, sometime in late 1856, this phrase was political dynamite. After all, the Republicans had fought the recent election on the issue of Bleeding Kansas. And Whitman repeatedly discussed Kansas and other issues relating to the slavery question in his editorials (not all of them identifiable with certainty, as was noted in chapter 2) for the *Brooklyn Daily Times* (1857–1859).[8] As he well knew, the West was the great contemporary arena of political conflict, and it was obvious to all that the increasingly bloody dispute between the America of slavery and the America of "freedom" would be decided there. By "singing in the west" and "striking up for a new world," Whitman was also striking a blow for that freedom. His "Proto-Leaf," like several of the other 1860 poems, was a considered political act. He was using his poetry to claim disputed territory and to occupy it in his imagination. He was out to preempt history and to secure the future of America as a democracy of "free men" living on "free soil."

As *The Eighteenth Presidency!* the unpublished personal manifesto he produced for the 1856 presidential election, shows, Whitman was an unwavering supporter of the campaign for a "democratic" new West. "Suppose you get Kansas, do you think it would be ended?" he asks (1322): "[N]ot one square mile of continental territory shall henceforward be given to slavery, to slaves, or to the masters of slaves—not one square foot" (1323). Instead, the new territories shall be filled, not with the financiers, entrepreneurs, and assorted "yuppies" who were the real leaders and beneficiaries of the new enterprise culture of America in the 1850s, but with the numberless members of the wage-earning underclass, who appear in Whitman's anachronistic imagination still to be the independent artisans, mechanics, and sturdy yeomen of a romanticized bygone age. They shall be given the freedom of the West. And in hymning the qualities of their free labor, Whitman was also pointedly countering the rhetoric of some pro-southern politicians who were asserting that the northern workingman was in reality no more free than the southern black slave. For him, this was part and parcel of the political attitude he savaged in *The Eighteenth Presidency!*: "All the main purposes for which the government was established are openly denied. The perfect equality of slavery with freedom is flauntingly preached in the North—nay, the superiority of slavery" (1310).

In actual historical fact, the eastern capitalists had, up to the end of the 1840s, opposed every attempt to provide workers with cheap western lands, as demanded by the labor leader George Henry Evans, because they feared it would mean the end of an abundant supply of cheap labor in the East. By the late 1850s, a wave of new immigrants guaranteeing low eastern wages, combined with a realization that western settlement meant new markets for eastern goods, caused industrialists to change their minds and raise their voices, too, in favor of homestead legislation. In his interest in such an issue Whitman was in the mainstream of northern political thinking during the 1850s. But his distinctive version of "the imagined West" was surely a result of his early education in what Eric Foner has called "the central ideas and values of artisanal radicalism." This shows in particular in his use of poetry to call into existence a western society that will be simultaneously individualistic and cooperative.[9]

"Workmen! Workwomen!" Whitman declaimed in *The Eighteenth Presidency!* "Those immense national American tracts belong to you; they are in trust with you" (1316). And the backbone of this vision is a straight line of thought linking the promise of the West with the repressed, authentically democratic underlife of the great northern cities: "From my mouth hear the will of These States taking form in the great cities" (1323). And how does the opening poem of the 1860 *Leaves of Grass* begin? With a verse paragraph in which the visionary speaker who was once a "Boy of the Mannahatta, the city of ships, my city," ends up, after a mental journey that embraces the whole continent, "[s]olitary, singing in the west," where he can "strike up for a New World" (*Variorum* 2, 273–274).

So wearily familiar are we by now with the tireless continental perambulations of Whitman's imagination in his poetry that we may, understandably, scarcely bother to listen when, in "Proto-Leaf," he once more rhapsodizes over his lands: "Land of wheat, beef, pork! Land of wool and hemp! Land of the potato, the apple and the grape! / Land of the pastoral plains, the grass-fields of the world! . . . / Lands where the northwest Columbia winds, and where the southwest Colorado winds!" (*Variorum* 2, 285). Such a numbingly predictable invocation can, however, take on a rather different complexion when it is placed in the context of the furious political debates of the day. The newly formed Republican Party, which Whitman was broadly inclined to favor, was routinely described by its opponents as the "northern, geographical, sectional party," in the words of that passage from the *New York Express* included in the original "Proto-Leaf" notebook. In its ostentatious embrace of the whole continent, "Proto-Leaf" therefore constitutes a poetic rebuttal of such an accusation. Whitman warned Frémont, as much as the pro-Southern Democratic candidate James Buchanan, in the *Eighteenth Presidency!* that "The Redeemer President of These States is not to be exclusive, but inclusive. In both physical and political America there is plenty of room for the whole human race; if not, more room can be provided" (1321). In 1860, Whitman appeared as redeemer poet by publishing poetry whose emphasis is consistently on the "inclusiveness" of the United States, primarily figured in "purely" geographic terms in order to avoid the fissures of the political mapping implicit in both the Democratic and Republican ideologies. And in claiming his poetry for the true "American" party, Whitman was simultaneously depriving the racist "American" Nativist Party, that had been in its politically sinister prime in the midfifties, of its arrogant right to that description. "Others are making a great ado with the word Americanism," he wrote heatedly in *The Eighteenth Presidency!* "a solemn and great word . . . using the great word Americanism without yet feeling the first aspiration of it" (1315). "The first aspiration of it": Whitman passionately believed that the proper noun "America" was forever synonymous with "aspiration."

During the course of his famous debates with Douglas in 1858, Lincoln was forced to answer his opponent's charge that in wishing to see a westward extension of the northern sociopolitical system he was really wanting to reduce all the states in the union to a single, dull, uniform pattern of life. "[Douglas] argues erroneously," Lincoln replied, "the great variety of the local institutions in the States, springing from differences in the soil, differences in the face of the country, and in the climate, are bonds of union."[10] In "Proto-Leaf" Whitman, too, shows regional differences as underlining rather than undermining the union between the states. "If they produce in one section of the country what is called for by the wants of another section, and this other section can supply the wants of the first," argued Lincoln, "they are not matters of discord but bonds of union, true bonds of union" (Stern, 463). "Interlinked, food-yielding lands!" writes Whitman, "Land of coal and iron! Land of gold! Lands of cotton, sugar, rice!" A few lines later, in the original draft, he adds, "Full-draped land, tied at the breast, with the belt stringing the oval lakes" (Bowers, 26). As noted in chapter 3, it is a fine illustration of one of the fundamental terms of his thinking—the belief that nature itself has destined these states, and eventually the whole of America, both North and South—to be a single vast country. Whereas conventional maps are concerned only to show the political geography of a continent, Whitman's poetic map is carefully drawn to illustrate what he regards as the predestined geographical politics of the Americas. He adopts a geopolitical outlook that may eventually derive from the work of the great geographer Alexander von Humboldt via the ecstatic political rhetoric of William Gilpin, the onetime friend of Jackson who was in 1861 to be one of the handful of men accompanying Lincoln on his journey from Springfield to Washington.[11] It is, indeed, worth recalling how Whitman's concept of "Cosmos"—a concept that proved of such value to him in 1860 as a geopolitical rhetorical tool—is partly modeled on Humboldt's great work of that name, the second part of which was published in 1847. As one of the recent editors of his *Cosmos (Volume Two)* has noted:

> Humboldt's picture of nature's unity—its reflection in the products of the artistic imagination and its gradual realization over the course of history—was "to strengthen the bond which, according to ancient laws governing the very core of the intellectual realm, ties the sensible world to the insensible" and to "stimulate the communications between that which the mind receives from the world, and that which, from its depths, the mind returns."[12]

It was on this organic sense of the "natural unity" of the North American continent that Whitman drew so incessantly and insistently in his 1860 edition.

How appropriate, then, that Whitman's favorite brother, Jeff (Thomas Jefferson

Whitman), should become a "topographical engineer" (1287). That is precisely what Whitman himself is in the realm of imaginative writing, and his stunning poetic cartographies of the United States, particularly as evidenced in "Proto-Leaf" (or "Starting from Paumanok"), have been brilliantly evoked (minus the political context that helps explain them) by William Boelbower. Discussing what he usefully calls the "ethnographic politics" of the poem, he identifies the "inspirational pathos represented by the hybris [*sic*] of flying that enables Whitman to invent his modern civic vision of 'this many-item'd Union.'"[13] For him, "toponyms became the tropes of connectivity" (42), and Boelbower explains how this works in the poetry:

> In comparison to common names, toponyms naturally refer to the political discourse of nationality in that they are indexically crucial to the territorial issue of boundaries. No boundaries, no nation, or state. The names semanticize what would otherwise be a geopolitical abstraction. Their meaning, in other words, is above all topological, the territory itself being the dynamic object to which they refer. In short, they not only place the nation but they also keep it in place; just as place gives toponyms their sole horizon of meaning. Given this cultural agency, it is apparent why their mere evocation can become an enchanting, even mystical act. This much Whitman assumes in chanting the country's name. (39)

This takes us to the very heart of Whitman's main politico-poetic concerns in the 1860 edition; and as Boelbower adds, "the more inclusive the catalogue, the more national the vista" (39).

As the first draft of "Proto-Leaf" shows, Whitman's dream of labor was at the literal center of his ethnographic politics, his geopolitical system: "The Kentuckian, Mississippian, Arkansian—the workwoman and workman of Iowa, Illinois, Indiana, Michigan" (Bowers, 28). But in the published version he substituted "woman and man" for "workwoman and workman," possibly because he realized that in its original form the politically loaded phrase might jar on the ears of the "Louisianian, the Georgian" who, he claims, are "as near to me, and I as near to him and her" (*Variorum* 2, 286). It is a small example of what is a large concern in the 1860 edition—Whitman's intermittent wish to conciliate southern opinion without compromising his "free soil" and "free men" principles. In *The Eighteenth Presidency!* he might uncompromisingly incite the "mechanics, farmers, boatmen [and] manufacturers . . . to abolish slavery, or it will abolish you" (1322). But after the word "manufacturers" he inserted "and all work-people of the South, the same as the North!" (1322). He thus clearly signaled he was a gradualist, not an abolitionist. As an ardent states' rights advocate he believed that, with regard to slavery in the South (as opposed to the unorganized territories of the new West), "We must wait, no matter how long. There is no remedy, except in The State itself: A corner-stone of the organic compacts of America is that a State is perfect mistress of itself" (1320). And it is this genuine concern that caused him in "Proto-Leaf" to exploit to the full the potential for ambiguity in the prophetic mode of utterance he carefully cultivated.

The ambiguity arises from uncertainties regarding time. When is the poetry referring to the present, when to the future; how distant is that future, and in what relation, precisely, does it stand to the present? It may be worth recalling that similar questions haunted, and bedeviled, the real, fateful political debates of the time—so much so that the Civil War itself could almost be said to have been precipitated by a confusion of tenses. It was on June 16, 1858, that Lincoln declared: "A house divided against itself cannot stand. I believe this government cannot endure permanently half slave and half free. I do not expect the Union to be dissolved—I do not expect the house to fall—but I do expect it will cease to be divided. It will become all one thing, or all the other" (Stern, 429). It was in vain that he later protested that his belligerent-sounding remarks applied not to the present or to the immediate future but to the predicted state of affairs a whole century hence.

If Lincoln was the victim of his ambiguous tenses, then in "Proto-Leaf" Whitman seeks to be the beneficiary of his. He defuses the bitter sectional conflicts of his time by gently imagining an indeterminate future when, by natural processes antithetical in spirit to the violent events of actual recent history, an America shall have emerged in which differences are honored but harmonized. Not only does he consistently go out of his way to include the southern states in this prospectus, he diplomatically avoids indicating the precise terms on which they have been admitted to his visionary union. Have they been accepted just as, in 1860, they stand, with all their sins still upon them? Or have they undergone extensive social and political reconstruction? Whitman's mode of writing ensures, of course, that such questions do not arise. Indeed, his poetic discourse is a medium in which the various, sometimes conflicting opinions Whitman had on the southern slavery question can be held in fluid suspension.

These opinions are clear enough in the prose and have a common origin in Whitman's belief that slavery is primarily to be judged—and condemned—with reference to its threats to the interests of free white labor throughout the states.[14] For this reason its western spread cannot ever be countenanced, but its persistence in the South must be accepted, until the mass of whites there realize both that they are being ruled by a tiny, powerful, slave-owning white elite and that slavery is damaging to white workers: "once get the slavery question to be argued on, as a question of White workingmen's Labor against the Servile Labor of the Blacks, and how many years would slavery stand in two thirds of the present slave-states?" (Editorial, May 6, 1858, Holloway and Schwartz, 90). In fact, Whitman foresaw a common "democratic" front eventually forming between the exploited and oppressed workers of both the northern and the southern states—a dream of labor that emerges in "Proto-Leaf," with all its frailty exposed. There Whitman finds in the Alabaman mockingbird, whose song is "[a] charge transmitted, and gift occult, for those being born," a tender secret analogue for himself: "Democracy! Near at hand to you a throat is now inflating itself and joyfully singing" (*Variorum* 2, 282). That the choice of Alabama is not merely coincidental seems to be confirmed by the evidence of the earliest extant version of this line, where the unspecified locale is vaguely northern in character: "As I have walked my walk through the rows of the orchard trees, I have seen where the shebird faithfully sat on her nest" (Bowers, 18).

The South again seems the "natural" setting for an experience of lonely, secret joy, in the famous "Calamus" poem, "I Saw in Louisiana a Live-Oak Growing." It would be transparently silly to read this simply as a political allegory, but Whitman's political sense of the South as a land where feelings of democratic comradeship were slowly cohering, visible as yet only in isolated cases, may have influenced his choice of Louisiana as the home of the live oak growing "without any companion": "I wondered how it could utter joyous leaves, standing alone there, without its friend, its lover near—for I knew I could not" (*Variorum* 2, 390). One's mind is, in fact, turned in the direction of the contemporary sociopolitical milieu by the poem that in the 1860 "Calamus" sequence immediately precedes "I Saw in Louisiana," since that is a piece in which Whitman presents himself as an isolated northerner—a dweller in populous Manhattan who is out of step with the "timid" life around him because he follows a different model that he offers to his lands. In spite of his unprepossessing outward appearance, there "comes one, a Manhattanese, and ever at parting, kisses me lightly on the lips with robust love, / And I, in the public room, or on the crossing of the street, or on the ship's deck, kiss him in return" (*Variorum* 2, 389). In other words, as Whitman affirms more explicitly elsewhere, there exists in the cities of the North a rudimentary, fugitive feeling of "brotherhood" among workers, out of which a new, extended American society of "comrades" will duly develop. Contrasted with this is the solitary, yet wondrously self-sufficient, state of the live oak in the Louisiana of the South.

On occasions, though, the South appears in the 1860 edition in a carefully neutral, vaguely benign, or quietly conciliatory light. This response to rising political tensions is consistent with several aspects of Whitman's complicated position on slavery in the South: his paramount concern with preserving the Union;[15] his perhaps exaggerated respect for states' rights; his rooted dislike of abolitionism; his belief in the inevitable but gradual decay of the institution of slavery; his liking for the supposed openness of the white southern character—in *The Eighteenth Presidency!* he nostalgically recalls "that great strong stock of Southerners that supplied the land in old times" (1313); his contempt for politicians and trust in the long-term triumph of working people, North and South, over a system that was inimical to their vital interests; and, of course, his fierce conviction that the situation of workers in the North urgently required as much remedial attention as the plight of the slaves. The nightmare of slavery was for him always inseparable from the dream of labor. At the same time, many of these publicly pronounced certainties were shadowed by corresponding private doubts—hence the presence in the 1860 edition of signs of disillusionment, distress, and confusion and the poetic evidence of a personal disintegration that obviously had its political dimensions. But as these features of the 1860 edition are already well-known and have been extensively discussed,[16] it is worth concentrating briefly instead on what might be called "the rhetoric of conciliation" in some of the poems.

Whitman's hatred of slavery is repeatedly and openly declared in 1860, most vociferously in the 1856 "Poem of the Many in One," a work, mostly consisting of phrases from the 1855 preface, which was pointedly made the first poem proper of "Chants Democratic." But historical hindsight has perhaps rather blinded us to the fact that he also needed somehow to develop a conciliatory discourse, the poetical equivalent, as it were, of his states' rights philosophy. The strangest and most blatant attempt to achieve this is the 1860 poem "Longings for Home," where Whitman unconvincingly impersonates a southerner nostalgically recalling the beautiful, colorful, faintly exotic landscape of the South. Needless to say, there are no great plantations to be seen, and the only black person mentioned is carefully set in a picturesque context designed to counteract and neutralize the political significance of the description: "The piney odor and the gloom—the awful natural stillness, (Here in these dense swamps the freebooter carries his gun, and the fugitive slave has his concealed hut) . . ." (*Variorum* 2, 409). As we shall see in chapter 6, this use of the swamp to image the South was to recur in Whitman. Since the fugitive slave figures so often in Whitman's work—most famously in "Song of Myself"—it may be worth suggesting that in "Longings for Home" the appeal of the figure of the swamp slave lay partly (though only partly) in the ambivalence of its political signification.[17] It immediately brought the reaffirmation and reinforcement of the Fugitive Slave Act in 1850 to mind—an act to which Whitman was opposed on the grounds of states' rights, while willingly conceding (on the same grounds) that once the act was repealed then northern states should readily undertake to return escaped slaves to their southern masters. In this context, to picture a fugitive slave was therefore less to indict the South than to raise, by implication, the whole issue of the invasive powers of the federal government, as of course Whitman does directly in "A Boston Ballad." A more interesting, extended example of his unionist strategy of political quietism is to be found in the important poem later called "Our Old Feuillage." As published for the first time in the 1860 edition ("Chants Democratic," 4), this poem consists of a captivating series of word pictures showing the beauties of the American natural and social landscape throughout the geographically diverse states of the Union. It includes several references to the South:

> There are the negroes at work, in good health—the ground in all directions is covered with pine straw;
> In Tennessee and Kentucky, slaves busy in the coalings, at the forge, by the furnace-blaze, or at the corn-shucking;
> In Virginia, the planter's son returning after a long absence, joyfully welcomed and kissed by the aged mulatto nurse. (*Variorum* 2, 295)

It is a recognition of the established facts of life in the South that amounts to a conditional, provisional endorsement of them. The earlier notebook version of the poem shows how Whitman eventually chose to print a highly selective, deliberately uncontroversial picture of slavery, because originally "Feuillage" (as it was then called) included the following three lines, only the first of which was published (in modified form) in 1860:

> The Texas cotton-field and the negro-cabins—drivers driving mules or oxen before rude carts—cotton bales piled on rude wharves,
> A slave approaching sulkily—he wears an iron necklace and prong—he has raw sores on his shoulders,
> The runaway, steering his course by the north star—the pack of negro-dogs chained in couples pursuing. (Bowers, 130)

Had these lines been included they would have shattered the decorum of a poem specifically intended to promote harmony between the states on existing, rather than on some distant future, terms.

There is even evidence, in the form of some of the earliest lines he wrote for the

1860 edition, that Whitman intended from the very beginning to build this conciliatory discourse into the fabric of his third collection. Originally "Proto-Leaf" (then entitled "Premonition") represented the composite speaker as "Boy of the Mannahatta—boy of the prairies, Boy of the southern savannahs / Looking friendlily southward . . ." (Bowers, 36). As well as reproducing with revelatory clarity the tripartite structure of Whitman's political thinking in *The Eighteenth Presidency!* (northern cities—the West—the South), these lines also illustrate his sporadic policy of appeasement. Yet his feelings about the South were at best equivocal, and nothing illustrates this better than the line he penciled in some time later as a substitute for "Looking friendlily southward": "Looking and longing southward" he wrote at the second attempt, revealing in the process how his affection for the contemporary South was really in anticipation of its emancipation from its enslavement to slavery. Indeed, as has already been suggested, he frequently confuses the present with the future, conflating the two until they are indistinguishable: "Still the Present I raise aloft—Still the Future of the States I harbinge, glad and sublime," as he exclaims in what is, perhaps, the key declaration and declamation of the whole poem (*Variorum* 2, 287). The present takes on the welcome attributes of the future, and the future is seen as a natural, easy extension of the present—which allows Whitman to minimize, to the point of ignoring, the trauma of revolutionary historical change that will be required if his vision of a thoroughgoing union is ever to become reality.

Conciliatory equivocations of this sort also appear in "Calamus." Take the well-known piece ("Calamus," 5) where Whitman proffers a love that is superior to the legal contracts that bind the states into mere nominal union:

> States!
> Were you looking to be held together by the lawyers?
> By an agreement on a paper? Or by arms?
>
> Away!
> I arrive, bringing these, beyond all the forces of courts and arms.
> These! to hold you together as firmly as the earth itself is held together.
>
> . . . Affection shall solve every one of the problems of freedom. (*Variorum* 2, 371–372)

The radical fervor of these lines is what is generally appreciated. Whitman is clearly anticipating a time when all the states, without exception, will be united by a common, comradely passion for freedom. But *The Eighteenth Presidency!* allows us to see the latent conservatism of these lines, by showing that they apply not only to the utopian future but also—in the unsatisfactory meantime—to the pragmatics of the present. In the 1855 pamphlet, Whitman had invited people to disobey the Fugitive Slave Act on the grounds that good faith and "friendship," rather than the crude compulsion of law, should require the free states to "deliver back" runaway slaves: "I had quite as lief depend on the good faith of any of These States, as on the laws of Congress and the President. Good faith is irresistible among men, and friendship is; which lawyers can not understand, thinking nothing but compulsion will do" (1320). Read with this in mind, the "Calamus" poem speaks with two voices. In the name of "friendship," it announces a future union of free states in which everyone will be joined in a glorious "companionship." But also in the name of "friendship" it persuades contemporaries that slave and free states should continue to coexist amicably, free of the coercion of federal law. In other words, Whitman is a conservative among radicals, the impetuous abolitionists who wanted federal action to dispose of slavery. But he is also a radical among conservatives, who were happy to see the Union continue half-slave and half-free indefinitely. In this "Calamus" poem, he uses his determined, confident vision of the future not only to predict change but also paradoxically to promote tolerance of what, in the perspective he offers, seems to be only a temporary difference between North and South.

What needs to be emphasized here, however, is that both Whitman's radicalism and his conservatism on the slavery issue were the direct result of his dreams of labor. "[A]ll attempts to discuss the evils of slavery in its relations to the whites," he insisted in *The Eighteenth Presidency!* had been deliberately sabotaged in the South, where "the three hundred and fifty thousand masters keep down the true people, the millions of white citizens, mechanics, farmers, boatmen, manufacturers, and the like" (1311). Implicit in such a comment is, therefore, the historically grotesque view—commonplace among the more radical advocates of the cause of white labor—that white workers were as much "kept down," as economically and politically subordinated, as were black slaves. But at least, Whitman added, in the South leading politicians openly declared that "the workingmen of a state are unsafe depositaries of political powers and rights, and that a republic can not permanently exist unless those who ply the mechanical trades and attend to the farm-work are slaves, subordinated by strict laws to their masters" (1316). Whereas in the North, leading political figures concealed similar beliefs under a "fog of prevarications" (1316). And it is at this point that we come to the very heart of Whitman's fears. Sensing that northern society had recently suffered a great sea change, that economic power was being concentrated in the hands of a new class, that his beloved working masses had been almost imperceptibly degraded into wage-slaves, and that politics had become the monopoly of cynical party professionals, Whitman looked for a simple dramatic explanation of what were, in fact, complex by-products of the advance of capitalism. He found it in his comprehensive theory of the leading political issue of the day: the issue of slavery. According to him, northern monopolists, who wanted to enslave the democratic masses, were conspiring with southern slave owners, with a view to taking the country over by political stealth.

In the Civil War, Whitman, of course, claimed to find confirmation of everything he had believed about the plight and the heroic potential of the northern worker. In the peace that followed, he overloudly asserted that the dreams of labor were well on their way to becoming reality. Yet, in *Democratic Vistas*, he faced up to a very different truth and heroically struggled to reconcile the facts of postwar society with his great expectations. The effort involved in this attempt was altogether too much for his poetry, and his later poems are interesting only when the full social and political pathos of their weakness is recognized. Betsy Erkkila has written well about the artisanal nostalgia in "Song of the Exposition," and Alan Trachtenberg has shown how "Passage to India" is "a poem of 'progress' [that] reverts obsessively to the past."[18]

These matters have already been so thoroughly discussed by recent criticism as to seem self-evident truths. It is best therefore to concentrate, in conclusion, on what seem to be neglected examples of Whitman's postwar disorientation. The bewildered state of mind that he generally took pains to conceal is conveyed with touching indirectness in two consecutive sections of *Specimen Days*. The first originated as a public lecture to commemorate Thomas Paine, the great hero of his working-class father. In it, Whitman casts his mind back thirty-five years to a time when he used to meet "Thomas Paine's perhaps most intimate chum" (797) in the back parlor of Tammany Hall (798). The image is such a politically suggestive one—Tom Paine's surrogate, as it were, symbolically attached to the Democratic Party. Those indeed were the days—the long-dead days of the 1840s, before Tammany (and the likes of Fernando Wood) had become synonymous with the politics of cynicism, when Whitman was still an idealistic young Democrat and the party seemed to him to be instilled with a Painite passion for the rights of workers. Yet by 1877 (the date of the lecture), Paine had long since been shown the door, ejected from political memory.

There then follows in *Specimen Days* a section that describes Whitman's return home to Camden across the frozen Delaware River on a winter evening:

> unable to make our landing, through the ice; our boat stanch and strong and skillfully piloted, but old and sulky, and poorly minding her helm. (Power, so important in poetry and war, is also first point of all in a winter steamboat, with long stretches of ice packs to tackle.) For over two hours we bumped and beat about, the invisible ebb, sluggish but irresistible, often carrying us long distances against our will. In the first tinge of dusk, as I looked around, I thought there could not be presented a more chilling, arctic, grim-extended, depressing scene. (799)

Anyone who has read his old-age poems will instantly realize that this scene is partly a trope for the aging Whitman's own crippled condition, but behind that, in turn, given the case made in the preceding section of *Specimen Days* for Paine as the kind of political figure "the season demands," may be a carefully occluded image of Whitman's powerlessness in the face of the socioeconomic currents of his age. If so, it wouldn't be the first time that Whitman had deliberately displaced his feelings of political impotence, placing the blame for his social despair instead on his physically shattered state: "I shall only be too happy," he had written earlier, "if these black prophecies and fears can be attributed, (as of course they will be,) to my old age and sickness & growling temper" (*NUP*, 3:1152).[19]

That remark appears in the extensive notes he prepared for a piece provisionally entitled "The Tramp and Strike Questions," and in the fragment published in *Specimen Days & Collect* (1882) he offered an incisive and nowadays well-known analysis of the "grim and spectral dangers" facing his society. Scorning euphemistic references to "the Science of wealth," he bluntly raised "the Poverty question" and proceeded to conclude that "[b]eneath the whole political world, what most presses and perplexes today, sending vastest results affecting the future, is not the abstraction question of democracy, but of social and economic organization, the treatment of working-people by employers, and all that goes along with it" (1063–1064). In his notebook entry on the same subject, he succinctly observes "that humanity in the U.S. is being divided merged more and more definitely into two marked divisions, the vast masses of employed persons, poor, ignorant, desperate, & dissatisfied / & the luxurious rich" (*NUP*, 3:1154). It is dispiriting that such comments, otherwise so evidently full of social understanding and compassion, show so little awareness of, let alone concern for, the plight of the blacks during the years of Reconstruction.

At the end of "The Tramp and Strike Question," a shocked Whitman speaks of seeing, in February 1879, three respectable-looking young men, "carrying chiffonier-bags on their shoulders, and the usual long iron hooks in their hands, plodding along, their eyes cast down, spying for scraps, rags, bones, etc." (1065).

What is arresting about this is the way it (knowingly? self-accusingly?) reverses a celebrated passage in "Song of Myself": "Shoulder your duds, and I will mine, and let us hasten forth; / Wonderful cities and free nations we shall fetch as we go. / If you tire, give me both burdens, and rest the chuff of your hand on my hip" (82). Nor is it the only instance of a chastened, not to say bewildered, postwar Whitman somberly revisiting the seminal, signature images beloved by his younger poetic self. At the end of "A Specimen Tramp Family," included in *Specimen Days*, he records "a queer, taking, rather sad picture" (821). This was a family of tramps, "in a rickety one-horse wagon." Stopping to buy a basket of theirs out of charity, Whitman notices that the woman, nursing an infant, is deliberately hiding her face in shame: "I could not see her face, in its great sunbonnet, but somehow her figure and gait told misery, terror, destitute" (822). In that failure to see her face is surely an unconscious admission by Whitman of another kind of failure; a crisis not so much of sympathy as of sympathetic intelligence—his inability to *comprehend* (in the sense of at once encompassing and understanding; encompassing *with* understanding) exactly what he is witnessing, and what, in postwar America, this figure is witness to. Faced by anonymity during the Civil War, in the form of figures draped in uniform, anonymizing blankets, Whitman had been able to lift those blankets, as he reported in "A Sight in Camp," and thus bestow the humanity of living recognition on those dead forms. But not so with this "tramp" woman. When she does reveal her face it is not to Whitman but to his traveling companion, who is thus able to glean some inkling of a story Whitman himself remains dumb to tell: "He caught a look of her face, and talk'd with her a little. Eyes, voice and manner were those of a corpse, animated by electricity" (822). And in that last figure, Whitman's great trope of the "body electric" is grotesquely transformed into a monstrous image.

Remarkable though such "portraits" are, there was, of course, nothing particularly remarkable about Whitman's analysis of the great problem endemic to the economic, social, and political order of the postbellum United States; indeed, his was the conclusion forced on many thinking people both inside and outside the labor movement by a complex series of developments that began in the early 1870s as the country entered what Trachtenberg has called "the age of incorporation." It was the end of the old republican dream of labor getting its just rewards and of *everyone* enjoying modest comforts—a dream that, incidentally, Trachtenberg specifically associates with Whitman. The mass of the people found themselves fixed immovably in their place as meager wage earners, helplessly dependent on large, impersonal business organizations. As Trachtenberg explains, "They tended to view wage labor as another form of slavery, of life-long dependency, and the monied classes as usurpers" (73, 72). The narrative of these times, from labor's point of view, can be simplistically summarized as follows. After the severe depression of 1873 had shaken everyone, the public euphoria associated with the centennial exposition of 1876 was ironically followed by the strikes of 1877, a year of labor violence that spurred the middle class to efforts of organized charity and cultural enlightenment. In spite of these ameliorative measures, the 1880s brought further unrest, culminating in the Great Upheaval of 1886. This was the year of the Knights of Labor's great strike against Jay Gould's railroad in the Southwest, of peak agitation for an eight-hour day, and of the Haymarket Riot in Chicago. It was the shape of things to come: between 1881 and 1905 there were to be 37,000 strikes involving seven million workers—"dramatic indices of turmoil" indeed, as Trachtenberg says (79), and incontrovertible evidence of a widening class rift. For most of the 1880s, Whitman's anachronistic dream of labor was shared to a significant extent by the Knights of Labor, who refused to accept the new economic order dividing owners from workers and strove to establish a single classless society. Out of the wreckage of that dream there arose the Amalgamated Union of Labor, which fatalistically accepted the status quo and was concerned only to defend the interests of its members.

Since scholars have traditionally been rather slow to consider the implications of these momentous developments for Whitman's later writings, it is good to see the subject receive illuminating attention from Betsy Erkkila and Robert Schulman.[20] It was not only through his writings, though, that Whitman struggled to come to terms with all this turmoil, and the story of one of his most interesting attempts to find an image to focus his confused feelings begins with him boarding a train in August 1881 to travel to Boston. It was an overnight sleeper that carried him in speed and in comfort—the very image, in fact, of modern progress, as indeed was the Boston in which he arrived early the next morning. Whitman marveled at its "immense material growth," seeing in it "the wand of future prosperity," and he registered with vivid appreciation the difference between the old part of the city and the new: "Old Boston with its zigzag streets and multitudinous angles, (crush up a sheet of letter paper in your hand, throw it down, stamp it flat, and that is a map of old Boston)—new Boston with its miles upon miles of large and costly houses—Beacon Street, Commonwealth Avenue, and a hundred others" (901).

Carefully overlooking the North End of Boston, already crammed with the Irish immigrants that have been noted in chapter 3, Whitman concentrated on the magnificent middle-class metropolis that had arisen from the ashes of the great 1872 fire and had been partly built on public lands created by the filling in, over a twenty-year period, of the marshes and bogs of the Back Bay. As noted in chapter 3, this elegant new Boston, with its handsome five-story brownstone houses in the French Second Empire style, intermixed with brick houses, Victorian Gothic mansions, and buildings in the Romanesque style, had been laid out by Arthur Gilman on the Paris model, an attractive feature of which was the wide tree-lined boulevards.[21] Farther out from the city center were new affluent suburbs like Brookline, Roxbury, and Dedham, and it was to the similar district of Jamaica Plain that Whitman traveled to visit "a home full of treasures: Japanese ware—lace decorations—the most incredible mass—the finest, rarest."[22]

This was the home of one of the wealthiest men in New England, Quincy Adams Shaw, and Whitman was later to doubt "that he has any deep artistic, aesthetic appreciation of the things he has collected there—doubt very much if he has." Indeed, Shaw, a retiring man, seems to have been quietly and decently dedicated to a view of culture perilously similar to the one Whitman had savagely attacked fifteen years earlier in *Democratic Vistas.* Forty years ago, in his classic study of nineteenth-century Bostonian culture, Martin Green accused people of Shaw's class of supporting a genteel kind of culture that cocooned them from the disturbing downtown realities of their city. More recently, Trachtenberg has seen them as steering an ineffectual middle way between the philistine plutocrats and the immigrant masses (142ff).[23]

Be that as it may, Whitman was to remember for the rest of his life what he saw in Shaw's house that day—and that memory became his precious stay in old age:

> "I was there with others," [he told Traubel seven years later]: "I wanted to be alone: I wiaved [*sic*] them all off"—here he gestured—threw his head back. "'Here you fellows,' I said, or something in that manner: 'I want you to all go out—to leave me alone: I want to be alone here': they went: and so I got an hour or two to myself—the sweetest, fullest, peaceablest: then I saw Millet." He ceased talking. I didn't break in.[24]

Earlier, in *Specimen Days*, he had given an equally moving account of the experience of seeing Jean-François Millet's work: "Two rapt hours. Never before have I been so penetrated by this kind of expression" (903).

Over the decade that followed this extraordinary shock of recognition, Whitman was to elaborate his sense of Millet's significance for himself into an ever more complex myth of the mystic union of the souls of two democratic artists. In this he was unhealthily encouraged by his coterie of cronies. And a bizarre apotheosis was surely reached when Richard Maurice Bucke produced an eleven-point checklist triumphantly proving that Millet was indeed Whitman's French alter ego or spiritual twin (3:93–94). There remains, however, an interesting question: why did Millet rivet Whitman's attention? And the answer may in part lie in the prominent attention Millet gave to work, in powerful pictures that allowed Whitman to focus his hopelessly confused postbellum feelings about labor in a single imperceptibly ambivalent image.

The frequent commentaries on Millet that appeared in American magazines in the late 1880s invariably praised him as "the Apostle of Work"[25] and, as was pointed out in the introduction to the catalog of the great Millet exhibition at Boston's Museum of Fine Arts, Shaw himself may well have been encouraged to collect Millet by his wife's passionate interest in this very aspect of the paintings. Pauline Agassiz Shaw (daughter of Louis Agassiz, the great zoologist and geologist) used to hang the pictures in the kindergartens and nurseries she ran in Boston, believing that they were useful for teaching children the dignity of labor.[26] This was very much in line with what has been called the "romantic capitalism" of the time—the assiduously cultivated belief that the lords of industry, the captains of commerce, and the kings of corporations during the Gilded Age were really genuine aristocrats of labor and had achieved success through hard, physical work. The corollary of this view was, of course, the belief that restless, dissatisfied members of the workforce should cease their envious agitation and obediently strive instead to emulate those who had risen through their own efforts.

There is plenty of evidence that Whitman was not immune to this kind of propaganda—the most nauseous example of it being, perhaps, the mutual admiration that developed between him and Andrew Carnegie. Or, to put the matter more kindly, it is probable that in the sentimentalization of labor Whitman found both relief from the real intractable labor problems of the day and grounds for a continuing belief in a "single society" theory of American life. Millet's paintings may, then, have appealed to him in much the same way that they did to the Shaws. But that is by no means the whole picture, so to speak. In order to see that, one needs to reexamine the passage in which Whitman recorded his first experience of seeing Millet's paintings:

> I stood long and long before "The Sower." . . . There is something in this that could hardly be caught again—a sublime murkiness and original pent fury. Besides this masterpiece, there were many others, (I shall never forget the simple evening scene,

"Watering the Cow,") all inimitable, all perfect as pictures, works of mere art; and then it seem'd to me, with that last impalpable ethic purpose from the artist (most likely unconscious to himself) which I am always looking for. To me all of them told the full story of what went before and necessitated the great French Revolution—the long precedent crushing of the masses of a heroic people into the earth, in abject poverty, hunger—every right denied, humanity attempted to be put back for generations—yet Nature's force, titanic here, the stronger and hardier for that repression—waiting terribly to break forth, revengeful—the pressure on the dykes, and the bursting at last—the storming of the Bastile—the execution of the king and queen—the tempest of massacres and blood. Yet who can wonder? (903)

This is one of those studied compositions, complete with a high-gloss finish, which Whitman went in for in his overelaborate postwar prose. The interest, however, is in the three different coats of paint that give the passage its rich emotional color. Two of these coats are easily discernible and have perhaps been too consciously applied. First, there is the ethereal hue of pathos in his treatment of *Watering the Cow*, a painting regarded as a solemnizing example of art hallowing the work of the poor. Second, there is the dark color associated with *The Sower* and the other paintings that Whitman sees as representing the life of the oppressed, repressed peasantry of prerevolutionary France. To the extent that Whitman believed the United States of the 1880s still to be a guiding light for corrupt, reactionary Europe, then implicit in this interpretation of Millet's paintings is Whitman's pride in his own politically emancipated and progressive society.

The third coat of paint, or level of feeling, in the passage, however, is the one that Whitman would probably not care to acknowledge, even to himself. One notices it only if one has other passages in mind that Whitman wrote around the same time, of which the following is the best example:

Two grim and spectral dangers—dangerous to peace, to health, to social security, to progress—long known in concrete to the governments of the Old World, and there eventuating, more than once or twice, in dynastic overturns, bloodshed, days, months, of terror—seem of late years to be nearing the New World, nay, to be gradually establishing themselves among us. . . . Curious as it may seem, it is in what are call'd the poorest, lowest characters you will sometimes, nay generally, find glints of the most sublime virtues, eligibilities, heroisms. Then it is doubtful whether the State is to be saved, either in the monotonous long run, or in tremendous special crises, by its good people only. . . . The American Revolution of 1776 was simply a great strike, successful for its immediate object—but whether a real success judged by the scale of the centuries, and the long-striking balance of Time, yet remains to be settled. The French Revolution was absolutely a strike, and a very terrible and relentless one, against ages of bad pay, unjust division of wealth-products, and the hoggish monopoly of a few, rolling in superfluity, against the vast bulk of the work-people, living in squalor. (1063–1065)

That is Whitman's attempt, in "The Tramp and Strike Questions," to come to terms with the labor unrest of the late 1870s; it turns on the painful parallels he uneasily draws between conditions in contemporary America and conditions in prerevolutionary France. His first reaction, on entertaining this comparison, is to be terrified by the specter of unbridled violence it releases. His second reaction is to discover, in the comparison of the French Revolution with the very different American Revolution, a hope that American labor will produce "heroic" leaders who will bloodlessly rectify the infamous inequities of American society. It is surely this volatile mixture of unacknowledged feelings that lends disturbing intensity to his description of Millet's *The Sower* as full of "a sublime murkiness and pent fury." And it could also well be that he saw the features of that "tramp" woman whose face had been rendered anonymous by her bonnet in those of the girl in *Watering the Cow.*

It is, then, useful to distinguish between three different layers of paint, or levels of feeling, in the "picture" Whitman offers of his response to the Millet paintings. At two of these levels he echoes the contemporary ruling class view by officially affirming that labor is assured of a central place in existing American society. But at the third level he expresses an unacknowledged, uneasy, and guilty wish to see labor reclaiming its redeeming place at the center of a society corrupted and distorted by wealth. Interestingly enough, Whitman's ambivalent response chimes with those of his French contemporaries, because from the very beginning Millet's work had lent itself, as Griselda Pollock has explained, to widely different political interpretations:

> Left-wing writers claimed him as the painter of the "Modern Demos," while conservatives decried the brutal picture of bestial humanity painted with what Théophile Gautier called "masonries of paint." Against both interpretations Millet was defended by his friend and biographer Alfred Sensie, who offered instead a picture of a man of deep piety and filial duty, more dedicated to the representation of the biblical injunction to Adam and Eve to "earn their bread by the sweat of their brow" than concerned with attempts to order more egalitarian distribution of both bread and sweat.[27]

As for Whitman's responses, the more radical directly contradicts the previous two, and the three taken together expose the deep confusion of mind and of feeling that characterized Whitman's attitude toward labor during his final years.

For final, comical, and pathetic proof of this, one need only turn to Sidney Morse's account of a visit paid to the sick Whitman by a labor agitator who

> was the happy possessor of a loud voice and in manner was quite imperious. The conversation ran somewhat like this: "I have solved the problem, Mr. Whitman." "Ah!" "In my own mind." "The right spot to begin." "I believe, in fact, I've settled the matter." "Oh!" "Now to convince the world. You yourself have struck the keynote." "Thanks." "Your words are a great reinforcement to the cause." "Thanks." And so on for ten minutes or more, the man standing with hat in hand orating, Whitman when there came a lull, looking up from perusal of his letters, interposing his "thanks." Finally, the man, grown weary or perceiving he was making little, if any, progress, suddenly brought up with: "Well, Mr. Whitman, I think I'll take my leave." "Thanks." Not until after he had departed did the inopportuneness of his response become manifest. He was not, however, greatly disturbed in consequence. . . . [Whitman felt that] the labor problem, as a practical question, belonged to younger heads than his, if there really was anything to be said or done about it. He was not sure but things were working well enough as they were, evolving in their natural course for better results than any theory of socialism could promise . . . so far as he could see there was as much "cussed selfishness" on the one side as the other. It was a question of manhood, if anything. Workingmen's strikes were apt to develop little of that. They would set on their fellow-workingmen who didn't belong to their "union" like tigers or other beasts of prey. It was their "union" against the world. The spectacle was not pleasing. . . . At other times he betrayed an anxiety in behalf of the "masses driven to the wall," and felt that somehow the Republic was not safe while "anybody was being so driven." He commended and gave me Carnegie's book on "Triumphant Democracy," as containing much that was "about so and gratifying."[28]

It is a commonplace of recent scholarship that, after the Civil War, prose replaced poetry as Whitman's chief medium for bringing his visions into living, mutually restorative contact with his times. In its turn, his prose also failed to cope with the economic facts and altered social mentality of a new age; Whitman's exhausted, superannuated imagination, the ideological product of an earlier period, was forced to look to art, specifically to Millet, for reinforcement and reinvigoration. We can thus usefully reverse Whitman's familiar remark and say that for him Millet's paintings were really only *Leaves of Grass* in another form.

In those pictures the dreams of labor, which had necessitated and sponsored so much of Whitman's mature work, found their final artistic image. And he himself confessed as much: "The *Leaves* are really only Millet in another form—they are the Millet that Walt Whitman has succeeded in putting into words . . . Millet is my painter: he belongs to me: I have written Walt Whitman all over him. How about that? or is it the other way about? Has he written Millet all over me?"[29] But to that one could add a codicil: the paintings viewed by the elderly Whitman, well past his antebellum prime as a poet, were in fact—and rather poignantly, one might perhaps say—the late *Leaves* that the dying, politically disorientated Whitman had failed "in putting into words."

Five. Fratricide and Brotherly Love

"Must not worry about George, for I hope the worst is over—must keep up a stout heart."[1] This jotting from Whitman's notebooks early in 1863 is a vivid reminder of the person around whom, for Whitman and his family, the whole of the Civil War seemed to revolve for the full four years of its duration. A great deal of attention has by now been paid to everyone and everything else that was of central concern to Whitman at this time. His fierce commitment to the Union cause; his boundless admiration for Lincoln; above all, his tender yet invigorating care for the sick soldiers in general and the complex passion of his attachment to a few individuals in particular—all these matters have been extensively studied, not only for the insights they offer into Whitman's character but also for the light they throw on his poetry. By contrast, Whitman's wartime connection with his younger brother George (who was thirty-two when he entered the army, to the poet's forty-two) has been treated as at best a relatively minor matter of merely biographical interest. On closer examination, however, this fraternal relationship begins to assume much greater significance. Indeed, it could be argued that it was at least partly through George that Whitman was led to an intimate understanding of the real, hidden nature of the war, and that it was around George that Whitman was able (perhaps unconsciously) to arrange several of those imaginative configurations that articulated his hopes and anxieties and that supplied the deep structure of his war poetry.

For the Whitman family the Civil War literally began and ended with soldier George; for them he was the measure of the conflict. Six days after the rebels fired on the flag at Fort Sumter, George was one of the first to volunteer for active service, initially joining the Brooklyn 13th Regiment before reenlisting with the 51st New York Volunteers when his original hundred-day term expired. Four years later, at the grand Victory Review in Washington, Whitman watched the parade with a pride doubtlessly intensified by relief that his younger brother had not only come safely through some of the fiercest campaigns of the war, but had also recently survived several months' incarceration in one of the notorious southern military prisons. (Whitman had worked diligently for his release.) Moreover George's war record had been a distinguished one, and his courage in the field had won him repeated promotion. Whitman's admiration of him extended to the regiment as a whole, and he carefully chronicled its battle honors. But this appreciation of what the veterans had suffered, and had achieved through the stubborn strength of their long endurance, was only one aspect of the complex insight Whitman had gained into the conditions of war through his close identification with his soldier-brother.

From the beginning, George was implicated (unwittingly, of course) in Whitman's work of creating in poetry a propagandist iconography for the Union cause. What Walt liked to think of as a "national uprising and volunteering" —namely, the frenzy of indignantly patriotic activity that immediately followed the firing on Fort Sumter—passed into *Drum-Taps* in the form of "First O Songs for a Prelude." There he showed "[t]he blood of [New York] city up—arm'd! arm'd! the cry everywhere," and the series of verbal snapshots he proudly displayed to back up his bellicose claims included one of "[t]he tearful parting, the mother kisses her son, the son kisses his mother, / (Loth is the mother to part, yet not a word does she speak to detain him)" (417). This minor melodramatic detail, probably based on George's own departure, matters, however, only for what it more generally signifies—a spontaneous unanimity of support in New York for the Union effort. Whitman's hysterical delight at this was proportionate to his previous despair at the city's selfish pursuit, before Sumter, of its mercenary commercial goals. Its change of heart (short-lived though it turned out to be) was typified for him by George's enlistment. And although "First O Songs" depicts a city in the grip of an enlistment fever that sweeps across occupations and ignores social classes, the emphasis is nevertheless on "[t]he mechanics arming, (the trowel, the jack-plane, the blacksmith's hammer, tost aside with precipitation)" (417). This was in keeping with Walt's deepest political conviction, his abiding belief (which the war was profoundly to confirm) that the true custodian of his visionary democracy was not the ruling elite but the working class, of which his brother was a representative member.

Although there is much heatedly aggressive talk in "First O Songs" and in the other poems in *Drum-Taps* that relate to the early phases of the war, there is scarcely a mention of the enemy. This is no accident. As has already been seen, Whitman's feelings about the South were so mixed and so complicated that he found it much easier to construct a positive rhetoric (in favor of union, democracy, liberty, etc.) than a negative rhetoric. Two poems in particular —"Virginia—The West" and "The Centenarian's Story"—represent interesting attempts to deal with the problem, and in both cases the figure of George Washington is crucial. The former poem constructs a tableau in which Virginia is depicted as "The noble sire fallen on evil days" who, in an amnesiac state of senile dementia, raises "[t]he insane knife toward the Mother of All" (429). She calmly rebukes him by reminding him that it was he who once famously supplied the greatest of all the defenders of her liberty, namely, George Washington. This tableau bears a curious resemblance to relations within Whitman's own family—as if, in creating the figure of the "sire," the poet had conflated his deceased father (moody, irascible, sporadically violent) with his oldest brother, Jesse, who eventually had to be committed to an insane asylum because of his increasingly violent attacks on his mother. What is really important, though, is that by figuring the North-South conflict as an internecine family drama, Whitman was able both to discount southern claims to independence and to make its "rebellion" seem a betrayal of its own history and of that "true self" symbolized by Washington. This was, of course, a propaganda ploy that ran directly counter to the South's image of itself. Confederates specifically saw themselves as the true heirs of the Revolutionary tradition, and found "an inspiring analogy between the struggle of the Confederacy and that of Revolutionary America under the generalship of Lee's great hero, Washington."[2]

The founding president of the United States is again the key figure in "The Centenarian's Story," a narrative poem set in Washington Park, Brooklyn, where an ancient veteran of the war against the British for independence watches young soldiers drilling before setting off for the front. Involuntarily the old man remembers the battle for Brooklyn, when the brigade of Virginia and Maryland, under the supreme command of Washington, marched out to meet the enemy, only to be decimated by murderous artillery (430–435). For Whitman the story is a nexus of meanings. The tragic irony is that southerners are about to march to their death once more, this time at the hands of fellow Americans who fight in the name of that very liberty that the South had so bloodily helped win. The North may, however, have to suffer defeat, like Washington himself, before final victory is won, and must therefore resolutely set its heart, like him, against the idea of capitulation. Thus in both poems, Whitman creates images of "the enemy" in which feelings of pity, sympathy, and condemnation commingle, and in both cases George Washington is the crucial common denominator between North and South, a historically connecting figure who brings out the tragic absurdity of the conflict. The full name of Whitman's brother was George Washington Whitman and it is difficult to believe that this fact didn't resonate in Walt's mind at some level when he was writing the two poems. What is at least possible is that his mixed feelings about fighting the South found expression in an unconscious association of the two George Washingtons. This may have helped him feel that the North, in the person of his soldier-brother, was setting out not to attack an enemy, but rather to liberate the South in the name of its true, libertarian, historical self.[3]

What is certain is that Walt believed that the Union army, whose formation was so joyously celebrated in "First O Songs," would be a revolutionary body—revolutionary in the sense that, unlike all the armies of history, it would be thoroughly democratic in spirit and in structure. When reality struck home, it therefore struck with a revelatory force that eventually dictated the vision, the terms, and the pattern of Whitman's war poetry. As the relevant passages in *Specimen Days* show, he blamed the debacle at the first battle of Bull Run (July 21, 1861) entirely on the officers, and in concluding that the northern armies consisted of superb fighting men with abominable leaders, he may have been eagerly building on information given by George, some of whose early letters contained similarly aggrieved sentiments. For instance, he wrote on December 13, 1862:

> I am pretty well satisfied that as yet we have had no one to command the Army of the Potomac that was a match for Lee, and it seems to me that in all the fights I have been in since we have been in the Potomac army (except the battle of South Mountain) we have been most terribly outgeneraled, the men fight as well as men can fight, and I firmly believe that all we want, is some one competent to lead, to finish up this work in short order.[4]

When Walt experienced this criminal incompetence for himself after moving to Washington, he was quick to inform his prospective publisher, James Redpath, that "[t]he officers should almost invariably rise from the ranks—there is an absolute want of democratic spirit in the present system & officers—it is the feudal spirit exclusively."[5] In fact, George did gradually win promotion in precisely this way, rising from private to acting lieutenant colonel of his regiment by dint of proven courage and recognized qualities of natural leadership. Walt, though, continued to be possessed by the desire to produce a revolutionary book that would "push forward the very big & needed truth, that our national military system needs shifting, revolutionising & made to tally with democracy, the people" (*Letters* I, 171). In a way, *Drum-Taps* was that book, undemonstratively egalitarian in language and in outlook, and bearing quiet testimony to the pure democracy of courage and of suffering Whitman believed he'd been privileged to witness in the hospitals.

Walt's journey to the hospitals started in December 1862, when he was aroused from the lethargy that had seized him virtually since the war began by a newspaper report the family in Brooklyn thought might possibly be a garbled account of a serious injury sustained by George during the recent fighting. Whitman immediately traveled down to Washington and then to the camp at Falmouth, where he met his brother, who, it transpired, had suffered only a superficial flesh wound six days earlier during the savage battle for Fredericksburg. As the surviving notebooks show, it was during this short visit to the front that Whitman collected the basic material for several of the best poems in *Drum-Taps*. It was also around this time that a pattern of reactions to the war began to form in his mind, a pattern that was to serve as the template for many of his future wartime experiences.

While Walt was searching for George, his mother received a letter from her soldier-son assuring her of his safety, "although I had the side of my jaw slightly scraped with a peice [*sic*] of shell which burst at my feet" (*Civil War Letters*, 75). It was to this letter Whitman alluded in a note he sent his mother after returning from Falmouth to Washington: "Mother, how much you must have suffered, all that week, till George's letter came—and all the rest must too. As to me, I know I put in about three days of the greatest suffering I ever experienced in my life" (*Letters* I, 58). Even after allowing for the exaggerated tones of familial concern that mark all Walt's correspondence with his mother, these sentences still strike one as basically genuine. The sincerity of the sentiments expressed seems to be confirmed by the pleas made in the postscript to the same letter: "Jeff must write oftener, and put in a few lines from mother, even if it is only two lines—then in the next letter a few lines from Mat, and so on. You have no idea how letters from home cheer one up in camp, and dissipate home sickness" (*Letters* I, 59). These pleas are all the more striking when one realizes that during the preceding few months, when Walt was still at home in Brooklyn, George had repeatedly, and fruitlessly, begged his family to be better correspondents. Indeed, the last of these notes home was written either on or about the day Walt actually arrived in Falmouth: "Mother why dont you write to a fellow I have not had a letter from you in a long time" (*Civil War Letters*, 77).

His arrival at the front brought home to Whitman what, in these circumstances, a letter really meant and what a vast psychological distance it had to cross. He realized, with a shock that galvanized his whole being and irrevocably altered his imagination, that the soldiers and civilians lived worlds apart from each other, separated by a fearful gulf of unknowing. Thereafter, much of his work for the remainder of the war consisted of attempts to connect these worlds—to build bridges, open lines of communication, establish lifelines—through his regular reports to the newspapers, by means of the poems he wrote, and, of course, via the innumerable letters he sent on behalf of the wounded and the dead. These famous letters lie at the heart of his enterprise and are a kind of synecdoche of all his wartime writings. His war poems became, in turn, his letters to the world that never wrote to him, just as Emily Dickinson's poems were hers. Yet, even before he went in search of George, Whitman already knew the anguish of being totally in the dark about what was really happening in that other world of the soldier. Some members of his immediate family, particularly his emotionally unstable sister Hannah, tended to become hysterical under the strain of such uncertainty. Her letters sometimes grew shrill with anxiety: "Mother, will you *be sure*; and send me word the minute you hear that he is safe. I am like you, I cannot see a bit of peace till I hear" (*Letters* I, 220n73). By traveling to Falmouth, Whitman completed his bipolar education. He now had both a combatant's and a noncombatant's experience of receiving letters.

On August 11, 1863, Whitman put his own nagging fears in writing: "I sent Jeff a letter on Sunday, I suppose he got at the office—I feel so anxious to hear from George, one cannot help feeling uneasy, although these days sometimes it cannot help being long intervals without one's hearing from friends in the army" (*Letters* I, 130). By suggestive coincidence, he had only the previous day sent a poignant yet carefully composed letter to Mr. and Mrs. S. B. Haskell informing them of the death of their son Erastus. In the accidental juxtaposition of these two letters, an important connection may stand revealed. It may well be that Whitman's self-assumed duties as secretary to the wounded were unconsciously informed by those worries about George that were themselves dramatically focused in the acts of sending and receiving a letter.

It is worth noting that Whitman began the habit of writing letters home on behalf of the soldiers as soon as he first arrived in Falmouth and found that George was alive and well. The professional writer had discovered his wartime vocation as amateur amanuensis. His quiet discovery of the depth of experience locked away in the muteness and inarticulateness of these soldiers corresponded to his more famous, dramatic discovery in the same camp of the heap of amputated limbs outside the Lacy House. Indeed, the tearing of youngsters violently away from their families produced a sort of psychological amputation, as Whitman was to realize later in the hosptitals. With reference to both kinds of maiming, physical and psychic, Walt discovered that the reality of the war continued to be unspoken because it was felt to be unspeakable and therefore remained unimaginable to the outside world. Whitman immediately set about breaking this taboo of silence, as this piece he sent to the *New York Times* shows:

> I do a good deal of this, of course, writing all kinds, including love-letters. Many sick and wounded soldiers have not written home to parents, brothers, sisters, and even wives, for one reason or another, for a long, long time. Some are poor writers, some cannot get paper and envelopes; many have an aversion to writing because they dread to worry the folks at home—the facts about them are so sad to tell. I always encourage the men to write, and promptly write for them.[6]

Indeed, George Whitman himself confessed in a letter to his mother that "I have often thought when I have been in a pretty hot place, how glad I was that none of you at home, knew anything about it" (*Civil War Letters*, 78). This feeling existed in tension, though, with a worry that "you would frett and worry about not hearing from me, and I have often thought, I would give almost anything to let you know that I was all right" (*Civil War Letters*, 120).

Such contrary impulses—to conceal and to disclose—were, of course, felt unbearably acutely by Walt when he had to communicate sad news of suffering or of death. He resolved the problem, as both his letters and his poems show, by telling the truth within what a modern psychiatrist might call a "holding environment." In other words, he tried whenever possible to set potentially demeaning and humanly devastating suffering in a redeeming context, emphasizing the transfiguring courage of the sufferer, the love and care that attended him. "The Wound-Dresser" is his great epic achievement in this vein—"Bearing the bandages, water and sponge, / Straight and swift to my wounded I go" (443). The poem is almost a conscious tour de force of sympathy, almost a tall tale of hyperbolic charity: "[I] Cleanse the [foot] with a gnawing and putrid gangrene, so sickening, so offensive, / While the attendant stands behind aside me holding the tray and pail" (445). To emphasize the extravagant, histrionic element in this writing is not, however, to question, but rather to affirm, the authenticity of the experience.

What Whitman here reveals is what he has to conceal in his letters, namely, the psychic economy of his acts of sympathy—the heavy price in internal strain he has to pay for remaining "faithful, I do not give out": "I dress with impassive hand, (yet deep in my breast a fire, a burning flame)." Accounts by other observers confirm that in the hospitals a mounting hysteria frequently underlay a surface calm that could sometimes appear brutal in character. The heartlessness of the field surgeons as they snatched the knife from between their teeth to dispatch yet more limbs was punctuated, said a contemporary observer, by the reaction of the occasional surgeon who, "having been long at work, would put down the knife, exclaiming that his hand had grown unsteady, and that this was too much for human endurance—not seldom hysterical tears streaming down his face" *(The Blue and the Gray*, 791).

The semiliterateness of many of the ordinary soldiers, which made them ill at ease with the written word, was another factor preventing their experiences from finding an effective voice. But if they needed a scribe, they also needed an interpreter—someone who could faithfully translate the reality of their situation into terms distant noncombatants could comprehend imaginatively as well as intellectually. Whitman's genius for doing this was inseparable from the humility of spirit with which he sought to adapt himself to the situation of the men—"With hinged knees returning I enter the doors, (while for you up there, / Whoever you are, follow without noise and be of strong heart)" (443). As well as suggesting a spontaneous genuflecting before a spectacle of courageous suffering, the "hinged knees" touchingly hints at the reluctant, involuntary, and automatic nature of the impulse to revisit traumatic scenes in memory; the hint of repetition compulsion in the "going," as in the retelling (the parallel with Coleridge's Ancient Mariner is an irresistible one to make). And yet, in spite of the heroic service he rendered, Whitman could not but remain centrally divided in feeling about his role as scribe. In *Drum-Taps*, the powerful crosscurrents of feeling Whitman associated with the sending and the receiving of wartime letters—feelings in which his own and his family's anxieties about George merged with his (impressively self-effacing) secretarial work in the hospitals—are most clearly apparent in "Come Up from the Fields Father."

"O mother," Whitman wrote in August 1863, "what would we [have] done if it had been otherwise—if [George] had met the fate of so many we know—if he had been killed or badly hurt in some of those battles—I get thinking about it sometimes, & it works upon me so I have to stop & turn my mind on something else" (*Letters* I, 137). In "Come Up from the Fields," Whitman does indeed live out precisely such an anxious fantasy in imagination, while at the same time putting himself in the place of those parents to whom he had sent news of their sons' serious injuries and even of their death (436–438).[7] The striking feature of the poem is the dramatic use made within it of two voices—the voice of the actual family receiving the letter and the voice of the observer who sympathetically watches their stunned reaction. There is already a suggestion of such a divide in the opening two lines of the poem: "Come up from the fields father, here's a letter from our Pete, / And come to the front door mother, here's a letter from thy dear son."

As the poem develops, the two voices grow more distinct, yet are carefully coordinated, and they precisely correspond to the dual relationship in which Whitman himself stands to the imagined scene. He is both the imaginary sender of the letter and the imagined recipient of it, being both the brother who received news in Brooklyn of George's injuries at the front and the person who later wrote innumerable letters from Washington hospitals on behalf of the soldiers. Indeed, the shock of premonition first enters the poem at the very point the mother realizes "O this is not our son's writing, yet his name is sign'd, / O a strange hand writes for our dear son, O stricken mother's soul!" (437). In context, that "strange hand" signifies the impersonal forces that have commandeered the soldier's life and that coldly govern his affairs at a remote distance from the fertile family farm in Ohio, "Where apples ripe in the orchards hang and grapes on the trellis'd vines" (436). This impression is reinforced by the sense given of the totally separate, unsynchronized lives lived by soldiers and civilians, who inhabit entirely different zones of experience: "While they stand at home at the door he is dead already, / The only son is dead" (438).

The poem concludes with a sensitive awareness of how the profound need of the bereaved to mourn is damagingly frustrated by the absence of the dead body: "In the midnight waking, weeping, longing with one deep longing, / O that she might withdraw unnoticed, silent from life escape and withdraw, / To follow, to seek, to be with her dear dead son" (438). As several powerful poems in *Drum-Taps* show, Whitman undertook in the hospitals to be not only a "psychological nurse" to the wounded (in Jerome Loving's excellent phrase) but also a surrogate mourner of the dead—one who took it upon himself to do what the relatives could not do: to remember the dead man in the very presence of his corpse. It is Whitman's psychologically perceptive understanding of the human need to do this that turns "Vigil Strange," for instance, into a poem *about* mourning as well as a poem *of* mourning.

During the war, Whitman many times took it upon himself to inform parents that their son had died and that he had been witness to that dying. In its pathos, therefore, the letter sent on August 10, 1863, to Mr. and Mrs. S. B. Haskell is typical of many over which he labored and anguished. But a short time earlier he had implored them to write to their son, who was critically ill with typhoid fever, and he had even gone so far as to "enclose you an envelope to send your letter to

Erastus—put a stamp on it, & write soon" (*Letters* I, 119). Now he ended his sadly graphic account of Erastus's final decline with the following explanation:

> I write to you this letter, because I would do something at least in his memory—his fate was a hard one, to die so—He is one of the thousands of our unknown American young men in the ranks about whom there is no record or fame, no fuss made about their dying so unknown, but I find in them the real precious & royal ones of this land, giving themselves up, aye even their young and precious lives, in their country's cause. (*Letters* I, 129)

These comments lay bare one of the deepest compulsions behind Whitman's wartime activities, namely, his passionate determination to record the achievements and sufferings of the "unknown" soldier and, wherever possible, to restore to those soldiers at least a trace of that personal identity that had almost been obliterated by the new techniques of mass warfare.[8] And here once again it was his concern for George that had been the means of initiating Whitman into a revelatory understanding of the unprecedented scale and terrifyingly modern character of the Civil War.

When Whitman first arrived in Washington posthaste from home in search of George, he hadn't the slightest idea where he might be. There were, he discovered, upward of fifty hospitals in the vicinity, each of which treated thousands of soldiers. Had he not stumbled, by the purest chance, on old friends who could tell him where he was likely to find his brother, he might well have failed entirely to locate him. A few months later, by which time he was a veteran of the wards, he reflected indirectly on what might have been under the ironically laconic heading of "hospital perplexity":

> To add to other troubles, amid the confusion of this great army of sick, it is almost impossible for a stranger to find any friend or relative, unless he has the patient's specific address to start upon. Besides the directory printed in the newspapers here, there are one or two general directories of the hospitals kept at provost's headquarters, but they are nothing like complete; they are never up to date, and, as things are, with the daily streams of coming and going and changing, cannot be. I have known cases, for instance such as a farmer coming here from northern New York to find a wounded brother, faithfully hunting round for a week, and then compell'd to leave and go home without getting any trace of him. When he got home he found a letter from the brother giving the right address. (739)

Having himself been very fortunate to escape this demoralizing extreme of disorientation in December 1862, he was able to make his way fairly directly to

George in camp at Falmouth. There he saw several bodies, each of which was covered by an identical brown woolen blanket. When he came to recreate this episode in "A Sight in Camp," he deliberately turned what had been an unexpected, unnerving encounter into a dignified ceremony of recognition (441). (One of the least appreciated aspects of *Drum-Taps* is the ritualistic and liturgical character of so much of the poetry; no wonder Whitman could refer to himself as writing "psalms of the dead," the "sacred" texts of his secular faith.) Instinctively in the poem he reverts to the ancient triadic pattern that for millennia, and through the myths and legends of many cultures, has signified a process of understanding that culminates in transcendent illumination. When he first lifts the blanket, he sees the gaunt face of an elderly man that leaves him wondering, "Who are you my dear comrade?" Next, he uncovers the face of a "child" and inquires, "Who are you sweet boy with cheeks yet blooming?" In both cases, he is therefore baffled in his urgent wish to bestow a fully humanizing individual identity on these dead forms. "Then to the third," and this time it is "a face nor child nor old," but rather a union of these opposites: "Young man I think I know you—I think this face is the face of the Christ himself, / Dead and divine and brother of all, and here again he lies." Whitman, we know, was not an orthodox Christian, and it will not do to read this line as routinely pious. What seems to happen is that in this final attempt—the third, as required by the ancient symbolism of numbers—Whitman finds a "name" that can give human meaning even to the irreducibly anonymous suffering and death that man visits upon his fellows. This is an occurrence best understood, perhaps, in relation to the instances of "displaced Christianity," along with the "plethora of very unmodern superstitions, talismans, wonders, miracles, relics, legends and rumors" that, as Paul Fussell has shown, was a feature of the soldiers' psychological reaction to that other "triumph of modern industrialism, materialism, and mechanism," the First World War.[9]

Whitman found this wholesale anonymity of the dead very disturbing. He returned to the subject repeatedly after the war in *Specimen Days*, noting, for instance, that in one particular war cemetery only eighty-five of the bodies were identified. A poem like "Vigil Strange" cries out to be read against this background. Then it can perhaps be appreciated that the emotional impulse behind the poem is partly the desire to ensure that the battlefield dead are individually recognized, remembered, and mourned: "Then on the earth partially reclining sat by your side leaning my chin in my hands, / Passing sweet hours, immortal and mystic hours with you dearest comrade—not a tear, not a word, / Vigil of silence, love and death, vigil for you my son and my soldier" (438–439). It is noteworthy that in draft form the poem referred to the dead comrade in the third-person singular, so that in altering it to the second-person singular, Whitman increased both the sense of mystery and the sense of intimacy, as Edward Grier remarked in his edition of the notebook (*Notebooks* 2: 611–613). Both versions are, in fact, highly significant because taken together they offer another example of that dual perspective that was noted in "Come Up from the Fields." Whitman both felt drawn toward a rapt immersion in the soldiers' experience (as expressed in the printed version of "Vigil Strange") and impelled to mediate their experience to the civilian world (hence the style of report of the original draft form).

The poetry of *Drum-Taps* is strongly marked by this quality of double vision. So, for instance, the entranced and entrancing little poem "Bivouac on a Mountain Side," in which Whitman loses himself in what he sees, is contrasted with "Cavalry Crossing a Ford" (435). The former opens with "I see before me now a traveling army halting"; the latter, however, deliberately omits any mention of personal sight/vision—"A line in long array where they wind betwixt green islands." In this interesting version of a pastoral, the (civilian) reader is brought into the poem to be the observer of the scene: "Behold the silvery river, in it the splashing horses loitering stop to drink, / Behold the brown-faced men, each group, each person a picture, the negligent rest on the saddles."

It has generally been accepted that "Vigil Strange" was very loosely based on an actual story, or perhaps several stories, Whitman had heard veterans tell. But one other possible source is also worth considering. When he moved to Washington directly after first finding George in Falmouth, Whitman sent a letter home to his mother in which he particularly mentioned the name of George's cook, Tom: "Tom thinks all the world of George—when he heard he was wounded, on the day of the battle, he left every thing, got across the river, and went hunting for George through the field, through thick and thin" (*Letters* I, 60). It seems very possible that other accounts Whitman may later have heard of soldiers scouring the battlefields for their wounded or dead comrades struck a particularly deep chord in him precisely because of this incident, about which he was told during his first, impressionable experience of life at the front. Here again, Whitman's close relationship with one very special soldier—his brother George—sensitized his imagination and prepared it to respond acutely to certain kinds of war experience.

Very shortly after arriving in Washington from Falmouth camp, Whitman began his unofficial visits to the hospitals, and so inaugurated a routine that lasted for most of the remaining two-and-a-half years of the war. In his letter of Saturday, January 3, 1863, he explained to his sister-in-law Martha why he had first gone into the wards. A note had come from Brooklyn boys asking him to visit them in the Campbell Hospital. There he found about one hundred sick and wounded soldiers lying in the one long, whitewashed shed. "One young man was very much prostrated, and groaning with pain. I stopt and tried to comfort him. He was very sick. I found he had not had any medical attention since he was brought there—among so many he had been overlooked" (*Letters* I, 63). What Whitman had once more discovered, but this time in a new setting, was the dangerously depersonalizing scale of operations during this war. His time thereafter was to be spent combatting this sinister and genuinely life-threatening aspect of the hospital scene. As he realized a few days after his first visit, the life of the youngster he'd befriended had indeed been hanging in the balance, not for want of medical care only, but also for want of solicitously individualizing attention.[10] Had he remained but a day or two longer without such encouragement, Whitman was convinced he would have lost heart entirely, and with it he would undoubtedly have lost his life.

Several of the great *Drum-Taps* poems enact a psychically healing process of bestowing a kind of identity on some poor unknown through a glance of sympathetic human recognition.[11] The key word in Whitman's wartime vocabulary to describe such an event is "sight." It is a word he first began to use deliberately in his Falmouth camp notes at a time when, it seems, he was considering preparing a book of wartime "sights." The pictorial, even picturesque, associations of the word were, however, subordinated from the very outset to the new meanings that accumulated around it as Whitman used it in a new, highly charged context. It came to stand for epiphany—for those rare moments of spiritual insight granted to Whitman, when the hidden inner meaning of the war seemed to be revealed to him. It also came to stand for the perfectly focused glance that was the gift of such insight.

The word occurs in a pivotal position in "A March in the Ranks," a poem that opens with a soldier's baffled sense of being at the mercy of immense forces bent on inscrutable ends (439–440). It is one of the passages where Whitman best suggests the impersonality of this war and the impossibility of the soldiers knowing where they were, both literally and metaphorically speaking: "A march in the ranks hard-prest, and the road unknown, / A route through a heavy wood with muffled steps in the darkness." This opening captures the bewildering speed with which the northern armies traversed the country, that impetus of modern warfare that is again registered in "As Toilsome I Wander'd Virginia's Woods": "Mortally wounded he and buried on the retreat, (easily all could I understand,) / The halt of a mid-day hour, when up! no time to lose—yet this sign left"

(441–442). As George tellingly wrote, "I believe I last wrote home from Lowell, but a fellow has to change about so often in this country, its [*sic*] hard work to remember where he was two days ago" (*Civil War Letters*, 93). It is therefore appropriate that no place names are ever mentioned in *Drum-Taps*. The action takes place in vividly realized yet carefully unspecified locations, thus creating a physical landscape that corresponds to the mental landscape of the soldiers. Indeed, the correlation between the general numbing of the mind and the weariness of the legs is suggested in the central lines from "An Army Corps on the March": "The swarming ranks press on and on, the dense brigades press on, / Glittering dimly, toiling under the sun—the dust-cover'd men, / In columns rise and fall to the undulations of the ground" (436). Under such circumstances of forced marching, the halts became a mental event of striking character and assumed a heightened, hallucinatory, almost psychedelic quality.[12]

When the army stops in "A March in the Ranks" the speaker stumbles, as it were, on an old church in a clearing, and "[e]ntering but for a minute I see a sight beyond all the pictures and poems ever made" (440). At first everything is shadowy and vague, until, that is, he is able to see "At my feet more distinctly a soldier, a mere lad, in danger of bleeding to death, (he is shot in the abdomen,) / I staunch the blood temporarily, (the youngster's face is white as a lily,) / Then before I depart I sweep my eyes o'er the scene fain to absorb it all" (440). Through this second glance, he is able to distinguish clearly the "faces, varieties, postures" (440) of the various separate individuals who on first glance had merely constituted one dark, undifferentiated mass. His recognition of the individual soldier has therefore resulted in a transformation of the whole scene. Shadows have been resolved into flesh and blood. Not only have his eyes become used to the gloom, his inner eye of the imagination has also readjusted, so that it is once more capable of registering the real, piteously human scale of this extensive scene of suffering. By concentrating on the individual youngster at his feet, the speaker has been able to get the whole picture into focus and can view it in its proper colors and perspective. This, in poetic microcosm, is precisely what Whitman spent his time doing in the hospitals.

Lastly, before again being propelled onward and away, the speaker bends "to the dying lad, his eyes open, a half-smile gives he me, / Then the eyes close, calmly close, and I speed forth to the darkness" (440). In his writings about the war, Whitman insisted almost obsessively that he was as much the consoled as the consoler in his work of caring for the dying. There was in him a kind of repetition compulsion, which seems partly to have stemmed from the need to overcome his fear of death by witnessing, time and again, the inspiring calm with which the soldiers faced their end. Another element in the obsession, however, may have been Whitman's need to prepare himself mentally to deal with the probable news of George's death. "I suppose it is idle to say I think George's chances are very good for coming out of this campaign safe," he wrote his brother Jeff in May 1864, "yet at present it seems to me so—but it is indeed idle to say so, for no one can tell what a day may bring forth" (*Letters* I, 225). He proceeded to fortify Jeff by drawing on his hospital experiences: "then one finds, as I have the past year, that our feelings & imaginations make a thousand times too much of the whole matter—Of the many I have seen die, or known of, the past year, I have not seen or heard of *one* who met death with any terror."

So concerned was Walt in June 1864 that George might be one of the casualties brought to Washington that he refused to return home to Brooklyn, although his health had by then broken down. In the event, George survived the war—and outlived his brother—to die eventually in 1902. It was with mingled relief and pride, therefore, that Walt watched the great Washington review that preceded demobilization. He recorded the emotional occasion in a poem: "How solemn as one by one, / As the ranks returning worn and sweaty, as the men file by where I stand, / As the faces the masks appear, as I glance at the faces studying the masks" (453–454). By that mention of "masks" Whitman overtly meant to indicate that it is always the indwelling spirit that constitutes essential identity, and not external features and manners: "How solemn the thought of my whispering soul to each in the ranks, and to you, / I see behind each mask that wonder a kindred soul, / O the bullet could never kill what you really are, dear friend, / Nor the bayonet stab what you really are" (454). But the poem is also about Whitman's pride in the unique intimacy of his knowledge of the soldier's life: If they present only a mask to public (civilian) scrutiny, to him they show a different, private face. "Easily all could I understand," he wrote in "As Toilsome I Wander'd"—he was skilled, through hospital experience, at deciphering the coded meanings, the "signs," of this closed society.

But could he really understand all? Could he truly penetrate the mask? Was he genuinely one of them? The agonizing answer to these questions was no, as Whitman realized when, on December 26, 1864, his brother's trunk was opened—George being by then an inmate of one of the notorious military prisons of the South. The trunk had just arrived and had "stood some hours before we felt inclined to open it." Eventually his mother and brother Eddy nerved themselves for the task and were confronted by papers, a diary, a revolver, photographs, and countless other private knickknacks that reminded them painfully of George, from whom they had not heard for almost three months: "whether living or dead, we know not." That evening Whitman settled down to read the diary, and found it contained the barest records of George's movements, along with a list of the campaigns in which he had participated:

> I can realize clearly that by calling upon even a tithe of the myriads of living & actual facts, which go along with, & fill up this dry list of times & places, it would outvie all the romances of the world, & most of the famous histories & biographies to boot. It does not need calling in play the imagination to see that in such a record as this, lies folded a perfect poem of the war, comprehending all its phases, its passions, the fierce tug of the secessionists the interminable fibre of the national union, all the special hues and characteristic forms & pictures of the actual battles, . . . & all the profound scenes of individual death, courage, endurance & superbest hardihood & splendid muscular wrestle of a newer larger race of human giants, with all furious passions aroused on one side, & the sternness of the unalterable determination on the other. (*Notebooks* 2, 745–746)

The paradox is clear. These are the sights that Whitman had not seen but George presumably had. In this respect, Walt had, after all, been able to follow George only so far: far enough to see what the war was really like, but not far enough to get to the heart of the soldier's experiences. But these are also the scenes that Whitman, the artist, can convincingly conjure into being by unfolding the perfect poems of the war, whereas the soldier simply records a "dry list of times and places." In fact, it was in part the very artistic sensibility that enabled Whitman to mediate aspects of the war to the civilian world that also set Whitman apart from the mental world of George and other soldiers—a world of frequently prosaic, practical effort. To set passages from George's letters alongside broadly corresponding experiences in Walt's poetry is to discover differences between the two that vary from the comic to the tragic. So, for instance, George's yearnings for home take the form of touchingly simple memories: "I often think that I can imagine just what you are all doing at home and ile bet now, that Mother is makeing pies I think Mat is putting up shirt bosoms like the deuce so as to get through before dinner I guess Sis is down stairs helping Mother mix the dough, Walt [then still at home] is up stairs writing, Jeff is down town at the Office, Jess is pealing potatoes for dinner, and Tobias has gone down cellar for a scuttle of coal, Bunkum I guess is around somewhere looking for a good chance to go sogering" (*Civil War Letters*, 71). Contrast that picture with Whitman's haunted and haunting account, in "By the Bivouac's Fitful Flame," of the way the ghosts of home throng the minds of soldiers in the field: "While wind in procession thoughts, O tender and wondrous thoughts, / Of life and death, of home and the past and loved, and of those that are far away; / A solemn and slow procession there as I sit on the ground, / By the bivouac's fitful flame" (436).

To put it crudely, George's work was to produce results, Walt's was to produce meanings. They were very different indeed in their temperaments and in their gifts. And the same difference manifested itself, to varying degrees, in Whitman's dealings with most of the soldiers he so lovingly tended in the hospitals. "Adieu O soldier," Whitman wrote in a poem that captures this difference poignantly, "You of the rude campaigning, (which we shared)." The painful truth was that he never could fully share in the "rudeness" of such campaigning, as the second verse paragraph tacitly admits: "Adieu dear comrade, / Your mission is fulfill'd—but I, more warlike, / Myself and this contentious soul of mine, / Still on our own campaigning bound" (456–457). Walt's campaigns were, of course, examples of what Blake called mental warfare—episodes in the politics of the spirit and attempts to change human society by transforming human consciousness. Although over a three-year period the soldiers he tended in the hospitals had been regularly recruited by Whitman for his campaigns, they themselves had no awareness of this and very little understanding of what he was about.

Implicit in Whitman's portrayals of men at war and in the military hospitals was the view that they constituted an alternative and superior society, the redeemed society of his visionary America. By contrast, the civilian society of actual wartime America was for him "the world of gain and appearance and mirth" (443) he stigmatized in "The Wound Dresser." His deep mistrust of the power of money in the booming capitalist society of the North led him to emphasize that a different "currency" circulated in the hospitals—a currency of love and affection symbolized, as he explained in *Specimen Days*, both by the little gifts he brought the men and the caresses he exchanged with them: "Another thing became clear to me—while *cash is* not amiss to bring up the rear, tact and magnetic sympathy and unction are, and ever will be, sovereign still" (750). *Drum-Taps* is, therefore, a book that sought to replace the cash nexus that was coming to dominate existing northern society with a network of intimate, comradely relationships.

Whitman's dream was that, once returned to civilian life, the soldiers would proceed to infuse it with a new, comradely spirit. However, what actually happened was well exemplified by what became of George in the months following demobilization. He sank part of his army savings into speculative building, only to find that the construction industry was already controlled by the New York bosses. This disappointment evidently left its mark on him, for his mother complained that her son's "wartime generosity had shrunken to insensitive frugality" (*Civil War Letters*, 28). Perhaps intuiting at heart that this would, after all, be the dispiriting course of postwar society, Whitman chose not to return to Brooklyn with his brother but to remain in Washington, where he continued to visit those increasingly forgotten soldiers who had been left behind in the hospitals. So Walt and George went the separate ways dictated by their different temperaments, with the latter never realizing the contribution he had inadvertently made to his brother's baffling poetry. But that he had indeed contributed is finally confirmed by the line about the Civil War that Whitman added to "Song of Myself": "Battles, the horrors of fratricidal war, the fever of doubtful news, the fitful events."[13] It was "the fever of doubtful news" about George that had so inflamed Walt's imagination in December 1862; and the outcome was a moving poetry of palimpsest in which brotherly love was overwritten by, yet never obliterated by, "the horrors of fratricidal war."

Six. Weathering the Storm

"Some are weather-wise, some are otherwise," observed Benjamin Franklin playfully in *Poor Richard's Almanac.* A keen keeper of daily weather records himself, Franklin helped inaugurate the great American tradition of weather diarists, among whom were Washington, Jefferson, and Walt Whitman. The letters, notes, essays, and articles produced by Whitman during the Civil War are studded with observations of, and on, the weather. And the poetry and prose he eventually produced to memorialize that war—*Memoranda*, *Specimen Days*, and *Drum-Taps* —are full of weather talk; that is, talk about the weather by way of seeking to articulate the unique meaning of an armed struggle that was for Whitman a world-historical event. It is therefore worth attending more closely to this particular discourse, this "weatherspeak," in an attempt to understand Whitman's own brooding interest in what he called "an unprecedented expression of the subtile world of air above us and around us" during the war years (759).

"An unprecedented expression of the subtile world of air": the phrase is a strange one, suggesting as it does that for Whitman the weather was the means by which the air expressed its feelings—just as the poems of *Drum-Taps* were Whitman's own "unprecedented expression" of the unprecedented world of modern, "democratic," war. The expressive phrase is, in other words, a warning that Whitman's "weather" is not simply the same as our own. It differs in at least two fundamental respects. First, what we blithely call the weather is in fact a complex socioscientific construct, and both the science of weather and the sociology of weather have changed radically since the mid-nineteenth century.

Second, out of this distinctively nineteenth-century discourse of the weather, this period-specific sociolect, Whitman develops his own personalized idiom, his own agonized wartime idiolect. And he typically does so by positioning his writing at the very point where there was a crossover from the real science of his time to older, prescientific modes of thinking. Hence his consuming, and by now well-documented, interest in semiscience and pseudoscience—phrenology, hydropathy, homeopathy. The phrase quoted above itself carries the tell-tale signs of that crossover. "Many an unprecedented expression of the subtile world of air": "expression" is a term that in this context can suggest that weather is a *manifestation* of such complex atmospheric processes as meteorology finds interesting, *and* that weather is expressive of the hidden life that air possesses in a much older, prescientific and pantheistic sense.

But before exploring such subtle issues, there are simple facts to be recorded that will further help us get our bearings. War conditions naturally promoted an intense interest in the weather. Attention was concentrated on the skies, whose changing modes and moods were anxiously scanned for both practical and psychological reasons. The dire circumstances were propitious for a rich interaction, in this weather zone, between fact and fancy, just as Paul Fussell notes in the First World War, when the ubiquitous mention of sunrise and sunset in war poetry was in part the result of the peculiar conditions of trench warfare. Huddled as they were at the bottom of a deep slit in the ground, the soldiers had nothing on which to fix their gaze except the sky directly overhead, whose signs they became adept at reading. Their consequently increased sensitivity to changes in light was then further heightened at every dawn and dusk, because these were the danger periods, when the enemy was most likely to launch an attack. Matter-of-fact, and matter for metaphor—the experience of weather in wartime was intensely both.[1]

"Cold, dark, heavy rain the past two days & nights—very bad for Hooker," reads Whitman's notebook entry for Wednesday, May 6, 1863.[2] In fact, and unknown to him—a time-lag factor that should be seriously noted—Hooker was that very day retreating from the Battle of Chancellorsville, leaving 17,000 men dead on the field, and prompting Lincoln's anguished cry: "My God! My God! What will the country say?"[3] Whitman's brother George was one of Hooker's men, having escaped, although not quite unhurt, from the carnage of the first battle of Fredericksburg five months earlier. As noted in chapter 5, it was the news of George's injury in that battle that brought Whitman hurrying from New York in search of him, desperate for accurate information. He finally located George in the Union camp before Fredericksburg, but only after first coming abruptly face-to-face with a mountainous pile of amputated limbs. Shaken and moved, Whitman adjourned to Washington, where he spent most of the remainder of the war selflessly, if not self-destructively, ministering to the wounded as a hospital visitor.

Shortly after Whitman left Fredericksburg, George, along with the Union troops under Burnside, became literally bogged down in the notorious "mud march." Attempting to outflank the Confederates on the left, the Union army was devastated by icy rain: "The wagons began to turn over," wrote Elisha Rhodes, "and mules actually drowned in the mud and water."[4] No wonder Whitman was so worried later about the "cold, dark, heavy rain" of May. With respect to the weather, as in so many other respects, Whitman had been especially sensitized to its wartime implications by the experiences of his serving brother, George (see chapter 5), whose own letters constitute a kind of wartime weather diary, full as they understandably are of comments—stoical and despairing by turns—on perversely unfavorable weather conditions.[5]

Burnside could not have forecast that heavy rain would ruin his march, because nobody could. Forecasting the weather, it is worth remembering, is a relatively recent—and still relatively imprecise—science. Although the Civil War produced the rifle, the great ironclads, the military telegraph, land mines, telescopic sights, and trench warfare, it failed to produce a single weather forecast, which would have been the most murderously successful invention of all, as Lincoln well realized. "It seems to me," he wrote tartly in his diary one wartime April day, "that Mr Capen knows nothing about the weather in advance. He told me three days ago that it would not rain again till the 30th of April or the 1st of May. It is raining now and has been for ten hours. I can not spare any more time to Mr Capen."[6]

Nevertheless, the kind of study of the weather that would in due course produce the weather forecast had been under way since the beginning of the nineteenth century and had made rapid progress, to public acclaim, during the antebellum years, as has been noted in the standard recent study of the subject:

> Meteorology in the nineteenth century experienced a rapid and dramatic expansion of its scientific horizons. On many levels—theoretical, empirical, institutional, technological—it encouraged inquiry, demanded discipline, and attracted controversy. Meteorologists were driven by fundamental questions about climatic change, the nature of storms, and the geography of health and disease.[7]

Particularly important was the fledgling development, in the immediate prewar years, of synoptic meteorology, that is a building up of a composite picture of weather systems by collating information collected from many, geographically scattered, sources. To this end, a substantial network of meteorological stations was established during the 1850s, partly in response to military demand. The wreck of a British and French fleet in that decade by an unexpected storm helped concentrate naval minds wonderfully. And weather also became a popular issue of the day, as evidenced by articles in the *Atlantic Monthly*, where it was noted that weather conditions "have had their part in deciding the destinies of dynasties, the fortunes of race, and the fate of nations. Leave the weather out of history, and it is as if night were left out of the day, and winter out of the year." The author of this essay on "the Weather in War" had been moved to embark on his survey by his compatriots' outrage at the "mud march":

> Americans have fretted a little because their "Grand Army" could not advance through mud that came up to the horses' shoulders, and in which even the seven-league boots would have stuck, though they had been worn as deftly as Ariel could have worn them. They talked as if no such thing had ever before been known to stay the march of armies; whereas all military operations have, to a greater or a lesser extent, depended for their issue upon the softening or the hardening of the earth, or upon the clearing or the clouding of the sky.[8]

In response to the new nineteenth-century interest in the weather, pop meteorologists began to appear, controversial figures like James Pollard Espy, to whom we will return and whose life and work has recently been treated as a case history of "the relation between science, ideology, government funding, and the popular imagination."[9] Espy's career is a reminder that at this time meteorology naturally kept company, at least at the popular level, with those other semisciences and pseudosciences already mentioned—phrenology and the like. But whereas their importance for Whitman as sources of trope and paradigms of experience have been brilliantly demonstrated by scholars from Aspiz to Reynolds, the significance of meteorology—along with the cognate subject of climatology—remains to be examined.

The weather at this time was a borderline phenomenon, as was implicitly admitted by Espy when he argued that "[a]mong the innumerable benefits arising from the adoption of a true system of meteorology, will be the *death of superstition*."[10] Meanwhile, the weather inhabited a limbo region between the inexplicable and unpredictable on the one hand, and the explicable and predictable on the other. "For," wrote the author of an *Atlantic Monthly* essay entitled "Meteorology. A Glance at the Science," "notwithstanding the rapid progress it has made within the last thirty years, it is far from having the authority of an exact science; many of its phenomena are as yet inexplicable, and many differences of opinion among the learned remain unreconciled on points at first sight apparently easy to be settled."[11] As such, it suggestively corresponded to Whitman's own relation to wartime events. Both psychologically and ideologically, he was in constant danger of being overwhelmed and undermined by the arbitrariness of events. His emotional survival depended on maintaining a teleology of conflict, on being credibly able to make the bewildering story of the war, as it actually unfolded, conform to Whitman's majestic vision of history, wherein the triumphant ineluctable progress of American democratic society was assured. How, then, account for military defeats and disasters that threatened to be terminal in their effect? The question became almost a desperate one for Whitman once he had reached the Washington hospitals, where only the belief that this previously unimaginable suffering was intensely historically purposeful could save him from psychic and physical collapse. But the question had presented itself to him from the very beginning of the war, and had from the outset elicited a response partly in terms of the weather.

The first battle of Bull Run stunned the North, and in recalling that humiliating first defeat Whitman painted it in terms of heat and rain. The defeated troops poured back into Washington on a "day drizzling all through with rain," whereas the Saturday and Sunday of the battle "had been parched and hot to an extreme—the dust, the grime and smoke, in layers, sweated in, follow'd by other layers again sweated in, absorb'd by those excited souls" (708). In fact, the weather is not incidental to this scene; it is essential to Whitman's purpose in recording it. He insists on the conditions—"the men with this coating of murk and sweat and rain, now recoiling back, pouring over the Long Bridge," these "defeated soldiers—queer looking objects, strange eyes and faces, drench'd (the steady drain drizzles on all day) and fearfully worn, hungry, haggard, blister'd in the feet" (709). This is, of course, an ideologically driven verbal composition—these are poor creatures who have been abandoned to the peltings of a pitiless storm, abandoned by their self-proclaimed "betters," those Union officers now retreated to the renowned comfort of Willard's Hotel in Washington. This is a bitter betrayal of northern democratic manhood, on the grand, "cosmic" scale; and the weather is eloquently "expressive" of it and of Whitman's fury at it. "Never tell me of chances of battle," Whitman snarls at the bleating officers: "I think this is your work, this retreat, after all" (710). The weather betrays their dirty work. Whitman's use of it is strikingly strategic—the very vagaries of the weather (so invitingly similar to the sheer chance of battle, which the officers plead as an excuse) are here triumphantly captured for Whitman's own ideological, teleological purpose. The defeat at Bull Run is revealed, in retrospect, to have been neither inexplicable nor unpredictable. In fact, it is presented as a paradoxical vindication of Whitman's belief in the inevitable military and political triumph of democracy, a corollary of which is the belief that anything less than a fully democratic military system is bound to result in some such disaster as Bull Run.

But in composing an account of Bull Run out of the materials of the weather, Whitman was doing more than simply recording the occasion: he was memorializing it. Weather served as a mnemonic device, ensuring that American society would not only recall the occasion but also bear vividly in mind its politico-spiritual meaning, its true, inner, ideological significance. Commemorating the war—that is, making it actively present to the noncombatants in Whitman's business-mad northern society—was an absolute obsession with him.[12] He had misgivings too deep for words about that society. And if his darkest fears—that northern society was fundamentally indifferent to the bloody sacrifice being made on its behalf—had ever been realized, Whitman's very sanity might well have collapsed. His wartime writings were an attempt to treat what was in stark reality a gulf in ideology (between the Yankee business ethic and Whitman's ethic of redemptive sacrifice) as if it were rather a mere breakdown in communications. Whitman knew from experience what it was to live in New York, having to rely on the newspapers for tardy and unreliable information about the geographically and psychologically distant war. As is made clear in discussions of the time, part of the appeal of the new art of photography was that it could seemingly annul distance by bringing graphically before the very eyes of anxious friends and relatives the remote "foreign" landscape in which their soldier boys were fighting.

Brady's photographic record of the 1864 Virginia Campaign was praised by *Harper's Weekly* in these very terms:

> The actuality of these views, the distant detail, and the inflexible veracity, make them invaluable to every student of the campaign; while all who follow the army with their private hearts as well as their public hopes will see with curious satisfaction the roads, the fields, the woods, the fences, the bridges, the camps, and the streams, which are the familiar daily objects to the eyes of their loved soldier boys.[13]

Whitman's writings were likewise attempts to impress his vision of war on "private hearts" rather than merely to address "public hopes." He knew, from Washington experience, what it was to be at the very hub, and not know what was going on all around him—not to know, for instance, that Hooker's army was being destroyed at Chancellorsville just as Whitman was needlessly worrying about wind and rain. As noted in chapter 5, he also knew, from Washington experience, the terrible difficulty of writing letters on behalf of "his" wounded soldiers, missionary missives that could make parents even half comprehend what their sons were enduring. These gulfs of unknowing were what he set out to bridge in his writings, in an attempt to close the ideological gap between northern society and the community of fighters and sufferers that Whitman served.

A key image here is that of Whitman himself receiving the news about the attack on Fort Sumter that triggered the Civil War. He was on his way home from the opera at midnight, when he heard the cries of newsboys. He bought a paper and crossed the street to the brightly lit Metropolitan Hotel. There he and others read the fearful report aloud to a rapidly swelling crowd, that was struck dumb by the news. "I can almost see them now," Whitman recalled in *Specimen Days*, "under the lamps at midnight again" (706). And he significantly adds that "for the benefit of some who had no papers, one of us read the telegram aloud, while all listen'd silently and attentively." It is an emblematic moment, anticipating as it does Whitman's subsequent service as an unofficial, and unorthodox, "war correspondent," whose most powerful bulletins, he came to feel, were in the form not of prose but of poetry. Indeed, all his writings from the front and from the hospitals during the war were a compulsive reenactment of that moment, that scene—an attempt to gather the whole nation "under the lamps at midnight again," to make the indifferent crowd listen and understand and remember and redeem the suffering by working to produce that new democratic society for which the Union troops were fighting, or so Whitman fondly believed. And the weather was for him a fixative of memory, defining and highlighting an occasion, just like those lamps at midnight. Or, to change the metaphor, the weather could be a means of conveying to a civilian audience not the bare facts of an event or occasion but its atmosphere, its climate, its inner ideological meaning. This use of weather is characteristic not only of prose passages such as that describing Bull Run but also of the *Drum-Taps* poems; and it reaches its apotheosis, as will be seen, in "When Lilacs Last in the Dooryard Bloom'd"—a poem that could, after all, be provocatively described as a kind of weather report and weather forecast rolled into one.

In that poem, as from the very beginning of the war, Whitman attempted to reach his public partly by sharing its discourse, and as Eduardo Cadava has pointed out,

> [the] recourse to the language of nature and climate—condensation, heat, crystallization—in order to figure not only the conflict between the North and South but also the passion and power of public opinion was pervasive during the early stages of the war and became a primary means for evoking what for many was the war's turbulent necessity. The *Syracuse Daily Courier and Union* proclaimed that the outbreak of war had "startled the public like the bursts of thunder in a still and cloudless night." The *Springfield Daily Republican* praised the men now surrendering themselves "to the patriotic thrill that leaps from heart to heart like lightning along a chain."[14]

As he goes on to point out, Whitman's own former paper, the *Brooklyn Daily Eagle*, figured the commencement of hostilities in exactly the same way, and so it is not surprising that in Whitman's "Rise O Days," one of the bloodthirsty "recruitment" poems he wrote during the euphoria of those early days, before the first battle of Bull Run sobered him forever, thunder and lightening are used as running figural motifs. "Thunder on! stride on, Democracy! strike with vengeful stroke! / . . . I waited the bursting forth of the pent fire—on the water and air I waited long; / But now I no longer wait, I am full satisfied, I am glutted, / I have witness'd the true lightning, I have witness'd my cities electric" (428–429). No wonder, then, that it was to the weather he again turned for clarifying, and thus comforting, expressive tropes when the war later turned savage, threatening to become an ever more bloody stalemate: "Year that trembled and reel'd beneath me! / Your summer wind was warm enough, yet the air I breathed froze me; / A thick gloom fell through the sunshine and darken'd me; . . ." (442).

But as well as serving as trope, the weather did have a direct physical effect on the war's progress. There was literal reason enough to think engagements were becoming bogged down, the soldiers ever more deeply mired. During Burnside's march after Fredericksburg, northern soldiers became veritable connoisseurs of mud. " 'Virginia mud,' a Union officer explained later, 'is a clay of reddish color and sticky consistency which does not appear to soak water, or mingle with it, but simply to hold it, becoming softer and softer' " (Ward and Burns, 184). The mud here becomes a synecdoche for the hostile and elemental foreignness of the South, that social, cultural, and political foreignness that had long found symbolic expression in climatic terms. Whitman himself registered his move from New York to Washington partly as a change of climate—the enervating heat of the Washington summer became an understandable subject for complaint. In old age, he could even explain the war in terms of "[t]he hot passions of the South—the strange mixture at the North of inertia, incredulity, and conscious power" (1037). These terms belong, of course, to primitive climatology—a protoscience that claimed to be able to classify cultures according to climate. This practice, as old as Aristotle, was vigorously developed in eighteenth-century thinking.[15] And in mid-nineteenth-century America, the supposed correlation between social character and climate was investigated in a skeptical and sophisticated way by an Emerson who was interested in "the influences of climate and soil in political history" precisely because during the antebellum years this topic gave rise to crude racial and political propaganda, allowing North to caricaturize South, and South, North.

But Whitman, in fact, invoked such socioclimatic stereotypes only in order to undermine their popular political signification. And he did so because during the war, as both before and after it, he held to a vision of a single reintegrated America in which northern characteristics were complemented and redeemed by southern characteristics, and vice versa, in a dialectical process that would in due course produce a single, augmented, diversified, and matured democratic society. Indeed, during the war he could even single out one aspect of the climate of Washington itself—that capital city set in border country—as prefiguring the blending of North and South.

Whitman's lengthy letter from Washington, published by the *New York Times* in October 1863, is an extraordinarily complex ideological structure, a deliberate exercise in propaganda, designed to counter the prevailing hostile popular view of Washington as the center of political bureaucracy and corruption. Whitman's praise of the city's architecture, and in particular the unfinished dome of the Capitol, is couched in terms that represent Washington as the truly "national city," a synthesis of North and West—and South. A month after Gettysburg he felt that the city "is conscious of a character and identity different from what it was five or six short weeks ago" (734). And at the end of "a year's residence" in Virginia, he announced that "the soil is yet far above the average of any of the northern States." The land was "prodigal in forest woods. . . . [t]he skies and atmosphere most luscious. . . . It is not the panting tropical heat, but invigorates. The north tempers it" (742).

This praise of a southerly climate is consistent with Whitman's prewar celebration of thoroughly southern climes in "Longings for Home," the 1860 poem later entitled "O Magnet-South." A poem in which Whitman impersonates a native of the South, it provides a striking example of that rhetoric of conciliation that, as has been argued elsewhere in this study, Whitman developed in 1860 in an attempt to reduce the intranational animosity that was then conspicuously threatening to rend the union asunder. When that rending moment came, with the firing on Fort Sumter, Whitman was himself fierce for war. But by the time he had settled in Washington, his earlier conciliatory impulses were reasserting themselves in drastically modified form; this time expressed as a sympathy for the southern people, in tandem with an implacable hostility to the Confederate cause and an almost fanatical commitment to the democratic Unionist struggle. And the more one studies the wartime Whitman, the more one feels that this southerly aspect of Whitman's wartime outlook has hitherto received insufficient attention from scholars.

The war was far less the fault of the southern people—particularly the poor whites—than of their leaders: thus Whitman rationalized it. Indeed, he held to his prewar belief that a true American democracy was already latent and potential in the southern character, as it so evidently was in the supposedly more highly developed northern character. Again, the border state of Virginia allowed Whitman, in *Specimen Days*, to give symbolical expression to this vision. Visiting Culpepper in 1864, he first hymns the heroism of the Union troops:

> I never before so realized the majesty and reality of the American people *en masse* [the phrase seems to be sadly predicated on the assumption that to be truly American is to be white]. It fell upon me like a great awe. The strong ranks moved neither fast nor slow. They had march'd seven or eight miles already through the slipping unctuous mud. (740)

But a couple of entries later, and the politico-meteorological focus has shifted. There has been a change in the weather. The emphasis is now on the fact that:

> the soil is yet far above the average of any of the northern States. And how full of breadth the scenery, everywhere distant mountains, everywhere convenient rivers. Even yet prodigal in forest woods, and surely eligible for all the fruits, orchards, and flowers. The skies and atmosphere most luscious, as I feel certain, from more than a year's residence in the State, and movements hither and yon. I should say very healthy, as a general thing. Then a rich and elastic quality, by night and by day. The sun rejoices in his strength, dazzling and burning, and yet, to me, never unpleasantly weakening. It is not the panting tropical heat, but invigorates. The north tempers it." (742)

And then the passage rises to its climax, as—over the dilapidated, fenceless, war-ravaged Virginian landscape—the moon rises: "the first of the new moon, the outlined old moon clear along with it; the sky and air so clear, such transparent hues of color, it seem'd to me I had never really seen the new moon before. It was the thinnest cut crescent possible. It hung delicate just above the sulky shadow of the Blue mountains. Ah, if it might prove an omen and good prophecy for this unhappy State" (742). It is a passage hauntingly consonant with passages in "When Lilacs Last in the Dooryard Bloom'd." And such echoes are not, perhaps, purely coincidental. This wartime rhetoric of sympathy with the South may help us hear in "When Lilacs" the related, and developed, tones of reconciliation with which Whitman greeted the ending of the war. "When Lilacs" may, therefore, perhaps be read as a poem for and from the South, as much as the North and West.

"No more for him life's stormy conflicts, / Nor victory, nor defeat—no more time's dark events, / Charging like ceaseless clouds across the sky" (468); so wrote Whitman in another of his Lincoln elegies, "Hush'd Be the Camps To-day." The storm may be clichéd as an image for the Civil War, but we ignore Whitman's use of it at our peril. As has been noted, the image is given the full treatment in "Rise O Days from your Fathomless Deeps." The first stanza depicts the prewar Whitman as exulting in an ocean storm, excited by the irresistible power of self-assertion that is absent from the business-enfeebled North, reluctant to assert itself decisively against an increasingly mutinous South, which is threatening to defect from the democratic Union. But by the second stanza the North's unanimous, tumultuous, commitment to war has more than satisfied a Whitman who now revels in a political sight that excels even that of an aroused and enraged natural world: "How the true thunder bellows after the lightning—how bright the flashes of lightning! / How Democracy with desperate vengeful port strides on, shown through the dark by those flashes of lightning!" (428).

Whitman's rodomontade is less than convincing, its bluster betraying an underlying nagging disquiet, his old chronic mistrust of northern society. But the poem anticipates his war-long attempt to understand, and to speak, the language of storms. And the deep structure of Whitman's interest is laid bare in a crucial passage he wrote in 1865 and later included in *Specimen Days*. It is entitled "The Weather—Does It Sympathize with These Times?":

> Whether the rains, the heat and cold, and what underlies them all, are affected with what affects man in masses, and follow his play of passionate action, strain'd stronger than usual, and on a larger scale than usual—whether this, or no, it is certain that there is now, and has been for twenty months or more, on this American continent north, many a remarkable, many an unprecedented expression of the subtile world of air above us and around us. There, since this war, and the wide and deep national agitation, strange analogies, different combinations, a different sunlight, or absence of it; different products even out of the ground. After every great battle, a great storm. Even civic events the same. (759)

It is a suggestive passage, and brings us back to the semiscience of meteorology in Whitman's day, a "science" uneasily (but fruitfully, for a poet) suspended between a new materialist and an old spiritual-animist view of the world. Of course, the word "sympathy," in the title question—"The Weather—Does It Sympathize with These Times?"—is a bridging term, equivocally situated between these two kinds of discourse. A term beloved by pseudoscientific phrenologists as well as by the devotees of the new semiscientific cult of electromagnetics, it always appealed immensely to Whitman.

James Pollard Espy, the controversial popular meteorologist previously mentioned, exulted in the title "The Storm-King," as he had been dubbed by the popular press following the success of his polemical 1841 volume, *The Philosophy of Storms.* That book was part of Espy's contribution to the great "American Storm Controversy":

> In the 1830s an international controversy developed among meteorologists over the nature and causes of storms. The American component of the controversy centered on competing theoretical positions advanced by three prominent scientists: William C. Redfield, James Pollard Espy, and Robert Hare. The dispute between Espy and Redfield held center stage between 1834 and 1841, then Hare entered the controversy with a vengeance and attacked both Espy and Redfield. American theorists argued over the *primum mobile* of storms: was it gravity, caloric, or electricity? They argued over methodology: were they searching for the *quo modo* or the *causa verum*? And they argued over basic definitions of the phenomena under investigation: were they looking at hurricanes, thunderstorms, tornadoes, winter storms, or some other "meteor"? (Fleming, 23)

The Philosophy of Storms exemplified the ambiguous status of meteorology as a science at that time. On the one hand, Espy made an original contribution to the understanding of the convective principle at work in the creation and movement of storms. On the other hand, he was wildly misled into advancing a theory of artificial rainmaking, based on the belief that the smoke produced by the factories of Manchester, England, generated rain clouds. He therefore proposed that in order to alleviate the Pennsylvanian drought, vast areas of forest should be burned to precipitate rainfall. Twenty years later, like theories still existed. In the 1860s, promoters claimed that the arid climate of the plains had been changed for good. "The increase of railroads," said one Colorado newspaper, "and also the increase of activity on the roads has the . . . effect of producing more showers. . . . The concussion of the air and rapid movements produced by railroad trains and engines affects the electrical conditions of the atmosphere."[16]

These theories provide a graphic illustration of the interest of the period in ways in which developments on the ground might influence events in the air. As Harold Aspiz has brilliantly demonstrated, ideas about electricity followed a like trajectory. "[E]lectricity was a mysterious power grounded in the earthly, material world and yet a part of the celestial ambience; . . . it seemed to be the link between the physical, mental, and spiritual worlds; . . . it seemed to constitute the very psychic essence."[17] Imagine, therefore, Franklin's famous kite experiment reversed. Instead of using a kite to demonstrate how electricity could be safely conducted down to earth, imagine instead using some device to demonstrate how the electricity abroad in the earth and all its creatures could be communicated to the very heavens. That is the kind of model Whitman has in mind in the passage about the weather sympathizing with the times. Aspiz has already memorably shown how semiscientific theories of electromagnetism could give rise, in "Song of Myself," to metaphors of human and celestial coupling. In that poem, "the electrical and spermatic 'threads' connecting the stars seem to be a projection of the persona's sexual and visionary powers. Just as the 'father-stuff' represents the electrical sources of human life, so the stars represent the electrical sources of universal life" (140). It remains, however, to apply Aspiz's insight to Whitman's talk of the heavens and its weather in *Drum-Taps*; to his use of the moon, and stars, and storms, in order now to suggest the electric and electrifying power not of an individual self but of a whole nation. "Convulsiveness" was the quality Whitman associated with the war years, a term suggestive of how his society had been electro-spiritually galvanized into action.

And key to Whitman's wartime reading of the semiotics of storms, of his fascination with "strange analogies" between politics and the weather, was his belief in a conflict whose wholly unprecedented character naturally produced wholly unprecedented results. The Civil War, like no other war in history, demonstrated "what affects man in masses"—by which Whitman meant not just the size of the armies involved but what that size signified; that here, in the northern states, was a whole society mobilized for the first time in history, because when a democratic society went to war it did so by turning itself into one huge citizen army. The *levée-en-masse* that had saved the French Revolution was as nothing in the eyes of a Whitman rendered willingly ignorant by prejudice. In the North, for the very first time in history in his impassioned opinion, a whole society had been electrifyingly aroused to fight. So what wonder this had resulted in spectacular storms? After all, in a section of *The Philosophy of Storms* entitled "Artificial Rain," James Espy had specifically concluded (on the basis of evidence taken from Scott's *Napoleon*) that military activity at the Battle of Valenciennes

(1793) had been intense enough to cause precipitation: "The allies employed two hundred heavy ordnance, and the besieged had above one hundred, and they were frequently all in action at one time. The rain, in the opinion of the combatants, was caused by the shaking of the clouds" (516).

If great battles produced such great storms, then so did "civic events the same," claimed Whitman. This he struggled with himself to demonstrate in two powerful but contrasting passages of wartime prose. The first, recorded in his *Notebooks,* concerns the last meeting of the 37th Congress, in March 1863. He there scornfully observed "the little mannikins, shrewd, gabby, drest in black, hopping about, making motions, amendments"; while all about the building broke a massive storm:

> Whither are we drifting? Who knows? It seems as if these electric and terrible days were enough to put life in a paving stone,—as if there must needs form, on the representative men that have to do with them, faces of grandeur, actions of awe, vestments of majesty—the day goes on, a strange, wild, smiling, promising, lowering, spitting, day—full of threats and contradictions—black at times as murkyest eve—then snowing in great flakes, obscuring the air, with fits of furious driving, and of whirls and eddies around and around as you look up—then a sharp short shower of rain. (*Notebooks* 2, 567–568)

The whole piece obviously turns on the ludicrous discrepancy between the pathetic antics of those toy figures, the agitated congressmen, and the great public events they have been charged with the responsibility of controlling: "These then are the men who do as they do, in the midst of the greatest historic chaos and gigantic tussle of the greatest of ages" (*Notebooks* 2, 567). All of Whitman's seasoned prejudices against centralized government can be felt informing the passage. His description of the pygmy congressmen as "representative men" is tragically ironic, echoing that earlier use of the phrase explored in chapter 1. Whereas the fighting, suffering soldiers were truly for Whitman representative men, these politicians are so only in the diminished sense of being officially elected political representatives. And whereas Whitman found in the hospitals a grand theater of suffering profoundly expressive of what the war was really about, here in Congress he found only the theater of political farce. Implicit in this whole scene is that recurrent anguish of his that the civilian world—here "represented" by its politicians—would never truly realize, let alone practically register, the inner justifying significance of this war's carnage. The description is fraught with the suggestion that this is one occasion when the storm, expressive of nature's sympathy with the suffering soldiers, vents only its contemptuous anger on the wretched politicians in their final congressional session.

Two years later, in March 1865, Whitman again made a meeting of Congress the subject of special comment, and once more freak weather conditions featured prominently in his verbal sketch, which was this time destined for publication in *Specimen Days.* There is even the same central pattern to the episode, as Whitman sets the nervous, exhausted, and sleepy representatives against the dramatic eruption of powerful forces in the natural world outside the eerily gaslit chamber. As the sudden storm batters the Capitol, startling the dopey speakers and dozing listeners into a momentary terror for their lives, Whitman strikingly makes of their sudden transition from torpor into jitteriness an image of the whole uncertain mood of this particular late phase of the conflict. But then the congressmen recover and compose themselves, prompting Whitman to a note of confidence in their courage and resolve, as he represents them as potentially equivalent in quality to the soldiers themselves: "One is not without impression, after all, amid these members of Congress, of both the Houses, that if the flat routine of their duties should ever be broken in upon by some great emergency involving real danger, and calling for first-class personal qualities, those qualities would be found generally forthcoming, and from men not now credited with them" (762). It is as if Whitman were desperately seeking to convince himself, as the war drew to its close, that the great yawning gulfs could be bridged: the gulfs between the hospitals and the Capitol, between the front line and the cities frantically in pursuit of wealth, between his own dreams for postwar society and the probably inimical future reality.

Whitman's greatest attempt to bridge these gulfs took shape as the poetry of "When Lilacs Last in the Dooryard Bloom'd," a poem that is the product both of Whitman's long-term pondering of the strange analogies between weather and war and of the meteorological portents that had accompanied Lincoln's 1865 inauguration. Indeed, "the heavens, the elements, all the meteorological influences have run riot for weeks past," wrote Whitman of that period. He recalled the astonishing brilliance at evening of "the western star, Venus," "as if it told something, as if it held rapport indulgent with humanity, with us Americans" (760). Remembering the wonder of that star, closely accompanied by "the moon like a young mother," Whitman also remembered how the "miracle" of the scene had somehow been completed by the "slow . . . clear . . . deliberate notes of a bugle come up out of the silence," floating out from one of the army hospitals nearby, where all the many wounded "from Illinois, Michigan, Wisconsin, Iowa, and the rest" were lying (760).

If space allowed, it would be revealing to track the search for portents undertaken by Whitman, as by virtually all combatants and noncombatants, North and South, during the Civil War. Think, for example, of the aftermath of the first Battle of Fredericksburg, when northern officers buried their dead by what they believed to be the cosmically comforting light of the northern lights, even as the Confederate soldiers, for their part, were simultaneously regarding that Aurora Borealis as celestial fireworks in celebration of their own victory. Which side owned the weather? The battle for the skies was a psychological and ideological reality in the Civil War many decades before airplanes turned it into a reality of a different kind. An amusing example of it is afforded by an incident recorded long after the event by one who had been a boy in New York during the Civil War:

> one day when a brisk west wind was blowing, we went to the top of our house on 12th street, taking with us a 3-foot kite. We flew it, letting out the cord till the kite was out of sight, and then we attached an American flag about 3 feet long to the string and let out another 200 feet of the kite string, thus suspending the flag over Fifth Avenue. There it hung, without any visible means of support. This caused a crowd to gather, and we tied the string to the chimney on the roof and went down to the street. We were in great glee at the remarks made: such as "A sign from heaven!" "We are sure to win the war now!" "Oh—it is only a reflection of a flag elsewhere, an optical delusion"—and many other remarks.[18]

This happened over a decade after Nathaniel Hawthorne had wryly reflected, in *The Scarlet Letter*, on the Puritans' fascination with supernatural omens:

> It was, indeed, a majestic idea that the destiny of nations should be revealed, in these awful hieroglyphics, on the cope of heaven. A scroll so wide might not be deemed too expansive for Providence to write a people's doom upon. The belief was a favorite one with our forefathers, as betokening that their infant commonwealth was under a celestial guardianship of peculiar intimacy and strictness.[19]

Through his omnipresent irony, Hawthorne asks leave to doubt, of course, whether mankind has indeed outgrown the habit of looking to nature for supernatural omens; and subsequent history was to justify his misgivings amply on this score. For instance, the soldiers of the First World War inhabited, according to Paul Fussell, a "myth-ridden world" that had taken shape in the very midst "of a war representing a triumph of modern industrialism, materialism, and mechanism." Out of these circumstances came, most unexpectedly, "a plethora of very un-modern superstitions, talismans, wonders, miracles, relics, legends and rumors" (Fussell, 115).

It was the very antiquity of such superstitions that appealed to a Herman Melville who, in his marvelous Civil War collection *Battle-Pieces*, wanted to emphasize that, far from being unique among the nations of the earth, the United States was simply exhibiting, in its fratricidal conflict, the savagery inherent in human nature. Hence his framing his collection along the lines of Shakespearean tragedy, complete with many of the conventions of the genre, including "A Portent" in the form of the swaying body of the executed John Brown, "The meteor of the war."[20] Hence, too, Melville's distinctive treatment of the trope of weather. In "Misgivings" the war becomes a storm "bursting from the waste of Time," in which nature shows its "dark side" and arouses the atavistic energies of precariously civilized human nature: "The hemlock shakes in the rafter, the oak in the driving keel" (37). By contrast, Whitman clung throughout the war to his salvific belief in American exceptionalism, and thus even while borrowing traditional tropes, such as those of portents, he attempted to imply that they were of an entirely different order, or character, from anything precedence might have to offer. So, after invoking 1859–1860 as "Year of Meteors," he was careful to embed mention of that ancient omen of disaster in a passage that stressed human progress:

Nor forget I to sing of the wonder, the ship as she swam up my bay,
Well-shaped and stately the Great Eastern swam up my bay, she was 600 feet long,
Her moving swiftly surrounded by myriads of small craft I forget not to sing;
Nor the comet that came unannounced out of the north flaring in heaven,
Nor the strange huge meteor-procession dazzling and clear shooting over our
  heads,
(A moment, a moment long it sail'd its balls of unearthly light over our heads,
Then departed, dropt in the night, and was gone . . .) (381)

By the time of Lincoln's assassination in 1865, the North was already victorious, and so Whitman was in one sense left, when writing "When Lilacs," in undisputed possession of the heavens and all their meteorological portents. By then, history itself seemed to have endorsed his rhetoric of weather, at long last underpinning metaphor with fact, even if, in the case of the assassination of Lincoln, it had done so to devastatingly unexpected and tragic effect. But shocked and saddened though he was by that catastrophe, Whitman was far from dismayed. Indeed, in a sense he could even be said to have welcomed the assassination, as his late lecture in commemoration of Lincoln makes arrestingly clear. What he appreciated was that Lincoln had been killed at a memorable time, under memorable circumstances, and in a memorable way; and that in being thus killed, Lincoln had become the means of rendering memorably visible both the vast suffering the war had entailed, and the meaning and purpose of that suffering. Here, wrote the aged and crippled Whitman, "the whole involved, baffling, multiform whirl of the secession period comes to a head, and is gather'd in one brief flash of lightning-illumination—one simple, fierce deed" (1045).

Indeed, Whitman's whole treatment of the episode of Lincoln's death in his lectures of 1879–1881 would bear extensive examination, not least because of the disclosure that "the immeasurable value and meaning of that whole tragedy lies, to me, in senses finally dearest to a nation, (and here all our own)—the imaginative and artistic senses—the literary and dramatic ones. Not in any common or low meaning of those terms, but a meaning precious to the race, and to every age. A long and varied series of contradictory events arrives at last at its highest poetic, single, central, pictorial denouement" (1045). Deliberately using the theatrical language of cathartic resolution, Whitman implicitly contrasts the authentic national theater of Lincoln's assassination with the actual tawdry theater, and farcical theatricality, of the setting in which it had occurred: "the audience and the crowd, the stage, and all its actors and actresses, its paint-pots, spangles and gas-lights" (1044). In his narrative, Whitman goes so far as to turn the occasion into a scene from the theater of the absurd, as, in the panic following the assassination, the soldiers "inflamed with fury, literally [charge] the audience with fix'd bayonets, muskets, and pistol, shouting *Clear out, clear out! you sons of*—" (1044). This, then, is the antimasque, so to speak, of "When Lilacs": the false art of the actual event, contrasted with the true art of "pictorial denouement" his recollection has to offer. And, as he emphasizes, that denouement derives its power from its (unique artistic) capacity to resolve "contradictory events." To register this is to realize anew why "When Lilacs" has the antiphonal structure that it does: the poem is Whitman's denouement, his climactic resolution of deeply conflicted feelings within him to Lincoln's death. And some of those emotions are hauntingly suggested by the very terseness of the strikingly brief entry on Lincoln's assassination in *Specimen Days* itself. Dignified in its spare, evidently sincere, eloquence, the tribute to Lincoln includes the comment that "By many has this Union been help'd; but if one name, one man, must be pick'd out, he, most of all, is the conservator of it, to the future." And the theme is picked up in the concluding sentence: "Death does its work, obliterates a hundred, a thousand—President, general, captain, private—but the Nation is immortal" (764). A deep, angry sadness at Lincoln's murder here clashes, as much as it blends, with a fear that the death of this one man might, after all, eclipse the deaths of the (probably hundreds) of ordinary soldiers Whitman had personally witnessed and the hundreds of thousands of corpses that had so lavishly strewn both battle fields and hospital beds. It was therefore vitally important in "When Lilacs" to register "the tragic splendor of [Lincoln's] death, purging, illuminating *all*" (764, my emphasis).

And here this chapter finally doubles back on itself, picking up several threads that were dropped earlier. The weather as a mnemonic device, designed to fix the inner meaning of an event in national memory; the weather employed as a symbolic means of creating a climate of sympathy in the civilian world for the conditions of living and dying at the front as in the hospitals; the weather as somehow mysteriously sympathizing with the Union cause, and signifying, in its own terms, the uniqueness of a democratic society; the weather as symbolically legitimizing and consecrating the northern effort through portents; the weather as a means of turning a sociopolitical struggle into a cosmically significant conflict, and in the process "naturalizing" northern, democratic society; the weather as offering the means of constructing cathartic "pictorial denouements." These features that have been discovered to be important constituents of the discourse of weather in Whitman's wartime writings are all again prominently apparent, though raised to an altogether higher level of significance, in "When Lilacs Last in the Dooryard Bloom'd."

The weather, one might say, rose magnificently to the occasion when Lincoln died, and thereby satisfied one of the needs we have already identified, namely Whitman's need for a sufficiently imposing outward sign of the inner meaning of the war. He was thus provided with adequate symbolical means of representing the significance of an assassination with which other writers could deal only by resorting to the trope of tropelessness; by speaking of a crisis of representation, since violence had been done to the very logic of symbolic discourse. This was the burden of the funeral ode published in *Harper's Weekly* on May 6, 1865. It began by explaining that when natural disaster, such as an earthquake, devastated towns, then:

The world may fitting emblems find
To speak the horrors of its heart
In cities craped, in banners furled
And all the solemn show of art.
But when a Human Hand was turned
Into a ruthless demon-power
And smites a nation in its Chief,
Even at his triumph's crowning hour,

What emblems shall Man fitting find,
What types sad, grand enough to show
The horror shaking continents
And their infinity of woe?[21]

Whitman had, however, been providentially supplied with appropriately expressive "types." Nor was it only the Washington weather that proved equal to the occasion. "When Lilacs" is as much a New York poem as it is a Washington poem, since Whitman was actually in New York when Lincoln was assassinated. He then made a hurried journey to Washington just in time to miss the train carrying Lincoln's body, as it left Baltimore on its long journey to Illinois. It was therefore Whitman's ironic fate to fail to participate in any of the impressive public ceremonies that attended Lincoln's funeral. Instead, he was in the city whose commitment to the Union had been as uncertain as its support for Lincoln had been notoriously unreliable—there had even been regular arguments on the subject between Whitman and his own brother Jeff. To see Manhattan and Brooklyn sunk in mourning was therefore to be able, at least briefly and perhaps quaveringly, to be convinced that a remarkable transformation had indeed occurred in the national temper.

Whitman's eager imagination seized upon every detail of the vast impromptu street theater of sorrow. He noticed "one large & fashionable picture store, all shuttered up close, except a broad square plate glass, in which hung a small grinning picture frame, vacant of a picture" (*Notebooks* 2, 765). Then, for the word "vacant," which simply denoted a space devoid of matter, he substituted the subtler word "vacuous," thus implying that President Lincoln's death had deprived even New York of a presiding image of its own character and destiny. Ever a connoisseur of mass spectacle, Whitman swept a discerning eye over the great panorama of a grieving city, and duly recorded the impressive semiotics of sorrow in his notebook. He was also recording, in the process, the temporary subduing, or tempering, of New York's recklessly entrepreneurial spirit: "All Broadway is black with mourning—the facades of the houses are festooned with black—great flags with wide & heavy fringes of dead black, give a pensive effect—towards noon the sky darkened & it began to rain. Drip, drip, & heavy moist black weather—the stores area all closed—the rain sent the women from the street & black clothed men only remained" (*Notebooks* 2, 763). For four years Whitman had, as we have seen, repeatedly attempted to find in the weather an appropriate symbolic expression of the war. Now, at last, even the ideologically fickle northern weather seemed to be sympathizing with the times. The "words," Whitman suggested in his notebook, "to describe the weather" for Lincoln's funeral, were "sulky, leaden, & dripping continually moist tears . . . black clouds driving overhead" (*Notebooks* 2, 763–764).

Fifteen years later, Whitman would begin his annual memorial lecture by harking back to "that dark and dripping Saturday—that chilly April day, now fifteen years bygone" (1036). And the New York weather replicated the weather conditions in Washington on the very morning of Lincoln's second inauguration, little over a month before his assassination. The papers were full of it:

> March 4, 1865 was a most inauspicious day, so far as the weather was concerned. . . . If you want to be disgusted with the place chosen for the Capital of your country, visit it in the spring time, near the close of a four days' rain, when the frost is beginning to come out of the ground. Whatever other objects of interest may attract your notice, the muddy streets and pavements will scarcely escape you, for if you do not see them you will certainly feel them, as you attempt to wade through them.[22]

But the day was to turn more "auspicious," after all:

> Just as President Lincoln took the seat assigned to him, in front, the sun in the heavens emerged from the clouds behind which he had been hidden for nearly two days, and shone forth in all its splendor and glory. It was a grand sight. The beautiful white Capitol seemed to assume a brighter hue, while the bronze Goddess of Liberty on the ample dome looked down for the first time on the inauguration of a president of the United States.

This was, of course, universally taken as an omen. Lord Chief Justice Chase remembered it, and, sending Mrs. Lincoln the Bible used for the inauguration ceremony, he both carefully marked the page Lincoln had kissed and accompanied the gift with a note:

> I hope the Sacred Book will be to you an acceptable souvenir of a memorable day; and I most earnestly pray Him, by whose Inspiration it was given, that the beautiful sunshine which just at the time the oath was taken dispersed the clouds that had previously darkened the sky may prove an auspicious omen of the dispersion of the clouds of war and the restoration of the clear sunlight of prosperous peace under the wise and just administration of him who took it.[23]

It is just such a popular rhetoric, in the form of a settled public discourse, of weather that not only underlies but actually informs Whitman's use of the weather in commemorating Lincoln: it is, perhaps, significant that in *Memoranda during the War* he actually placed "The Weather—Does It Sympathize with

These Times?" directly next to his discussion of Lincoln's second inauguration.[24] As to the weather descriptions in both the prose passages on Lincoln's assassination and "When Lilacs," these may be regarded as Whitman's moving attempt to superimpose an image of its better self upon the business-driven civic society to which the future was now to be entrusted; a society whose spiritual fitness Whitman much doubted. Correspondence is, surely, the key word for understanding Whitman's Civil War experience. As has been noted in chapter 5, the correspondence he sent from Washington—his own letters, prose writings, and poems, as well as the letters he wrote for his soldiers—was an attempt to make correspondents of his civilian readers; that is to make them respondent to the war's meaningful suffering and thus to make them co-respondent, with the soldiers, to the redemptive anguish involved. But if, in superimposing grief on business, "When Lilacs" becomes a palimpsest of a poem, it is also so in another sense. Twinned with a portrait in *Specimen Days* of Lincoln as the embodiment of the northern people is a portrait of John C. Calhoun, represented as one who had bequeathed the legacy of a shattered South to a people he had not so much led as misled. Purporting to report the words of a young Connecticut veteran in conversation with a Confederate soldier, "Calhoun's Real Monument" speaks of "the desolated, ruined south; nearly the whole generation of young men between seventeen and thirty destroyed or maim'd" (773). It is worth remembering that wasted southern land when reading great, familiar passages like this:

> Now while I sat in the day and look'd forth,
> In the close of the day with its light and the fields of spring, and the farmers preparing their crops,
> In the large unconscious scenery of my land with its lakes and forests, . . .
> And the streets how their throbbings throbb'd, and the cities pent[.] (463)

More or less consciously composed of the populist images of Lincoln's own campaign rhetoric for a free soil, and implicitly representing Lincoln as "the conservator of [the Union] to the future," this passage is also a poignant reverse image of a southern landscape and a southern people supposedly shattered by *un*representative leaders such as Lincoln's polar opposite, Calhoun:

> "All the old families used up," continues the Union veteran in Whitman's account: "the rich impoverished, the plantations covered with weeds, the slaves unloosed and become the masters, and the name of Southerner blackened with every shame—all that is Calhoun's real monument." (773)

The words are, it must be scrupulously noted, attributed to a northern soldier. But they do seem to be endorsed, to some degree, by Whitman's sympathy. Which leads us to the vexed, and complex, question of Whitman's attitudes toward blacks.[25] To read "When Lilacs" in the light of the passage relating to Calhoun is to at least be troubled by the shadow of the possibility cast across the text that Whitman is so anxious to return his strife-torn American to "normality" after the Civil War that he prefers not to factor into his picture such troublesome unknown quantities as "unloosed slaves." Certainly the human landscape of his poem in no way substantially anticipates that of racially inclusive "reconstruction," and he elsewhere displays scant sympathy with those abolitionists he contemptuously dubbed "the extreme Philo-African element of the North," (1206) who were determined on radical reconstruction at whatever cost. Profoundly regrettable though such a temporizing attitude may seem to be to us today, it should not, however, be allowed to centrally affect feelings about "When Lilacs." Rather, it simply highlights the particular, limited, and therefore all the more movingly human, conditions under which the poem was historically produced. For clarification of those conditions, it might be worth recalling Melville's words in the supplement to *Battle-Pieces*:

> Those of us who always abhorred slavery as an atheistical iniquity, gladly we join in the exulting chorus of humanity over its downfall. But we should remember that emancipation was accomplished not by deliberate legislation; only through agonized violence could so mighty a result be effected. In our natural solicitude to confirm the benefit of liberty to the blacks, let us forbear from measures of dubious constitutional rightfulness towards our white countrymen—measures of a nature to provoke, among other of the last evils, exterminating hatred of race toward race. In imagination let us place ourselves in the unprecedented position of the Southerners—their position as regards the millions of ignorant manumitted slaves in their midst, for whom some of us now claim the suffrage. Let us be Christian toward our fellow-whites, as well as philanthropists toward the blacks, our fellow-men. (Melville, 200)

It is not necessary to endorse Melville's every word (he elsewhere mentions "the blacks, in their infant pupilage to freedom" and recommends "paternal guardianship" of them [199]) to feel the power of his decency in this passage, which thus seems to offer a salient gloss on Whitman's feelings at the end of a war in which he himself, after all, had been tortured witness primarily to the suffering of whites.

And to begin to readmit the South, in this way, to the postwar Union, which is being celebrated in "When Lilacs," is to begin to read that poem with different eyes. It does, for instance, seem to have been altogether too long regarded as exclusively a poem of the North-East and of the West, with readers hypnotized, perhaps, by such invocations as those of Whitman to "Sea-winds blown from east and west" (462). Critics have accordingly mostly responded in limited, and limiting, terms. Thus, in his brilliant, authoritative book on *Whitman's America*, David Reynolds has suggested that the hermit thrush singing of death in the swamp derives from Whitman's memories of early life on Long Island.[26] But does it? Is it that simple? Could not those passages about the bird also be redolent of Whitman's experiences in the hospitals in a Washington whose rural hinterland his close friend, John Burroughs, was to emphasize and to celebrate in his first book, *Wake-Robin*?

> One need but pass the boundary of Washington city to be fairly in the country, and ten minutes' walk in the country brings one to real primitive woods. The town has not yet overflowed its limits like the great Northern commercial capitals, and Nature, wild and unkempt, comes up to its very threshold, and even in many places crosses it.[27]

It was Burroughs, of course, who first interested Whitman in the hermit thrush, which he characterized in *Wake-Robin* as follows:

> It is quite a rare bird, of very shy and secluded habits, being found in the Middle and Eastern States, during the period of song, only in the deepest and most remote forests, usually in damp and swampy localities. On this account the people in the Adirondack region call it the "Swamp Angel." Its being so much of a recluse accounts for the comparative ignorance that prevails in regard to it.[28]

In pointing out elsewhere that even the great ornithologists Wilson and Audubon had "little or nothing to say of the song" of the hermit thrush, Burroughs gives the impression that he himself is one of the chosen discriminating few to have become intimately familiar with this particular bird. And this is surely also the impression given by Whitman in "When Lilacs." The song of the "Swamp Angel" is represented as being for his ears alone, that is for the ears of one uniquely attuned by hospital experience to what Burroughs called "the pure, serene, hymn-like strain of the hermit."

Such, indeed, are the strains Whitman eventually reproduces, or rather translates, toward the conclusion of "When Lilacs," but only after repeated, protracted postponements of that moment of naked, vulnerable exposure to the hermit's song. It is as if Whitman had read the words of an anonymous author whose mention of the hermit thrush in an *Atlantic Monthly* article (December 1858) was noted by Burroughs in *Wake-Robin*. "It is certain that any one who stops to listen to this bird," wrote the anonymous essayist, "will become spellbound, and deaf to almost every other sound in the grove, as if his ears were enchained to the song of the Sirens."[29] Whitman protects himself from that song, half stopping his ears against it until he is psychically ready to listen. This rhythm of deferred listening enacted in the poem ("Sing on there in the swamp, / O singer bashful and tender, I hear your notes, I hear your call, / I hear, I come presently, I understand you" [461]) also corresponds to the actual rhythm of the hermit's song as described in the *Atlantic Monthly* essay: "The song of the wood-thrush [*sic*] consists of about 8 or 10 different strains, each of considerable length. After each strain the bird makes a pause of about 3 or 4 seconds." Whitman finally "receives" the song at the psychological juncture when he has worked his way through the emotional turmoil that had threatened to disintegrate his core psychic being. The hermit's chant is therefore heard not as a dangerously depressive dirge but rather as calm, healing affirmations signifying the beginning of a process of psychic reintegration.

Appropriately enough, the *Atlantic Monthly* essay explains that the hermit thrush "delights in a dusky retreat, and is evidently inspired by solitude, singing no less in gloomy weather than in sunshine." And just as its song is suited to all weather, so, through its migrations, does the bird span and connect different climes. Hence John Burroughs's observation on hearing it sing in the Adirondacks in late summer: "Here also I met my beautiful singer, the hermit thrush, but with no song in his throat now. A week or two later and he was on his journey southward" (1: 93). With this in mind, it is worth reconsidering Whitman's "swamp angel," with particular reference to the extensive and complex antebellum tradition, highlighted by David C. Miller in his recent groundbreaking study, that treated the swamp as signifying the whole climate of southern culture.[30]

Miller strikingly explores the political iconography of the swamp, its use, by antebellum northern writers and painters, to signify a whole nexus of negative values. The swamp is the location of fetid sensuality and lush, lascivious, fertility; it is the malarial, miasma-ridden kingdom of stifling death; it is the refuge of the desperate fugitive slave. Hence such verse as "The Swamp Angel," published in a wartime number of *Harper's Weekly*:

And many a mother has the angel blessed
Of the dark swamp, as, with convulsive strain,

She clasps her wandering infant to her breast,
While baffled blood-hounds lick their chops in vain.[31]

"The piney odor and the gloom," wrote Whitman in the prewar "O Magnet-South," "the awful natural stillness, (here in these dense swamps the freebooter carries his gun, and the fugitive has his conceal'd hut)" (584). Taken out of context, this image could be read as antislavery propaganda along the lines of the portrait of the swamp-slave Dred, in Harriet Beecher Stowe's celebrated Abolitionist novel. But in context, the image is deliberately merged into an indiscriminate paean of praise for the southern landscape, a striking example of what has, in chapter 4, been termed Whitman's prewar rhetoric of conciliation.

The Whitman of "When Lilacs" is also, very possibly, using the image of the swamp to construct another rhetoric; a rhetoric of reconciliation—and very significantly so bearing in mind, of course, that Lincoln had been assassinated as an act of southern vengeance. Whitman's line, at war's end, was that soldiers North and South had been united in death and by suffering; and that furthermore the suffering of the South had not really been by the people's volition, but had rather been the fault of its leaders, who had eventually resorted to an antidemocratic policy of enforced conscription. This had been the revelation that had come to Whitman through the deathly hospitals, in swamp-surrounded Washington, where "some of my best friends were probably Southern boys."[32] The hermit thrush's hymn of praise to the kindly death that ends all suffering is therefore a song that reunites North and South. It readmits the South to the Union. It reclaims the swamp from sectional propaganda, and implicitly proclaims that the southern climate is as naturally part of an all-American biodiverse democracy as are the climates of the North and the West. Hence the significance of the fact that the hermit thrush breeds across northern North America in mixed woodlands, but winters in the Gulf states.

"When Lilacs Last in the Dooryard Bloom'd" is a moving demonstration that Whitman and his democratic vision had indeed weathered the storm, in more than one sense. And so, in the very last lines of his concluding *Drum-Taps* poem, "To the Leaven'd Soil They Trod," Whitman not surprisingly turned, but now for the last time, to the weather, in the settled form of climatology rather than the unpredictable wartime form of meteorology:

The prairie draws me close, as the father to bosom broad the son,
The Northern ice and rain that began me nourish me to the end,
But the hot sun of the South is to fully ripen my songs. (458)

Whitman U.K.

Seven. The English Whitman

Long recognized as significant, the relationship between Edward Carpenter (1844–1929) and Walt Whitman has been explored by scholars over the last decade or so through studies of the homosexual, the homosocial, and the homoerotic within the context of an examination of growing nineteenth-century concern with gender roles, constructions of masculinity, and the process of (re)writing the body. The most dramatic episode in this connection has probably been the 1966 publication of a memoir by Gavin Arthur, *The Circle of Sex*, in which the aged Carpenter admitted to having enjoyed with Whitman a sexual caress that resulted in "a far more intense orgasm of the whole nervous system, in which oneself, as a unit, reunites with the Whole."[1] And while the reliability of the aging Carpenter's memory has been repeatedly questioned by scholars, it is at least interesting to note—in the light of the discussion to follow—that the active, stereotypically masculine, role in this encounter is attributed to Whitman and the passive, stereotypically feminine, role to Carpenter.

Influenced by theorists and historians such as Foucault, Dollimore, and Showalter, contemporary Carpenter scholars have done much to place his almost obsessive interest with Whitman in the setting of rapidly and radically changing conceptions of sex and gender at the end of a century when "the various constructions of same-sex desire . . . functioned with ambivalence and antagonism."[2] As William A. Pannapacker has pointed out, Carpenter's own writings offer discursive instances of like ambivalences and in the printed record of his meeting with Whitman are inscribed "the visual and textual complexities of Whitman's significance in the emerging discourses of same-sex desire."[3] Carpenter's visits to Whitman in 1877 and 1884 "enabled him to construct a new identity for himself, paradoxically, as the 'English Whitman'" (281). But it also highlighted the tension within that identity, because "Carpenter's conception of the Uranian [personality of female soul in male body] seems contradictory; at times polemically masculine and homosexual, at times androgynous and bisexual, the Uranian is generally portrayed as an *Übermensch*, belonging to a 'third' or 'intermediate' sex" (283). Building on the work of George Chauncey,[4] Pannapacker shows how implicit in Carpenter's development of the "Uranian" ideal, partly as a result of his meeting with Whitman, was a reaction against contemporary imaging of homosexuals as effeminate "fairies" and an assertion of his own socially transgressive preference for roughly masculine working-class men. As the following discussion will show, these are refinements important for the appreciation of the terms of Carpenter's textual reproduction of Whitman in his celebrated "poetic" text *Towards Democracy.*

Alongside and overlapping this interest in the male sexual bonding of Carpenter-Whitman runs a well-established scholarly interest in Carpenter as a highly significant figure of the political left, characterized by Raymond Williams as "to an extraordinary extent, a prefigurative man."[5] As Anthony Wright has trenchantly noted:

> The history of socialism is the history of socialisms. Moreover, it is a history not of fraternal plurality, but of rivalry and antagonism. The battle lines have changed (Marxists versus anarchists, collectivists versus syndicalists, reformers versus revolutionaries, communists versus social democrats, Trotskyists versus everybody else . . .), but battle lines there always have been.[6]

In his masterly survey of socialism, Wright notes all its shifting terms and categories, and the instability of its political vocabulary, before concluding that the sole common factor in this bewildering array of options is "an assault on [competitive] individualism, the ideology of capitalism" (23). However, he proceeds to emphasize that socialism's alternative program of "human socialty" stood in an ambivalent relationship to the Enlightenment individualism to which it was opposed: as well as seeking to replace it, socialism also sought to extend it into a new kind of universality. The difficulties of such an attempt are, of course, well illustrated in the way in which "human socialty" is characterized in the writings of Carpenter and Whitman alike.

How and where, then, to place Carpenter on this map of the socialist world? His admirers were extraordinarily wide ranging, and included "R. B. Cunninghame-

Grahame, Havelock Ellis, Roger Fry, John Galsworthy, Harley Granville-Barker, Keir Hardie, Peter Kropotkin, Jack London, Sidney and Beatrice Webb, and W. B. Yeats."[7] His friends ranged from the Leeds working-class leaders Alf Mattison and Tom Maguire, through radical sexual thinkers like Olive Schreiner, Arthur Symons, and Havelock Ellis, vegetarians and antivivisectionists like Henry Salt, and lower-middle-class reformers like the Bolton Whitmanites, to the Bloomsbury aesthete Roger Fry. He was at once a mystical middle-class utopian, a practical commune dweller, and (during certain phases of his career) a militant educator and campaigner who was an active participant in working-class organizations and fledgling unionism, particularly in the Midlands, Leeds, and Sheffield. The influences upon his thought extended "through Shelley, Whitman, Thoreau, Ruskin, Lewis Morgan, Olive Schreiner, William Morris, H. M. Hyndman, Buddha, Havelock Ellis, J. H. Noyes, Ulrichs, to Kraft Ebing and Moll. A motley crew . . ."[8] And in confirming that his was a "very sociable politics," the socialist scholar Sheila Rowbotham provides a vivid imaginary snapshot of him in his prime:

> "Simplification of life" was at once a moral pursuit—it signified a better life—and a practical one—it was the means of ensuring some independence from domestic labor of others. Carpenter's attempt to practice his own message appeared startling to contemporaries. It was after all unusual—in the 1880s and 1890s—to find a middle class man who wandered the streets in sandals and broad hats copied from the American poet Walt Whitman, who tried to live intimately with people of a lower social station and combine intellectual and manual labor.[9]

Ethical, utopian, romantic—all these adjectives and more can be applied to a Carpenter whose thinking had in some ways been indelibly marked by his upbringing in a Broad Church Anglicanism and by his own brief period as a Cambridge curate. Nor did he ever fully shed those upper-middle-class variants of Victorian radicalism to which his undergraduate life at Cambridge had introduced him. And he was never really to keep pace with the changes in socioeconomic conditions that, by 1914, had led to an increasingly organized, centralist, and unionized working class. Throughout his life, Carpenter, the individualistic collectivist and communitarian anarchist, could never reconcile himself to any form of state socialism, government control, or disciplined working-class action. He believed in a "non-governmental society," spontaneously produced, voluntarily maintained, and antinomian in spirit: hence his deep sense of spiritual kinship with Whitman. Perhaps the best attempt to place him in the socialist movements of his period is that by Marie-Françoise Cachin. She pays sensitive attention to the way in which guild socialism and Christian socialism—a leading figure of which was the F. D. Maurice who was vicar in the Cambridge parish where the young Carpenter briefly served as curate—blended increasingly in his work with Eastern yogic mysticism. These were in turn fused with a benign version of Kropotkin's version of anarchism and a heady mix of other ideologies in Carpenter's distinctively eclectic, resolutely unsystematic, and unyieldingly antiscientific brand of religio-ethical socialism:

> If we look at Carpenter's career, we see that he always chose to side with those socialists who attached the highest price to the freedom of the individual. Despite his association with [the Marxist-inspired] Hyndman, he was closer to William Morris' Socialist League than to [H. M. Hyndman's] S[ocial] D[emocratic] F[ederation]; he felt more akin to revolutionary syndicalism than to official trade unionism or the Labor Party, and continued to develop in this direction. Paradoxically, however, despite his remaining on the fringes, Carpenter is nonetheless a fairly typical representative of what was called "ethical socialism" in Britain at that time, and which disappeared with the development and official recognition of the Labor Party, for which political action and national material issues took precedence over moral problems and individuals' self-realization.[10]

It is not difficult to see why an emergent Labour Party should wish to ensure that the Carpenter who had evolved such controversial ideas about sex should become strictly a closet socialist. Otherwise, he could easily have been used to add substance to Conservative accusations that Socialists favored the sharing of sexual partners as well as a sharing out of property. It is true that Whitman was a revered figure whose work was cited by many "ethical socialists" during the phase of British socialism that was at its height in the 1890s. But his reputation faded from the scene (as did Carpenter's) following the rise of a class-conscious, socially militant, politically hard-line, and heavily unionized Labour movement that produced a new machine politics after the First World War, as an industrial capitalist class under increasing pressure from the world economy showed its true colors. As the 1890s progressed, so a capitalist class threatened by workers' organizations tried to dismantle trade unions, cooperative movements, friendly societies, and other instances of working-class self-help. Faced with this aggressive counterattack by the ruling class, the kind of ethical, voluntarist socialism Carpenter—and "his" Whitman—represented was found wanting. Emphasizing personal psychological and spiritual change, it proved to be relatively ineffectual in equipping the working class to deal with the brutal realities of industrial circumstance and the realpolitik of class warfare. As Stephen Yeo has pithily remarked, such a socialism had been characterized by a fatal internal contradiction between "the power of the vision and the short-sighted blur on the problem of agency."[11] In addition, the kinds of issues on which ethical socialism concentrated—such as vegetarianism, antivivisection, and a protoenvironmentalism—served only to bring a more hard-headed program of socialism (concerned with improving working conditions, securing social welfare provisions, etc.) into popular disrepute.

Yeo is, however, concerned that the socialism of the 1880s and 1890s should not be dismissed as dreamily impractical; nor, in his view, should it be regarded as a mere historical stage in the transition to the "mature," politically effective Labour politics of the twentieth century. In an outstanding essay on the "new life" that the socialism of the late Victorian and Edwardian period so passionately advocated, he sets out to show it enjoyed "its own special dynamism which became a wistful memory soon afterwards." For him, the phrase that best conveys the character of the emergent ideology of the period is "religious socialism"—a phrase first coined by William Morris in 1885 in the manifesto of the Socialist League, an organization that Carpenter immediately joined upon its foundation. The year 1883 came to be regarded as the date clearly marking the unmistakable emergence of British socialism; and it was in that very year that Carpenter was himself converted to this new secular faith, the spirit of which he was eloquently to convey from the pulpit of his texts, as the influential Labour Member of Parliament Fenner Brockway was fervently to testify in 1929:

> His *Towards Democracy* was our Bible. We read it aloud in the summer evenings when, tired by tramping or games, we rested awhile before returning from our rambles. We read it at those moments when we wanted to retire from the excitement of our Socialist work, and in quietude seek the calm and power that alone gives sustaining strength. We no longer believed in dogmatic theology. Edward Carpenter gave us the spiritual food we still needed.[12]

Robert Blatchford, one of the most prominent and successful polemicists for the Socialist cause during the 1890s, later wrote to Carpenter after reading *Civilization, Its Cause and Cure* (1889) in terms that further underlined the religious "illumination" that such texts could afford the devout: "It has given me a lot of light . . . [and helped me understand myself]." He demurred, however, at Carpenter's frank address of sexual subjects, pleading that "I am radical but . . . the whole subject is 'nasty' to me. Be charitable. I can't help it."[13] Blatchford was author of the best-selling *Merrie England*, a collection of papers from the *Clarion*, one of the most influential mass-circulation papers of the early Labour movement. In the penny edition of 1894, the book sold 700,000 copies and by the third edtion had reached the million mark. It broadcast Blatchford's belief in what, in his *Clarion* papers, he styled "The New Religion," one of the major prophets of which was Walt Whitman. Deliberately echoing St. Paul's famous First Epistle to the Corinthians, Blatchford declared that "[i]n place of Anglicism with its gentility, Romanism with its pomp and circumstance, and Calvinism with its fire and brimstone, it gives us a charity which 'beareth all things, believeth all things, hopeth all things' *of men* and endureth all things *for men.*"[14] After quoting Whitman's passage about "a great city is that which has the greatest men and women," he goes on to another quotation from the same author during the course of asserting that "[w]e are the party of humanity. Our religion is the religion of humanity. 'The black with his woolly head, the felon, the diseased, the illiterate are not denied'" (15). However, in a rhetorical and polemical move to establish a native and national socialism parallel to that of Whitman's American vision rather than subordinate to it, Blatchford concludes with Milton's magnificent charge to the "Lords and Commons of England" to "consider what the nation it is whereof ye are, and whereof ye are the governors: a nation not slow and dull, but of a quick, ingenious, piercing spirit; acute to invent, subtle and sinewy to discourse, not beneath the reach of any point, the highest that human capacity can soar to" (15).

When, therefore, Blatchford pays tribute to Whitman he is careful to associate his vision with that of the English prophets of socialism: "the new religion, which is Socialism, and something more than Socialism, is more largely the result of the labors of Darwin, Carlyle, Ruskin, Dickens, Thoreau, and Walt Whitman" (4). It is a textual ploy to which he repeatedly reverts, declaring that "we are indebted to the idol-breaking of Carlyle, to the ideal-making of Ruskin, and to the trumpet-tongued proclamation by the titanic Whitman of the great message of true Democracy and the brave and sweet comradeship of the natural life" (4); the Socialist Party "will rather honour the giver than the getter, rather love the man-helper than the self-helper; will put the names of John Ruskin, Thomas Carlyle, Walt Whitman, and Erasmus Darwin above those of all the money-spinners, fame-winners, blood-shedders, and self-makers that ever encumbered the earth" (8).

Implicit in such strategies is a repudiation of the Americanness of Whitman the prophet, and, as we shall, see, Carpenter's textual relationship to Whitman —infinitely more intimate though it be than Blatchford's—is marked by similar rhetorical maneuvers.

Blatchford's pamphlet affords classic utterance to that "new religion" of socialism the main features of which Yeo has so meticulously recorded. And Carpenter's life and work conform to all the main specifications. In a series of "confessional" texts (from the endnote of *Towards Democracy* to *My Days and Dreams*) he detailed his "conversion experience," attributing his "illumination" in major part to the impact of the secular "texts" of Whitman and testifying to the salvific power of Whitman's physical presence. He produced his own "hymns" of his new faith in *Chants for Labor*, including a poem, "England Arise," that came to rival Blake's "Jerusalem" as the great labor hymn of national revival. He exhibited a consciousness of sin—not, as Beatrice Webb remarked, that individual sin of which a Christian convert was made so acutely aware, but the sin of class consciousness and of class identity (Yeo, 10). His peripatetic preaching of his new faith was powerful, as C. T. Cramp, later Industrial General Secretary of the National Union of Railwaymen, recalled:

> In a curious way he seemed to take one both forward and backwards; forward to a freer and less care-worn world, yet backwards to something which all of us had lost. [As we shall see, this was perhaps one of the ways in which his ideology most exactly and revealingly matched that of Whitman.] One lost the sense of the grimy city with its jostling thousands living under a pall of smoke and earning their scanty livelihood by sweating at mill or forge, amid sulphur and gases. One lost the sense of those small worries and oft-time ridiculous conventions which oppress the soul and make of life a weariness. One saw a reconquest of the green and beautiful England by a happy and healthy people. . . . (Yeo, 29)

"At that time," Cramp remembered, "he lived at Holmesfield, situated in the peaceful Cordwell Valley in Derbyshire, and his house was a rendezvous for all sorts and conditions of men, particularly at week-ends. The Sheffield cutler, engineer, miner, or railwayman met poet, musician, or dramatist beneath his roof and were all made to feel one of a great family" (Yeo, 29). In his advocacy of "Simplicity of Life," a Carpenter otherwise dedicated to a salvific liberation of self through the cultivation of the capacity for sensuous pleasure evidenced the moral asceticism typical of the new religion, and, as Yeo has well noted, his passionate concern to establish unity by breaking down the false categories of his society was an important characteristic of a brand of socialism for which this was a precondition of the remaking of society. But whereas the mainstream of the movement confined its efforts to connecting "activities normally held separate in the culture," by organizing labor outings, socialist ramblings, games, brass bands, choirs, and the like (the form of healthy socialism promoted by the Clarion Scouts [1884] and the Clarion Fellowship [1900]), Carpenter, following in part in Whitman's footsteps, explored such controversial new unities as same-sex relations. However, the Englishman ventured much further than the American when he expressly advocated a wholesale reconsideration of the "norm" of heterosexual relations.

Yeo notes how "a language and style of religiosity surrounded" the "altruism" of this new religion, and nowhere is this better exhibited than in Carpenter's *Towards Democracy*, challengingly based as it is on a secularized millenarianism and including attacks on organized, established religion in the form, for instance, of a caustic sketch of York Minster. Throughout, a Carpenter who had in the 1870s written a drama effectively representing Moses as "the greatest of Labor Leaders,"[15] humanizes the divine, and sees the elect in the outcasts and underclass of society, most notably working men, and women of every class.[16] And in treating Christ as the perfect man, not only does he follow Whitman but may also, like Whitman, be indebted to one of his earliest Christian teachers. Just as the radical Quakerism Whitman had encountered as a boy in Elias Hicks had contributed to the development of the poet's later secular faith, so too in "the Anglican minister, Frederick W. Robertson," a friend of Carpenter's parents noted for his "incarnation-centered theology" (Pierson, 301), young Edward found an early model for his own mature socioreligious creed. Moreover, Carpenter's early experience as an ordained Anglican priest ensured that the language and spiritual and ethical outlook of Christianity continued to inform all of his thinking, acting, and writing when later he became an ethical Socialist.

Christianity was not, however, the only spiritual belief system that significantly inflected early socialist creed and practice. It was also sometimes infected by a spiritualism of an altogether more esoteric, exotic, not to say colorfully bizarre, kind that looked to the ancient, mystic Orient for inspiration and found in remote antiquity the purest sources of universal Gnostic wisdom. As Peter Washington has accurately noted, "radical politics [often] went with a strong religious bent in this period" and—as may be seen in the case of the prominent radical and pioneer of contraception, Annie Besant, who turned Theosophist—"Theosophy and Fabian socialism were [not] that far apart."[17] Even Shaw's theory of creative evolutionism bore a strong resemblance to Theosophist doctrine. And one of the fundamental attractions of Spiritualist and Theosophist movements is that they offered a single key to all the mysteries, thus purporting to uncover the underlying unity craved for by an age whose dominant scientific, economic, technological, and social systems appeared only to promote fractures and divisions that traditional Christian faith seemed helpless to withstand. The lure of a healing universalism is succinctly expressed by the cofounder of the Theosophical

Society (1875), the astonishing Madame Helena Petrovna Blavatsky, in the introduction to the celebrated bible of her syncretic faith, *The Secret Doctrine*, itself tellingly subtitled *The Synthesis of Science, Religion and Philosophy*:

> The aim of this book may be thus stated: to show that Nature is not "a fortuitous concurrence of atoms," and to assign to man his rightful place in the scheme of the Universe; to rescue from degradation the archaic truths which are the basis of all religions; and to uncover, to some extent, the fundamental unity from which they all spring; finally, to show that the occult side of Nature has never been approached by the Science of modern civilization.[18]

While never wrecked on the wilder shores of such beliefs, Carpenter was undoubtedly attracted to "Oriental wisdoms" and his devotion to his own guru, Whitman, was due in no small part to his conviction that Whitman was a reincarnation of ancient truths and uniquely empowered to recover ancient universals. Such a shared interest in both orthodox and heterodox spiritual faiths owed not a little to shared historical circumstances. The failure of the 1848 revolutions seems to have played a part (along with the failure of the Free-Soil Movement and the mainstream Democratic Party's disavowal of radical policies) in Whitman's turn away from politics, and in his resultant increased interest in transcendentalism, phrenology, Egyptology, spiritualism, and other midcentury fads. As David Reynolds has so powerfully shown, these then fed directly into the great poetry of his first and most innovative period. And it was likewise the failure of the revolutionary politics of 1848 that in part intensified British interest in "an 'alternative synthesis'" that included not only phrenology but "vegetarianism, feminism, dress reform, homeopathy and every variety of social and religious dissent" (Washington, 11). This was the very time when spiritualism, "having taken root in America[,] . . . rapidly colonized Europe" (Washington, 11). In looking to America for sources of sociospiritual illumination, Carpenter was therefore following in a well-established British tradition of looking across the Atlantic for radical inspiration. Not only could the United States be said to have effectively introduced spiritualism to Britain (even Madame Blavatsky had assumed her final incarnation as a Theosophist in New York), but Henry George's *Poverty and Progress* was a key text for early British incipiently socialist radicals.

There are, then, not only broad historical circumstances but suggestively precise symmetries of historical circumstance that partly help explain how Carpenter came to achieve such an extraordinarily intense psycho-textual twinning with Whitman. And a further historical symmetry may be detected in the terms in which the two constructed and textually expressed their vision. Whitman's stubborn attachment, in the face of aggressive new developments in the capitalist order, to an idealized form of artisanal republicanism has repeatedly been stressed in previous chapters of this volume. And as Stanley Pierson has explained, Carpenter was one of those

> sensitive members of the middle class [who] were increasingly torn between the norms associated with an advancing industrial urbanized society and the moral and social values inherited from older, simpler forms of communal life. In the middle decades of the century Victorians had tended to compartmentalize the two sets of values, applying the utilitarian ethic to the public realm and confining the personal virtues, often with the aid of Evangelical religious sanctions, to the private sphere. But the collapse or attenuation of the older religious doctrines, with their sobering and reconciling notions of sin and an other-worldly salvation, made this dualism less tenable. Young men from the middle classes, especially where affluence or strong personal drives had freed them from the ordinary pressures of social conformity, were entering onto a new quest for integrity. (317)

As a result, one of the most striking and central aspects of the vision of Whitman and of Carpenter is the attempt to reconcile a discourse of progress and sociospiritual evolution with a nostalgic, retrogressive, collectivist ideology. This is the tense, taut paradox uncoiled through the complex dynamics of their intimately corresponding textual rhetoric.

But interestingly enough, it is this correspondence of vision as it operates at the most fundamental, quintessential level—that of text—that has continued to be overlooked in all the writing about Whitman and Carpenter. While *Towards Democracy* is acknowledged to be not only the founding text of Carpenter's sociospiritual vision but also the most radical, original, and striking instance of Whitman's influential presence in British literary and political culture, very rarely has it been examined in any textual detail. Concentration has almost inevitably been on ideological correspondences between the two authors. And yet, as Carpenter pointed out during the course of what is one of the best nineteenth-century discussions of Whitman's forms (Carpenter sensitively notes the varieties of form used), Whitman's "message" or "vision" was essentially inseparable from his style: "The underlying and dominant mood of Whitman's poems, corresponding to his theme, is extraordinarily vast and inclusive—and it requires for its expression a rhythm of similarly broad and flexible character. It is obvious that such emotions as he deals with could never be engaged in a symmetrical stanza or verse."[19]

What is singular about *Towards Democracy*,[20] at least in some places, is its uncanny textual approximation to *Leaves of Grass*. What is accomplished is not, however, replication but reproduction—a re-producing of the text from a significantly different kind of "source": the source of Carpenter's own personal, distinctive, and English imagination. It is extraordinary testimony to the way in which Carpenter's encounters with Whitman had resulted in a conversion experience of more than one kind—bringing not only a spiritual conversion but also the discovery of means of converting Whitman's American poetry into the different sociopolitical idiom of Carpenter's English culture. It is, therefore, a fascinating instance of cultural translation. What is interesting is not merely Carpenter's adoption of Whitman's long poetic line, of course; rather, it is what Carpenter does with it—his mastery of some of the kinds of rhetorical strategies Whitman favored being evident in his convincing ability to build panoramas, to produce unexpected exclamations, boldly to apostrophize Democracy and Freedom, to sculpt the body in loving verbal detail, to infuse landscape with homoerotic longing, and to draw insinuatingly close to his readers. It would be interesting to see how many Whitman scholars could on every occasion tell Carpenter from Whitman himself, were select phrases or brief passages to be secretly smuggled into Whitman's slightly lesser-known texts. The following might just possibly escape notice even if discreetly insinuated into "Song of Myself":

> The guides are all talking. They are settling the affairs of the universe (They never cease).
> They have not settled yet which way to go themselves; how shall they give help to an ignorant child?
> Lovers of all handicrafts and of labor in the open air, confessed passionate lovers of your own sex,
> Arise!
> Heroes of the enfranchisement of the body (latest and best gift long concealed from men). Arise!
> Come! I too call you, I too have looked in your eyes, O you of great faith and few words; you cannot escape, now.
> I weave these words about myself to form a seamless web without beginning or ending. I do not spin a yarn for you to reel off at your leisure; nor do I pour out water into pots.
> This is one of my bodies—of the female—which if you penetrate with true sexual power, clinging it shall conceive, and you shall know me in part—by the

answer of the eyes of children, yours and mine, looking up from the grass and down from the sky upon you as you walk.[21]

Built from lines taken almost at random from "Towards Democracy," such a passage would be very easy to assemble from any number of that poem's materials and could as easily be dismissed perhaps as inspired pastiche. But Carpenter is also capable of genuinely beautiful phrases in the Whitman manner:

For the face of the farm-lad who came and sat beside me, the handfuls of pease that he offered me—for the taste of their juicy pods;
The thick-thighed hot coarse-fleshed young bricklayer with the strap round his waist.
The diamond that you wear in your hair, the gold piece you hold so solid in your hand—they are no more solid than a swarm of bees is solid, of which the units are in constant motion to and fro, some leaving and some joining the swarms.
The rocks flow and the mountain shapes flow,
And the forests swim over the lands like cloud-shadows.
When the awful vision moves across the sky, and the earth is electric under it —and the grass stands stiffly, and the blue thistle in the hedge is erect with meaning.[22]

To come across such passages may be to grow dissatisfied with the "Whitman and water" gibe famously aimed at Carpenter by his friend and comrade-in-arms the Victorian "sexologist" Havelock Ellis, and to appreciate how *Towards Democracy* may be read as Carpenter's love-poem to Whitman. And to perceive that Carpenter is at least capable of lines of this quality is next to wonder whether when Carpenter seems to be writing in a sub-Whitmanesque manner elsewhere, he may not, possibly, be rather writing *differently* from Whitman. (Which is not at all to suggest that he is remotely Whitman's equal as a poet.)

The key to the fundamental difference between *Towards Democracy* and *Leaves of Grass* may be found in the following revealing comment by Carpenter on weaknesses in Whitman's poetry:

in parts he "set himself" very deliberately to do certain things. And it is in these parts that I think he is least successful. Thus he set himself to vaunt and magnify "these States" in season and out of season (a good purpose in moderation, but rather overdone). (*Days*, 133)

Lover of Whitman Carpenter may have been, but he was no particular lover of America. Resolutely opposed to nationalisms of every kind, he clearly sensed in

Whitman a nationalist poet, and could not accept the latter's vision of America as being in the vanguard of human progress and already prefiguring the future of mankind. So when Carpenter writes his poem "On an Atlantic Steamship," he draws upon his own experience of traveling steerage to the United States in 1877 to present vivid vignettes of the huddled masses from Europe that are bound for America. But he pointedly refrains from the slightest suggestion that they may be bound for a better life—instead, the whole tone and stylistic demeanor of the poem makes this passage across the Atlantic no more hopeful than is the train journey "From Turin to Paris" for the passengers Carpenter also vividly etches (*TD*, 315–321). And when his vision did find part of itself embodied in a country, it was preindustrial peasant China, "rooted in the land, rooted in the family," that became the custodian of his hopes and not the United States (*TD*, 471–475). Published in 1901, the poem was also a radical's response to the "land-grabbing" intervention the previous year by British and other Western powers, to suppress the Boxer Rebellion and to safeguard imperial interest in maintaining the opium trade and safeguarding entry for Western commerce through Chinese ports.[23]

Carpenter's misgivings about the United States may have their roots in his recollections of his father's obsessive worry over the vagaries of the market value of the shares he held in American railway companies—the shares upon which the Carpenter family's fortunes were based. From such intensely personal experiences, in part, sprang his total opposition to modern capitalism and his consequent disbelief that "the world was somehow going to be saved by Trade and Commerce" (*TIF*, 18). For him, these were nakedly "founded on greed and self-seeking, and chicanery and the law of devil-take the hindmost . . . the principle of *Internecine Competition*" (*TIF*, 20–21). And the basis of the whole system was the pernicious belief in the sacredness of property—which was, to one of Carpenter's millenarian vision, the very Antichrist itself. In one of his many jeremiads against property, Carpenter quotes in passing Whitman's reference to "the [modern] mania for owning things" (*TIF*, 51), but he very well knew that the quintessential American could not believe, as he did, in the abolition of all property except for that "supported by no apparatus of armed authority, but as far as it exists is . . . a perfectly spontaneous arrangement" in the interests of "Community of life and Interest in life" (*TIF*, 87–88). By contrast, Whitman's rooted commitment to property was tellingly recorded by his great Socialist friend and chronicler in old age, Horace Traubel:

> The old man "looked forward to a world of small owners," but Traubel asserted that a world of "no owners at all" might be even better. The suggestion stunned the poet.

"What do you mean by that? no owners at all?" he mused. "Do you mean common owners—owning things in common? . . . [I]t *sounds* best: could it *be* best?"[24]

Once again, Whitman, cute as an old hen, had evaded Traubel's attempts to pin socialism on him.

Property was, for Carpenter, the chronic systemic disease destroying humans' body and soul, "the condition of health [being] loyalty to the divine Man within it."[25] Disease is disunity, and property causes it because it draws "Man" away "(1) from Nature, (2) from his true Self, (3) from his Fellows" (*CCC*, 27). For Carpenter, the communal and universal had to reassert its power in human beings over the atomizing forces of socioeconomic individualism: "The mass-Man must rule in each unit-man, else the unit-man will drop off and die" (*CCC*, 28). That is why the war against property is waged mercilessly and incessantly throughout the pages of *Towards Democracy*; with a passion that derives in substantial part from his own family background. And that is why, being the angrily confrontational, radically anticapitalist text it is, it is fundamentally different from *Leaves of Grass*. There would, for instance, seem to be strong parallels between Carpenter's call for free land and Whitman's obsession with Free Soil, but such an analogy, though inviting, is also deceptive. Whereas Carpenter saw the British land question as exposing the very heart of capitalism, Whitman tended to see slavery's threat to the new territories in terms of a struggle between progressive modern libertarian capitalism and a reactionary social and economic order that was precapitalist and feudal in essence. That is, insofar as Whitman ever clearly (yet alone systematically) thought in these categories, or used this lexicon at all—tellingly enough, there is no entry on Capitalism in the recent Whitman *Encyclopedia*, and his sparring with Traubel in old age took the form of his resisting Traubel's attempts to introduce him to this "new" vocabulary and outlook. For him, that way extremism lay, as he clearly and repeatedly warned Traubel, and he, Whitman, mistrusted extremists, not least because he felt they were by nature authoritarian, anti-individualistic "enforcers." He made this perfectly clear to Carpenter in several of their meetings. For instance, he was adamant that "it was no good trying to *benefit* people (laboring people for instance) who did not feel the need of any change" (*Days*, 26). And, even when faced with the Carnegies and Rockefellers of late nineteenth-century American monopolistic capitalism, he was reluctant, as noted in chapter 4, to confront their power at root. Witness his comments to Carpenter on June 18, 1884:

> Talked a little about social questions. W.: "I believe, like Carlyle, in *men*; I think that notwithstanding all set-offs the great capitalists and masters of private enterprise have, in America at least, been useful. I have myself had all along a tender feeling for Co-operation, but for that doubt whether a committee or an elected person could or would do the work." As to England, he seemed to think that emigration would relieve it, and he looked upon the law and custom of *entail* as "the hard-pan underlying your social institutions." "I like and welcome all agitation, even the fiercest, but like Carlyle have little belief in reform talk. Society, like a person in middle life, is *set*, and you have to make the best of it. I am, I hope, a bit of a reformer myself. Yes, we must *grow* generous, ungrasping masters of industry; absurd as the idea would seem to most now-a-days. I believe that is the upshot of what is going on. The creation of a large, independent democratic class of small owners is the main thing—though is never once mentioned by our economists and politicians." (*Days*, 38)

A Carpenter who had opted out of the capitalist economy by creating his own self-sufficient smallholding at Millthorpe where he grew his own produce was hardly likely to agree that the industrial garden of England was ever likely to "grow generous, ungrasping masters of industry."

Everywhere in Carpenter's text may be found his anticapitalist rhetoric, sometimes specifically targeting his England: "The puppet-dance of gentility—condescension, white hands, unsoiled dress, charitable proprietorship—in the street, the barracks, the church, the shop, the house, the school, the assembly" (*TD*, 26). But the textual markers of this animus also take subtler forms. His oppositional anger is present as a style of vision embodied in a style of writing, as when he sees a wealthy woman emerge from a church service:

> The dress of the elder one especially is a study—the flounces, the innumerable quantity of beads, the formless mass of plaits and gaiters, the wonderful arrangement of whale-bones in the body, the strict lacing down the back, the frills and lace round neck and shoulders, the several rings seen on the for a moment ungloved hand, the lump of trinkets suspended from her waist, and the usual headgear (— one cannot help thinking of the chaotic mass of human work this idle easy-tempered woman carries about on her body). (*TD*, 117)

This discourse constructs the woman in terms of both predator and prey. This is partly because Carpenter felt all women, regardless of social status, belonged to the capitalist underclass by virtue of their very gender. But it is also partly because Carpenter saw all human beings in this dual vision: "Villeins and thralls become piece-men and day-tal men, and the bondsmen of the land become the bondsmen of Machinery and Capital; the escaped convicts of Labor fit admiringly the bracelets of Wealth round their own wrists" (*TD*, 107). Even as Carpenter seems to be adopting Whitman's characterization of modern Europe as "feudal," he sees, as Whitman does not—*will* not—that it is capitalism itself (American capitalism included) that is to blame. And however Whitmanesque Carpenter's paeans to nature may sometimes sound, they, too, are indictments of property, as Whitman's are not. In his important millenarian poem "The Coming of the Lord" (*TD*, 337), it is "the Lord Demos" that takes the place of the Lord Christ as redeemer of mankind, and what he means by "Demos" in this particular instance is the liberating spirit of the land itself: "For the land (the Demos) is the foundation-element of human life, and if the public relation to that is false, all else is of need false and inverted" (*TD*, 390). The divine liberating word comes from this source: "I the Lord Demos have spoken it: and the mountains are my throne" (*TD*, 340). "My feet tread naked the grass of the valleys, the trees know me by name—they hear my voice—the brook with heaped up waters rush past me" (*TD*, 339). And the companion poem "The Curse of Property" begins with the announcement: "Are they not mine, saith the Lord [Demos], the everlasting hills?" (*TD*, 340). Here, as in many places in *Towards Democracy*, Carpenter reveals himself to be the heir not so much of Whitman as of Blake and Shelley—and also, like them, the heir of Milton.

American nature was not British nature. It must be remembered that "the Land Question" was one of the hottest political topics of nineteenth-century Britain and Ireland, since a vast percentage of acres—an area greatly augmented under the Enclosure Acts of the late eighteenth-century Agrarian Revolution that helped make the Industrial Revolution possible—was in the possession of the wealthy, and often titled, propertied classes. Some members of this class were grasping absentee landlords who screwed their tenant-farmers and evicted them if, following the Second Reform Bill of 1868, they dared to vote for the wrong political party. No wonder Carpenter strongly asserted that "civilization" (a pejorative term in his vocabulary, denoting a stage of social evolution earlier than that marked by the emergence of "democracy") "dates roughly from the division of society into classes founded on property, and the adoption of class-government" (*CCC*, 5). It is this ineradicable awareness of division that scars Carpenter's vision and is everywhere reproduced in his text, as when the class divisions of industrial society are mirrored textually in Carpenter's hard unyielding division between the present capitalist order and a future communal, or communitarian, postcapitalist society.

This division operates as a structural principle both of his thinking and in his writing, and marks his confrontational, adversarial, oppositional politics and poetry very clearly from the largely consensual rhetoric of Whitman. When Whitman *is* oppositional it is on an occasional basis; and never, of course, is he opposed to the capitalist order of his society as such. Everywhere, and at every rhetorical level, in *Towards Democracy* one finds Carpenter's binary thinking clearly inscribed. For instance, in opening *Towards Democracy* with a millenarian vision of a redeemed human and natural order, Carpenter speaks from the vantage point of a remote future and makes clear that a gulf stands between it and the historical present in which he was actually writing—a gulf that nothing less than a revolution could possibly bridge. Thus the poem starts:

> Freedom at last!
> Long sought, long prayed for—ages and ages long:
> The burden to which I continually return, seated here thick-booted and obvious yet dead and buried and passed into heaven unsearchable . . . (*TD*, 3)

Already, then, a contrast—between Carpenter's body, "thick-booted," fixed leadenly in the present, and his mind, or imagination, that has already achieved passage to a redeemed future. And nowhere in his poetry does one find the "thick-booted" speaker from the present achieving union with the liberated mind that "conceive[s] a millennium on earth" (*TD*, 5). There is none of that skillful blurring of future prospects and present actualities that one everywhere finds in Whitman (see chapter 3 of the present study), and that was (and is) one of the most seductive features of his poetic rhetoric. There is rarely a sense of imminent millennium in Carpenter's writing, let alone the immanent millenarianism that some of Whitman's greatest poetry seems (however misleadingly) to convey. Take, for instance, a powerful passage from *Towards Democracy* such as the following:

> The blacksmith blows up his fire; he listens for the sound of the great heat. He taps the glowing iron in advance of the blows of the striker, and turns it deftly with the tongs. . . .
> The tall thin grey-bearded man I meet daily in the street—with lined brow, silent, full of experience;

> The stout matron in the greengrocer's shop, loquacious, clear-eyed, with clear indubitable voice;
> The thick-thighed hot coarse-fleshed young bricklayer with the strap round his waist . . . (*TD*, 68–69)

More than capable of Whitman's "cosmic mooning" (to quote E. P. Thompson), Carpenter is also, as this passage shows, capable of Whitman's physical relish. The passage seems strikingly Whitmanesque, until one realizes that Carpenter relates to these workers both as flesh-and-blood sources of inspiration and as instances of the kind of life that is yearning for a *future* fulfillment only the loving word of intimate recognition he as a poet can utter is capable of defining and of delivering. "Touching" them in, or with, his imagination, Carpenter dreams "the dream of the soul's slow disentanglement" (*TD*, 71). This dual aspect of Carpenter's relation to the working classes he adored is beautifully encapsulated in another similar passage:

> I will be the ground underfoot and the common clay;
> The ploughman shall turn me up with his ploughshare among the roots of the twitch in the sweet-smelling furrow;
> The potter shall mould me, running his finger along my whirling edge (we will be faithful to one another, he and I);
> The bricklayer shall lay me: he shall tap me into place with the handle of his trowel;
> And to him I will utter the word which with my lips I have not spoken. (*TD*, 73)

With its light suggestion that Carpenter is a kind of Piers Ploughman of a poet, this beautiful homoerotic passage, characteristically tactile, dramatizes an act of double, or mutual, redemption as an act of lovemaking between Carpenter the poet and his (male) workers.

And the following passage very clearly follows the same pattern, providing anyone accustomed to reading Whitman with the shock of surprise at a delayed recognition of fundamental difference between the American's vision and that of Carpenter in a rhetoric that had seemed so invitingly to be indicating sameness (if not virtual identity):

> Brawny figures move to and fro in the iron works, half-seen through clouds of flying steam or against the glare of furnaces;
> The flame of the Bessemer cupola roars, with showers of sparks, and rattling of cranes, and shouts of men; . . .
> The man in a corner washing his shoulders and head in a bucket of water;

> The steam-hammers, the blocks of yellow-hot iron shimmering in the heated air;
> The steel-melter's men around the crucibles with their tongs—their feet and legs swathed in rags to keep off the heat, their sweat-handkerchiefs held between their teeth; . . .
> And he at the forge streaming with sweat, the striker, with bared breast, turning out claw-hammer heads by the score,
> Keeps dreaming and dreaming all day between the strokes, of love which is to come and change our earth into heaven;
> But his brother who works with him laughs at his dreams—and the spring comes in the woods to all alike:
> The gnarled oak breaks into pale yellow buds against the blue, the mouse stirs under the dry grass, and the corn-crake runs with head erect among the young green blades of corn. (*TD*, 298–300)

Very much an example of how Carpenter had become a son of Sheffield, the great city of steel, this passage shows us not just, as Whitman does, the beauty and dignity of labor but also the desperation underlying the seductive energy: Carpenter's is a picture of a slave society, in which

> [p]ale and desperate in the cutlery buffing shop boys and girls bend over their wheels; . . .
> The master looks round with his hands in his pockets, well satisfied;
> The cheap goods ready to fall to pieces as soon as used are duly packed and despatched to African and Pacific Island traders. (*TD*, 298)

Nowhere, of course, does Whitman include "master" and "wage-slave" in the same verbal "shot" to this effect—so as violently to highlight directly opposed class interests.

And the homoeroticism of that first passage makes clear the internal link for Carpenter between sex—not least "transgressive" sex—and politics. For him, "deviants," whether same-sex lovers or criminals, were in some ways among the most hopeful of what he styled "the spirits of the suffering brotherhood," the most obvious and thus the most dangerously oppositional victims of the way established society was constructed—and policed. Carpenter repeatedly attacked the police, treating the constabulary as nothing but the enforcers of a law fashioned exclusively to protect the interests of the elite of capitalist society. He dreamt of a "non-governmental society" "in which . . . Private Property is supported by no apparatus of armed authority" (*TIF*, 87). Thus in *Civilization: Its Cause and Cure* he devoted a chapter to a "Defence of Criminals," rejoicing in their violation not only of the laws of property but also those of capitalist bourgeois respectability, because "the respectability of today is the respectability of property" (108).

"O disrespectable Democracy! I love you," he exclaims in *Towards Democracy* and, needless to say, Carpenter rejoiced in a scandalous, outrageous celebration of that most jealously policed of human features, the body. He was acutely conscious of what today is referred to as the "social construction" of the body, and thus of sexual experience and of gender identity. It is a great theme in *Towards Democracy*, where he again explicitly sets out to liberate the body from capitalism—or from "civilization" as he witheringly styles Victorian society elsewhere:

> Wondrous is Man—the human body: to understand and possess this, to create it every day afresh, is to possess all things.
> The tongue and all that proceeds from it: spoken and written words, languages, commands, controls, the electric telegraph girding the earth;
> The eyes ordaining, directing; the feet and all that they indicate—the path they travel for years and years;
> The passions of the body, the belly and the cry for food, the heaving breasts of love, the phallus, the fleshy thighs,
> The erect proud head and neck, the sturdy back, and knees well knit or wavering. (*TD*, 359–360)

This passage culminates in a diagnosing of the disease of Victorian industrial society—that high point of "civilization"—as directly causing, as well as being symbolized by, the misshapen, disease-ridden body. And the poem from which the passage comes concludes with a remarkable section where Carpenter imagines himself wrestling with Satan, just as Jacob had wrestled with an angel, in order to regain his true identity—in order to reclaim his body, in all its aspects, as his own. It is Carpenter's record of his past, successful struggle both with social convention and with internalized social convention—the insidiously "respectable" side of his own mind, imagination, and being. And once Carpenter is victorious, Satan reveals his own identity:

> Then he ceased, and said, "I love thee."
> And lo! his form changed, and he leaned backwards and drew me upon him,
> And bore me up into the air, and floated me over the topmost trees and the ocean, and round the curve of the earth under the moon—
> Till we stood again in Paradise. (*TD*, 364)

It is a triumphantly transgressive moment, and the whole structure of this dramatic occasion is clearly based on, and seems deliberately to echo, the structure of Blake's *Marriage of Heaven and Hell.*

The vision is not only Blake's but also that of the Shelley who asserted in *A Defence of Poetry* that in ancient Hellenic Greece erotic poetry (along with "bucolic poetry") had served as a site of resistance to social corruption of the human spirit:

> For the end of social corruption is to destroy all sensibility to pleasure; and, therefore, it is corruption, it begins at the imagination and the intellect as at the core, and distributes itself thence as a paralyzing venom, through the affections into the very appetites, until all becomes a torpid mass in which hardly sense survives.[26]

Thus did malign Victorian "respectability" spread corruption in Carpenter's England, and the echoes, at least to a British ear, of Blake and Shelley in *Towards Democracy* are not unimportant coincidences. They are testimony to Carpenter's central belief in tradition which was, as will be seen, a central element in his rhetorical strategies to "de-Americanize" Whitman.

Love, then—most particularly including same-sex relations—offered, for Carpenter as for Blake and Shelley, the most visceral, vital means of resistance to the antihuman threat of social convention; it was a healing, annealing presence in a world wounded, scarred, and disfigured by all the forces of "disunion." The following passage clearly shows how Carpenter instinctively, but also consciously, linked the bridging of the great British social divide of class division to the act of breaking down conventionally sanctioned sexual roles and sexual identities:

> The young heir goes to inspect the works of one of his tenants;
> (Once more the king's son loves the shepherd lad;)
>
> In the shed the fireman is shoveling coal into the boiler furnace. He is neither specially handsome nor specially intelligent, yet when he turns, from under his dark lids dimmed with coal-dust shoots something so human, so loving near, it makes the other tremble.
>
> They only speak a few words, and lo! underneath all the differences of class and speech, of muscle and manhood, their souls are knit together. (*Towards Democracy*, 397)

There are clear parallels, of course, between this relationship and that of the bourgeois Carpenter to his lifelong partner, the working-class George Merrill.[27] The passage comes from the poem "A Mightier than Mammon," which lists innumerable other examples of cross-class, same-sex relations, including the following. It needs to be quoted in full for reasons that will become apparent:

> The graduate from Cambridge is a warm-hearted impulsive little woman, genuine and human to the core. Having escaped from high and dry home-circles, she found curiously the answer of her heart in a wage-worker of an East London workshop—a calm broad-bowed woman, strong, clearheaded, somewhat sad in expression, and a bit of a leader among her trade-mates.
>
> Having got in touch with each other, the two came at last to live together; and immediately on doing so found themselves a focus and center of activities—like opposite poles of a battery through which when in contact the electricity streams.
>
> So the news and interest of the two classes of society streamed through them. Through them too, folk from either side, especially women, came into touch with each other, and discovered a common cause and sympathy amid many surface differences.
>
> Thus by a thousand needs besides their own compelled, was their love assured, their little home made sacred. (*Towards Democracy*, 402–403)

The passage would seem to be a gift to those who argue that not only is Carpenter no Whitman, he is simply no poet. But that is, perhaps, where an important misconception lies, the correction of which further assists us to modify the "received" impression of the Carpenter-Whitman relationship. In his prose work *Angels' Wings*, Carpenter could be said to be struggling toward a concept nowadays fashionably explored under the term "hybridity"—that is, the concept that the breakdown of established categories, resulting in the intermixing of two elements, may produce not an impure amalgam but an entirely new entity, which is sui generis and thus forces the rethinking not only of all categories but of the very concept of fixed categories. The title of Carpenter's work is an image of this, referring as it does to what he regards as traditional Western artists' failure to convincingly (that is, with anatomical conviction) portray that body-soul, earth-heaven hybrid, the angel. And Carpenter's argument is that only the New Democratic Age, of which Whitman is the great prefigurative poet, will be capable of this radical reappraisal, this reconceiving both of the body-soul relationship and of the relationship between the real and the ideal. Along with Whitman he couples Millet and Wagner as major modern artists whose works are prophetic of the "new man," and notes that the reformation of man is inscribed in their re-formed art through the production of radically new, and yet anciently primal *forms* of artistic expression. But he goes on to note polarizations, too, that were being produced in progressive art and that needed to be reconciled. Most notably, he cautiously, reservedly praises the new "obscenely" frank realism of Zola's prose for its disclosure of the hard unsavory truths of contemporary life, but he regrets that, except to a degree in Whitman, such realism was never successfully fused with a sense of the beauty inherent in those features of life being described. And in looking forward to a new realist poetry, Carpenter observes that "[n]o absolute line of course can be drawn between the forms of Prose and Poetry. Wherever there is emotion concerned in the thought there will be emotional effects in the language—that is, there will be rhythm—and the wavelike rhythms and rhymes and recurrences will take on the simplest and briefest or the most complex and far-reaching forms according to the character of the emotion concerned—just as they do in Music."[28] Read in the light of such a remark, the long passage quoted above may, perhaps, be best understood as Carpenter's (in this case manifestly unsuccessful) attempt at a new synthesis—or at a "hybrid" form—that of the prose poem; and this helps explain the tendency throughout *Towards Democracy* for Carpenter to produce those connecting chunks of "prosaic" poetic text that have provoked so many of his readers to lament his total want of Whitman's "ear" for rhythm, and his failure to reproduce the electrifying power of Whitman's writing.

Even in the form of his writing, Carpenter seeks to join and fuse all of those elements his society was so intent on keeping apart, and same-sex relationships were, for him, models of the kind of socially transgressive, consciously anticapitalist behavior his crusading social vision actively advocated. Whitman's "In Paths Untrodden" may express the wish to escape "From all the standards hitherto publish'd, from the pleasures, profits, conformities, / Which too long I was offering to feed my soul," (268) but nowhere in Whitman does one feel that hostile, threatening pressure of a society specifically defined as capitalist that one feels in those poems and passages of *Towards Democracy* that are most reminiscent of *Calamus*. "As It Happened," for example, imagines a young man sitting "Cross-legged in a low tailor's den, gasping for breath—The gas flaring, doors and windows tight shut, the thick sick atmosphere" and "stitching, stitching" in a cameo scene almost literally enacting that strangling "entanglement" of human beings in the capitalist system that Carpenter so fears and fiercely fights. And as he stitches, the young man experiences the "deep deep hunger" of his dream of love—a dream that takes the form of a homoerotic, sadomasochistic vision of "a garden and at the gate stands a bearded man, dagger in hand, saying 'Thou canst not enter here, except thou pass the Ordeal.' / And he in his dream, beholding

Love beyond, bares his breast gladly to the knife, and feels the sharp point turn within his heart" (*TD*, 280–282). (This sadomasochistic homoeroticism finds further expression in a neighboring poem, "Summer Heat" [*TD*, 284].)

And in "The Dead Comrade," one of Carpenter's loveliest poetic conversations with Whitman, there is another interesting aspect of the Englishman's un-Whitmanesque stance. The poem is clearly modeled on "Vigil Strange." In that poem, however, the persona is a combatant hurried on in the excitement and heat of battle and allowed time to grieve his dead comrade only after victory has been won; in "The Dead Comrade" the persona speaks as one appalled by "the splintered trees, the blood-smeared corpses, the devilish noises and the sights and smells." It is these that remain strewing the scene of his lover's death, where grows a memorial emblem of the dead man's beauty:

> . . . on the stained red ground, in the midst of the clotted precious blood, not even yet dry, stood a small yellow flower—
> The little Cow-wheat they call it, with its slender yellow blossoms in pairs, and its faint-tinged lips. (*Towards Democracy*, 412)

Whereas the *Drum-Taps* poem is written by one who, however reluctantly, accepts the necessity of war in defense of freedom, Carpenter's poem dramatizes its author's unqualified objection to war as an obscene product of the "internecine strife" between nations that was a direct expression of the capitalist system.

If "The Dead Comrade" is one of Carpenter's poems that deserves very serious consideration for inclusion in any anthology of Victorian poetry, then "Wings" is another. It opens with a delicately moving evocation of a homoeroticized landscape:

> Wings, wings!
> I beheld the young leaves breaking from the buds and poised on the tips of the branches;
> I saw a squadron of anemones in the meadows all waving in the wind as impatient to take flight together;
> I looked at the acorn buried in the earth, and lo! it divided and put forth two seed-wings; and the embryo plant resembled the penis and dual testicles of man and the animals;
> And the starling like-shaped flew overhead through the trees, and the lark hung, a cross, in heaven;
> And the butterfly flew by—emblem of the soul—and the bee hung downwards in the wind-flower cup . . . (*Towards Democracy*, 201)

Unable to see his millennial new world as immanent in the working population of Britain, Carpenter instead saw the unsubdued natural world as instinct with exactly that potential. In this poem nature awakens in the speaker an awareness of "the wings of Man distinctly unfolding," a stirring of imagination that produces the poem's fine millenarian conclusion with "universal man" manifesting itself to him:

> And as I gazed—lo! slowly all these other things swam with me and became incorporate with that figure, and the clouds floated and the streams ran down from ledge to ledge within it;
> And the trees with their square arms took on a new signification, and the little seeds with their twin cotyledons were for [me] an emblem, and I saw whither the birds were hastening, and the direction of the index of all generation,
> And the starlings flew through the spaces of its thoughts, and the anemone squadrons trembled along its flanks . . . (*Towards Democracy*, 202)

Maybe such a passage would not have been possible without Whitman, but it is not a Whitmanesque passage; it is unmistakably Carpenter's. And it stands, as all such passages in his work do, in implicit contrast to his dark vignettes of actual social circumstance in late Victorian England. Thus, in "In a Manufacturing Town," urban space is specifically, and accurately, mapped as demarcated and divided along class lines. Carpenter's opening—"As I walked restless and despondent through the gloomy city"—is deliberately reminiscent of the opening of that bible of proletarian resistance, Bunyan's *Pilgrim's Progress.*[29] This leads on to a visit to "the Capitalist quarter," before "a little ragged boy" becomes his guide into the labyrinth of "the smoke-blackened walls and the tall chimneys" of the proletarian district (*TD*, 144–146). And just as nowhere in Whitman does one see New York's urban space starkly charted in these class terms, so nowhere in the American's work are there the equivalent of Carpenter's poetic vignette of Sheffield (*TD*, 450–452), or of his prose poem on a Lancashire mill hand (*TD*, 452–454). Nor does a Whitman intent on making American slang and urban cant his own, ever make Carpenter's (occasional) attempt to provide the subaltern with a voice, to allow the subject of one his poems actually to speak in the very language of the "illiterate" working class.

Carpenter's relationship with Whitman grew out of a period of profound personal crisis. He had greeted *Leaves of Grass* ecstatically as a sexually liberating text from the very first moment in 1868 when, a repressed and depressed Cambridge curate, he opened the Rossetti edition a friend had given him. However, it was in 1873 that the poetry began to demand urgent expression in his own life. After rereading Whitman in Cannes, while nursing his sister, Lizzie, it "suddenly flashed upon me," he wrote in *My Days and Dreams*, "that I would and must somehow go and make my life with the mass of the people and the manual workers" (77). He determined to leave Cambridge as soon as possible, and it was at the very moment of standing on the threshold of the new life he was to make for himself in the northern industrial cities that Carpenter wrote his famous confessional letter of 1874 to Whitman. That letter has received considerable attention from critics, but Carpenter's relationship with Whitman was far more complex, and far more delicately modulated, than has generally been realized, let alone properly explored. At the risk of crude simplification it may be put simply: Whitman's Americanism was, for Carpenter, not a neutral factor, nor a positive (let alone an inspirational) one, but an actual obstacle. This is not for one minute to deny that, for Carpenter, Whitman (both in his texts and in person) had been his personal savior and that he continued to regard him so throughout his long life. He had first read Whitman in 1868, and what he wrote to him in 1874—three years before first meeting him and seven years before beginning "Towards Democracy"—remained true for Carpenter to the very end:

> There are many in England to whom your writings have been as the waking up to a new day . . . [and have] become the central point of their lives. . . . Here, though dimly, I think I see the new open life which is to come, the spirit moving backwards and forwards beneath the old forms, strengthening and reshaping the foundations before it alters the superstructure. . . . You have as it were given me a ground for the love of man.[30]

And yet, perhaps the account Carpenter offers, in *Days with Walt Whitman*, of Emerson's influence on Whitman may also offer insight into Carpenter's own case: "[He] did give to Whitman just what he might have been waiting for (though probably in any case it would have come to him some time), the magic touch and inspiration which set his kosmos in order. No doubt an outside push of some kind is often required for the launching of a big ship" (163). And if Whitman was Carpenter's savior, it was in some such sense of the term as he outlined in *Civilisation: Its Cause and Cure*:

> this divinity in each creature, being that which constitutes it and causes it to cohere together, was conceived of as that creature's saviour, healer—healer of wounds of body and wounds of heart—the Man within the man, whom it was not only possible to know, but whom to know and be united with was the alone salvation. (14)

"Walt Whitman, a kosmos, of Manhattan the son, . . .": thus it was that, some twenty pages into "Song of Myself," Whitman first made his personal identity electrifyingly known, and felt, in the otherwise anonymously published 1855 *Leaves of Grass.* Thus did he "identify" himself. And, significantly enough, a Carpenter who never names himself in "Towards Democracy" suddenly introduces Whitman's name more than ninety pages through his poem: "The savage eternal peaks, the solitary signals—Walt Whitman, Jesus of Nazareth, your own Self distantly deriding you—/ These are always with you" (94). It is a striking moment, as if Whitman was being invoked at the very point where a Carpenter whose poem is so obviously haunted by "Song of Myself" might reasonably have been expected to identity himself. And there is indeed a sense in which Carpenter wants to acknowledge Whitman as the author of his poem, and wants to do so in these precise terms, not only identifying Whitman but identifying Whitman *with* both Jesus and the "Self." And here lies the clue to the psychological and textual strategy Carpenter evolved for dealing with Whitman's presence in his life, a strategy that also accomplished the de-Americanization of Whitman that was necessary from the point of view of Carpenter's socialist, anticapitalist convictions. Because here, as throughout his works, Carpenter treats Whitman as the modern prophetic incarnation of "the eternal Saviour, the sought after of all the world, dwelling hidden; (yet to be disclosed) within each" (*Towards Democracy*, 253).

In *Civilisation*, Carpenter distinguishes between "the little mortal man who dwells here and now, and the divine and universal Man who also forms a part of consciousness" (13). For him Whitman was, like Christ (and in *Days* Carpenter refers to Ann Gilchrist's exclaiming at Christ's likeness in a Whitman portrait), the very personification of that man. The wisdom that Whitman voiced was therefore ancient as well as culturally universal; it was "A new conception of Life—yet ancient as creation (since, indeed, properly speaking, there is no other)" (*TD*, 396). Carpenter believed in going back to the future, since prophets such as Whitman, who "marks a stage of human evolution not reached" (*Days*, 55), nevertheless showed "the way back to the lost Eden, or rather forward to the new Eden, of which the old was only a figure" (*Civilisation*, 35). In *Days*, Carpenter cites Whitman's own words that "[t]hese thoughts are really the thoughts of men in all ages and lands, they are not original with me" in support of his observation that "he speaks not merely as a successor of him that was crucified, but as a continuer of some world-wide and agelong tradition" (76). Carpenter came to revere India (which he visited and about which he wrote several celebrated books) as "the wisdom Land" (*TD*, 440) and felt that "gentle and venerable India [was] well pleased now at last to hear fulfilled the words of her ancient sages" (*TD*, 13). Therefore, he was obviously delighted to discover that Whitman, the modern American sage, had at least dipped into the Vedic Scriptures (*Days*, 76) and that he spoke knowledgeably of "*Sakúntula*, the Indian drama" and "of the great Hindu epic, the Ramáyana" (*Days*, 23). But whereas Whitman shared the wisdom of the ancient prophets of every culture and civilization, he was for Carpenter unique in his consciousness that his role totally transcended nation and culture, an awareness he owed to the modern technological developments that had made global intercommunications possible. "The Press, the Locomotive, the Wire" were the great enablers and sponsors of universalization and "of this new Era, with its splendours and terrors, Walt Whitman may be said to be the prophet" (*Days*, 83–84).

Carpenter was thus able to create a Whitman who was in essential ways supra-American, a universal seer, and it was to this Whitman that he related. It was a reading of Whitman that made it possible, as was noted earlier, for Carpenter to value (selectively constructed) tradition as not only the "great expressional effort of the human race" (*Angels' Wings*, 960) but as that which kept "Man" "in touch with that immense field of the Collective Consciousness of the race, which is in fact Religion, and from which the individual—however great his genius—may not stray too far" (*Angels' Wings*, 114). Furthermore, it was a reading of Whitman that made Carpenter's own writing possible as a writing distinctively his own, even as it openly acknowledged an intimate internal link with that of Whitman. Both were writing from the same aboriginal source, so to speak, which makes *Towards Democracy* an interesting case of (cultural) translation, in the sense in which Walter Benjamin famously understood translation. In "The Task of the Translator," Benjamin notes that translation possessed the power to demonstrate "the kinship of languages."[31] But he adds that such kinship does not, could not, mean "alikeness," nor is it accounted for by tracing languages back through history to the same primal root. "Kinship" rather signifies that every language's very being *as language* dumbly witnesses to that which no language can by definition possibly express: the original and eternally recurrent *desire* to speak, and to speak that which is fundamentally and everlastingly true: "If there is such a thing as a language of truth, the tensionless and even silent depository of the ultimate truth which all thought strives for, then this language of truth is—the true language. . . . And this very language . . . is concealed in concentrated fashion in translation" (77). Elsewhere Benjamin identifies this unspoken and unspeakable ur-speaking as the "expressionless and creative Word, that which is meant in all languages" (80). Hence for any translation to aim at "fidelity" to the source text is to attempt that which is philosophically mistaken as well as practically impossible. Rooted in Jewish mysticism, Benjamin's theory of translation has its much cruder equivalent in that secularized version of the Pentecostal experience that one finds in "Towards Democracy" in the passage that, appropriately enough, immediately follows the one in which Whitman is named:

> Words unspoken, yet wafted over all lands, through all times, eternal; no more mine than yours—I give them again, to the wide embracing Air.
> Haply a little breath for you to breathe—to enter, scarcely perceived, into your body—a little time to dwell, transforming, within you.
> Haply mementos, indications, broken halves of ancient changeless Symbols, eternal possessions, treasures incorruptible,
> Of Love which changes not—to be duly presented again—the broken halves to be joined. (*TD*, 95)

There is, therefore, a sense in which for Edward Carpenter *Leaves of Grass* and *Towards Democracy* are examples of Pentecostal utterance; both are linked not through alikeness but through "kinship," because both spring from the same "root": the primal desire to speak the single word of universal truth.

In his endnote to *Towards Democracy*, Carpenter admits that *Leaves of Grass* had changed his life: "I find it difficult to imagine what my life would have been without it" (518). Every word and line in his book bears witness to that truth. And yet, as Carpenter goes on to say, in discussing the form of his poetry, "I did not adopt it *because* it was an approximation to the form of 'Leaves of Grass.' Whatever resemblance there may be between the rhythm, style, thoughts, constructions etc. of the two books, must I think be set down to a deeper similarity of emotional atmosphere and intension in the two authors" (518). This form of phrasing makes it perfectly clear that the "intentions" of Carpenter and Whitman were "akin" (in Benjamin's sense) and yet not identical. Carpenter then proceeds to emphasize the marked difference in temperament between himself and Whitman, and does so primarily by offering images from nature, representing Whitman as elemental, earthy, rocky, whereas "'Towards Democracy' has a milder radiance, as of the moon compared with the sun—allowing you to glimpse the stars behind. Tender and meditative, less resolute and altogether less massive, it has the quality of the fluid and yielding air rather than of the solid and uncompromising earth" (519).

These images work to construct Whitman as, in terms of conventional gender stereotyping, masculine and Carpenter as feminine. And as such they may illuminatingly be read in the light of Carpenter's interest in Karl Ulrich's notion of the "Uranian" personality, an evolutionarily advanced being in whom stereotypically "masculine" (body) and "feminine" (soul) characteristics were combined. The "Child of Uranus" is hymned in *Towards Democracy* as a lord whose second coming is awaited, and also imagined as "wanderer down all times . . . outcast and misunderstood of men." "With man's strength to perform, and pride to suffer, without sign, / And feminine sensitiveness to the last fibre of being," he is "twice-born" and a "song of heaven," and awaits the day when "thy form in glory clad shall reappear" (*TD*, 410–411). In *Days with Walt Whitman*, Carpenter carefully constructs a Uranian image of Whitman, representing him as sensitive to women and tender with children but also as formidably craggy, precipitous, forbidding, hawklike, and so on; and he makes these "masculine" characteristics predominate. In other words, for Carpenter, Whitman was a Uranian in whom the "masculine" side predominated and Carpenter was the Uranian in whom the "feminine" side predominated. The truth, of course, may have been somewhat different—certainly Carpenter's presentation of himself as yieldingly "feminine" does not fully accord with the description of friends, who testified to his capacity for brusqueness and periods of frostily authoritative distance.[32] But such antithetical constructions of self and other were particularly important to Carpenter in relation to Whitman as a means of establishing a meaningful "working relationship" with the American. And moreover, inscribed in such gendered stereotypical distinctions were national stereotypes of the kind Henry James was at that time ingeniously exploiting in his fiction—of the brash American and the more cultured, sensitive, subtle European. This, again, was a distinction that enabled Carpenter to mark a social difference, and a psychic distance, from the powerful poetic personality that had so indelibly marked his own and so irrevocably changed his life.

And these strategies did work. *Towards Democracy* possesses none of Whitman's genius, but it is not a negligible text, nor is it a pallidly derivative one. It deserves serious attention. Not only is it a book of historic importance in its own right, a book that reached the hands of those workers that Whitman's *Leaves of Grass* very rarely reached (to its author's lasting chagrin), and that in the process genuinely changed proletarian lives. It is also noteworthy as a collection of poetic experiments, a handful, at least, of which are genuine poetic achievements. And achievements on Carpenter's own separate, distinctive terms. This was very well understood by a reviewer in the important reformist-radical journal of the late nineteenth and early twentieth century, *The New Age*—a periodical that, as the next chapter will show, significantly influenced the development of D. H. Lawrence and other writers:

> Mr Edward Carpenter holds a unique place in English letters. At once he is our great democratic poet, the singer of revolutionary ideals, a prophet of the days that are to be and a brilliant satirist of modern British civilization. . . . [T]here is no one in England that stands nearer to Walt Whitman, the virile American, and to Tolstoy, "the great mujik," than Edward Carpenter; and no one of living writers in England has exercised greater and more lasting influence on the men and women of his generation than the author of "Towards Democracy."[33]

In coupling Carpenter not only with Whitman but also with Tolstoy, the reviewer at least demonstrates an understanding of the plural contexts to which Carpenter's life, work, and books in fact belonged, and thus avoids narrowing him condescendingly down to an "English Whitman." He deserves better than that, as he deserves to be treated with proper respect and close attention by Whitman scholars and, indeed, by any committed reader of late Victorian poetry.

Eight. Lawrence's Whitman

"Whitman, the great poet, has meant so much to me. Whitman, the one man breaking a way ahead. Whitman, the one pioneer. And only Whitman. No English pioneers, no French." The truth of Lawrence's admission in *Studies in Classic American Literature* (1923) has been confirmed by many scholars. In his essay "Lawrence's Whitman," George Y. Traill even concluded that Whitman was "Lawrencian" to the core, "so Lawrencian, I suggest, that for [him] to admit the depth of [Whitman's] influence he would be forced to deny a large part of his own originality, to see himself as a disciple, an interpreter, derivative."[1] Hence, Traill argues, Lawrence imputed to Whitman phantom weaknesses, since to have read him fully, honestly, and accurately Lawrence would have to face up to his own enormous debts to his American predecessor. While hesitating to go so far, Richard Swigg saw Lawrence's interpretation of classic American writers as closely interwoven with his own writings, from interpretative essays such as *Study of Thomas Hardy* to creative work such as *Women in Love*. In the caustic tone of the published *Studies*, Swigg found no "flowing ease of humour," only scourging passages of ridicule, "the effort of a man attempting a purgative, confessional laugh at himself," if only by proxy, as he attacks "dreamy, idealist husbands."[2] His effort to stop "putting a phantom wholeness around experience" is begun with the Whitman essay and is completed with the writing of *Kangaroo* (362). Lawrence's "poetry and his aesthetics owe much to Whitman," agrees Émile Delavenay, but he proceeds to qualify the remark: "The influence of the great American . . . is often indistinguishable from that of his English disciple Carpenter."[3]

Only two of Lawrence's essays on Whitman were known to Traill, Swigg, and Delavenay. But the publication in 2003 of the definitive Cambridge edition of *Studies in Classic American Literature* has, for the very first time, made available to scholars four of the five versions of the essays on Whitman that Lawrence is known to have written.[4] Completing this body of writing is Lawrence's important letter to Henry Savage in 1913, his essay on "Democracy" of 1919, and "The Poetry of the Present," Lawrence's introduction to the American edition of *New Poems* (1918).

Since Mark Kinkead-Weekes had access to all of these materials when completing the second volume in the authoritative, three-volume, multiauthored Cambridge biography of Lawrence, his discussion, in conjunction with the outstanding introduction and notes to the recent Cambridge edition of *Studies*, provides us with an incomparable wealth of understanding of the personal, social, political, and economic contexts of Lawrence's writings on Whitman. It is, in particular, salutary to be reminded of the impact of financial concerns on his whole method of working. Repeated revision of the essays finally published as *Studies* (1923) was dictated, in no small part, by his concern to escape prosecution (on the grounds of obscenity), to satisfy publishers, and to find a substantial paying readership. Moreover, in style as well as in content, *Studies* in its final form bears the marks of Lawrence's (in some ways disillusioning and embittering) exposures to America—an America he had not visited when first he began work on the book. The streetwise aggressiveness of the essay on Whitman in its final form is in part Lawrence attempting to write in the kind of terse, hard-hitting style he believed American readers preferred.

Yet, when all is said and done, Lawrence's writings on Whitman bear, from beginning to end, the lurid stigmata of a personal, self-wounding obsession. That Lawrence's Whitman is just that—a Whitman created in Lawrence's own singular image, as an expression of compelling psychic needs—is self-evident. Equally significant, but less widely appreciated, are the ways in which Lawrence constructed Whitman not only out of the materials of his own culture but in conversation with those images of Whitman already so well established in that culture as to be subtly influential within it. Scholars have been unable to determine when exactly Lawrence first encountered *Leaves of Grass*, for the significant reason that Whitman's poetry permeated the thinking of several of the intellectual circles in which the young Lawrence moved. It is therefore as impossible to pin down the instant of recognition as it would have been impossible at the time for Lawrence long to have remained ignorant of Whitman's existence. Thus, while the quotations from his work in *The White Peacock* (1911) provide the first extensive textual evidence of his acquaintance with the poetry, a letter to Jessie Chambers in 1908 (when he was twenty-three) already reveals a familiarity with "I saw in Louisiana" (*Studies*, xxvi). As for the extensive discussion of Whitman in the letter to Henry Savage (December 22, 1913), not only does it establish the main terms of Lawrence's preoccupation for the next ten years, it also shows him already weaving personal and cultural elements into the complex "reactive" image of Whitman he then proceeded to develop. After exclaiming at the "rumness" of Savage's sudden addiction to Whitman, he warns against being taken in by the doctrine that "all men are brothers":

> Don't let yourself in for a terrific chagrin. But I'm glad you've discovered Humanity: it is fearfully nice to feel it round one. If you read my poetry—especially the earlier stuff which was published in the *English Review*, and isn't in the book of poems, you would see how much it has meant to me.[5]

There, at the very outset of Lawrence's protracted mental wrestlings with Whitman, it is established that he intends to read against the grain not only of Whitman's poetry but also of his own earlier poetry in the Whitman vein.

But to pin down the English cultural sources of Lawrence's early reading of Whitman is inevitably as impossible a task as exactly to identify the date and origin of his first awareness of the American poet. However, one of the leading literary-political journals of the first decade of the twentieth century was *The New Age*, a journal Lawrence is known to have read regularly, and to which he subscribed in 1908–1909. During that decade, mention of Whitman was frequent in the journal's pages, and regardless of whatever precise influence—if any—such discussions had on the young Lawrence's thinking, they are of considerable value in themselves, as evidence (never hitherto examined) of the views of Whitman prevailing in progressive intellectual circles at the time.

Until May 2, 1907, *The New Age* was the organ of nineteenth-century radicalism, and thus of the progressive, reforming wing of the powerful Liberal Party. From that date onward, under the new editorship of A. R. Orage and Holbrook Jackson (who left in 1908), it metamorphosed into the "cultural weekly" of the intellectual wing of a politically emergent Socialist movement destined to eclipse liberalism over the coming decades.[6] Whitman intriguingly continued to serve as an important point of reference for contributors to the journal both before and after that revolutionary change. The Liberal "Whitman" differed profoundly from the Socialist "Whitman," however, thus offering valuable insight into the way his work was viewed from different points on the ideological spectrum of progressive thinking during the first decade of the twentieth century.

Before 1907, *The New Age* advertised itself as a "Democratic Review," pledged to the promotion of such virtues as Human Brotherhood, Political Liberty, and Economic Justice (Nov. 16, 1900, 591). The figures most revered by it included William Cobden, Michael Davitt, William Lloyd Garrison, John Ruskin, Leo Tolstoy, and John Greenleaf Whittier, and the origins of its prevailing ideology in what its socialist enemies dubbed the "Manchester" school of economics is as evident as is its indebtedness to the longstanding nineteenth-century rationalist tradition of a robust individualism with a social conscience. Hostile to the triumphant globalism of international capitalism in its assertively nationalist and imperialist late nineteenth-century form, *The New Age* fiercely opposes the Boer War; and the move by the great Western powers to crush the Boxer Rebellion is seen as a naked attempt to force the Chinese, at the point of a bayonet, to keep their ports open for the lucrative opium trade. The journal therefore repeatedly looks elsewhere for alternative models of modern "democracy." But although contributors sometimes even advocate the formation of a Liberal-Socialist alliance, in the light of the Liberal Party's domination by conservative pro-Boer imperialists, such sporadic outbreaks of sympathy with Socialists is always offset by the kind of deep mistrust that caused one reviewer to prefer the anarchist Kropotkin's *Memoirs* to the "squabblings of the British Labour Movement." This was not least because the Russian's work seemed to him close in spirit to "Whitman's 'Whoso touches this book, touches a Man'" (Feb. 7, 1907). Whitman is thus implicitly associated with an ideology in which a liberated, libertarian individualism is seen as happily resulting in spontaneous social cooperation. Elsewhere, another reviewer objects to Newell Dwight Hills's *Great Books as Life-Teachers*, because the author "hurls" Lowell, Longfellow, and Emerson at his reader as great American seers but omits mention of Whitman (May 10, 1900, 283). Another review, this time of a book by Edward Carpenter, significantly describes him not as a proto-Socialist but as "our great democratic poet, the singer of revolutionary ideals, a prophet of the days that are to be." The review then adds that "there is no one in England that stands nearer to Walt Whitman, the virile American, and to Tolstoy, 'the great mujik,' than Edward Carpenter" (May 31, 1900, 241). There is a certain irony, of course, in this interpretation not only of Whitman but of *Carpenter's* Whitman as the very model of stereotypically desirable masculinity, but such an image was a commonplace of mainstream cultural thinking in the period, and is here clearly linked to a Liberal's admiration for the American's robust self-reliance. The invocation of Whitman when some notion of "democracy"—a very heatedly contested term at this time—is being advanced, is another recurrent feature, and needs to be borne in mind in view of Lawrence's later centering of his own important essay on "Democracy" on Whitman's poetry.

The casual, passing mention of Whitman in instances such as these is intriguing testimony to his ubiquitous, and therefore paradoxically elusive, presence in intellectual discussions of this period, but of different interest are those articles in the Liberal *New Age* specifically devoted to considerations of the poet's work. One such is the substantial review by "J. C." of Bliss Perry's *Walt Whitman: His Life and Work*. "J. C." prefers this new study to recent ones by Binns and Carpenter, partly on the grounds that it "takes Whitman's greatness for granted. . . . We are no longer concerned to prove Whitman a super-man; his character is too big, his gifts are too magnificent" (Nov. 29, 1906, 134). But precisely because "the glamor and rapture of the days when the book was first made known to us are departed," the reviewer feels Whitman is now ripe for discriminating criticism, recognizing the unevenness of his writing and unafraid to "admit some of it dull." And the review concludes with a quotation from "By Blue Ontario's Shore," followed by advice: "When there is any heart failing for democracy, let the reader turn to *Leaves of Grass* . . ." Again, then, radical liberalism displays a tendency to produce Whitman as evidence of the progressiveness of its own enlightened agenda to establish a socially reformed but still essentially individual-centered version of British "Democracy."

In April 1907, a bare month before the Socialist takeover, *The New Age* again featured Whitman, and again—but for the last time—he appeared in the guise of a hero of reform liberalism, with its dream of rescuing "democracy" from the clutches of a reactionary international capitalism: "The forces which make for the future and for the universal as they gathered together in the nineteenth century found no greater expression than in the life of Walt Whitman, the greatest Democrat, the tenderest lover that the Earth he so much loved ever produced" (April 4, 1907, 424). There follows an ethereal poetic effusion on these themes addressed to Whitman by Amy A. Locke. It begins with an invocation: "Far soaring Spirit, thou dost stand / Gazing upon the Earth, watching the round / Of all the mighty spheres, hearing the sound / Of heavenly melodies, as the blest spirit band / Takes up the lark's sweet Song." Whitman is evidently being seen through the lens of Shelley—one of the libertarian poetic heroes of late nineteenth-century radicalism. The second stanza envisions Whitman as there "by my side— / Lover of lovers, comrade of comrades." It then modulates gracefully into melancholy by imagining him as "Lying entranced beneath the darkening shades / Of night as daylight slowly fades / From the horizon—like a retreating tide," before it ends on an upbeat note:

At other times thou treadest lovingly
The busy thoroughfares of restless city life,
Or marchest with the regiments lustily
To soothe with tender hands those wounded in the strife,
Of battle, staying beside them as their spirits flee.
Walt Whitman, in thy breath we feel our life! (April 4, 1907, 424)

By this point, Shelley seems to have given way to the Matthew Arnold of "The Scholar Gipsy," that great nineteenth-century poem of melancholy protest, as Lionel Trilling has observed, against the remorseless advance to power of "the manufacturing Whigs," with their callously selfish version of the ideology of economic individualism.[7] Whitman is thus made to seem the heir to a great English tradition of writers who emphasized the sense of social obligation implicit in any civilized economic, social, or political assertion of individual interest. It is a classic expression of the ideology of reforming liberalism.

On May 2, 1907, *The New Age* underwent a change of editors, and was duly advertised henceforth as being *An Independent Socialist Review of Politics, Literature and Art.* From May 16, it was incorporated with *The Labor Record*, and with the change of ideological allegiance came a change of heroes. Out went Cobden, Davitt, and company and in came Arnold Bennett, Edward Carpenter, G. K. Chesterton, George Bernard Shaw, and H. G. Wells. While the very first issue featured an editorial on socialism, it was not until the autumn that the journal offered a comprehensive eight-part account (October 3rd–November 21st) of the highly distinctive version of the Socialist vision animating the thinking of A. R. Orage, the most influential of its two new editors. Orage declared a belief in a "solidarity of souls." Nevertheless, a passionate commitment to the individual was, he insisted, the necessary precondition of a belief in the inherently social nature of individual being. The "Individualism" of both liberalism and conservatism, he explained, was "merely a dark shadow of the real individuality": "True individuality is not a claim to possess but a claim to give. Being itself complete as a ripe fruit is it demands no more than to be allowed to scatter itself" (October 17, 393). Orage here touches on an issue of much concern to Lawrence, and one expressed through his aggressively critical engagements with Whitman's model of social democracy. And indeed Whitman is actually mentioned by Orage in the third part of his disquisition. It is Carpenter, Shaw, Whitman, and Shelley, he explains, who have convinced him of the inadequacies of a merely economic conception of socialism. This serves in his view only to perpetuate "those radical [in the discredited nineteenth-century Liberal sense], time-dishonoured, and most damnable beliefs . . . that the individual belongs to himself alone" (October 17, 393).

Knowing his views were very much at odds with the "mainstream" Labourite socialism of his time, Orage preempts criticism from that quarter in the next issue by defiantly declaring "we are proud of being Utopians. . . . Every good Socialist is a Utopian!"—a declaration with which Lawrence, a perversely unorthodox Socialist and incorrigible utopian, would surely come to agree (Oct. 24). Orage's assertion in the next issue follows naturally on from this. "All our institutions, without exception," he writes, "are the work primarily of imaginative people, who invented the State, the Nation, Religion, Love, Art, Business, and all the rest" (Oct. 31, 16). It is a very significant statement. It explains the coupling of the term "Socialist" with the categories "Politics, Literature, and Art" on the journal's new masthead. It also account for *The New Age*'s appeal to writers (including the young Lawrence). This was due in no small measure to its unswerving belief in the social and political centrality of the creative arts. It was thus genuinely pioneering in the way it encouraged artistic experiment by putting writers in touch with exploratory (and often controversially unorthodox) thinking in "new" disciplines such as theosophy, anthropology, and psychoanalysis.[8] The breaking down of traditional category distinctions was a central aim of an A. R. Orage who argued in an editorial of June 13, 1907 that the Independent Labour Party was admirable on "Socialist economics" but of no use on "Socialist sociology" or "Socialist aesthetics" (104).

An example of *The New Age*'s commitment to transgressive thinking can be found as early as May 23, 1907, in a review by "R. M." of Edward Carpenter's *Iolaus: An Anthology of Friendship* (55). This review begins with the observation—seriously intended but expressed with a kind of defensive facetiousness—that love is not naturally English. Rather, the reviewer claims, it is the sign of the corruption of the healthy Anglo-Saxon mind by Arthurian chivalric romance. The result is a sickly "Celtic" sentimentality—the reviewer here invoking the racially marginalizing and condescending image of the colonized but uncomfortably subordinated "Celt," a dominant image in English thinking about the Welsh and the Irish at least since the time of Matthew Arnold. "The typical British capacity is not for love at all, but for friendship," states the reviewer as he deplores "the poetic glamor thrown over sex-love in England." This has "diminished the value of our peculiar fate for friendship . . . In plain words, passion in friendship is taboo exactly to the extent to which passion is supposed to be confined to love." "One of the first instinctive moves of the Socialist spirit was the flat repudiation of sex-tyranny, and the substitution of friendship," notes the reviewer. "The dominant idea of Whitman, for example, is undeniably friendship, or what he calls camaraderie." The establishing of "a Socialist State" would therefore be possible only for those who "have realized the meaning of friendship and de-throned sex-love; this enthronement of the sex-emotion being, as it were, a kind of free republicanism in matters of the affections." This is why Carpenter's "ideas of friendship apart from sex . . . appears to me of . . . importance. The politicians may make Socialism; but such a spirit as Carpenter's is required to make Socialists."

The discussion is a suggestive one. In reminding us that Carpenter's attempts to advocate an "Uranian" version of gay identity (see chapter 7) could be comfortably (mis)interpreted, even by his more orthodox left-wing contemporaries as merely an argument in favor of asexual friendship, and in showing us how Whitman's poetry could be understood by "straight" Socialists in the same disarming terms, it also alerts us to the fact that it was not only homosexuals and believers in the "New Woman" who were at this time mounting an attack on that lynchpin of bourgeois Victorian society, the family. In openly questioning the sufficiency for men of heterosexual love, implying it might need to be complemented and completed by the experience of male-male friendship, the review anticipates the issues covertly raised by Lawrence in the very title *Women in Love* and overtly addressed in the body of that extraordinary novel. The conventional tone and familiar discourse of the discussion reminds us that its concept of what Melville had called "the paradise of bachelors" is in many ways neither modern nor modernist in character but is rather a natural consequence of male Victorian society's infatuation with establishment fraternities, from all-male dining clubs, through the regiments of the all-conquering British armies, to the best of all gentleman's clubs, the Houses of Parliament. And finally, we are alerted to the fact that by the Edwardian age a sophisticated understanding had already developed, particularly among Socialists, of the ways in which the family functioned as the key socioeconomic unit of the industrial capitalist order to which many of them were implacably opposed.

Lawrence's dissatisfaction with the family unit is evident in all his writing. It is linked both to his obsessive interest in what it meant to be a "man" (and a "woman") in his time, and to his concern to redefine "relationship" in ways that recognized how, in interconnecting intimately *as* two who remained essentially distinct and separate individuals, a couple actually came to constitute a third, oxymoronic, being. Sexuality and sexual identity were, for Lawrence, inescapably implicated, at very root, in these and related issues, and homosexuality was for him a particularly fraught and problematic area in this connection. Therefore, bearing in mind the ways in which Whitman had, not least through the ministrations of Edward Carpenter, Havelock Ellis, and others, assumed considerable significance for those most concerned to reconfigure male sexuality, it is reasonable to suppose Lawrence's complex view of his sexual signification was developed, at least in part, in counterpoint with their version of Whitman's significance.

Homosexual identity was, to an important extent, associated by Lawrence with leading figures in those social groups he most loathed and despised, namely the Bloomsbury set and the Cambridge coterie that included Keynes, Strachey, and E. M. Forster. The latter's diaries for 1907 record that he had recently read the work of Carpenter and Whitman (whom he later described as "a grand old man"[9]) with considerable interest.[10] Despite briefly seeming to make enthusiastic common cause with Forster on a number of fronts when they actually met in early 1915, Lawrence took the homosexual novelist's abstinence from sex as evidence of a deep creative sterility, a fear of entering into a soul-altering encounter with another.[11] Lawrence further suspected that sexually active homosexuals suffered from the same psycho-spiritual disease, since they treated partners as no more than convenient means of sexual gratification. Similarly, he was to assert that "Ego-bound women are often lesbian, / perhaps always. / Perhaps the ego-bound can only love their own kind, / if they can love at all."[12] Homosexuals were therefore inherently incapable of what Charles Olson was later to call "forwarding," an openness to new, potentially self-transfiguring encounters with others, evidence of which Lawrence so welcomed in the poetry of "his" Whitman. He found late expression for this in "Sex and Trust," a poem from *Pansies*:

> If you want to have sex, you've got to trust
> at the core of your heart, the other creature.
> The other creature, the other creature
> not merely the personal upstart;
> but the creature there, that has come to meet you
> trust it you must, you must
> or the experience amounts to nothing,
> mere evacuation-lust. (466)

At best capable of "mere evacuation-lust," a homosexual like Forster, Lawrence concluded, "*does not believe that any beauty or any divine utterance is any good any more*" (Kinkead-Weekes, 192). This observation is interesting, bearing in mind that only a few years earlier Forster had published "The Beauty of Life," an essay centering on Whitman.[13] There, while on the one hand praising Whitman for the omnivorous inclusiveness of his affirmations, Forster confesses on the other hand that "We may follow [such a] whole-hogger at moments, and no doubt it is our fault and not his when we don't follow him; but we cannot follow him always." Forster then proceeds to settle instead for "[b]eauty in scraps. It may seem a little thing after the comprehensive ecstasies of Whitman, but it is certain." There is poignancy to such a conclusion, resonant as it is with Forster's palpable wish that he possessed Whitman's reckless faith in the possibilities of life. But it is precisely the kind of (humane) caution evidenced here that Lawrence the passionate "whole-hogger" came so to despise and to associate with the homosexual "character." "His" Whitman therefore included very pointed homage to those qualities Forster, although wistfully admiring, was never willing to embrace.[14]

"Poetry of the Present," the introduction to the American edition of *New Poems* (1918), is one of the pieces in which Lawrence gives most compelling expression to this aspect of his vision. There he famously speaks of

> the unrestful, ungraspable poetry of the sheer present, poetry whose very permanency lies in its wind-like transit. Whitman's is the best poetry of this kind. . . . The clue to all his utterance lies in the sheer appreciation of the instant moment, life surging itself into utterance at its very well-head. . . . The quivering, nimble hour of the present, this is the quick of Time. This is the immanence. The quick of the universe is the *pulsating, carnal self*, mysterious and palpable. . . . Because Whitman put this into his poetry, we fear him and respect him so profoundly. (*Poems*, 183–184)

The passage is an invitation to scholars to investigate the relationship of Lawrence's poetry to that of Whitman. But that subject is as complex as it is fascinating, and must therefore be recognized as beyond the scope of the present chapter. Instead, it is important to note how echoes both of Forster's reading of Whitman and of Lawrence's own negative verdict on that reading are to be heard in the final sentence of the passage. Equally, the whole passage brings to mind a discussion in *The New Age* at the time when its pages were also full of discussions of the philosophy of William James and of Henri Bergson, both of whom were interested in the concept of "flux" (a recurrent term in Lawrence's passage) and the élan vital (Lawrence's "quick of the universe"). The dancing of "Madame Magdeleine" is the subject of a review by W. R. Tittston:

[I]n her tragic movements there is a rhythm not of the music—a big rhythm, with irregular cadences, to be fitted to no formal rule. You will find its parallel in the poetry of Whitman, with whom in many other ways her art has much in common.

And here I note a point of comparison with Isadora Duncan. The rhythm of Isadora is lyric, it runs, the rhythm of Whitman, of the Magdeleine, is epic, it strides, it grows. . . . [O]ne is perplexed to find in each instant's pose a something eternal, of the rock, and yet to find it perpetually changing with the swiftness of smoke windblown. (April 22, 1907, 527)

This kind of response to Whitman's poetry anticipates that of a Lawrence who found in his free verse "the insurgent naked throb of the instant moment . . . [it] has its own *nature*, that it is neither star nor pearl, but instantaneous like plasm. . . . It does not want to get anywhere. It just takes place" (185). Even better, perhaps, is the marvelous passage from the conclusion of the "Intermediate" Whitman essay (1919). Speaking of "Out of the Cradle" and "When Lilacs," Lawrence writes:

There is the sheer creative gesture, moving the material world in wonderful swirls. The whole soul follows its own free, spontaneous, inexplicable course, its contractions and pulsations dictated from nowhere save from the creative quick itself. . . . This is the greatest poetry. (*Studies*, 369)

"All this should have come as a preface to *Look! We Have Come Through*," writes Lawrence at the end of his essay on "Poetry of the Present," and indeed it is in that remarkable volume, along with *Birds, Beasts and Flowers* and *Pansies*, that he was most memorably able to "translate" Whitmanesque free verse into his own "original" idiom. This was one sign of his genius, not least because so many of Whitman's admirers who attempted this ended up writing something very different, and incomparably inferior. One such was Whitman's important English biographer, Henry Binns, who in 1908 published *The Good Companions*, a volume that led F. S. Flint to conclude in *The New Age* that "Mr Binns is rather created than a creator: he is a disciple of Walt Whitman." Unwilling, however, to damn Binns entirely with such faint praise, Flint later repents of suggesting "that Mr Binns is only a reflection of the Good Grey Poet," and claims some of his prose-poetry "enter[s] the brain like a drench of perfume." As proof, he quotes a passage from "Envoi":

Words were worth nothing if words could say all; ever behind our singing is the silence out of which it broke.
So too, behind this little book with its words of franchise, my enfranchisement remains untold.
The trees swing in the gale and make music in it; but in the Earth abiding they keep their silence.
So for you, beloved, abiding in your love, my heart keeps silence while I sing.
(August 15, 1908)

If this passage is not evidence enough for a modern reader of Binns's unconscious claim to be a failed Whitmanian, then the following, quoted in a prospectus for *The Good Companions* in the March 21, 1907, issue of *The New Age*, would appear to clinch the matter:

I carry an Unknown Voyager whose errand I know not, save that he crieth to me continually as I do, "have faith, little brother! Have faith!"
Flower-like becomes the body that understands, the flesh wherein He awakens.

But the case is not as simple and certain as it here seems. Binns may not be a good poet, but his *The Good Companions* is a truly fascinating, and hitherto wholly unexplored, example of English Whitmanian writing.[15] Not only its prose poetry but its basic philosophy is entirely, and entirely consciously, Whitmanesque, as is evident from its dismissal of books in favor of nature (10); its celebration of life and death as part of a single natural process; its anthem to democracy (31); its celebration of (primarily male) "fellowship," and comradeship (passim); its celebration of "the living labor of true men and women, comrades" (43); its valorization of "Love's Body" (58ff); its belief in a sustaining superior consciousness; and a myriad other features. Many of Binns's phrases carry with them vague echoes of passages from *Leaves of Grass* ("So that my hand may only touch thine for support and courage as a comrade's should" [78]), and, yes indeed, grass itself duly figures as an important trope for the wonderfully indomitable, rank profusion of the ordinary: "I was seeking a rare flower, and ever dissatisfied; but now the mere grass itself—the mere wonderful innumerable living blades, the tall jointed stems and flowery spears, the grass of the field—is my joy all the day long" (85). The very last section of the book is duly entitled "Vista." And then, to cap it all, in the section/chapter "Love's Body," after proclaiming "I saw the Great Fellowship—the fellowship of Divine People—how it impassions those strong shining ones," Binns pays open homage to Whitman, in a millenarian passage that deserves to be quoted in full, as it is hitherto unknown:

> Then I remembered how Walt Whitman, when his people was responding to war's wild challenge, his soul responding also, made oath and answer for himself in solemn words, to build his body up into an altar that should sustain that changeless fire.
>
> And now—his outer body broken, shattered, dead—the inner, one and constant—I see him stand, holding his beacon high above the clouds of Time, not for America alone, but as a sign to every nation:—a man responsive to Love's lightest breath, a man for Love's most fierce demand, patient, enduring.
>
> He heralds the new day when comradeship shall be established among men, and Man the Divine Being, shall awake in them and rule.
>
> When, beholding Love no longer as though bound and blinded amid the jealousies and lusts of lovers, but as He truly is, we shall misunderstand our passion no more, but to us it will be sacred, reverent, immortal, not to be refused.
>
> Nor shall we miss any longer the wondrous uses of the bodies of His dwelling, the symbols of His mystery, but enter through them into His delight. (58–59)

There is much here of relevance to an understanding of how Lawrence, also a prophet of "Love's Body," may have been engaging as much with English Whitmanians as with Whitman himself in his historic essay in *Studies*. But also interesting is Binns's emphasis (redolent, of course, of scripture) on Whitman's significance "not for America alone, but as a sign to every nation." Because Binns's significance lies not in his being a mere pale imitation of Whitman but in his being, like Carpenter, a conscious adaptor, or transposer, of Whitman to English cultural conditions. The Quaker Binns was all the more conscious of the need thus to translate Whitman as he himself was a committed anti-Marxist utopian Socialist, who could write, in *The Great Companions*, "For the red flag is flying, the pass-words are chosen, the revolution has commenced" (43). And in one of the eloquent, and fascinating, passages in his text, Binns seems deliberately to be "translating" (and conflating) key passages and images from both "When Lilacs" and "Out of the Cradle" into English terms, because when he imagines viewing the "beloved" in "Love's mirror," he writes:

> I sat in my porchway, with the odours of the night and the body of the earth fragrant anew from the warm rain, stealing thro' all my senses to let loose the soul within me; and all about, the windy sound of the dark trees.
>
> And as I sat there, listening to the divine bird, the hazel-haunting nightingale, whose song bubbled up in quick jets out of the joyous earth, my soul at large, I knew it was not only to his mate upon the nest in the thick leaves and dark he sang, pouring that music forth, but yet without his mate there close beside him he would not sing at all.

> O bird and brother, so possessed by song that spasm on spasm break the brave notes forth—the untameable demonic passion of you and of the trees and of the earth's wild heart breaking up through your little pulsing throat. (73)

And in the "warbling" of his "little brown brother," lost in "ecstasy," Binns hears the certain note of "Life's mystic meaning."

That a writer of a distinctively English kind of Whitmanesque free verse should appeal to some of *The New Age*'s readers is not, perhaps, so surprising considering the anti-American prejudice regularly voiced in the paper, most particularly by the editors. President Theodore Roosevelt may be sporadically recognized as a good president, but even he is scoffed at as "Teddy the Rough-Rider— [who] would enhance his popularity by punching a prize-fighter's head as surely as he would lose it by telling the American people what he must think of their political capacity" (January 25, 1908, 243). "America deserves nothing but the execration of civilisation for permitting such horrors as lynching and convict-leasing in its own land," trumpets an editorial on August 22, 1908, adding "what has America done for civilisation, or what is she doing?" (322). An essay on the "American Scene" (October 24, 1907) paints a very hostile picture of American contemporary capitalism and economic individualism. From this it concludes that the United States is a socially backward country, in spite of such recent successes as the *Lusitania*'s reducing the transatlantic run to fewer than five days and Marconi's wireless telegraphy link between Cape Breton and Clifden, County Galway. "Unconstrained competition in the commercial sphere" has turned "the 'land of liberty' . . . into the land of liberty for property and capital, and of economic servitude for the labor dependent on them." But redemption from "a gross kind of individualism" is at hand, in the form of the Socialist revolution of which Upton Sinclair's novel *The Jungle* is the most promising augury. And in an essay on "American Literature" in *The New Age* (November 19, 1908), Sinclair duly declared that "Whitman himself . . . would if he were alive today, be stumping the country for the Socialist ticket; nearly all his followers are doing it" (69).

While he could never have shared such a Socialist dream, Lawrence did share *The New Age*'s view of the United States as ripe for a violent revolution. This is the assumption on which the whole of *Studies in Classic American Literature* is based, from its inception in 1917. It is also given powerful expression in "The Evening Land" (289). America is there seen as constituting "the grave of mingling," since no one realizes "that love should be intense, individual / Not . . . this philanthropy and benevolence on other people's behalf" (291). Lawrence is at once "half-cajoled" by this seductive United States and yet "I am so terrified, America, / Of the iron click of your human contact. / And after this / The winding-sheet of your self-less ideal love. / Boundless love / Like a poison gas" (291). But lurking in the undergrowth of this continent, and in the unconscious of its psyche, is the figure that will bring release and redemption not just to Americans but to the whole white race:

> Nascent American
> Demonish, lurking among the undergrowth
> Of many-stemmed machines and chimneys that smoke like pine-trees,
>
> Dark, elvish,
> Modern, unissued, uncanny America,
> Your nascent demon people
> Lurking among the deeps of your industrial thicket
> Allure me till I am beside myself,
> A nympholepht,
>
> "These States!" as Whitman said,
> Whatever he meant. (293)

What Whitman "meant" was a question that preoccupied Lawrence for the best part of a decade, and the resulting body of work leaves us with the mirroring question: "What was it, then, that Whitman 'meant' to D. H. Lawrence?" So complex in its implications is such a question, it would take a whole book even to begin to answer it. However, within the limiting terms of the present discussion, it might be reasonable to suggest that for him, in some small yet significant part, Whitman "meant" England, in the sense that his Whitman was to some extent constructed as a reaction against those images of Whitman that, as brief examination of *The New Age* has shown, had deeply embedded themselves in English culture by the first decade of the twentieth century. To read Lawrence's writings on Whitman in this way will undoubtedly be severely limiting, but may be nonetheless useful for that.

In some ways, reaction may be said to function as an organizing principle, as well as a rhetorical strategy, in *Studies in Classic American Literature.* As Lawrence's biographer, Mark Kinkead-Weekes, has usefully explained, reaction (negation, polarization, contrariety, dialectic) was very actively interesting Lawrence by the summer of 1915, not least because of his readings in Heracleitus, Nietzsche, and Blake (371ff). (The latter two were also regularly featured in *The New Age.*) "Without contraries is no progression," Blake had famously written, and such aphoristic formulations of the principle of contrariety proved deeply seductive to a Lawrence whose nature was part irrepressibly contrary, as well as edgily, not to say violently, combative. This side of his nature, powering a dialectical style of writing, is evident in virtually everything he writes about Whitman, as indeed it is throughout all the several versions of *Studies in Classic American Literature*. Moreover, it is *meant* to be evident. So, for instance, the final (1923) version opens with the aggressive assertion, "We like to think of the old-fashioned American classics as children's books. Just childishness, on our part." Reference is then specifically made at several points in the text to Lawrence's own childish exposure to such writers. His father first put "Old Daddy Franklin's" (20) book in his hand, and the whole discussion at this point is infused with a spirit of contrariety derived from Blake's *Marriage of Heaven and Hell*. So Lawrence duly counters Franklin's moral maxims with diabolic proverbs of his own invention: "TEMPERANCE: Eat and carouse with Bacchus, or munch dry bread with Jesus, but don't sit down without one of the gods" (27). Elsewhere in the 1923 edition, Lawrence recalls his childhood reading of Cooper, while his discussion of Crèvecoeur plays off such dreams of utopian community as seduced not only by the gullible transcendentalists but also by the Lawrence of the "Rannanim" period. As for the first version of *Studies* (1918–1919), it begins by observing, "It is natural that we should regard American literature as a small branch or province of English literature" (167), thus preparing the way for Lawrence to argue reactively for the irreduceably American, foreign character of the literature if properly read. Similarly, the earliest surviving Whitman essay (1919) opens reactively with an indication that its argument will run counter to the belief of "many really thoughtful men, in Europe, . . . that he is the greatest of modern humbugs" (358). Reflective as it may be of the views of people in those circles in which Lawrence had moved from 1913 onward, this assertion conveniently overlooks the strong parallel current of pro-Whitman opinion to which the younger Lawrence had been regularly exposed. His writings on Whitman draw extensively on these opinions (such as that the American was a "prophet") even as Lawrence reacts strongly against the ways in which they had been formulated. And central to his reformulation is the consciously paradoxical view ("this is the age of paradoxes") that Whitman was paradoxically *both* humbug and prophet (358).

The reactive principle is again evidenced in Lawrence's governing belief, as a critic: "Never trust the artist, trust the tale." The assumption here is that "[a]n artist usually intellectualizes on top, and his dark under-consciousness goes on contradicting him beneath" (34). Although Lawrence believed this to be especially true of American artists, his phrasing of it as a universal truth necessarily implies an acceptance of it as a self-description as well. And the reactive character of *Studies* includes other similar instances of self-recognition. Thus, when Lawrence uses a snake sloughing its skin to image the process of shedding an old, constricting, false consciousness and emerging into new truth, he is implicitly characterizing a process he, as artist, was continuing to undergo; a process of which the several versions of *Studies* were themselves an expression: "The two processes go on, of course, simultaneously . . . And sometimes this immortal serpent feels very happy, feeling a new golden glow of a strangely-patterned skin envelop him and sometimes he feels very sick, as if his very entrails were being torn out of him, as he wrenches once more at his old skin, to get out of it" (57). Believing that polarization of opinion, to create a violent current or "circuit" of energy between the opposite extreme poles, was an integral part of the process of developing a new consciousness (without contraries is no progression), Lawrence evolved, through the successive versions of *Studies*, a style of writing designed to elicit strong negative reactions in his readers (especially his American readers): "[o]nly savage humour has connected us" (415). Partly a rhetorical strategy to provoke the reader, this was also, in its mature form, an attempt to tap what "takes place *beneath* the consciousness" (79)—a critical style analogous at once to the creative style Lawrence had developed through writing *The Rainbow* and *Women in Love* and to the spontaneous, impetuous "poetry of the moment" Whitman himself had so helped him capture in his poetry. "Of course I am being personal, I intend to be," he snaps in the penultimate (1922) version of the Whitman study (424).

Inscribed in Lawrence's adventuring style of critical writing, as well as in the deep structure of *Studies*, the principle of reaction also governs Lawrence's relationship to past phases of his own life and personality, and to settled features of his character in constant need of correction (his instinct to moralize, his yearning for mutuality, his attractions toward primitivism). Above all, it is seen in his oppositional response to the regnant assumptions and values of his society. It is in this latter connection that Lawrence engages with some of the images of Whitman most powerfully operative in his culture. From the evidence afforded by discussions of Whitman in *The New Age*, the English Whitmans that most concerned Lawrence could be said to include the Democratic Whitman (beloved alike of Liberals and Socialists), Comrade Whitman (the darling of Socialists and gays), the loving Whitman (attractive to more conventional mainstream progressives such as Amy Locke), Whitman the Nature Poet (also sentimentally admired by mainstream readers), and the Prophetic Whitman (acclaimed by any number of progressive movements, including the reforming democratic Liberals and the utopian Socialists). And in considering Lawrence's reactions to these different images it is important to make reference to the whole spectrum of his writings on Whitman—not only the different versions of *Studies* but also the essays on Democracy and "The Poetry of the Present."

Lawrence uses most of his writings on Whitman to give short shrift to political democracy. As his poem "True Democracy" shows, he was very well aware that the nature, and the future, of democracy was one of the commonest topics of the period (434). As for his essay on that very subject, it was completed partly as a reaction to the First World War and the mob rule that seemed to Lawrence to characterize it.[16] Moreover, it was an offshoot of the work he was doing on Whitman for inclusion in *Studies* at the time. (Lawrence even considered including it in *Studies* as a substitute for the Whitman essay, unpublishable in its earliest version since it would have unfailingly attracted prosecution.) In "Democracy" he takes as axiomatic Whitman's assertion that political democracy was founded on: "(1) the Law of the Average and (2) the Principle of Individualism, or Personalism, or Identity" (63). He then proceeds to key the entire essay to Whitman's work, even to the extent of borrowing (and sarcastically interrogating) such items of Whitman's vocabulary as "eidolons" (punningly construed by Lawrence as involving democracy's idolatry of the Average). The standardization involved in such thinking is mocked: "Now for the Average Man himself! He is five-feet-six-inches high: and therefore you, John, will take an over-size pair of trousers, reach-me-downs, and you, *François mon cher*, will take an undersize" (64). Such a statistical concept of the Average (Lawrence's mockery of it echoes Dickens's attacks in *Hard Times*) is then seen as symptomatic of a reductive, materialistic, and mechanized conception of the human, exclusive of "all Spiritual and Mystical needs" (65). By linking the treatment of man as mere unit to the controlling power of the collectivist modern state, Lawrence is able to blame the First World War on democracy. The Great War had been nothing but a nationalist orgy, a conflict between states needing to conceal their mere functionality by fostering an aggressive ideology of nationhood. Stripped of this ideological superstructure, the modern state is nothing but a political contrivance, and "Politics—what are they? Just another, extra-large commercial wrangle over buying and selling—nothing else" (67). Thus far, Lawrence could be said to have been engaging with Whitman indirectly, via progressive Liberals' notions of him as prophet of a reformed democracy in which a centralized welfare state, while still respecting private property, would supply the needs of every individual. (After all, it was the greatest of reforming Liberals, David Lloyd George, introducer of the People's

Budget, who—first as Minister for Munitions and then as Prime Minister—had served as the architect of Allied victory in the First World War.)

So much for Whitman's notions of the Average. Lawrence next turns to Individualism, Personalism, or Identity:

> Whitman insisted on raising Democracy above government, or even above public service or humanity or love of one's neighbor. Heaven knows what his Democracy is—but something as yet unattained. It is something beyond governments and even beyond Ideals. It must be beyond Ideals, because it has never yet been stated. As an idea it doesn't yet exist. Even Whitman, with all his reiteration, got no further than *hinting*: and rather bad hints, many of them. (69–70)

Such an account of Whitman's democracy is strikingly reminiscent of the version of Socialist society that A. R. Orage and other contributors had developed—and identified with Whitman—in *The New Age*. "Democracy, which is only the political device of elective institutions, has no more necessary relationship with Socialism than walking has with any given place," one contributor notes (May 2, 1907). Democracy meant not "government by the people" but "government by permission of the people." "[T]he business of a democratic government is to divine and provide for needs before they become articulate" (4). Such Socialist dissatisfaction with (established) democracy prompted Orage to observe in his opening editorial that "while Socialism has immensely gained in intensity by [workers'] advocacy of democracy or of labor, of the rights of the disinherited and the wrongs of the poor, the awakening determination of Society to transform itself will be carried out by no one of them" (May 2, 1907, 5). Orage then proceeded to the kind of vatic rhetoric Lawrence was later to satirize: "The society of the future will be even more complex than the infinite potentialities of individual difference will begin to be unfolded. . . . Socialism as a means of the intensification of man is even more necessary than Socialism as a means to the abolition of economic poverty" (ibid.). It was the task of "genuine philosophic reformers" and creative artists (such as Whitman, Orage suggested elsewhere) to engineer such a society. Lawrence's riposte is that this notion of democracy is as fallacious as it is necessarily (and revealingly) vague, an instance of the kind of thinking concerned not with "provisioning the body, this time, but of provisioning the spirit, the consciousness. We are all one, and therefore every bit partakes of all the rest. That is, the Whole is inherent in every fragment. That is, every human consciousness has the same intrinsic value as every other human consciousness, because each is an essential part of the Great Consciousness. This is the One Identity which identifies us all" (70). Cue Whitman, of course, who, failing to recognize how "every living creature is single in itself, a *ne plus ultra* of creative reality, *fons et origo* of creative manifestation," fatally believed in "One-Identity, the En-Masse . . . a horrible nullification of true identity and being" (73). This was precisely the kind of Whitman worshipped by Henry Binns. In the introduction to *The Good Companions* appears the following: "But every poet hears, flowing amid the silence, the living intricate rhythm of the immortal song; its words progress together in a cosmic fellowship, inseparable, moving forward in the liberty of a living thing" (7; quoted in *The New Age*, August 15, 1908, 313). Only in the final section of his essay does Lawrence let Whitman off the hook.

> It is obvious that Whitman's Democracy is not merely a political system, or a system of government—or even a social system. It is an attempt to conceive a new way of life, to establish new values. It is a struggle to liberate human beings from the fixed, arbitrary control of ideals, into free spontaneity. So, the ideal of Oneness, the unification of all mankind into the homogeneous whole, is done away with. (78)

Lawrence then proceeds briefly to outline the kind of vision of the good society given eloquent symbolic expression in his poem "Bare Fig Trees": "Oh weird Demos, where every twig is the arch twig, / Each imperiously over-equal to each, equality over-reaching itself / . . . Wicked fig-tree, equality puzzle . . ." (298–300). Expressed in prose, as in the second surviving version (1921–1922) of the Whitman essay, the vision sounds considerably less enticing, since it includes an unappetizing variant on the cult of leadership. For this Lawrence, a leader-follower relationship is a core feature of true comradeship: "the next great epoch" will be produced through "the great inspiration of a culminating leader" (415). There are shades here of the "great men" cult, some forms of which had in fact left their mark on Whitman's thinking. But far from seeing this, Lawrence associates Whitman with a concept of comradeship that falls well short of his own evolved and matured version. On such occasions he may be seen as reacting against the cult of Whitman as prophet that thrived among English admirers of Whitman, whatever their political color. One of the prominent exponents of such a view was, of course, Edward Carpenter, as was shown in chapter 7.

Fiercely denying that Whitman was a harbinger of an advanced human society, Lawrence was nevertheless prepared to grant him prophetic status—and if the concession is somewhat grudging in the case of the final (1923) version of *Studies*, it is much more generous, bordering on the fulsome, in some of the earlier versions. In the first surviving version of the Whitman essay (1919), even the Whitman of "oneing" (so mercilessly mocked and excoriated by 1923) was pronounced "a true prophet" (361). His mistake had simply been to take union as a goal, "and not as a process, a means to a different end altogether." As for the 1921–1922 Whitman, he, too, was "a wonderful poet . . . [who] brought us to the world's edge, beyond where any other man has gone . . . [a] Columbus of the soul" (417). And judging by what Lawrence himself rather nauseatingly promises to those who venture further (or back, in his image), it is just as well Whitman's open road did come to a final precipitous roadblock:

> Not any more mob-humility. But leaping up in each soul like a flame, leaping flame by flame, towards the heroic soul that burns the very zenith. The grand culmination of soul-chosen leaders up till we reach the perfect leader, the tyrannus who when he looks round has love in his face, and a wonderful light of purpose that is beyond even love, beyond all love, beyond all men's understanding. The light in the soul of the greatest hero: that the beacon of all our faith . . . let us catch the flame of belief from eye to eye, leaders seeking for leaders, for a leader. Let us cry out to our leaders whom we love, our leading comrades whom we more than love, whom we fiercely believe in. Let us cry out to our leaders whom we passionately love and believe in, to take our love and give us leadership. (417)

A cross between imperialist *Boy's Own Fantasy* and sub-Nietzschean rant, this must be one of the more embarrassing passages of a writer (of genius, nevertheless) notorious for the high embarrassment quotient of his writing. Nietzsche had, in fact, been one of the writers most assiduously featured in *The New Age*, thanks in part to A. R. Orage's intense interest in him. In 1907, Orage published *Consciousness: Animal, Human and Superman. The New Age's* reviewer, Florence Farr, noted its indebtedness to Nietzsche and Shaw, in its treatment of a "transcendental consciousness, the morning star, which precedes the dawn of day." She then noted how leading thinkers imaged this state of consciousness as "mystically feminine. It is Isis, who will bring forth Horus the Saviour. . . . It has often been said jokingly that Superman is Woman" (June 6, 1907, 92).

The comment exposes the heavily patriarchal bias of Lawrence's thinking. It also reminds us that, while it is now temptingly easy to see this cult of leadership as "prophetic" of Nazism, it was in fact characteristic of progressive thinking in a period when the mind-body relationship, the relation of conscious to unconscious, the concept of gender identity, the future of social organization, and a myriad other issues (some just beginning to be "scientifically" investigated by the emergent disciplines of anthropology and psychoanalysis and by the pseudosciences of theosophy and spiritualism) formed an intricate nexus of "enlightened" contemporary concerns. Lawrence was steeped in this culture of (frequently bizarre) inquiry, and his writings on Whitman evidently derive from it. Nowhere is this more evident than in the extraordinary first surviving essay on Whitman (1919). This may be thought of as constituting a hostile investigation of the "Comrade Whitman" image, cherished for its sexual implications by heterosexuals and gays and for its sociopolitical promise by Socialists.

In this essay Lawrence most fully confronts the "issue" of homosexuality—an issue that, as Mark Kinkead-Weekes has so scrupulously shown, troubled him psychically throughout the decade of his intimate imaginative engagement with Whitman. Indeed, as the 1919 essay makes clear, his wrestlings with Whitman were an important means for him to get a psychic grip on the subject, and over the course of the essays he tries many different "holds." Back in 1913, Lawrence's reigning belief was that "sex is the fountain head, where life bubbles up into the person from the unknown," and true sex involved exposure to and respect for the "unknown" in one's partner ("so that one is free from oneself" [quoted, 103]). This had led him to conclude it was virtually impossible for same-sex relations to be life-affirmingly creative in this way, since it was inherently narcissistic, like incest. In the Poe essay in *Studies*, Lawrence likens Poe's marriage to his cousin Virginia as spiritually incestuous: "[B]eing his cousin, she was more easily keyed to him" (69). And in a late poem, "The Noble Englishman," he has a woman ask, "[I]f a man is in love with himself, isn't that the meanest form of homosexuality?" (447). However, even as he saw homosexual relations as the sterile projection of a man's "own image on another man," with the resultant "extinction of all the purposive influences," he also openly admitted his own deep attraction to homoerotic experience: "I should like to know why nearly every man that approaches greatness tends to homosexuality, whether he admits it or not: so that he loves the *body* of a man better than a body of a woman" (103). Evidence of this passion in Lawrence is provided in a text more or less contemporary with this passage, the astonishing unpublished "Prologue" to the first version of *Women in Love* (a novel whose later forms were to be significantly influenced, particularly in its characterization of the Birkin-Gerald relationship, by Lawrence's reading of Whitman). For this Birkin, "it was the men who roused him by their flesh, and manly, vigorous movements" (104). He keeps "a small gallery of such men: men whom he had never spoken to, but who had flashed themselves upon his senses unforgettably," and Lawrence vividly renders through Birkin's response to Gerald "this secret of his passionate and sudden, spasmodic affinity for men he saw."[17] Birkin, however, "kept this secret even for himself. He knew what he felt, but he always kept the knowledge at bay. His a priori were: 'I *should not* feel like this'" (107). (For discussion, see Kinkead-Weekes, 329.)

Here would seem to be the crux of the continuing debate over whether or not Lawrence was himself, perhaps unconsciously, a "suppressed homosexual." In his temperate biography, Kinkead-Weekes is adamant, however, that it is not as clear-cut a case as this. Insisting on clearing a bisexual Lawrence of the charge of homophobia, he argues that he was fully aware of his homoerotic feelings and that his understanding of homosexuality changed significantly over a period of time, even as at any one time his feelings were deeply conflicted. The earlier Lawrence associated homosexual practice with individuals such as John Maynard Keynes, in whom he sensed a hard intellectual arrogance and whose callous class-based predatoriness (of mind, spirit, and flesh) disgusted him. He recoiled from his pederasty, and so visceral was his revulsion that thought of Keynes and his kind made his mind creep, as well as his flesh; he had nightmares about black beetles crawling everywhere (quoted 213). He reluctantly linked E. M. Forster with this "Apostolic clique . . . the Trinity clan of philosophers, classicists and mathematicians, within the privileged concourse of Cambridge, in a class-ridden English society" (208). And this seems to have resulted in his early linking of Forster's "Whitman" to coldly "masturbatory" homosexual practices. Certainly, Lawrence has no time for the kind of Whitman English homosexuals such as Carpenter had been constructing over the previous decades.

As Kinkead-Weekes points out, the 1919 Whitman essay marks a highly significant turning point in Lawrence's attitudes toward the poet and toward homosexuality. But it takes very heavy machinery to accomplish this turn. He constructs this machinery out of materials in pseudobooks of Gnostic wisdom by the theosophist Madame Blavatsky and, most importantly, her acolyte James Pryse. Lawrence believed in an ancient body of supreme knowledge carefully protected by sacred priesthoods but lost to the modern world, save for its debased remnants in "primitive" societies (such as those of the Native Americans). This made him a sucker for Pryse's Hindu theories of the chakras (the human body's nervous system as known to and controlled by initiates). But Lawrence's interest was not quite as crazy as it sounds, as one reads the 1919 essay today. In his time, the developing deep-mind explorations of Freud and Jung, for instance, owed something to alchemists and occultists. Comparative anthropology was interested in myth systems containing stories and symbols analogous to the materials with which theosophists worked. With the proliferation of theories of evolution (some of a distinctly non-Darwinian character), the line between genuine speculative scientific investigation and pseudoscience was sometimes blurred at points intimately relating to the mysterious relationship of life to the inert, of mind to body, and of spirit to matter. A similar blurring was produced by other category breakdowns, such as the collapse of hard-and-fast distinctions between gender identities. Lawrence himself had, like Pryse, received a training in science but had gone on to write not only novels but *Fantasia of the Unconscious* and similar studies.

Through all the endless pages of talk in the 1919 essay of the "cerebellum," of the "hypogastric plexus and the sacral ganglion" (365), and of Whitman operating "almost [like] the esoteric priest-hoods of the past" (361), Lawrence was patently trying to rewrite the body quite radically. As Kinkead-Weekes has usefully put it, "he would develop from these sources a new *physical* psychology" (389). He was attempting a psychosomatic remapping of the body that would enable him to rethink sexual relationship and gender identity. One outcome of this was a valorization of anal sex between men, advocated on the basis that it made possible forms of knowing not available through any other kinds of heterosexual or homosexual activity:

> The vagina, as we know, is the orifice to the hypogastric plexus, which, in the old words, "is situated amid the waters." It is the advent to the great source of being, and it is the egress of the bitter, spent waters of the end. But beyond all this is the cocygeal center. There the deepest and most unknowable sensual reality breathes and sparkles darkly, in unspeakable power. Here, at the root of the spine, is the last clue to the lower body and being, as in the cerebellum is the last upper clue. Here is the dark node which relates us to the center of the earth, the plumb-center of substantial being. Here is our last and extremest reality. And the port, of egress and ingress, is the fundament, as the vagina is port to the other center. (365–366)

While crediting the Whitman of *Calamus* with a kind of uncomprehending intuition of such "truth," Lawrence denies him credit for actually understanding, expressing, and acting upon it. Instead, Whitman's wistful dream of comradeship comes to a melancholy dead end. He is defeated at the very point where Lawrence has managed to break through to a final "sparklingly dark" psychophysical illumination. In other words, Lawrence had found a way past his own impasse: his homoerotic inclinations and his disgust at what he (mis)took to be established homosexual practice.

In interpreting Whitman's poetry of comradeship in this extraordinary way, he was reading directly against the grain of writing on Whitman by such campaigning gays as Edward Carpenter. As was shown in chapter 7, by Carpenter's (questionable) account, sexual congress between Whitman and himself, itself based on superior "Eastern" models, was diametrically opposed to what Lawrence is here advocating. And while there are certain affinities between Lawrence and Carpenter in their shared dislike of camp, or "feminized" homosexual identity, Carpenter did nevertheless give the impression that homosexual relations were based on a reproduction of conventional gender distinctions. He himself was inclined to take the passive, "female" role, and even "straight" readers seem to have intuited this aspect of his personality. After mentioning the "Socialist Spirit" of Whitmanesque notions of comradeship and approvingly noting how "early Socialists call each other Comrade without distinction of sex," the *New Age* reviewer of Carpenter's *Iolaus: An Anthology of Friendship* then passes a different comment: "I remember making in a moment of dubious inspiration an epithet for Carpenter that appeared to me at the time essentially true. I called him Mrs Whitman. Whitman certainly impressed one with the sense of masculinity; and equally certainly there are qualities in Carpenter that strike one as womanly" (May 23, 1907, 55).

Lawrence's Whitman was equally at odds with culturally established views of the virile "masculine" Whitman as gentle lover—a view implicit in Amy Locke's effusions in *The New Age*. He would go to shocking lengths to shatter all such illusions, convinced as he was that this lover was a fraud, a humbug, an intellectual masturbator, a nasty idealist who dreamed of blissful fusion with the beloved. Indeed, so scandalous did Lawrence himself deem the following disclosure in the penultimate (1922) version of the Whitman essay, he never sought to put it into print:

> I remember an American girl whose parents had lived in the town where Whitman (resided) when he was old, told me that the neighbors fairly hated Walter because he used to walk in his little back yard—he lived in a row—stark naked and fat and excited with his own nudity and his grey beard. "His nasty little back yard," Arabella said. And that he used to stop the little girls coming home from school, with senile amorousness. (423)

This then becomes a kind of running motif, culminating in the admission already quoted: "Of course I was being personal, I intend to be" (424). As has been explained, this is not only a rhetorical strategy (and perhaps a kind of self-exculpatory gesture of confession, an apology for Lawrence's verbal act of gross indecency). It is also a climactic accusation, because the whole thrust of the essay has been the charge that for all his advocacy of identity and doctrine of personalism, and for all his professions of love, Whitman failed in fact to become an authentic "person." For Lawrence, this meant discovering, through one's creatively open, exploratory relationship with another, that "[w]hen we are living from our very deepest selves, there is no comradeship, there is no friendship, there is no equality. For comradeship, equality, friendship, and love all presume equality between lovers and comrades. And in the deepest self, there is no sense of equality left, there is no possibility of equal Communion" (429). Poor old Amy Locke, who had imagined that "Again I see thee, thou art by my side— / Lover of lovers, comrade of comrades" (April 4, 1907, 424).

She had also imagined Whitman "lying entranced" upon "the wide, / Low-lying plains" beneath "the darkening shades / Of night as daylight slowly fades / From the horizon—like a retreating tide." But Whitman the nature lover was also anathema to Lawrence, who homed perceptively in, like a heat-seeking missile, on important aspects of Whitman's attachments to the American land. Most of the best discussions of this occur not in the Whitman essays but obliquely in various versions of the opening essay in *Studies*, "The Spirit of Place." The concluding part of the 1920 foreword to *Studies* furnishes another example. Americans are urged to "embrace the great, dusky continent of the Red Man . . . it is a theme upon which American writers have touched and touched again, uncannily, unconsciously, blindfold as it were. Whitman was almost conscious: only the political democracy issue confused him" (385).

"The Spirit of Place" obviously derives from the centuries-old European cultural practice of rooting nations "volkishly" in the "organic life" of particular "national" landscapes. It is very well attuned to Whitman's fundamental belief that American democratic society is (or rather should be) a natural human expression of the vast, geographically varied, infinitely grassy continent with its teeming wildlife and huge range of natural habitats. Particularly acute is Lawrence's suggestion that such intense attachment to the landscape carried within it a terrible anxiety. White Americans feared the land might be theirs but they were not the land's. It still belonged in spirit to the aboriginal inhabitants, the Native Americans (see chapter 3). But Lawrence never explicitly links this perception to Whitman either in his essays on the poet or in "The Spirit of Place." The comment from the 1920 foreword is therefore particularly revealing, as it clearly shows Lawrence believed there was this undercurrent of anxiety in Whitman's nature writing.

An analogous case of Whitman's implicit, rather than explicit, presence in Lawrence's thinking can be found again in the 1920 foreword, which could be read as a brilliant riposte (*avant la lettre*) to the theory of tradition in Eliot's celebrated essay, "Tradition and the Individual Talent." "[T]here are quite as many wonders enfathomed in the human spirit as ever have come out of it; be they Milan Cathedral or the Coliseum or the Bridge of Sighs," Lawrence asserts (382).

He sympathizes with "the barbarian rage against the great monuments of civilization" and rejoices that, for a true American, any one of the wonders of Europe can "be no reproach. . . . It isn't *his*. . . . It is ours. And we like crabs ramble in the slack waters and gape at the excess of our own glory." As a result, "Happy is the nation which hasn't got a tradition, and which lacks cultural monuments" (383). And America is urged to look not to dying Europe but to its aboriginal peoples for inspiration, and to its continent for its true genius loci. Whitman himself could scarcely have put it better. Lawrence's is a truly *American* Whitman, constructed though he (and his America) may in part have been in terms of Lawrence's reaction against alternative English models: "[w]hat would you not give, O America, for our yesterdays? Far more than they are worth, I assure you. What would not *I* give for your tomorrows" (383).

Insofar, then, as modern translation studies would encourage us to view Lawrence's writings on Whitman as acts of translation, or instances of cultural transposition, the discussion so far has helped identify one of the enabling factors in the process of intercultural transfer. By approaching Whitman partly via assimilated versions of him already circulating widely in his own culture, Lawrence was helped in the work of constructing what turned out to be an exceptionally subtle and complex "Whitman" of his own, one who functioned within Lawrence's creatively enabling system of "root-myths and . . . root-utterances" (289). But many overlapping and interacting factors are obviously necessary before any such translations can be as culturally profitable as those of Lawrence. And one other factor of significant importance in his case would seem to be the system of broad correspondences between his culture (as received and perceived by Lawrence) and Whitman's culture (as mediated through his poetry). It was this attunement between cultures that helped promote a kind of intimate, unconscious harmony between their respective outlooks, mediated in turn through Lawrence's "translations," his writings on Whitman.

Background to this harmony was their common fundamental belief that they lived in apocalyptic times, when the collapse of an established order caused deeply unsettling fluidities of belief, value, and practice prefiguring the coming of a new order. Lawrence approvingly mentions how "All the Americans, when they have trodden new ground, seem to have been conscious of making a breach in the established order . . . They have felt they were trespassing, transgressing, or going too far" (403). This is obviously a self-portrait of Lawrence the transgressor, and is part and parcel of his apocalyptic imagination. As has been made evident in chapter 2, such a transgressive, millenarian belief is powerfully operative in Whitman's first and greatest editions of *Leaves of Grass*, and the historical reasons for it (at once economic, social, political, and more broadly cultural) have been very well rehearsed by many recent Whitman scholars. Lawrence scholars have similarly explored his root obsession with contemporary millennial and apocalyptic beliefs. The outcome, for both writers, was an endlessly branching complex of intellectual interests. These ranged through a common interest in evolutionary theory, pseudoscience, heterodox spiritual teachings, ancient cosmology with its "root-myths and . . . root-utterances" (289), esoteric body-maps, cross-gender identities, versions of primitivism, occult nature philosophies, vitalism (Lawrence's concept of "inorganic consciousness"), and many other kinds of exploratory intellectual models, particularly those deriving from what one might appropriately, if anachronistically, style the "alternative cultures" of their respective periods. Such an awareness of the broad historical symmetries between them helps demystify (but not to invalidate or dispel) the impression of intimacy between Lawrence and Whitman that otherwise leads commentators to attribute a kind of uncanny power of intuitive sympathy to the Englishman. To read Lawrence's writings on Whitman is certainly to be deeply struck by how the frequently bizarre and seemingly inappropriate systems of explanation he employs to account for the power of the American's writing nevertheless succeed in producing quite extraordinary results. It is as if Lawrence possessed the ability of a spiritualist, or psychoanalyst, or mind-reader (to name three figures from the "fringe culture" of his time that were congruent with Lawrence's own deepest interests). He seems able to access prohibited areas of Whitman's preconscious mind and to map a hidden field of psychic energy.

Take the intense interest of both creative writers in what would nowadays be termed the "pseudosciences" of their day. Both were notably interested in the remodeling of the mind-body relationship[18]—Whitman's interest in phrenology finding its counterpart in Lawrence's lover's quarrel with emergent psychoanalysis; and both felt the need to reconfigure the "Self." Behind Lawrence's critical fascination with psychoanalysis lay the feeling that he had "a strange and fugitive self shut out and howling like a wolf or coyote under the ideal windows . . . the self who is coming into his own" (20). He was therefore hypersensitive to the impression he got from American writers, including Whitman, that "every man as long as he remains alive is in himself a multitude of conflicting men" (20). Lawrence and Whitman shared a fascination with spiritualism, mediums, and the symbolically powerful worlds of ancient cultures. (Here, bear in mind Whitman's interest in Egypt.) Whitman's maverick transcendentalism is paralleled by Lawrence's modernized vitalism—and herein perhaps lies a clue to a concern underlying and determining so many of their unorthodox interests.

They were both ambiguously fascinated by the developing power of contemporary science to explain life. Their common problem was that the physical sciences seemed to be in the ascendancy, so that materialist, and even determinist, theories of human life and of the human habitat threatened to prevail. Lawrence summed the issue up colorfully: "[O]ur science tends all the time to the assertion that life is a mere outcome of certain conjunction of specific forces: a made thing, manufactured in the great and fascinating factory of the cosmos, at a certain point in time." Ancient science believed the opposite and a debased form of that earlier, deeper truth survived in modern alchemy and astrology: "To the ancient scientist, *life* was the first mover. It was life which produced the universe, not the universe which produced life" (394). This is a crucial issue for a Lawrence who, while insisting on accepting that material science had effectively despiritualized the cosmos (including the human mind, soul, and body), still fought desperately to resist the consequent reduction of "life" to a material phenomenon. Similarly, Whitman favored the teleological, pre-Darwinian idea of evolution advanced by Lamarck. He also turned to transcendentalism and other forms of late-Romantic philosophy sanctioning a continuing belief not only in the human "soul" but in a "cosmos" so permeated by spirit it was the externalized symbolic expression of human psycho-spiritual existence. Obviously, a Lawrence who was in these respects aggressively post-Romantic found Whitman's "solution" not only unacceptable but unhealthy and potentially deadly. Hence his sustained attack on him. Whitman represented a real threat to the very different kind of "scientific" synthesis of spirit and matter for which Lawrence constantly sought to find an adequate terminology and language, not least in his American essays. Thus he excoriates Whitman obsessively, for refusing, despite all his pioneering love of the sensuous body, to recognize that its essential value is not dependent on its remaining twinned with spirit. While never being other than physical, the body had a "religious" authority: "[T]he Lord Almighty [himself] has a bottom," as Lawrence wittily puts it (109). But, perhaps feeling he hadn't managed to nail Whitman on the score of his absurd "idealism," he then tries to nail him on his corresponding "materialism." In the 1922 essay, he argues that in some of the poems from *Children of Adam*, Whitman fails to observe the vital distinction between life and inert matter. In their amorous yearning, individuals are represented as "all helplessly hurtling together into one great snowball" (422). There is a note of panic in the writing at this point, as Lawrence strikes out blindly—as he always did—at any idea threatening his free will or curbing him in any way.

Nevertheless, given this great divide between the ways they confronted the scientific revolution of their respective times, there was also a deep accord between

Whitman and Lawrence, in the form of their dark fear of a merely material, mechanical (and therefore dehumanizing) cosmos. One of the most powerful tokens of this is the term that was key to both their vocabularies: "electricity." For both of them, electricity was a scientifically verifiable and respectable material "force," but it seemed also to have qualities analogous to those of psychosomatic "life." It was therefore the indispensable "middle term," mediating between life and matter, mind and body. Lawrence was always insistent that electricity belonged to the world of material forces, of "dynamic physical events." It could not help one finally understand "the being of men" (119). Nevertheless, in elsewhere posing the question, "What is the breath of life?" he could answer "[an] electric vibration . . . the strange current of interchange that flows between men and men, and men and women, and men and things" (109). "Vibrations" was for Lawrence another handy term, cognate with "electricity." Hence his sympathetic interest (however carefully qualified and ostensibly skeptical) in telepathy, ghosts, oracles, mediums, trances, and all the other paraphernalia of spiritualism and theosophy (102 ff). Sick "psychic tricks" they might be, but to describe them as such implied that theirs was a negative validation of the "psychic" and of its connection to "health"—another of the key terms in the psychosomatic vocabulary of both Whitman and Lawrence.

"Vibrations" also helped Lawrence rescue the concept of "spirit of place" from the wreck of a spiritual universe: it allowed him to use a pseudoscientific language to imbue the material universe with a form of consciousness. This was precisely the use Whitman had made of transcendentalism to construct "cosmos," a term he adopted because it implied some kind of universal binding, organic life. And just as Whitman imagined this "cosmos" as being profoundly cognate with the human, so Lawrence was interested in the occultists' talk of a "universal mystic language" of the cosmos, "known to the initiated, or to the adept, or to the priesthood of the whole world, whether Chinese or Atlantean or Maya or Druid" (169). The supposition—upon which his art was founded—that the ancient language must have consisted of "symbols or ideographs" (the mythic language of artists), had its counterpart in Whitman's mention of the universe's secret "hieroglyphs" and his ability both to read and reproduce them in his poetry. Lawrence's pious hope was that "it may be possible, as the scientists of the subtler psychic activities desire and need to do, to discover a universal system of symbology; for practically the whole of psychometry and psychoanalysis depends on the understanding of symbols" (169). But lest future science take the path he himself dreaded, Lawrence hastens to bestow on artists the ultimate power of speaking truth: "art-speech, art-utterance, is, and always will be, the greatest universal language of mankind, greater than esoteric symbolism" (169). And Whitman makes precisely the same move to outflank science. He elevates the poet, in case the science which he always carefully professes to worship should treacherously break troth by finding truth only in matter.

Industrial capitalism, with its intensive mechanization of so many aspects of what by Lawrence's time had become mass production was, for Lawrence, the soulmate and handmaiden of modern science. Already violently opposed to it before 1914, he found his fear and disgust confirmed by the international carnage of World War One. And as the editors of the Cambridge edition note, his plans for *Studies* changed significantly owing to "a profound transformation experienced by Lawrence during the spring of 1918 as he read deeply in works of psychology and cosmic history that resonated with his revulsion from war-torn Europe" (xxxv; also see Kinkead-Weekes, 438–440). So when he speaks of modern America as "tangled in her own barbed wire, and mastered by her own machines" (30), he has in mind not only the fencing in of America's grasslands but also the soldiers hideously crucified on the Western front's barbed wire defenses. Since he had originally seen the United States that stood aloof from the conflict as a force for sanity and a kind of mental refuge, the bitterness of his disillusionment when it was later drawn in was all the deeper, and marked his writing of the early versions of *Studies*. And just as he saw militant unionists simply as the repellant converse of the industrial magnates and managerial class, so did he see in Woodrow Wilson's postwar internationalism only the peacetime equivalent, on a global scale, of the kind of deadly leveling that mass war and mass production produced. Moreover, in the state mobilization of industry organized by the architect of victory, the wartime Minister for Munitions David Lloyd George, he saw the dread image of a new, dehumanizing mass society. This kind of vision finds expression through the character of Gerald in *Women in Love*, the novel upon which he was working contemporaneously with the earlier versions of *Studies*. Whereas the Lawrence of *Sons and Lovers* could at least balance his fierce dislike of his native coalfield society with an enchanting image of industrial craftsmanship, in the form of his father gently, lovingly fashioning fuses, the Lawrence of *Women in Love* could find no such redeeming image of gentleness and love in that "developed" form of mechanized production imported from Germany by the new breed of industrial managers that Gerald Crich represents.

In these respects, too, there are suggestive parallels between the socioeconomic experiences of Lawrence and Whitman. Lawrence's hatred of unionism as a symptom of mass society was shared (if not in intensity) by the aging Whitman who, again like Lawrence, had lived through a violent transformation of the capitalist order he had known as a youth. And like Lawrence, Whitman had continued in many ways to weave his insistent images of a more humanly fulfilling future out of the sociocultural materials of his early life. They were alike, too, in suffering the tensions of the contradictions that lay at the very core of their beliefs. One was the tension between their commitment to unfettered "evolution" and their need to *control* it; to dictate to the future. While both proclaimed a belief in openness, in process, in endless becoming (it is precisely what Lawrence admired in a Whitman from whom he accordingly borrowed key images like the open road), both were secret essentialists and authoritarians, as prophets by definition are. Multiple selfhood or not, they believed there was only *one* road open to human beings if they were to realize what both conceived of as essential human nature. By speaking of the road as "open," and avoiding the mistake of setting for it any particular destination, both thought they imaged human freedom. The trouble is that for a *terminus ad quem* they substituted an equally determining *fons et origo*, an originating impulse that, however delicately and flexibly they tried to define it, preordained the direction the human road was "destined" (by whatever unpredictable creative unfolding) to take. It was not for nothing that they were both raised on a belief in the straight and narrow. And moreover, just in case those on the road seemed inclined to wander (Whitman's America was rapidly proving as unreliable in this respect as Lawrence's England), the road was fiercely policed by each of them—think of Whitman's attempts at controlling the future in "Crossing Brooklyn Ferry" and Lawrence's in all his apocalyptic novels. Such a response is due, in no small measure, to the fear they both felt at the fragmenting impact on values and beliefs of a modern industry and science that were simultaneously totalitarian in their effects on social organization and production. Both Whitman and Lawrence were at bottom healing integrationists, holistic in their vision. As Kinkead-Weekes has remarked, Lawrence believed that "both cosmically, and within the person, 'as life moves on its creative singleness, its substance divides and subdivides into multiplicity'; yet at each creative moment, all comes together with all, anew" (449). Whitman's vision was very similar.

To explore these initial points of interconnection between Whitman and Lawrence, is to be led by degrees into the labyrinth of interconnections between their respective understanding of their different cultures. It is out of this labyrinth that Lawrence brings his remarkable "translations," with the help of the Ariadne's thread of the extant English images of Whitman. Fuller investigation would need to concentrate, in particular, on the way that, for both men, inherited notions of sex and gender were among the categories of established "reality" that were most vulnerable to the psychoculturally liberating process of "trespass" and "transgression" (to borrow Lawrence's own phraseology). Their implicit interest in bisexuality and in same-sex relations comes into clear focus here, as does their struggle to find adequate ways of imagining and articulating these alternative ways of organizing one's sexual "being" and relating. One of Lawrence's greatest strengths as a reader of Whitman is his grasp of the intimate significance of these issues in the poetry—a grasp we feel is profoundly intuitive, even though it may in fact have been a function of the symmetries in their respective psychocultural situations. At the same time, Lawrence probably misconstrued the exact nature of their significance and of Whitman's manner of dealing with them, even as he misses the potential relevance of Whitman's example to his own case. Nevertheless, there is a real sense in which to read Lawrence on Whitman is to feel that they were what Joseph Conrad would term "secret sharers," in the multiple sense of sharing specific secrets, of secretly sharing, and of sharing a need to deny they *had* the secrets that most mattered to them, even as they openly confessed to being secretive. It seems necessary to put it in this tortuous, convoluted fashion in order to convey the full extent of that extraordinary intimacy Lawrence both consciously and unconsciously displays with the hidden life of the Walt Whitman whose work haunted, tortured, and inspired him for the best part of a decade.

Nine. "What a Welshman You Would Have Been"

"Those blessed gales from the British Isles probably (certainly) saved me," wrote the elderly Whitman. And then he added: "That emotional, audacious, open-handed, friendly-mouthed, just-opportune English action, I say, plucked me like a brand from the burning, and gave me life again."[1] For British Isles read England: it continues to be a common enough tendency in England itself, let alone in the United States. But it won't do. Nor, therefore, will any discussion of Whitman's impact on the British Isles that is conducted, in fact if not in frankly proclaimed intention, in these falsely homogenizing, distorting terms. And for that reason, it may safely be asserted that the response to Whitman of what Les Murray has more accurately termed "the Anglo-Celtic archipelago" has to date been inadequately understood, reported, and analyzed.

But at least the promising conditions for just such an exercise seem, now, to have been created. As one would have expected, Ireland (the independent Republic of Ireland in its present form and throughout its antecedent history) has already received very substantial attention, not least from Joann P. Krieg.[2] Her excellent study of *Whitman and the Irish* includes a strong chapter on Dublin's response to Whitman. Moreover, in her coda she briefly considers the distinctive response to Whitman of Northern Ireland, the region of the Emerald Isle that is not part of the Irish Republic.

Implicitly recognizing that a full understanding of Ulster's reading of Whitman is beyond her (and therefore remains to be achieved), she sensibly homes in on that significant contemporary writer, Tom Paulin. She sees him as typical of his country in that he feels himself to be stateless, "marginalised, adrift between two political bodies and a part of neither" (234). Her perception is worth developing further. Passionate advocate though he is of a secular, nonsectarian republicanism—a pointedly different use of the term from the one preferred by the IRA (Irish Republican Army)—Paulin is, in fact, of Protestant stock: "I'm aware [of the] buried Anglican within me," he wryly notes in his essay on Geoffrey Hill.[3] This may well have sensitized him to the bigotry not only of Ulster Protestants and Unionists like Ian Paisley (decidedly non-Anglican in spirit) but also of the Irish State, intolerantly Catholic and nationalist for so much of its twentieth-century existence. For Paulin, the bigotry of the one is identical to the bigotry of the other, and both are products of the Minotaur, the monstrous ideology of the modern nation state. Carefully avoiding the jingoistically nationalist and expansionist aspects of Whitman's writings, Paulin therefore finds in him, and in Milton, a utopian alternative to state-worship: "a generous, wonderfully innocent optimism, that springs from their absolute confidence in the liberating possibilities of the free individual conscience" (31). Of course, the precise cultural source of this reading of Whitman becomes only the more apparent when one notes the (presumably unconscious) irony of this secularized expression of what is, nevertheless, a distinctly Ulster Protestant (and un-Catholic) commitment to the primacy of individual conscience. Such are the intricacies and complexities of any culturally situated response to Whitman, once minutely examined; hence the pressing need to undertake precisely such a close examination.

All the more's the pity, therefore, that the fullest study to date of Scotland's response to Whitman remains relatively inaccessible, in the form of a section of an unpublished doctoral thesis by R. H. Jellema on "Victorian Critics and the Orientation of America."[4] (His interesting conclusion is that "the Scots were naturally disposed to take a keen interest in what was taking shape in America. While sprawling America virtually ignored Walt Whitman, tiny Scotland produced a number of articles and three books on him in his own lifetime" [270]). However, the raw materials made available by Jellema's study would need now to be processed by an understanding informed by recent sophisticated and highly productive analyses of Scottish-American literary relations. Robert Crawford has emphasized the politico-cultural similarities between the fledgling United States and Scotland after the Act of Union with England:

> If one might suggest that the eclectic impulse behind Scottish encyclopaedism, anthologism, and anthropology, as well as behind the fictions of Scott and Carlyle, played a strong part in the building-up of a wider perspective in which Scottish

> culture could fulfil its role without being surpassed by England, then there was certainly a reason for some of the major American eclectic urges also. American writers were anxious to compare a wide variety of other cultures, including that of the native Americans, with English culture, so as not to be subject to the sole model offered by Old England.[5]

"To call Whitman an eclectic is to state the obvious," adds Crawford (204) and, in assimilating Whitman's prominent interest in Scott's *Minstrelsy of the Scottish Borders*, the poetry of Burns, and the prose of Carlyle to his dominant model of international politico-cultural symmetries, he paves the way for an interesting explanation of a phenomenon noted by Jellema; that a disproportionate number of Whitman's earliest and most discriminating critics were Scottish. The recent work of Susan Manning would seem at bottom to reinforce Crawford's promising master narrative of Scottish-American cultural relations. Recognizing a fundamental concern with "gathering the nation" in both the United States and Scotland, she notes the role played by geography in America's attempt to resolve the issue of connection and argues for a comparison in this respect of *Leaves of Grass* with Thomas Jefferson's *Notes on the State of Virginia* and St. John de Crèvecoeur's *Letters from an American Farmer.* "I shall argue," she states, "that these works establish different versions of an American 'syntax of space' whose stylistics derive from Anglo-Scottish structures of thought."[6]

So what, then, of Wales's reaction? How did Whitman and his work prove instrumental from the point of view of Welsh culture? This subject is virgin soil, and all the more potentially fertile for that.[7] This chapter attempts to initiate investigation of the subject, without claiming to exhaust it. And the interest of such an exercise should lie not only in itself (since, as should appear, Welsh culture is sufficiently complex for its response to Whitman to prove intriguingly various), nor in its contribution to a more complete understanding of Whitman's reception in the British Isles, but also in its fruitfully indicative nature.[8] An awareness of the complexity of the case even in a country as small as Wales should help deepen appreciation of how international response to Whitman has always been subtly inflected by a whole complex of cultural factors. The lesson is therefore clear: to be truly meaningful, future consideration of Whitman's multiple significance worldwide will need always to be based in a deeply inward understanding of the cultural infrastructure of the "receiving" country.

Some time in 1876, Whitman was persuaded to read some of his poems aloud to his friend Samuel Morse in the sculptor's Philadelphia studio. The performance attracted a crowd that included the chambermaid. Apparently intrigued by her absorption, Whitman asked where she came from. All the way from Wales, came the reply, in hopes of making her fortune at the Philadelphia Centennial Exposition. Moved by her words and by her condition, Whitman exploded into anger at such sad evidence of the fateful lure of money.[9]

According to some of his biographers, Whitman was himself of Welsh descent on his mother's side.[10] Whether the story is true or not, there seems to be no record of Whitman priding himself on any such ancestry. But there is evidence enough in his writings, including the very first edition of *Leaves of Grass*, that he knew of Wales and the Welsh. And there is evidence, too, of his having met and corresponded with at least one proud Welshman. Ernest Rhys was a young unknown of twenty-six when first he introduced himself by letter to Whitman. Having recently given up his secure, respectable position as a mining engineer in the Durham coalfield in order to enter the risky, unstructured world of freelance writing in London, he was busily trying to secure a foothold there as an editor. A Tyneside publisher, Walter Scott, had shortly before made Rhys's friend, the former miner Joseph Skipsey, general editor of a popular classics series called *The Canterbury Poets.* Seeing Whitman listed as one of the authors Skipsey proposed to include in the series, Rhys had eagerly volunteered to edit the volume, and on May 31, 1885, he wrote Whitman a long letter requesting permission to make a selection from *Leaves of Grass.* W. M. Rossetti had already published a bowlderized edition of this poetry in 1868, and Rhys probably had this in mind as a model for his own selection, although he seems also to have been familiar with the complete, unexpurgated 1882 (Philadelphia) edition of *Leaves of Grass.*

Unsuccessful in eliciting any reply, Rhys sent the mute Whitman another beseeching letter, this time seductively outlining the social vision behind his proposed enterprise. After apologizing for the "cheap and prettified" design of *The Canterbury Poets*, totally out of keeping with the long lines and rough-hewn character of Whitman's revolutionary verse, Rhys proceeded to share with the poet his young man's dream of a cheap edition of his poetry that would "put it in the reach of the poorest member of the great social democracy. . . . You know what a fervid stir and impulse forward of Humanity there is today in certain quarters! and I am sure you will be tremendously glad to help us *here*, and in the very camp of the enemy, the stronghold of caste and aristocracy, and all selfishness between rich and poor!"[11] There were those, he suggested, who wanted Whitman's work to be available only in prohibitively expensive editions, and so kept well out of the reach of the ignorant, impressionable, inflammable masses. But his aim was "an edition for the poor" as it was his "great love and desire to help the struggling mass of men, to be a true soldier in the War of liberation of

Humanity." The sentiments, however naively expressed, were genuine and resilient ones. Having not gone to university, Rhys retained throughout his long life the Victorian autodidact's passion for intellectual self-improvement. His most lasting success in later years was his founding (for J. M. Dent) of the enormously influential Everyman's Library, which he then proceeded to edit for the first forty years of its life.[12]

Whitman shared this missionary zeal. Largely self-taught himself, and a visionary believer in democracy, he yearned to see his poems lovingly embraced by the masses—particularly by the proudly masculine "coal-miners and shepherds" of whom Rhys spoke. Yet although, as he later confessed, Whitman's imagination was kindled by the idea of supplying "a gospel of life for the [English] poor" (Traubel 1: 453), it took a third letter from Rhys to get him to respond to these impassioned overtures. Once proper contact had been formally established, further negotiations followed, with the result that Rhys eventually undertook not only to bring out a selection of Whitman's poems, but also to supervise the London publication of *Specimen Days* and *Democratic Vistas.* All these works appeared in 1887, roughly two years after the initial approaches had been made. Whitman was impressed. Rhys, he wrote to William Sloane Kennedy on February 21, 1887, "makes the impression on me of a deep true friend of L of G and of myself."[13]

By the time, therefore, that Rhys actually travelled across the Atlantic to visit the old man, in December 1887, he was as eagerly expected as he was eager to arrive. If Whitman was just a little disappointed in his admirer when, at last, they actually met, then he concealed it with his customary good nature. "Rhys," he later told his young local friend Horace Traubel, "is very interesting to me—I easily love him. He is not original—brilliant. He is young—he may still go on to great things—but he is rather a plodder than a dreamer."[14] When Kennedy, another of Whitman's stalwart friends, quarreled with the interloper and pronounced him selfish, stolid, and dull, the poet was more amused than offended. Kennedy had "got his glasses on his nose upside down," he told Traubel. "Rhys should come to America and stay—he belongs here. He is bright, smart, wide-awake, with an instinct for new things, delighting in strange doctrines" (Traubel 2: 28). While shrewdly noting that Rhys, like Rossetti, had fought shy of publishing his poetry in unexpurgated form (Traubel 1: 124), Whitman still staunchly championed his young admirer, satisfied that he was one of "the New Guard": "Rhys is the type of the young men who are come our way and learn the best we have to teach—of the young men who will rightly perceive, measure us, and then go back and indoctrinate Great Britain" (Traubel 1: 221). When pressed by Kennedy to admit that his visitor was in fact selfish, Whitman refused: "I can realize that Ernest has the English acquisitiveness—and Lord knows! our own is great enough—and I don't see how I can object to it either."[15]

"The English acquisitiveness." Whitman tended to think of Ernest Rhys at this stage as being almost quintessentially English in character, characteristically referring to him in a letter as "my English friend" (*Letters* 4: 190). In turn Rhys could, in 1889, address a poem "To Walt Whitman from some young English friends." But, although born in Islington, he was half Welsh, having a Welshman for a father and having lived for almost all the first six years of his life in his father's hometown of Carmarthen. It was, however, the experience he had gained from living in England, and specifically from working in the Durham coalfield, that informed his first enthusiastic response to Whitman. The young Rhys moved in Socialist circles. An ardent admirer of Edward Carpenter and of William Morris (whose arts and crafts movement easily translated into the kind of celebration of labor that so excited early Socialist admirers of Whitman's poetry), Rhys was on the fringes of such groups as the Social Democratic Federation, the Fellowship of the New Life, and the Fabian Society.[16] When Morris pressed him to join the Socialist League, however, he declined: "something in me, the arrant touch of the individualist, rebelled" (*WEW*, 94). Such, too, would have been Whitman's response. Yet, Rhys worked in his own way for radical social change. He established "the college of a village" by starting a lending library full of educational, improving books for the miners in the pit village where he lived and worked, and to it he attached a club program of lectures (*WEW*, 56). It was out of such a background that his early enthusiasm for Whitman came, and his initiative to bridge the class divide between himself and the miners (closing, in the process, the gap between Whitman and that genuine Tyneside miner-poet Joseph Skipsey) is best understood if placed alongside the analogous work of the celebrated Bolton Group. (Indeed, in view of the attention now understandably lavished on the latter, it may be time to emphasize that they were by no means unique: similar groups and enterprises were scattered throughout industrial England, from Nottingham to Bristol and from Leeds to Sheffield.[17]) Rhys entertained a genuine affection and respect for the miners and this found late expression in *Black Horse Pit* (1925), his splendid collection of reminiscent tales of the experiences he had garnered as a young mining engineer. Published only a year before the great, historic General Strike—climaxing in an epically brutal confrontation between miners and government—it features a revealing preamble in which Rhys, as if sensing encroaching catastrophe, elegizes the passing of "the pitman" with "his qualities, his humours, virtues and vices."[18] And in turning to Border Ballads and the ballads of Skipsey himself for adequate expression of his sense of the heroic dimensions of the miners' "coal-dark underworld," Rhys illuminates for us the sources of his earlier interest in the poetry of a Whitman who had produced magnificent magnificats of the laboring life.

In these respects, then, Rhys's early enthusiasm for Whitman may be seen as adding interesting detail to an already familiar picture—the picture scholars have painted of early English reception of the poetry. But there was an entirely different side to Rhys's enthusiasm. This is related exclusively to his Welshness and has hitherto received no scholarly attention. Evidence for it may be found not so much in his published work as in the letters he addressed to Whitman subsequent to his visit and that are lodged in the Library of Congress Feinberg Collection. These make fascinating reading. The first was dispatched in October 1888, from Llanddeusant, Llangadog, where Rhys was staying on a farm called Blaen Sawdde. "The life of the farmer, which you know so well in the States, is essentially the same here no doubt," he told the poet, before proceeding to dwell on the hardiness of seventy-year-old William Williams the farmer, "a typical Welsh peasant of the better class." Having no doubt already divined Whitman's partiality for robust young workingmen, he expatiated on the "self reliance and manly sufficiency" of the farmer's two sons, who, "like most Welshmen," were both "good singers and [took] bass in the parish Church on Sundays." Recording a visit to the local market, he explains it provided him with the chance of "picking up the Welsh idiom, difficult as it is," with a view "in a month or two, to be able to read the old Welsh Mss, poetry and romances chiefly, at the British Museum."

Although his letters may seem to suggest that his expeditions into Wales at this time were no more than picturesque tours or holiday jaunts, Rhys was in fact beginning the (to him) serious work of reconnecting himself to his Welsh Celtic background. Excited by his discovery of a rich ancient literary culture dating back to the very earliest Christian centuries, he was to pour out a torrent of translations of Welsh Anglophone poetry, romances set in Wales, lyrical plays on Welsh topics, and Welsh ballads over the next twenty-five or so years. The visits to Wales that Rhys described to Whitman were, therefore, for the serious purpose of discovering more about the land of his father.

Where all this was tending begins to be evident in a letter of September 1889:

> There is great store of the antique in Wales, as you know: and it is good on these sunny autumn afternoons to climb up to some old castle, and imagine the Medieval bards and warriors parading there as of old. I have been dipping more and more into the old Welsh romance and poetry of late; eking out with a dictionary my small store of the vernacular as now spoken. There is great wealth of metaphor, and exces-

> sive metrical finesse in some of these old Welsh poets. Indeed, Welsh poetry is far more intricate and distinctive in its way than the English, while of course wanting in many things that the best Elizabethans knew.

Thus did Rhys bravely attempt to enlighten Whitman about *barddas*, the magnificent body of Welsh-language poetry in the unique *cynghanedd* forms that constitutes one of the glories of European literature. A month later, he enthuses about his stay in Carmarthen (popularly referred to in English as "Merlin's town") and, recalling ancient Welsh legend, claims he has acquired "a new sense of human destiny, and of the epic continuity from old Wales to new America." In such letters as these he therefore consciously appeals both to Whitman's enthusiasm for and scorn of "simple," "primitive," "feudal" societies, seeking always to make some sort of common cause with him. The reasons for this will shortly become apparent.

During the idyllic summer of 1890 he reported to Whitman his engagement to an Irish girl, his future wife, mentioned his attendance at the National Eisteddfod in Bangor, and explained he was busily at work studying "Taliesin and the medieval fathers of Welsh poetry." To give Whitman some "idea of early Welsh poetry," he quoted several extracts, in the original Welsh, from the "famous *Awdyl Vraith* [*sic*]," and added his own rough translations. He concluded by remarking that "the more I read of these Old Welsh bards, the more I think of their fine imagination, their music, their wonderful art of verse. But as yet I am only at the beginnings of a very difficult study."

What Whitman thought of Taliesin is not, unfortunately, recorded, but he was certainly intrigued by the accounts of the Eisteddfod. He was already aware of the existence of Wales as a separate, ancient culture. His "Salut au Monde" referred to the time when "druids walk'd the groves of Mona. I see the mistletoe and vervain" (291), and in the pamphlet intended to be included in the London edition of the 1876 *Leaves of Grass*, he spoke of sharing the book "with the English, the Irish, the Scottish and the Welsh—the highest and the lowest, of these Islands."[19] There is even a reference in "Proud Music of the Storm" to his visionary seeing and hearing of "old harpers with their harps at Welsh festivals" (526). But now he was fascinated to hear from Rhys that such antique festivals were still held in contemporary Wales. (He had, of course, completely misunderstood the real nature of an eisteddfod.)

On Tuesday, September 24, 1889, Whitman told Traubel he had received a good, long letter from Rhys in Wales. "They have been holding a harp festival there in Wales—they have them, I understand, both in North and South

Wales—a sort of equivalent for the Roman, Grecian games. The Welsh people are animated, gesticulating people." At this point Traubel expressed some mild surprise: was not Rhys, after all, rather a quiet, undemonstrative kind of man? "Well," said Whitman quickly, "Ernest was practically raised in England. They call these games, Eistedfodd [*sic*]. I have met harpists—I remember they coached me in the pronunciation of the word, which is not as we would pronounce it, though what I could no more tell now than fly!" (Traubel 6: 18). Four days later he was still sufficiently involved in the whole subject to raise it when visited by a local Unitarian minister. Again he pondered aloud the mysteries of the pronunciation of the word "Eistedfodd," and once more he approved of the character "of the Welsh people, as Rhys makes them out . . . warm, flush—not flamboyant—but flowing, radiant—in their poetic, musical forms" (Traubel 6: 28). He had much more to say along the same lines, but Traubel, wearying of his inexplicable enthusiasm for a remote, insignificant people, refrained from recording it.

So what have these attractively gossipy letters and casual comments to tell us about any distinctively Welsh response to Whitman's work? To answer such a question one needs to be able to place Ernest Rhys's reports to Whitman in their proper cultural and political context. By 1889 Rhys was well on the way to becoming what he was throughout the 1890s: a passionate believer in pan-Celticism and a supporter of the Cymru Fydd/Young Wales movement whose members frequently aspired not only to greater cultural autonomy for their country but also for Home Rule within the British Empire. This was the Rhys who sought to make common cause with his fellow founding member of the Rhymer's Club, his young friend W. B. Yeats. And it will be remembered that Whitman was admired by the young Yeats not because he seemed to adumbrate a Socialist vision but because he was the powerful poet of national affirmation and liberation. It was to Whitman and his like in America that Yeats looked for "hope for the de-Anglicising of our people," believing that their work showed how "to build up a national tradition, a national literature, which shall be none the less Irish in spirit from being English in language."[20] Wavering between support for Irish separatist aspirations and belief in "Home Rule for all" the nations of Britain, and between a cultural and a political nationalism, the young Yeats also veered between a celebration of the Irish as the true, quintessential Celts and a recognition that the (Highland) Scots and the Welsh had equal claims to being Celtic. (In English cultural circles, "Celtic" became, of course, a conveniently flexible and modishly fashionable term of supposed ethnic identity in the 1890s.) "The mutual understanding of the Scotch, Welsh and Irish Celts," Yeats noted in 1896, was "a matter I have myself much at heart."[21] Such a feeling was shared at that time by prominent members of the Gaelic League, who implicitly recognized that if Ireland was setting the pace politically, then it was Wales who exemplified best practice in cultural matters, with its vigorous institutions (most notably the National Eisteddfod) for supporting its native Celtic language. It was with this pan-Celtic Yeats that Ernest Rhys formed a kind of uneasy cultural alliance that extended to include the Scot William Sharp (alias "Fiona Macleod" the novelist), and it is the lineaments of a Welsh version of Yeats's Whitman that may be seen emerging between the lines of Rhys's letters to the American. Between the visit to Whitman in Camden and the letters to him from Wales, Rhys's center of cultural gravity seems therefore to have shifted radically, causing a similar shift in his perception of Whitman's relevance to his own case and cause. Implicit in those letters he addresses to him is a new recognition of Whitman as a national "bard" (an English word partly deriving, after all, from the Welsh "bardd," and permanently entering the English language thanks in part to Gray's famous and influential eighteenth-century poem based on the legend of the slaughter of the Welsh poets by Edward the Conqueror).

Rhys's position on Welsh politics and culture is made most explicit in the important article he contributed to the very first issue of *Young Wales.* As its title suggests, the journal was the official organ of a very powerful political movement taking its inspiration from such key nineteenth-century nation-building programs as had been promoted by Young Italy and Young Ireland. The leading figures in Cymru Fydd/Young Wales included Welsh Liberal politicians of genius, such as Tom Ellis (later Liberal Whip at Westminster) and, of course, David Lloyd George, the Welsh wizard himself, so often likened to a latter-day Merlin.[22] *Young Wales* was launched in 1895, when the power of the Liberal Party (to which virtually the whole of Wales was in thrall) was at its height and when Welsh politicians wielded incomparable power over that party. Its hold over Wales was largely due to its virtual monopoly of the support of Welsh (and Welsh-speaking) Nonconformity, thanks to its popular association with radical causes such as land reform, a public program of education (culminating in the establishing of a national university), and (however guardedly) the disestablishment of the Church of England (viewed by Welsh Nonconformists as the alien church of an alien English state).

Writing in *Young Wales*, Rhys reminisced about his search for the home of that great hero of Welsh cultural (and political) independence, Owain Glyndŵr, known to the English as Owen Glendower. To his dismay, he had found people in Owain's very own Glyndyfrdwy who not only had not known of the house's location but who had never even heard of Glyndŵr himself. Such was a subordinated "peasantry's" state of cultural amnesia. Rhys refuses, however, to believe in Glyndŵr's final defeat: "[O]ur pulses expand today at his name; that old, red-handed, fighting spirit of his, converted into other forms of energy, will carry us far into the Wales that is to be."[23] The fight now, for Rhys, is not primarily a political one (and here Welsh Cymru Fydd supporters parted company from militant Irish separatists). Rather, it is a cultural struggle against the forces "that seek to destroy the national sentiment, and make Wales into a London suburb, and Snowdon—the sacred mountains of our fathers!—into a railway station!" By providing a forum for Wales's cultural and political aspirations, *Young Wales*, he concludes, is the modern successor to that independent Welsh parliament Glyndŵr had briefly succeeded in establishing at Machynlleth.

Whitman's name is specifically associated with that of Rhys in an interview with the London Welshman by the editor of *Young Wales*, J. Hugh Edwards, who sees in Rhys a fine example of the missionary work being done among the alien Saxons by expatriate Welshmen in London (*Young Wales* I, 132). And when Rhys mentions how the Welsh King Arthur is stirring in his sleep prior to his messianic return, one recalls how, in a letter of February 2, 1889, he had mentioned to Whitman his intention of visiting "King Arthur's Seat [*sic*]" on Cefn Bryn, in Gower. In the interview, Rhys's main emphasis is, however, on the Arnoldean concept of the Celts as the dreamy idealists who provide the powerful, materialistic English with a kind of spiritual ballast. Implicit in such a notion is the concept of a "Britain" to which England, Scotland, Wales, and Ireland all continued to belong. This contributionist strain in his thinking is confirmed when he urges the Welsh to fight against mass modern cosmopolitan society, "not only in self-preservation, but to preserve the health of other people, its English cousins and the rest." This is the culmination of references in his letters to Whitman to being refreshed by "the quiet of the mountains." Remembering Whitman as the poet who loved to "lean and loaf at his ease, observing a spear of summer grass," he could conclude that "such fits of lazy satisfaction with the idle spirit of sunny summer days spent by lake and mountain and seashore, are not sins in your code of life! It is this wretched commercial demand for unceasing work and worry that make that best of all types, the vagabond, seem nowadays a weak and unsatisfactory creature. But vagabondage has a notable encouragement in L. of G.; and I for one hope to keep up its honourable reputation."

In interviewing Rhys, J. Hugh Edwards asks his opinion of the recent politicizing of the Cymru Fydd/Young Wales movement by its amalgamation with the Liberal Party; and in his reply Rhys reluctantly recognizes that Wales's struggle to establish cultural autonomy may necessitate political expression. Little was either of them to know that this amalgamation, masterminded by Lloyd George, would bring disaster to Cymru Fydd/Young Wales within a matter of months. At a meeting in Newport, southeast Wales, Robert Bird, Bristol-born chairman of the Cardiff Liberal Association, thwarted Lloyd George's plans to commit the whole of Liberal Wales to the Cymru Fydd Home Rule platform, when he stated that "[t]here are from Swansea to Newport, thousands upon thousands of Englishmen, as true Liberals as yourselves . . . who will never submit to the domination of Welsh ideas" (quoted, Williams, 13). Bird's was the voice of the new, industrialized, Anglophone Wales of the south Wales coalfield and its great urban centers. It was therefore also the voice of the future. And through Bird it declared its total opposition to the language, religion, politics, and culture of nineteenth-century Welsh Nonconformity and its Liberal representatives. Moreover, Bird was, unknown to himself, prophesizing the death of Welsh liberalism. Over the next decade, the proletariat of the new commercial and industrial Wales, whose voice Bird claimed to be, was to desert the Liberal Party in favor of the emergent Labour Party: as early as 1900, Merthyr—one of the oldest industrial communities in the modern world—returned the Socialist Keir Hardie, miners' leader and founder of the Independent Labor Party, as one of its members of parliament.

Defeated in his attempt to make Welsh Home Rule a plank of mainstream liberalism's platform, Lloyd George threw in his lot with Anglophone Britain and its Empire, and went on to international fame and success in its service. With that defeat, a wedge was driven between Welsh cultural and political nationalism. The latter largely disappeared underground, only to reappear thirty years later in the form of a militantly political Plaid Cymru (Party of Wales), led by Saunders Lewis, a controversial political figure, a cultural visionary, and giant literary talent. As for Welsh-language literary culture, divorced from politics but inspired (exactly as Rhys and others had dreamt) by scholarly rediscoveries reconnecting it to a rich, ancient literary tradition, it blossomed in the twentieth century into achievements the likes of which had not been seen since the golden age of the fourteenth century. Wales was slower to develop a rich distinctive literature in English, but this began to appear during the 1930s not, as Ernest Rhys had hoped (following Yeats's example), by drawing upon the legends and literary achievements of Welsh-language culture, but as the by-product of massive population- and culture-shift, and as the unique cultural expression of one of the world's earliest and greatest industrial societies, established in the coalfield valleys of south Wales. Modern Welsh responses to Whitman cannot be understood without an understanding of these developments and the linguistic, cultural, and political divisions attendant upon them, already apparent in that historic confrontation between Lloyd George and Robert Bird.

Welsh-language culture, in both its rural and its industrial aspects; Anglophone Welsh culture, in its industrial and urban strongholds: all these found significant points of self-recognition in Whitman's writing. Moreover, his vision seemed to speak particularly potently to those, like himself, conscious of being caught up in bewildering processes of economic change, cultural transformation, and social transition—the condition of many in a Wales experiencing massive immigration and violent wholesale reconfiguration. Between 1851 and 1914, the population of Wales increased from 1,163,139 to 2,523,500, an increase of 117 percent; the same period saw 380,000 attracted from the rural areas of Wales to the new industrial boom valleys of the southern coalfield, while 320,000 immigrants (most from England) swelled the labor force even further.[24]

The widespread popularity of Whitman's social gospel in these industrial areas may be illustrated by examining the situation in the Amman Valley, an anthracite district in the far western corner of the south Wales coalfield and home to a remarkable Welsh-speaking industrial community. Indeed, such was Whitman's popularity among the industrial working class in that area that as early as 1903 the important workers' periodical *Llais Llafur* (*The Voice of Labor*) could carry an inventive and affectionate parody of his poetry entitled "Walt Whitman Up-to-Date":

> O my bicycle!
> O thou who attractest with a curious undeniable attraction!
> I sing of thy wheels—revolving, circumambient, belligerent, essential,
> omniovorous—
> (Or if not these—then any other five-syllabled adjectives which will do as well
> to fill up a line);
> Of thy handles—upturned, umbrageous, resilient, vivific;
> Of the curious sympathy one feels when smoothing with the hand thy naked
> enamel.
> Camerado! away with thee, shuddering equine thing that neighest a long finale
> to the roadway, . . .
> Allons! I see thee hurtling away over the plain, and after thee come strong men,
> maidens, mothers, church wardens, and sacred idiots
> On Bicycles,
> Transcendent bicycles.[25]

And so, amusingly, on to a catalog of the riders exhilarated by "the invigoration of the wheel": "Shapes of aged, respectable and much-venerated matrons . . . / Shapes of aproned bishops, and gaitered deans, and stout rectors, and hungry-eyed curates—shapes of all things shovel-hatted; . . . / Shapes that puff, and pant, and blow, and lean well over their handlebars in a manner truly and eccentrically frog-like."

Whereas by the end of the nineteenth century the valleys at the very heart of that coalfield (second in Europe only to the German Ruhr in industrial muscle) had attracted a huge cosmopolitan workforce to mine the steam coal needed by the British Navy, and society there had consequently adopted English as its lingua franca, the population in the anthracite mining townships of the western coalfield had been drawn mostly from the Nonconformist society of the surrounding rural areas and had therefore remained Welsh-speaking. This meant that while the Amman Valley eventually became as fiercely working class in character and as unswervingly Labour in politics as the valleys to the east, it nevertheless featured a society strikingly different in social temper and cultural character from theirs.[26]

In his strong Nonconformist faith, his Socialist politics, his staunch unionism, and his love of Welsh literature, David Rees Griffiths (or "Amanwy" to give him the bardic name by which he became known and loved throughout Wales) was a largely self-taught miner-poet who typified the upright values most highly cherished not only by his distinctive industrial society but also by Welsh-language culture at large at the beginning of the twentieth century. His equivalent could not be found among the English industrial proletariat, since the English class structure did not really translate into indigenous Welsh social terms. Through his authoritative physical presence, impressive personal qualities, moral integrity, moderate political activism, and above all his prominent success at eisteddfodau (major literary festivals), Amanwy became a nationally respected figure: indeed, the Welsh contribution to the Festival of Britain of 1950 was a powerful film (*David*) celebrating his life. He seemed the perfect example of the "gwerin"—that dominant ideological construct of nineteenth-century Welsh-language culture, signifying a highly moral, naturally cultivated, egalitarian society of ordinary people. There was as much historical truth as falsehood in this construct. The literary, cultural, and intellectual life of Amanwy's working-class society was indeed sophisticated, impressive, and rich, movingly sustained as it was by workingmen (women were marginalized) who had received little or no formal education. (The popular lyric poet "Watcyn Wyn," for instance, was working underground at the age of eight.) Moreover, in an age when poets were the pop idols of a Wales besotted with its image as one of the most civilized regions of the British Empire, national success at poetry brought with it the kind of social prestige enjoyed elsewhere in the industrial valleys by boxers, rugby players, and singers. In the absence of any real upper class or even middle class on the English model, this society could legitimately feel that it was heir to, and sustainer of, a complex poetic tradition extending back to the sixth century, as well as the inheritor of the popular ballad and lyric verse of neighboring rural society. Indeed, the "gwerin" had originally been associated exclusively with rural Wales, but Amanwy quite consciously proffered proof, particularly through his poetry, that the qualities that characterized it could be reproduced in an industrial environment hitherto believed by traditional Welsh-speaking society to be morally suspect. Such a reassurance was all the more necessary at the very time when the Welsh industrial proletariat was being driven by economic conditions to become more militantly confrontational in its relationship to industrial management: this was the very period when "working-class" consciousness was assuming a potent politico-economic form, and a new kind of radically leftist unionism was developing. In the poetry of a Whitman who seemed as formally unlettered yet as naturally "educated" as himself, Amanwy felt he discovered in part models for celebrating the industrial "gwerin" of which he was so proud a member.

The young Amanwy turned to Whitman at a point of emotional, intellectual, spiritual, and political crisis. In 1908, his gifted older brother was killed in a terrible pit explosion in which Amanwy himself was severely injured.[27] During his protracted recovery period he had the leisure for the first time to immerse himself in reading, including the poetry of Whitman, whose work was then exciting young miners in the Amman Valley. He thus provided himself with the means of resolving a dilemma. He was at this time in effect caught between two gospels, confused by two conflicting conversion experiences: on the one hand he had been permanently marked by the powerful religious revival of 1904–1905 led by Evan Roberts, on the other he was profoundly moved by R. J. Campbell's "New Theology," a major influence on socialists throughout industrial Britain in the first decades of the twentieth century. While the former preached a Calvinistic doctrine of sin and repentance, the latter emphasized divine human potentiality based on a gospel of social, rather than personal, transformation. Whitman's poetry seems to have offered, for Amanwy, a poetic discourse that fused the spiritual passion of the revivalist with the comradely social vision of the more modern minister's program. Whitman's rather vague, unfocused "spirituality" helped Amanwy infuse a new Socialist proletarian politics with the kind of religiosity of feeling that best satisfied a Nonconformist conscience newly sensitized by the impact of the Revival.

Although Amanwy took to composing some of his earliest eisteddfod-winning pieces in free verse, on the model of Whitman and Carpenter, it is in its sentiment rather than in its form or vocabulary that his youthful poetry is most consciously Whitmanesque. But as is disappointingly apparent in "Y Ddaear Newydd" ("The New Earth"), a poem about the spiritual carnage of the First World War, Amanwy simply translated vaguely Whitmanesque sentiments into the conventional language of the versifying religious lyric so beloved of Victorian Wales:

> The most beautiful ideals of the ages have become livingly realized,
> And the loveliest flowers of heaven spring up on mankind's path.
> The judges' robes no longer adorn the wolves of savage war,
> Worldwide, the hearts of low and mighty are united in the bonds of love;
> No more will blood turn streams ruddy on the pebbles,—
> The peace of glades will not be broken by the wailing of a nation in flight,
> The "gwerin" of all kingdoms are journeying arm in arm,
> And the shoulder of intense sympathy is lightening every burden.[28]

In view of this kind of effusion, it is worth recalling that Amanwy had been introduced to Whitman's poetry by "Gwili" (John Gwili Jenkins), a "poet-preacher"—that cult figure in nineteenth-century Wales. Gwili taught at a school in the Amman Valley to train youngsters for the ministry, and by advocating a revolutionary social gospel he helped produce an important generation of consciously Welsh Socialists and Labour leaders. Reading Whitman may, for Gwili, have initially been a means of extending the vocabulary of "y Beirdd Newydd" ("the New Poets"), neo-Hegelians who had favored interminably long poems stuffed full of exalted philosophical abstraction, with abstruse discourse to match. He would therefore have been primarily interested in Whitman as a source of abstract Platonic speculation. But it seems likely that on inspection he found in him a humanist of incipiently Socialist sympathies and that Whitman thus provided Gwili with a bridge between the "Bardd Newydd" (such as he himself had been) and the emergent Labour culture to which the later Gwili was to make a significant contribution.

It is, though, a Welsh "poet-preacher" of an entirely different, and wholly unconventional, stamp who offers the most striking example of Whitman's influence on Welsh industrial culture during the early decades of the twentieth century.[29] T. E. Nicholas (1878–1971)—affectionately and universally known as "Niclas y Glais"—was a colorful figure. Of west Wales farming stock, he was prepared for the Congregational ministry at a Nonconformist academy before serving as a minister in several places, including Dodgeville (United States) and Glais (lower Swansea Valley). The experience of living in this working-class village—surrounded as it was by coal mines and steel and tin-plate works, and horribly subject to the poisonous by-products of the metallurgical industry—was an educational experience for the young Niclas. He identified totally with the workers in their struggle with capital, joined the Independent Labour Party (whose leader, Keir Hardie, became a close friend of his), and began to preach a fervent social gospel, not only from the pulpit but also through popular journalism and popular crusading verses. Appalled not only by the First World War, but also by the way in which establishment Nonconformity responded to it by spearheading a recruitment drive throughout Wales, he fiercely voiced his objections and was in consequence persecuted by religious, military, and political bodies. This effectively drove him out of the recognized ministry and so he retrained as a dentist, while continuing to preach. In the meantime, he had converted to communism, following the Bolshevik Revolution of October 1917, and became a founding member of the Communist Party of Great Britain, remaining a Christian Communist for the remainder of his long life. Since the Second World War seemed to him essentially a repeat of the first, involving further exploitation of a working class that had borne the brunt of the Depression, he again forcefully registered his objections and was imprisoned for two months on trumped-up charges. Although he was a fierce campaigner, his underlying good nature and undeniable moral integrity made him a favorite with people of many political persuasions in Wales.

True to his proselytizing beliefs, Niclas was a prolific versifier throughout his life, addressing his "psalms" (as he liked to style them) to "the people."[30] The main burden of his message was the international brotherhood of man, which he expected to be realized once the masses joined together to overthrow their oppressors. Although Niclas employed Marxist forms of analysis after his conversion to communism, his beliefs never entirely lost the marks of their origins in a Christian socialism very much colored by the writings of authors like Tolstoy and Whitman. Niclas's Whitman was a Whitman of the late nineteenth-century Labour movement and of the Independent Labour Party. He was the forerunner of socialism; the prophet of a new, people's age of social cooperation. What he was *not*, however, was Whitman the great poet. His Socialist supporters (such as Amanwy) quarried his poetry for ideas, sentiments, and uplifting phrases, but were rarely comfortable with the unconventional style of *Leaves of Grass.* Niclas's early poetry was written almost exclusively in popular Victorian verse forms, while his later poetry consisted mainly of sonnets.

There was, however, one notable exception that makes his an interesting case. In 1920, Niclas closed his collection subtitled *Cerddi Rhyddid* (*Songs of Freedom*) with a thirty-three page, savagely antiwar, poem in free verse entitled "Gweriniaeth a Rhyfel" ("Republicanism and War"). It opens as follows:

> I shall sink my own personality in the republic of the people.
> I shall escape from narrow limits; in me shall the people's democracy live.
> I shall spread myself over continents, I shall learn the language of the toys and the lambs and the flowers,
> Like the sea's tides entering the narrow straits, I shall invite true democracy into my life.
> Hills and estuaries, springs and deeps, the heather of the mountain and the shells of the seashore, come and speak through me.
> It is I who own the earth—I claim it;
> It is I who own hell—and when I go there, Love shall drag itself thither too.
> It is I who own heaven—and both men and demons shall be allowed to enter it.
> From now on it is I who am the republic of the people.[31]

The word repeatedly used here—"Gweriniaeth"—nowadays simply means "Republic" or "Democracy," but it is derived from "gwerin"—always a key term in Niclas's political rhetoric—and there is no doubt that he wants to reactivate the original meaning, just as Whitman wanted to put the "demos" back into "democracy."

Throughout the poem, Niclas strives to turn apocalyptic war into an occasion for millenarian vision, and section 7 includes passages in which despair and hope are beautifully blended:

> Pleasant, pleasant it was to search for birds' nests on spring mornings, and to count the eggs every day; this year there is no charm for children in birds' nests, nor in the song of the cuckoo;
> The cruel god of war came by and damned the world.
> His shadow fell upon the play of children and on the hard labor of workers;
> Will the song return?
> A new greenness flows over hedgerow and hedge; the leaves tremble in the breezes from heaven; the trees and forests are arrayed in blue and green garments; away over the wave the green and the blue are red with blood.

The trees are stripped of their bark by the fireballs; it is the god of war who accomplished this . . .
Who will dare to kill his fellow while the birds are singing? Who will dare thrust a bayonet into a brother's heart while the hedges are bright with life?
Mars is pitiless: he knows not what gentleness is. I believe in the spring and the primroses, in the nests and the birds and the trees—
For this reason I cannot believe in war.

The work concludes with a visionary verse paragraph in which Niclas hears the approach of a new age and sees that a social revolution is at hand. The poem is dated 1916. Almost exactly a year later Russia was to experience the Bolshevik Revolution.

The influence of Whitman on "Gweriniaeth a Rhyfel" is in one sense easy enough to see—mediated though it may have been by Carpenter's *Towards Democracy*—but it is very difficult to isolate, so blended is it with influences from other sources. And it is precisely this difficulty, arising from such an intermixing, that makes the poem a very instructive example of the complexities of "influence," particularly when that involves "translation" from a foreign language and a foreign culture. Whitman's poetry has here been received, and naturalized, by a mind steeped in the rhythms, images, and values of the Welsh Bible, so that *Leaves of Grass* is being read as an additional chapter to the Book of Revelation. Of course, Whitman himself owed a great deal, as poet, to the Bible, to radical forms of Protestantism, and to a Christian millenarian tradition, and Niclas anticipated the findings of later scholars when he unconsciously intuited this. But what is interesting is the way in which Whitman's poetry seems to have enabled Niclas, at one of the most critical points in his life, to discover in the Welsh Bible styles of writing that allowed him to develop radical new forms of expression for the radical sociopolitical ideas he had also partly derived from biblical sources. In other words, the foreignness of Whitman paradoxically helped to make aspects of Niclas's own native Nonconformist culture newly visible to him, and available to him, as a poet. The result is a Welsh poem that has certain affinities with famous early examples in English of a poetry revolutionized, in style as well as in sociopolitical content, by radical Protestantism—Blake's *The French Revolution* and Shelley's *The Mask of Anarchy.*

In the last essay he ever wrote, Waldo Williams (1904–1971), one of twentieth-century Wales's preeminent poets, recalled the thrill he experienced as a boy when he heard his father read "Gweriniaeth a Rhyfel" aloud to his mother during the First World War.[32] A product of the same region of rural west Wales as Niclas, an area noted for a religious and political radicalism that had several times found expression in militant direct action, Waldo had no doubt been unconsciously prepared for the experience by exposure from his earliest years to the writers that were his father's passion: William Morris, Ruskin, Shelley, Tolstoy—and Walt Whitman.[33] A respected headmaster, Waldo's father nevertheless remained a member of the group of largely self-educated workingmen of progressive views who provided this farming community with its intellectual leadership. A local discussion group met in a convenient carthouse to discuss theology, politics, and literature, and Whitman's work figured in these informal discussions. The evidence comes from the writing of Edwal's brother William, an ardent Socialist, who was, in 1892–1893, the first writer to experiment, under the Whitman-Carpenter influence, with free verse in Welsh; and Waldo was himself to produce similar Whitmanesque poetry during his callow years as a poet.[34] As he matured, however, he seems to have taken a more objective and mixed view of Whitman's achievement, remarking that "when a mere cry, as in Whitman sometimes, gets us on the raw, we feel that it is not poetry but a protoplasm from which poetry might be organized."[35]

Such reservations were understandable. After all, Waldo developed as a poet under the twin influences of English Romantic poetry and the traditional, epigrammatic poetry of Welsh strict-meter poetry, with a third influence—the revisionary work done by several outstanding Welsh-language poets of his own generation—in the end proving particularly decisive. But friends have testified that he never lost his enthusiasm for Whitman and that he could quote admiringly from his work. This was largely due to the close spiritual affinity he had with Whitman, and to similarities in their social vision.

Throughout his life, Waldo based his vision of the brotherhood of man upon a belief in the inborn divinity, and goodness, of every individual. Persuaded early of the truth of the inner light, he eventually joined the Quakers, discovering in their socially active faith the kind of mystical attraction Whitman had also felt toward the teaching of the controversial Quaker Elias Hicks. But for Waldo, as for Whitman, the corollary of spiritual immanence was what, with his genius for succinctness, he called "Awen adnabod." Unlike English, Welsh distinguishes between the act of knowing a thing ("gwybod") and that of knowing a person ("adnabod"). "Awen" can mean muse, or spirit, or genius, or gift. Hence "Awen adnabod" means the spiritual-poetic gift of creatively apprehended human recognition, involving an existential gesture of generous "fellow feeling" that goes as deep as a profound understanding of our fellow men—a humanly comprehensive act of "knowing" that was for Waldo, as it was for Whitman, the very essence of writing poetry. To "know" in this way was to know oneself to be inextricably part of what in Welsh is epigrammatically called "cwlwm cymdeithas," literally "the knot of community/society." And again like Whitman, Waldo tended to see his own society—the actual rural society of west Wales—as instinct with the potential for visionary community. In this he saw the hope for a redeemed Wales and a redeemed world, just as Whitman extrapolated a future cooperative American order and a transfigured world order from his visions of contemporary New York.

Waldo's visionary communitarianism was an amalgam of many different sources, including his radical Nonconformist background, his family involvement in the early Socialist and Welsh nationalist movements, his wide reading in Welsh literature, in English literature, in anthropology and in Eastern religions, and his interest in the philosophy of international figures such as Gandhi and of international thinkers such as Buber and Berdyayev. But although it would not do, in the face of all of this, to overemphasize the influence of Whitman on his thinking, it is important to remember Waldo's very early and enduring affection for him. He had absorbed Whitman's poetry, one suspects, to a point where he was no longer fully conscious of its presence within him, or of its contributions to the color and movement of his own highly original and distinctive imagination.

Whitman's indirect presence is most creatively apparent in Waldo's masterpiece, "Mewn Dau Gae" ("In Two Fields"), his response to contemporary events. In 1946, the British government requisitioned large areas of land in Waldo's native Pembrokeshire (where American troops had been stationed during the Second World War) in order to establish several military bases. In 1950, the Americans, along with their allies in the UN, became embroiled in a war in Korea. Waldo, who had been a pacifist throughout the Second World War,[36] was appalled by both events—indeed so disturbed was he by the latter, so racked and prostrated by personal guilt, that for some time he felt unable to walk the streets of his small town because he shrank from the ordeal of having to face his neighbors. Eventually he decided, in his own words, "to turn guilt into conscience, and conscience into responsibility" by refusing to pay his taxes while a part of them went toward equipping the military machine. Consequently, his goods were first seized and then he was imprisoned. During this grim period in his life, he virtually gave up writing poetry, and his imagination was troubled by hideous childhood memories of reports from the front he had read during the First World War. In particular he recalled 1916—the very year in which Niclas wrote "Gweriniaeth a Rhyfel." It was, Waldo remembered, a terrible year, when the allies seemed literally hell bent on capturing a certain "Hill 60," and he specifically associated the horror of it all with Niclas's apocalyptic poem. But he also remembered that Niclas had managed to find grounds for visionary hope even in Armageddon. It was a feat of transmutation which Waldo was to repeat, at an infinitely deeper spiritual level, when he returned to poetry in 1956 to write "Mewn Dau Gae."

The poem begins by wondering from what deep source had come the "sea of light" that Waldo remembered once seeing "rolling its deep" over two ordinary fields in his youth. It signified, he felt, the coming of the field's "life-giving hunter," present as much in "the host of rushes dreaming the blue sky" as in the stirrings of the human creative imagination. This it was that had been the "tranquil soother of a troubled self," and with its coming had come an ineffable spirit of beatitude:

> Till at last the whole world came to the stillness
> And on the two fields his people walked,
> And through them, among them, about them spread
> A spirit rising from hiding, conjoining all,
> As it was with the few of us once, in the plying of pitchforks
> Or the tedious tugging of thatch out on the heavy moor.
> How close to each other we came—
> The silent hunter was casting his net about us.[37]

Pivoting on this moment of vision, the poem then turns, in conclusion, to an anticipation of the day when such a presence will become a lasting, transfiguring one, transforming the world into millennial peace and harmony.

In an excellent study, Ned Thomas has shown how Waldo is here reappropriating and regenerating several of the great seminal images of European Romanticism, as he works to bring an experience of illumination he had as a boy into a saving relationship with his traumatic adult experiences of human cruelty and aggression.[38] Knowing of Waldo's longstanding interest in Whitman, one no doubt could, if one chose, hesitantly identify specific parallels between the poem and *Leaves of Grass.* For example, Waldo's ecstatic affirmations seem, both in spirit and in the terms in which they are expressed, to be consonant with Whitman's. Both poets are fascinated by the relationship between the one and the many; both conceive not only the cosmos but also human society in these terms; both see the presence of the whole as informing each part of life, magnifying its rich singularity of being; both regard the creative imagination as in essence a religious power through which the visionary unity of all existence is revealed.

This kind of analysis is, however, as superficial as it is beside the point, since Waldo has absorbed aspects of Whitman's poetry so completely that they have become flesh of his imagination's flesh and soul of its soul. Or, to use an entirely different metaphor, "In Two Fields" offers us a fine example of the way in which a great creative writer's imagination is authentically a Celtic cauldron of rebirth, in which past writers are constantly being brought back to life, only insofar as it is first a crucible of meanings that operates by smelting everything down to produce the molten materials of new creation. Consequently, when the works of other writers reemerge from this crucible-cauldron, it is frequently in a form in which their own author fathers and mothers would not recognize them. Rather, therefore, than search for identifiable parallels, it would be better to re-view Whitman in the light of Waldo's achievement, allowing the Welsh poem to suggest to us new contexts in which Whitman's poetry could be read. So, for instance, we are led by Waldo to see Whitman as a kind of latter-day Langland, and to see sections of *Leaves of Grass* as resembling passages from *Piers Ploughman*, since these are connections that seem to have been made unconsciously by Waldo's imagination. We are encouraged to see in Whitman's democratic vistas the millenarianism of a secular society whose utopian faith is in historical progress.[39] And we may also be moved to reinvestigate the sources of Whitman's affirmations—to see his poetry at its best as surging up, like Waldo's, from a wellhead of suffering, until the falling tears are turned before our very eyes, as they are in "Mewn Dau Gae," into the joyous leaves of a healing tree.

The unsubduable spirit of affirmation in Whitman's poetry could prove attractive to the new Anglophone writers of the south Wales coalfield as well as to poets from the rural, Welsh-speaking west. "Ah, Walt [Whitman], why were you never a Welshman? What a Welshman you would have been," wrote the Merthyr writer Glyn Jones in 1973,[40] and Whitman's "Welsh" presence may, indeed, be felt in the following extract from the rhapsodic conclusion to Glyn Jones's notable short story "The Water-Music":

> I lie like sand-eel, water-snake, or Welsh Shelley under the ten-foot slab of transparent green, watching it reach the world of my God whom I continue to praise, whom I praise for the waters, the little balls of dew and the great wave shooting out its tassel; I praise him for the big boy-bodied beeches, and all trees velvet in sunshine and shying like mad when the grass is flat under the wind; I praise him for the blooms of the horned lilac, for the blossomed hawthorn with the thick milks of spring ris-

ing over her, and the blood-drop of the ladycow bled on the white lily. I praise him for the curving gull, the brown coat of the sparrow and the plover with wings like blown hair.[41]

The passage is a conscious blend of English writers such as Hopkins, Shelley, and Whitman with the great Welsh-language tradition of "praise poetry." As such it is a cultural product that deliberately mimics in its hybridity of discourse the mixing of peoples Glyn Jones knew had produced his native early industrial township of Merthyr. In this sense, Jones's evocation of Whitman is relevant not only at the level of discourse but also in terms of the ideology inscribed in the whole cultural, as well as literary, style of the passage. Like Whitman, Jones is pointedly celebrating a world that is produced by an endless, indiscriminate "breed of life," the "procreant urge of the world," a promiscuous intermingling of races and peoples. He praises a God who "leaves no stretch of water unmarked, no sand or snow-plain without the relief of interfering stripe, shadow or cross-hatch, no spread of pure sky but deepens it from the pallor of its edges to its vivid zenith. I praise him that he is never baulked, never sterile never repetitious."

Glyn Jones's implied Whitman is therefore the muse of that new, hybrid Wales of the industrial coalfield, where—as Jones knew from personal experience—Jews, Italians, Spanish, English, and many other nationalities all fused with the native Welsh to produce an extraordinarily dynamic new "Welsh" society. Hence the frequent description of this region as "American Wales." And Jones was particularly interested in producing the kind of Welsh modernist art and literature that seemed to him to be, in its eclecticism, the cultural medium most appropriate for expressing this new hybrid society.[42] At the very same time that he was reading James Joyce and D. H. Lawrence and visiting London and Paris to view post-impressionist painting and experience the Dadaist and surrealist movements, the young Jones was putting himself to school to improve his relatively slight grasp of the Welsh language (spoken by his parents) and to educate himself in the great poetic tradition of Dafydd ap Gwilym and medieval Wales. The result was a Welsh modernist poetry that Jones modeled partly on Welsh *cynghanedd* writing, and a fiction (such as *The Valley, the City, the Village*) that is a deliberate bricolage of mixed vocabulary and styles, as if Jones were sometimes foregrounding words and discourse in the way cubist painters foregrounded form and color.

No wonder, then, that the young Dylan Thomas felt a strong artistic kinship with the Glyn Jones who became his friend. And what did Dylan Thomas pin above his desk in that famous boathouse at Laugharne where, in later life, he produced some of his most popular work, but "a big photograph of Walt Whitman. . . . There are also pinned about, pictures of monkeys & naked women."[43] In 1940, Thomas sent Vernon Watkins a satirical poem, explaining:

> I've got little to say about it myself: you'll see the heavy hand with which I make fun of this middle-class, beardless Walt who props humanity, in his dirty, weeping, expansive moments, against corners & counters & tries to slip, in grand delusions of all embracing humanitarianism, everyone into himself. (*Letters*, 445)

But he had preceded these comments with the qualifier that "this [is] a half comic attack on myself."

Soulmates though, in one sense, Thomas and Glyn Jones may have been, in another sense they were chalk and cheese as people and as artists, and their relation to Whitman differed accordingly. Something of their difference is caught in a very early letter Thomas wrote to Jones:

> I refuse on paper to quarrel with you about obscurity, fluid verse, T. S. Eliot, Walt Whitman, Worker's Party, my own anatomic slap-stick, and other controversial points mentioned in your letter, especially as you're coming down. (I would far rather be Eliot than Whitman, if only because Eliot has a very splendid sense of form.) (*Letters*, 117)

Although there is youthful attitudinizing in these remarks, along with the dramatic scoring of a debating point, Thomas's comments on Whitman and Eliot should not be lightly disregarded. He was always to feel a deep ambivalence about Whitman's sprawling, garrulous free verse. The immediate context of these comments, however, was a disagreement between a Glyn Jones who was desperately resisting his own inclinations toward obscure modernist experimentations because these scarcely promoted that artistic solidarity with the workers in which he believed, and a professedly modernist and experimental Thomas who was impatient with all such sentiments. Moreover, Glyn Jones was to remain a practicing Welsh Nonconformist all his life, identifying not with the darkly oppressive Calvinism of its remarkable religious civilization but with the distinguished humane, radical, egalitarian, and proto-Socialist record of Nonconformity's liberal, progressive wing. Thomas, by contrast, not only reacted violently against a Welsh Nonconformity he could imagine only as malign but actually defined himself as a writer partly through that very reaction. When, in "After the Funeral," Thomas announces himself to be "Ann's bard on a raised hearth," not only is he identifying with the praise poetry tradition of medieval Welsh writing, he is also pitting his powers to "call all/ the seas to service" against those of the Nonconformist minister officiating at his aunt's funeral. At a time when cancer was popularly supposed to be produced by repression of physical desires, Ann's death from that disease is treated as a sign that she was killed by her inhibitions, her fierce, loving passions thwarted by soul-crippling Nonconformity, so that her dead hands are seen as lying "with religion in their cramp." Thomas, by contrasts, sings to set her love free to "sing and swing through a brown chapel" and to "bow down the walls of the ferned and foxy woods" so that her spirit may at last be granted liberating passage. It is a deliberate echo of Dafydd ap Gwilym's celebrated, repeated trope of the greensward as the true, pagan church of love.

The same anti-Nonconformist animus is apparent in a Whitmanesque passage from Thomas's *Portrait of the Artist as a Young Dog* where a young boy from an Anglophone, urban town, on a visit to his Welsh-speaking country relatives, plays hide-and-seek in a meadow's long grass:

> I felt all my young body like an excited animal surrounding me, the torn knees bent, the bumping heart, the long heat and depth between the legs, the sweat prickling in the hands, the tunnels down to the eardrums, the little balls of dirt between the toes, the eyes in the sockets, the tucked-up voice, the blood racing, the memory around and within flying, jumping, swimming and waiting to pounce. There, playing Indians in the evening, I was aware of me myself in the exact middle of a living story, and my body was my adventure and my name.[44]

The boy and his friend Jack are hiding from his cousin Gwilym, "one-eyed, dead-eyed, sinister, slim, ten-notched Gwilym, loading his guns in Gallows Farm"; and Gwilym is the glowering cousin who has just thundered out a (comical) imitation sermon from his "pulpit cart," his chapel being an old barn. The boy's pagan awakening to bodily identity functions as Thomas's answer to the dark puritanism of the Nonconformity that Gwilym represents. And as this passage suggests, the Whitman who was one of the muses of Thomas's writing was therefore the great celebrant of the flesh who had found his identity in the body; a Whitman who was the welcome liberator, releasing Thomas from the clutch of Welsh puritan Nonconformity. That carnivalesque Whitman who identified body with cosmos and cosmos with body, and who delighted in physical process and sexual generation, was, from the beginning, a significant sponsor of Thomas's imagination both as poet and as prose writer.

In *Start with the Sun: Studies in the Whitman Tradition,* an important academic by-product of the "alternative culture" of the early sixties and a polemical blast against the "New Puritanism" of twentieth-century American poetry, Bernice Slote and James E. Miller exhaustively listed Thomas's debts to Whitman, from the level of "ideas and theme" to that of "word and image."[45] Beginning by recalling how Thomas had once styled himself "A singing Walt from the mower . . . / Beardlessly wagging in Dean Street," they sensibly put this down to self-mockery before proceeding to emphasize how "the poetry of both Thomas and Whitman becomes itself a part of the creative body of the world, image creating image, word bursting into word, in a spiral plunge out of the dark seed to the larger, encompassing light."[46] But while rightly concluding that "the world and universe of Thomas's poetry are astonishingly similar to the world and universe of Whitman's" (190), they wholly failed to see how the "world and universe" of Thomas's poetry had a local habitation and a name in the Wales of the twenties and thirties, just as Whitman's cosmic philosophy was solidly embedded in the socioeconomic conditions of the New York of the 1850s. The interesting fact, surely, is that two writers of backgrounds that seem, at least, to be geographically, culturally, and historically remote from each other, should nevertheless have shared a vocabulary of the imagination. And one way to begin exploring this coincidence would be to understand Thomas as being, like Whitman, a self-styled "provincial," living in a puritan society undergoing violent change.

A recent critical essay may help us place Thomas's Whitmanesque "poetry of the body" in an appropriate historico-cultural context. This discussion emphasizes "the liminal and hybrid qualities of Thomas's early work," suggesting that it is possible to read "the radical and disruptive qualities" of the poetry "in the context of the mainstream *New Country* reaction against experimentalism and the social crisis of the 1930s."[47] Just when the poets championed in Michael Roberts's influential *New Country* anthology (1932) were rejecting modernist formalism in favor of a poetry of social message, the young "Thomas was deliberately opposing what he saw as their presumptive rationality" (86–87) by choosing instead to turn to Freud (read in the 1930s as "a champion of individualism and freedom and as an honorary socialist") and to a politically subversive surrealism. And in Thomas's poetics, the essay suggests, may be discerned telltale signs of his ambiguous (or uncertain) national identity: "[H]is poetic identity, or rather *process*, is precisely this mediation between the bardic and the banal, the balance of *hywl* [*sic*]-inflated rhetoric and literary *lèse majesté*" (89). In this sense, too, then, Thomas found a useful model in Whitman, as had his friend Glyn Jones. What the essay does not see, however, is that Thomas's Whitmanesque (and Freudian) concerns with the body constitute the return of the repressed; a journey into the unconscious of his Welsh puritan society. This was an important source of his Welsh modernist writing, and it was to take a comic turn, of course, in *Under Milk Wood*. If it was Stalinism that moved Bakhtin to develop his theory of the carnivalesque, then it was against the totalitarian moral authority of Welsh Nonconformity that Thomas was reacting when writing his aggressively carnivalesque poetry. Not that he was the first such Welsh rebel. Even before it had been fatally undermined by its vociferous support for what turned out to be a murderous First World War, Nonconformity had come under sustained attack from Welsh-language writers. But whereas they had turned to Ibsen as the great unmasker of hypocrisy and liberator of the imprisoned self, Thomas turned instead to such writers as Whitman.

Moreover, in Whitman's body poetry, Thomas found a new model of the "bardic." In his time, prominent Welsh "bards" were more likely than not to be ministers, academics, or other similarly respectable products of the Welsh Nonconformist middle class, and Thomas (affectionately) satirized the sanctimoniousness and conventionality of their kind in the prayer of the Reverend Eli Jenkins in *Under Milk Wood.* But Thomas entertained the notion that the true Welsh bards of the Middle Ages, such as the textually inventive philanderer Dafydd ap Gwilym, had been of a very different ilk. Many Anglo-Welshmen of Thomas's period believed (unhistorically) that preindustrial and pre-Nonconformist Welsh society had been essentially "pagan," Celtic, and druidic, and Dr. William Price of Llantrisant, a prominent nineteenth-century eccentric (or some might say schizophrenic), was fondly regarded as the very reincarnation of its spirit. Price (known to history as "the father of cremation," because by publicly cremating the body of his son, Iesu Grist [Jesus Christ], he paved the way for the eventual legalization of that practice) was an extremely colorful character; a qualified doctor, Chartist agitator for political reform, and vocal advocate of free love who had once lectured in the nude and was given to walking the streets of industrial Pontypridd garbed in "druidic" costume and sporting a fur cap.[48] Dylan Thomas was fascinated with Price, and his story repeatedly crops up both overtly and covertly in Thomas's writings, most notably in the short story "The Burning Baby."[49] He shared the highly romantic view of him held by Rhys Davies, an important Anglophone fiction writer contemporary with Thomas himself:

> William Price did not lose faith in the old druidic gods. Such gods alone had respect for sacred bards and their riddles which were linked to the principles of life. He wanted the old race back, with its bright-striped coats and purple cloaks, its lime-washed dyed hair and its circumspect hospitality to strangers at the gate.[50]

So Price became a significant figure for "Anglo-Welsh" writers alienated by Welsh Nonconformist society, and it is possible that in Whitman Thomas found a "bard" after William Price's own heart; a bard like the "sacred [Welsh] bards of old" and wholly unlike those to be found at the National Eisteddfod, whose eminently respectable Gorsedd (bardic circle) was, as Thomas memorably quipped, "black with *parchs*" (reverend ministers), garbed though they might be in the fanciful druidic costume dreamt up in the late eighteenth century by Iolo Morganwg—a wonderful poetic forger and fantasist of Welsh cultural identity, and one of Williams Price's heroes.

And there are further interesting twists to this "bardic" story. In a brilliant obituary essay published in 1954, Karl Shapiro laid bare the process by which Thomas, following his sensationally successful American tours, had been translated into American cultural terms. By virtue of his Welshness, Shapiro suggested, Thomas was an outsider to English culture, just like Americans: "[H]e was another *naïf*, like Rimbaud, a countryman [*sic*] who, having left the country wanders over the face of the earth seeking a vision."[51] "And there are suggestions of Druidism . . . and primitive fertility rites, apparently still extant in Wales [!], all mixed up with Henry Miller, Freud and American street slang" (177). Noting Thomas's interest in the "animal" self, Shapiro observes: "It is the authentic symbol for a poet who believes in the greatness of the individual and the masses. It is Whitman's symbol when he says he thinks he could turn and live with animals" (281). This connection of Thomas with Whitman via the bardic (defined in primitivist terms that are, in fact, significantly at variance with the classical Welsh style, and cultural style, of the "bardd") resurfaces in Shapiro's essay in *Start with the Sun*:

> "Thou orb aloft, full dazzling!" [Whitman] begins his bardic invoction, "Strike through these chants." Writers in the Whitman tradition [like the Thomas who is specifically mentioned] make the strongest affirmation possible: that we do not live by either illusion or disillusion; that no life is cheap or need be separate; that in the earth we may grow into possibilities; that we take nothing secondhand. (238)

During his visits to the United States, Thomas had given poetic performances of inimitable power. In the flesh, and in full voice, he transformed arid intellectual text into emotionally compelling oral utterance, thereby helping to reawaken Americans' excited interest in their own bardic tradition, stemming from Emerson and Whitman.[52] As Karl Shapiro put it in his obituary essay: "[I]t is one thing to analyse and interpret poetry and keep it in a book: it is another to watch that poetry enter an audience and melt it to a single mind" (270). Thomas the bardic performer "was the master of a public which he himself had brought out of nothingness" and as such he may legitimately be claimed as the grandfather, if not the father, of the Beats. And when Allen Ginsberg visited Swansea in 1995, it was to Dylan Thomas's grave in Laugharne that he insisted on making a pilgrimage. Arrived there, he sank to his knees and chanted a mantra in memory of the Welsh Whitmanesque bard who had helped restore Whitman and bardism to American poetry.

If Dylan Thomas was the greatest Welsh Anglophone poet of the first half of the twentieth century, then R. S. Thomas was that of the second half of the century, and his relation to Whitman was entirely different from that of his predecessor. An early convert to the cause of Welsh-language culture and the political nationalism that sought to protect it, Thomas was strongly inclined to share that culture's deep mistrust of the threatening power of Anglo-American linguistic and cultural imperialism.[53] As such, he was in later life disinclined to indulge in unqualified admiration of a poet such as Whitman, whose expansive internationalism could be reasonably claimed in fact to conceal precisely such imperial ambitions. (Whitman shows no real understanding of the valuable irreducible "otherness" of non-American cultures.)

Indeed, there was for this reason a very strong impulse in Welsh-language culture from the very beginning of the twentieth century to reject American cultural products. This is symbolized by an interesting incident. Whitman's death was promptly reported in *Y Faner* (April 6, 1892), the paper that was at that time virtually the official organ of radical (i.e., Liberal), Nonconformist Wales. Of particular interest is the fact that the routine report was by T. Gwynn Jones, who was at that time a working journalist (largely self-educated, like Whitman), but who ten years later scandalized traditional Nonconformity when his controversial *Ymadawiad Arthur* (*The Departure of Arthur*) won the premier award for poetry (the chair) at the National Eisteddfod. This event is generally regarded as having initiated the great twentieth-century renaissance of Welsh-language literature, a cultural revival in which Jones became a dominating figure. During those ten years reports suggest that Jones, who was an active supporter of the new labor movements, had attempted some poems in a Whitmanesque style. But *Ymadawiad Arthur* marked a decisive turn back to Welsh legendary materials and Welsh *barddas* (strict-meter poetry). Modern Welsh literature may thus be said to have begun with the rejection of Whitman and the Anglo-American literary culture he represented.

It was therefore to be expected that, after his passionate identification with the values of modern Welsh-language culture, R. S. Thomas should also have rejected America and Whitman. Such an attitude grew pronounced during his middle and later years, as the conviction settled upon him that the Anglophone inhabitants of Wales could never be considered Welsh.[54] (He therefore despairingly concluded that his own Anglophone poetry belonged to the literary culture not of Wales but of England.) The younger Thomas had, however, entertained a different belief. Enthused by his readings in "Fiona Macleod" (William Sharp) and the authors of the modern Scottish Renaissance (such as Hugh MacDiarmid), and inspired by the romantic nationalism of Yeats and his contemporaries, he had in that period hoped to see a correspondingly national literature in English develop in Wales. In "A Time for Carving," a radio broadcast in April 1957, Thomas stated: "As a Welshman living in Wales, whose first language is nevertheless English, I find the history of American literature particularly instructive." In building on this observation, he repeatedly referred to Whitman approvingly as one of the literary begetters of this new nation, but for him Whitman's significance for Wales did not lie in the self-proclaimed eclecticism of his cultural outlook. Rather, Thomas placed emphasis on the assimilative powers of Anglophone America, as evidenced in Whitman's work:

> One of the most noticeable features of American history has been that of men coming from other cultures, other languages, finding themselves in this new land and taking inventory of themselves and their surroundings. Need one say how necessary it is that the non-Welsh speaker in Wales should do the same? . . . One might quote . . . Whitman's memorable words in "By Blue Ontario's Shore": "Who are you indeed who would talk or sing to America? Have you studied out the land, its idioms and men? / Have you learn'd the physiology, phrenology, politics, geography, pride, freedom, friendship of the land? its substratums and objects?"[55]

In an earlier version of this statement, appearing in a published essay on "Anglo-Welsh Literature" (1952), Thomas had followed this quotation from Whitman with the tart comment: "The signs of having done this are too scarce in the work of the majority of the English-language Welsh. For one thing, too many of them come from the industrial areas. They tend therefore to give an unbalanced picture of Wales, creating the impression that it is a land of coal-mines. But to me, the true Wales is still to be found in the country" (*Selected Prose*, 43). The "Anglo-Welsh" therefore lacked that holistic vision of the nation that Thomas so prized; and he found the main thrust of Whitman's nationalism was best encapsulated in a phrase by Marianne Moore, repeated twice for emphasis in the radio talk in order to underline its significance for himself: "Patriotism is a matter of knowing a country by perceiving the clue."

Thomas's mistrust of the Anglophone Welsh is mirrored in the work of his close friend Emyr Humphreys, the preeminent Welsh novelist of the twentieth century. It is, though, in one of his poems that Humphreys turns to Whitman for clarification of his critical vision. It takes its title, "A Democratic Vista," from Whitman's writings and is here quoted in full:

> Strange sanctuary this, perched on the rising cornstack,
> Like a desert saint on a broken pillar
> Staring, eyes unstirring until hill field sea are one
> The procession of thought blurred
> Into the regular rising and falling of a sinewy arm
> And the dry rustle of sheaves.
> Tom Williams, Guto, Dick Williams, Wil Fach, Dafydd Dew and me,
>
> We are the people; our conversation is smooth and superficial
> Like a veneer of grained wood, curves leading nowhere
> Which was where they started.
> We are the people for whom politicians shout and soldiers fight
> We sow and reap, eat and sleep, copulate in secret, think
> In circumference of one dimension.
> We are the sacred people, the secular mystery, the host,
> Whitman's elastic deity, Marx's material, Rousseau's noble savage
> Mayakovsky's beloved—
> Tom, Guto, Dic, Wil, Dafi and me—
> Reasonably efficient between dawn and sunset,
> God chewing tobacco, God drinking tea, digesting rice.
> We are the people.
> God is not mocked.[56]

This poem (which may now be seen to conduct a conversation with the concepts of the "gwerin" and the "proletariat"—two dominant and sacred ideological terms in twentieth-century Wales) comes from a sequence called *Ancestor Worship.* One of the recurrent themes in the more than twenty novels Humphreys has so far written is the eminently corruptible will of the Welsh people—a people whom he sees as comfortably succumbing to various temptations to desert their ancient, rich, indigenous culture.[57] The Welsh language has, therefore, in his view, been left behind in his nation's selfish and self-destructive stampede toward the glamour, power, and wealth obtainable only through the medium of English. The radical democratic politics for which late nineteenth-century Wales was famous—a politics that at its best originated from and was sustained by the libertarian, humanitarian values of the Nonconformist chapels—has, in Humphreys's view, degenerated during the twentieth century, first into a spuriously international socialism and then into the hedonistic consumerism of present-day Welsh society. Hence his democratic vista is seen from a politico-cultural perspective pointedly different both from that of Waldo (whom Humphreys admires, but with whose great poem "Mewn Dau Gae" his poem may be seen as holding a sardonic conversation) and from that of Whitman, who is here implicitly associated with the spiritually empty populist rhetoric of Anglo-American cultural hegemony. It is fascinating, therefore, to see how, over the period of a century, Welsh writers discover—and uncover—between them, in the features of Whitman's writing, the Janus-face of America's benign and baleful influences on the modern world.

Welsh response to Whitman has, then, been as varied as is the culture of the country. In this instance, to understand any particular interpretation or reaction it has proved necessary to understand the exact social, cultural, and political positioning of the respondent. And the same would obviously be true of any attempt to comprehend this quintessential American's impact on another country. The Welsh case is perhaps all the more interesting because it affords examples of the two different kinds of acts of translation that are bound to be met with if one undertakes a wide-ranging study of Whitman's reception "abroad." As has been seen, Wales affords examples of both "intralingual translation" and of "interlingual translation," to adopt Roman Jackobson's classification. The main emphasis in these last three chapters has, however, been on the former, on what Michael Cronin has termed "writers who travel within their own language."[58] And what has emerged is what Cronin predicted would appear:

> intralingual travel accounts highlight not the limited repetitiveness of the travel experience but the endless series of finer discriminations that become apparent as the travelers chart the social, regional and national metamorphoses of the mother tongue. The language of home becomes stranger and more labyrinthine in the mouths and minds of others who ostensibly speak the same language. The language of origin becomes fragmented and plural and the potential for creative journeying in language gradually reveals itself to be inexhaustible. (3)

Through its two contrasting sections, this book has, then, sought to heighten but also to explore the paradox of Whitman's "travels across the lines," to adopt Michael Cronin's metaphor. And it has done so by emphasizing, with reference to a single cultural example, the peculiar phenomenon of Whitman's "American internationalism"; a nineteenth-century New Yorker's enduring ability to convince people of other times and of other cultures that he is really one of *them.* What has in the end hopefully been shown is that not the least intriguing aspect of this enigma has been Whitman's compelling power to appeal to societies that also speak English, but an English very different from his own.

Notes

Preface

1. Walt Whitman to Ernest Rhys, February 2, 1889 (Library of Congress, Feinberg Whitman collection).

2. M. Wynn Thomas, *The Lunar Light of Whitman's Poetry* (Cambridge, MA: Harvard University Press, 1987).

3. See, for instance, such works by Paul Giles as "Two-Way Mirrors: British-American Literary History and the Ideology of Exchange," *Yearbook of Research in English and American Literature* 14 (1998), 269–286; *Transatlantic Insurrection: British Culture and the Formation of American Culture, 1730–1860* (Philadelphia: University of Pennsylvania, 2001); *Virtual Americans: Transnational Fictions and the Transatlantic Imaginary* (Durham and London: Duke University Press, 2002).

4. Betsy Erkkila, *Walt Whitman Among the French* (Princeton, NJ: Princeton University Press, 1980); Walter Grünzweig, *Constructing the German Walt Whitman* (Iowa City: University of Iowa Press, 1995). The best summary of response to Whitman worldwide is Gay Wilson Allen and Ed Folsom, eds., *Walt Whitman and the World* (Iowa City: University of Iowa Press, 1995). See also "'Teach Me Your Rhythm': The Poetics of German Lyrical Responses to Whitman," in Ed Folsom, ed., *Walt Whitman: The Centennial Essays* (Iowa City: University of Iowa Press, 1994), 226–239, and essays on Whitman's influence on Chinese culture in Ed Folsom, ed., *Whitman East and West: New Contexts for Reading Walt Whitman* (Iowa City: University of Iowa Press, 2002).

5. For an attempt at beginning this work, see M. Wynn Thomas, "Walt Whitman and Risorgimento Nationalism," in Winnifred M. Bogaards, ed., *Literature of Region and Nation: Proceedings of the Sixth International Literature of Region and Nation Conference* (Saint John: University of New Brunswick in Saint John, 1998), 345–367.

However, for a useful summary of the controversial issues raised by any attempt to draw comparisons between North America and Latin America see J. H. Elliott, "A Pan-American Flight," *New York Review of Books*, February 26, 2004, 38–40. The early growth of American nationalism is admirably traced in Susan-Mary Grant, *North and South: Northern Nationalism and American Identity in the Antebellum Era* (Lawrence: University Press of Kansas, 2000).

6. Murray Sayle, "Introduction," in Philip Jones Griffiths, *Dark Odyssey* (Cardiff: National Museums and Galleries of Wales, 1996). For Welsh images of the United States, see M. Wynn Thomas, ed., *Gweld Sêr: Cymru a Chanrif America* (Cardiff: University of Wales Press, 2001), and M. Wynn Thomas, "Wales's American Dreams," *Corresponding Cultures: The Two Literatures of Wales* (Cardiff: University of Wales Press, 1999), 214–251.

7. Herbert Bergman, ed., *The Journalism: I (1834–1846)* (New York: Peter Lang, 1998), 449. Whitman typically characterized Owen as "a fine old man, but too enthusiastic" (446). Whitman was always conservative in his assessment of society's capacity for radical and wholesale reform: "The Reformer, the aged Robert Owen, is stirring up the people with a long pole, again, about the need of a 'complete social and political revolution.' Ah, Mr. Owen! when God has ordained that evil should exist, do you think that *you* can banish it altogether!" (435).

8. George Steiner, *After Babel: Aspects of Language and Translation* (London: Athlone Press, 1975).

1. A Tale of Two Cities

1. Dylan Thomas, *Quite Early One Morning: Broadcasts* (London: Dent, 1954), 8.

2. Emory Holloway and Ralph Adimari, eds., *New York Dissected* (Folcroft: Folcroft Library, 1972), 136. In his early journalism, Whitman frequently emphasized and mapped the dark side of New York City: see Herbert Bergman, ed., *The Journalism: I (1834–1846)* (New York: Peter Lang, 1998), 63–64; 162ff.

3. See particularly David Reynolds, *Walt Whitman's America: A Cultural Biography* (New York: Knopf, 1995). For other significant studies see the bibliographical essay in David Reynolds, ed., *A Historical Guide to Walt Whitman* (Oxford: Oxford University Press, 2000).

4. Peter Conrad, *The Art of the City: Views and Versions of New York* (New York: Oxford University Press, 1984), 13.

5. Edward K. Spann, *The New Metropolis: New York City, 1840–1857* (New York: Columbia University Press, 1981), chapter 1; Edwin G. Burrows and Mike Wallace, *Gotham: A History of New York City to 1898* (Oxford: Oxford University Press, 2000), 735ff.

6. For Whitman's sketch of boardinghouse culture (of which he had extensive personal experience) see *Journalism*, 60–61, 70–71. He also described "boarding-house

life" as "simply a place to keep a man's trunk and his wife while he is at work, and where he has breakfast, tea, and sleeping-room" and campaigned for proper decent housing at affordable prices for New York's working class: see *New York Dissected*, 92–102.

7. Anon., *Sketch of the Resources of the City of New York* (New York: no publisher, 1827).

8. He wrote interestingly about the monotony of an omnibus driver's life (*Journalism*, 67).

9. Ezekiel Porter Belden, *New York As It Is* (New York: no publisher, 1849).

10. Junius Henri Browne, *The Great Metropolis: A Mirror of New York* (Hartford: no publisher, 1869), 92.

11. Anon., *A Sketch of the Resources of the City of New York* (New York: no publisher, 1827).

12. B. A. Botkin, ed., *New York City Folklore: Legends . . . and Sayings* (New York: Random House, 1956), xviii.

13. Stephen Spender, *Love-Hate Relations: English and American Sensibilities* (New York: Random House, 1974), 13.

14. See Peter Buckley, "Culture, Class, and Place in Antebellum New York," in John Hull Mollenkopf, ed., *Power, Culture, and Place: Essays on New York City* (New York: Russell Sage Foundation, 1988), 25–52.

15. Thomas Bender, "The Culture of the Metropolis," *Journal of Urban History* 14 (1988): 492–502.

16. Ezra Greenspan, *Walt Whitman and the American Reader* (Cambridge: Cambridge University Press, 1990), chapter 3; Shelley Fisher Fishkin, *From Fact to Fiction: Journalism and Imaginative Writing in America* (Baltimore: Johns Hopkins University Press, 1985), chapter 2; Stephen H. Jaffe, "'The History of the Future': Whitman and the New Journalism," *Seaport: New York's History Magazine* 26: 4 (1992), 26–31; Gunther Barth, *City People: The Rise of Modern Culture in Nineteenth-Century America* (Oxford: Oxford University Press, 1980), chapter 3; *Gotham*, chapter 39.

17. Emory Holloway and Vernolian Schwarz, eds., *I Sit and Look Out: Editorials from the Brooklyn Daily Times* (New York: AMS, 1966 reprint), 39.

18. George G. Foster, *New York in Slices* (New York: no publisher, 1849), 56.

19. Stuart M. Blumin, Introduction to George G. Foster, *New York by Gas-Light and Other Urban Sketches* (Berkeley: University of California Press, 1990), 56.

20. Emory Holloway, ed., *Uncollected Poetry and Prose of Walt Whitman* (Gloucester: Smith, 1972), vol. 2, 201.

21. See, for instance, *Journalism*, 63–64, 70–72.

22. George G. Foster, *Celio: Or, New York Above Ground and Under-ground* (New York: no publisher, 1850), 89.

23. George Ellington, *The Women of New-York: Or, The Under-World of the Great City* (New York: no publisher, 1869), chapter 68. See also Eric Homberger, *Scenes from*

the Life of a City: Corruption and Conscience in Old New York (New Haven: Yale University Press, 1994).

24. Graham Clarke, *Walt Whitman: The Poem as Private History* (London: Vision, 1991), chapter 5.

25. Peter J. Schmitt, *Back to Nature: The Arcadian Myth in Urban America* (New York: Oxford University Press, 1969), chapter 1.

26. William Bobo, *Glimpses of New York City* (Charleston: no publisher, 1852), 19–20. Whitman repeatedly visited Greenwood and hymned its delights in his journalistic pieces. See *Journalism*, 9ff, 190ff, 421ff.

27. Lydia Maria Child, *Letters from New York*, 2nd series (New York: no publisher, 1845), 69.

28. Georg Simmel, "The Metropolis and Mental Life," in Richard Sennett, ed., *Classic Essays on the Culture of Cities* (New York: Appleton-Century-Crofts, 1969), 47–60.

29. M. Wynn Thomas, *The Lunar Light of Whitman's Poetry* (Cambridge: Harvard University Press, 1987), chapters 1–3; Sean Wilentz, *Chants Democratic* (Oxford: Oxford University Press, 1984), chapter 1.

30. John C. Gobright, *The New York Hand Book and Merchant's Guide* (New York: no publisher, 1869), 10. The section describing the great "manufacturing establishment" of Robert Hoe's famous steam printing press (97–103) is equally interesting and particularly relevant to Whitman.

31. See *Lunar Light* and Alan Trachtenberg, "The Politics of Labor and the Poet's Work: A Reading of 'A Song for Occupations,'" in Ed Folsom, ed., *Walt Whitman: The Centennial Essays* (Iowa City: University of Iowa Press, 1994), 120–132.

32. One of the earliest and most influential descriptions of this cityscape was that offered by Dickens in 1842. See John H. Whitley and Arnold Goldman, eds., *American Notes* (Harmondsworth, Eng.: Penguin, 1972), chapter 6.

33. From Whitman's own anonymous review of the 1855 *Leaves of Grass*, in Francis E. Murphy, ed., *Walt Whitman: A Critical Anthology* (Harmondsworth, England: Penguin, 1969), 29.

34. The fullest account is by David Reynolds, *Walt Whitman's America*, 508–516.

35. Richard M. Dorson, "Mose the Far-Famed and World-Renowned," *American Literature* 15 (1943–1944), 288–300. See also *Gotham*, 752–760.

36. George G. Foster, *New York by Gas-Light: With Here and There a Streak of Sunshine* (New York: no publisher, 1850); *New York in Slices* (New York: no publisher, 1849).

37. As Blumin notes: "[W]hat Foster finds to celebrate in [the Bowery B'hoy and G'hal] are traditional virtues suggestive of the village or small town independence, spirit, honesty and directness of speech, simplicity in feelings and taste, loyalty and generosity to friends and neighbors. The b'hoy and the g'hal recreate the traditional community within the non-traditional spaces of the Bowery. And in doing so they carry into this alien and unpromising world of tenements, factories, gas houses, and endless city streets, a reassuringly American presence" (55–56).

38. In a recent interesting article, Andrew Lawson has questioned whether Whitman was able in his poetry to resolve the contradictions in his "ambiguous social identity" and ideological stance: "'Spending for Vast Returns': Sex, Class, and Commerce in the First *Leaves of Grass*," *American Literature* 75: 2 (June 2003), 335–365.

39. Edwin Haviland Miller, ed., *The Correspondence* (New York: New York University Press, 1961), I, 242.

40. "In Memory of W. B. Yeats," Edward Mendelson, ed., *W. H. Auden: Collected Poems* (London: Faber and Faber, 1976), 197.

2. The New Urban Politics

Sections of this chapter were originally delivered in the form of a lecture at the University of Peking (1998).

1. *American Phrenological Journal* (July 1855), 5–7. I am very grateful to Peter Black for drawing this portrait of Wood to my attention.

2. Although no sustained attention has yet been paid to Wood by Whitman scholars, there is an interesting mention of him in Paul Benton, "Whitman, Christ, and the Crystal Palace Police: A Manuscript Source Restored," *Walt Whitman Quarterly Review* 17 (Spring 2000), 147–165; and Joann P. Krieg mentions Wood several times in *Whitman and the Irish* (Iowa City: University of Iowa Press, 2000), calling him someone Whitman "heartily despised."

3. Amy Bridges, *A City in the Republic: Antebellum New York and the Origins of Machine Politics* (Cambridge: Cambridge University Press, 1984), 46.

4. For an account of this society in relation to Whitman's poetry, see M. Wynn Thomas, *The Lunar Light of Whitman's Poetry* (Cambridge, MA: Harvard University Press, 1987).

5. Jerome Mushkat, *Fernando Wood: A Political Biography* (Kent, Ohio, and London: Kent State University Press, 1990), vii–viii; see also E. K. Spann, *The New Metropolis: New York City, 1840–1857* (New York: Columbia University Press, 1972).

6. Thomas L. Brasher, ed., *Whitman as Editor of the Brooklyn Daily Eagle* (Detroit: Wayne State University Press, 1970), 427.

7. Emory Holloway and Ralph Adimari, eds., *New York Dissected* (1936; reprinted Folcroft: Folcroft Library, 1972), 80–84.

8. Sean Wilentz, "Artisan Republican Festivals and the Rise of Class Conflict in New York City, 1788–1837," in Michael H. Frisch and Daniel J. Walkowitz, eds., *Working-Class America: Essays on Labor, Community, and American Society* (Urbana: University of Illinois Press, 1983), 33–77, quotation, p. 38; and Sean Wilentz, "The Rise of the American Working Class, 1776–1877," in J. Carroll Moody and Alice Kessler-Harris, eds., *Perspectives on American Labor History* (De Kalb: Northern Illinois University Press, 1989), 83–151. The political importance of street festivals in the United States ever since the republic was founded is demonstrated in Simon P. Newman, *Parades*

and the Politics of the Street: Festive Culture in the Early American Republic (Philadelphia: University of Pennsylvania Press, 1997). See, for instance, his explanation that it is "by exploring the political badges, songs, and toasts, the partisan parades, feasts, and crowd actions that we can begin to see what politics was all about for ordinary Americans. Only then can we begin to see how these Americans pulled politics out of the corridors of power and onto the streets of the new republic" (43).

9. For a detailed consideration of this whole momentous, tumultuous process of change, see Sean Wilentz, *Chants Democratic: New York City and the Rise of the American Working Class, 1788–1850* (New York and Oxford: Oxford University Press, 1984).

10. A magisterially comprehensive account of such changes, set in the context of the history of development of nineteenth-century New York, may be found in Edwin G. Burrows and Mike Wallace, *Gotham: A History of New York City to 1898* (Oxford: Oxford University Press, 2000). For readings of "A Song for Occupations" in the light of these circumstances, see *Lunar Light* and Alan Trachtenberg, "The Politics of Labor and the Poet's Work: A Reading of 'A Song for Occupations,'" in Ed Folsom, ed., *Walt Whitman: The Centennial Essays* (Iowa City: University of Iowa Press, 1994), 120–132.

11. Charles Dickens, *All the Year Round* (March 16, 1861). For the change in firefighting during Whitman's early years from volunteers to municipal employees see Mark Tebeau, *Eating Smoke: Fire in America, 1850–1950* (Baltimore: Johns Hopkins University Press, 2003).

12. The details that follow are all taken from Alvin F. Harlow, *Old Bowery Days* (New York and London: D. Appleton and Co., 1931).

13. Emory Holloway and Vernolian Schwarz, eds., *I Sit and Look Out: Editorials from the Brooklyn Daily Times* (1932; reprint New York: AMS, 1966), 59.

14. See the note on the omitted passage in Harold W. Blodgett and Sculley Bradley, eds., *Leaves of Grass: Comprehensive Reader's Edition* (New York: New York University Press, 1965), 624.

15. Michael F. Holt, *The Political Crisis of the 1850s* (London: Norton, 1978).

16. "The New World and the Old," in Herbert Bergman, ed., *The Collected Works of Walt Whitman: The Journalism, Vol.1 (1836–46)* (New York: Peter Lang, 1978), 338.

17. *Journalism*, 441–443.

18. For Whitman's attacks on Nativism see *Journalism*, 124ff, 442ff.

19. Jerome Loving, *Walt Whitman: The Song of Himself* (Berkeley: University of California Press, 1999), 227.

20. Parts of the following discussion first appeared in "Representatives and Revolutionists: The New Urban Politics Revisited," Ed Folsom, ed., *Whitman East and West* (Iowa City: University of Iowa Press, 2002), 145–158.

21. Ralph Waldo Emerson, *Representative Men*, Riverside ed. (London: Routledge, n.d.), 4:36.

22. Scully Bradley, Harold W. Blodgett, Arthur Golden, and William White, eds.,

Leaves of Grass: A Textual Variorum, I (New York: New York University Press, 1980), 219.

23. See Donald E. Pease, *Visionary Compacts: American Renaissance Writings in Cultural Context* (Madison: University of Wisconsin Press, 1987), chapter 4.

24. Edward Grier, ed., *Walt Whitman: Notebooks and Unpublished Prose Manuscripts I* (New York: New York University Press, 1984), 272.

3. Leaves of Grass and The Song of Hiawatha

Thanks are due to my friends and colleagues Robert Penhallurick and Glyn Pursglove for some of the materials upon which I draw in this chapter.

1. Francis E. Murphy, ed., *Walt Whitman: A Critical Anthology* (Harmondsworth, Eng.: Penguin, 1969), 29.

2. *Letters*, 503 (November 30, 1855).

3. Reginald Horsman, *Race and Manifest Destiny: The Origins of American Racial Anglo-Saxonism* (Cambridge, Mass.: Harvard University Press, 1981); Reginald Horsman, "Scientific Racism and the American Indian in the Mid-Nineteenth-Century," *American Quarterly* 27: 2 (May 1975), 152–168.

4. For instance, Richard Slotkin, *Regeneration through Violence* (New York: Harper Collins, 1996); Joshua David Bellin, *The Demon of the Continent: Indians and the Shaping of American Literature* (Philadelphia: University of Pennsylvania Press, 2001); David T. Mitchell, "Colonial Savages and Heroic Tricksters: Native Americans in the American Tradition," *Journal of Popular Culture* 32:4 (Spring 1999), 101–117.

5. Leslie Fiedler, *Waiting for the End: The American Literary Scene from Hemingway to Baldwin* (Harmondsworth, England: Penguin Books, 1967), 128.

6. Daniel Aaron, ed., Henry Wadsworth Longfellow, *The Song of Hiawatha* (London: Dent, 1992). All quotations will be taken from this edition.

7. Included in the text of "Excelsior" in 1856 but removed in 1882. For this and other aspects of Whitman's response to Longfellow see the entry by Julie A. Rechel-White in J. R. LeMaster and Donald D. Kummings, ed., *Walt Whitman: An Encyclopedia* (New York and London: Garland Publishing, 1998).

8. Virginia Jackson, "Longfellow's Tradition: Or Picture-Writing a Nation," *Modern Languages Quarterly* 59: 4 (1998), 471–496.

9. David Reynolds, *Walt Whitman's America: A Cultural Biography* (New York: Knopf, 1995), 353.

10. Kenneth M. Price, *Whitman and Tradition: The Poet in His Century* (New Haven: Yale University Press, 1990).

11. Horace Traubel, ed., *An American Primer by Walt Whitman* (Stevens Point, Wisconsin: Holy Cow! Press, 1987).

12. See the Longfellow entry in *Walt Whitman: An Encyclopedia.*

13. One of the few extended comparisons of Longfellow and Whitman is by Angus

Fletcher, "Whitman and Longfellow," *Raritan* 19:4, 131–145. His is an excellent essay, but takes a very different approach from that followed in the present chapter.

14. Philip Rahv, ed., *Literature in America* (Cleveland, Ohio: World Publishing Company, 1975), 11.

15. J. D. McClatchy, ed., Henry Wadsworth Longfellow, *Poems and Other Writings* (New York: Penguin, Library of America, 2000), 793. All quotations from text, apart from *The Song of Hiawatha*, will be taken from this volume.

16. It would be interesting to compare, at length, Longfellow's interpretation of Native Americans with that of Whitman. For the latter, see the relevant chapter in Ed Folsom, *Walt Whitman's Native Representations* (Cambridge: Cambridge University Press, 1994) and the same author's entry on "Native Americans (Indians)" in *Walt Whitman: An Encyclopedia* (New York and London: Garland Publishing, 1998).

17. Keith Bosley, trans., *The Kalevala* (Oxford: Oxford University Press, World's Classics, 1989), xxiii.

18. See, for example, the passage in *Specimen Days* dated November 1881 and entitled "An Ossianic Night—Dearest Friends": "a real Ossianic night—amid the whirl, absent or dead friends, the old, the past, somehow tenderly suggested—while the Gael-strains chant themselves from the mists" (915–916).

19. Valentina Bold, "'Rude Bard of the North': James Macpherson and the Folklore of Democracy," *Journal of American Folklore* (Fall 2001), 464–477.

20. Newton Arvin, *Longfellow: His Life and Work* (Westport, Connecticut: Greenwood Press Publishers, 1963), 22.

21. Henry Wadsworth Longfellow, ed., *Poets and Poetry of Europe* (Philadelphia: Porter and Coates, 1871 edition), vi.

22. Robert Ferguson, "Longfellow's Political Fears: Civic Authority and the Role of the Artist in *Hiawatha* and *Miles Standish*," *American Literature* 50, 189.

23. It was actually to Sumner that Longfellow wrote on June 25, 1854, requesting his help to "get a copy of Schoolcraft's great work on the Indians published by [the] Gov't." (468).

24. On February 21, 1854, he reported to Sumner that he had given an unnamed visitor "such a lecture on the Nebraska business that I am afraid he will never come again" (415).

25. See for instance Betsy Erkkila, *Whitman: The Political Poet* (New York: Oxford University Press, 1989).

26. These attitudes and practices are usefully examined in Gregory Eselein, *Literature and Humanitarian Reform in the Civil War* (Bloomington and Indianapolis: Indiana University Press, 1996).

27. Linda K. Kerber, "The Abolitionist Perception of the Indian," *Journal of American History* 62: 2 (September 1975), 276.

28. Oliver Wendell Holmes, "The Physiology of Versification," *The Writings of Oliver*

Wendell Holmes VIII: A Collection of Essays, 1857–1881 (London: Sampson, Low, Marston, Searle, and Rivington, 1891).

29. As Holmes further writes: "[T]he early poems of a people are recited or sung before they are committed to writing, and even if a versifier does not read aloud as he writes, he mentally articulates every line, and takes cognizance instinctively of its physiological adjustment to respiration as he does of its smoothness or roughness, which he hears only in imagination" (318); "All the early ballad poetry shows how instinctively the reciters accommodated their rhythm to their breathing" (319).

30. George B. Hutchinson, *The Ecstatic Whitman* (Columbus: Ohio State University Press, 1985).

31. I am, of course, using the term very loosely. For influential attempts at a more precise definition, and for taxonomies of different sorts of fantastic fiction, see Tzvetan Todorov, *The Fantastic: A Structural Approach to a Literary Genre* (Ithaca, NY: Cornell University Press, 1975); Neil Cornwell, *The Literary Fantastic* (New York: Harvester Wheatsheaf, 1990); Lucie Armitt, *Theorising the Fantastic* (London: Arnold, 1996).

32. See, for instance, John Garth, *Tolkien and the Great War* (London: HarperCollins; New York: Houghton Mifflin, 2003).

33. Quoted in Anthony Grafton, *The Footnote: A Curious History* (London: Faber, 1997), 70.

34. Constance Rourke, *American Humor: A Study of the National Character* (New York: Harcourt, Brace and Company, 1931), 172.

35. See Donald Pease, *Visionary Compacts: American Renaissance Writings in Cultural Context* (Madison: University of Wisconsin Press, 1987).

36. Eve Patten, "'Flying to Belfast': Audience and Authenticity in Recent Northern Irish Fiction," in Tony Brown and Russell Stephens, eds., *Nations and Relations: Writing Across the British Isles* (Cardiff: New Welsh Review, 2000), 30.

37. Edward Thomas, "I Never Saw That Land Before," in *Collected Poems* (London: Faber, 1965), 100: "I should use, as the trees and birds did, / A language not to be betrayed; / And what was hid should still be hid / Excepting from those like me made / Who answer when such whispers bid."

38. George Burke Johnston, ed., *Poems of Ben Jonson* (London: Routledge and Kegan Paul, Muses Library, 1962), 77.

39. M. Wynn Thomas, *The Lunar Light of Whitman's Poetry* (Cambridge, MA: Harvard University Press, 1987).

40. See *Lunar Light.*

41. Sam Bass Warner Jr., *Street Car Suburbs: The Process of Growth in Boston, 1870–1900* (Cambridge, MA: Harvard University Press, 1978), 1.

42. Andrew Buni and Alan Rogers, *Boston: City on a Hill* (Boston: Windsor Publications, 1984).

43. Marjorie Drake Ross, *The Book of Boston: The Victorian Period, 1837–1901* (New

York: Hasting House Publishers, 1964), 50; see also Llewellyn Howland, ed., *A Book for Boston* (Boston: David R. Godine, 1980); anon., *Fifty Years of Boston: Issue in Commemoration of the Tercentary of 1830* (Boston: no publisher, 1937); Stephen Thernstrom, *The Other Bostonians: Poverty and Progress in the American Metropolis, 1880–1970* (Cambridge, MA: Harvard University Press, 1973).

44. Martin Green, *The Problem of Boston: Some Readings in Cultural History* (New York: Norton and Co., 1966), 103.

4. The Dreams of Labor

1. *Selected Poems* (Harmondsworth, England: Penguin, 1963), 25.

2. Irving Howe, *The American Newness* (Cambridge, MA: Harvard University Press, 1986), 65–70.

3. M. Wynn Thomas, *The Lunar Light of Whitman's Poetry* (Cambridge, MA: Harvard University Press, 1987).

4. Fredson Bowers, ed., *Whitman's Manuscripts, Leaves of Grass (1860): A Parallel Text* (Chicago: University of Chicago Press, 1955), xxxv, note 2.

5. Edwin Haviland Miller, ed., *Walt Whitman: The Correspondence* (New York: New York University Press, 1961–1977), 1: 41–42.

6. Quoted in R. B. Nye and J. P. Morpurgo, *A History of the United States* (Harmondsworth, England: Penguin, 1965), 2: 442.

7. Scully Bradley, Harold W. Blodgett, Arthur Golden, William White, eds., *Leaves of Grass: A Textual Variorum of the Printed Poems* (New York: New York University Press, 1980), 2: 273.

8. Emory Holloway and Vernolian Schwartz, eds., *I Sit and Look Out: Editorials from the* Brooklyn Daily Times (New York: Columbia University Press, 1932), particularly the sections on "Slavery" and "National Politics."

9. For the contributions of Evans, the Free Soil movement, and the political parties to these debates, see Eric Foner, *Politics and Ideology in the Age of the Civil War* (New York: Oxford University Press, 1980). Ray Allen Billington, *Westward Expansion: A History of the American Frontier* (New York: Macmillan, 1974), provides a full history of the homesteading movement. Various versions of the "imagined West" are usefully summarized in Rush Welter, *The Mind of America: 1820–1860* (New York: Columbia University Press, 1975), 298.

10. Philip Van Doren Stern, ed., *The Life and Writings of Abraham Lincoln* (New York: Modern Library, 1940). Interesting comparisons are made between poetry and politics in Allen Grossman, "The Poetics of Union in Whitman and Lincoln," in Walter Benn Michaels and Donald E. Pease, eds., *The American Renaissance Reconsidered* (Baltimore: Johns Hopkins University Press, 1985), 183–208.

11. Henry Nash Smith, *Virgin Land* (New York: Vintage Books, 1950).

12. Michael Dettelbach, introduction to E. C. Otté, trans., Alexander von Humboldt,

Cosmos: A Sketch of the Physical Description of the Universe, Vol. 2 (Baltimore and London: Johns Hopkins University Press, 1997), xvii.

13. William Boelbower, "Scenes of Origin: Ethnographic Politics in the Whitmanian Mode," in Stephen Fender, ed., *American and European National Identities* (Kiel: Kiel University Press, 1996), 37–56.

14. Whitman's position on these matters is succinctly summarized by Daniel Aaron, *The Unwritten War* (New York: Knopf, 1972), 59–62.

15. Herbert J. Levine, "Union and Disunion in 'Song of Myself,'" *American Literature* 59 (December 1987), 570–589. See also Jerome Loving, "Whitman's Democratic Vision in the First *Leaves of Grass*," in Joann P. Krieg, ed., *Walt Whitman: Here and Now* (Westport, Conn.: Greenwood Press, 1985), 139–146; George B. Hutchinson, *The Ecstatic Whitman: Literary Shamanism and the Crisis of the Union* (Columbus: Ohio State University Press, 1986).

16. See, for example, Betsy Erkkila, *Whitman the Political Poet* (New York: Oxford University Press, 1989); Dennis K. Renner, "Lear and the *Leaves of Grass* Poet" in Krieg, 185–191.

17. For thoughtful discussions of the subtle implications of Whitman's treatment of slavery in key passages in his poetry, such as the "Lucifer" passage from "The Sleepers," and the slave auction passage in "I Sing the Body Electric," see Kerry C. Larson, *Whitman's Dream of Consensus* (Chicago: University of Chicago Press, 1988). The fullest account, however, is found in Martin Klammer, *Whitman, Slavery, and the Emergence of* Leaves of Grass (University Park, PA: Pennsylvania State University Press, 1995).

18. Erkkila, 274–276; Alan Trachtenberg, *The Incorporation of America* (New York: Hill and Wang, 1982), 61.

19. This was also a characteristic of Whitman's late poetry. See M. Wynn Thomas, "A Study of Whitman's Late Poetry," *Walt Whitman Review* 27 (March 1981), 3–14.

20. Erkkila, passim; Robert Schulman, *Social Criticism and Nineteenth Century American Fiction* (Columbus: University of Missouri Press, 1987).

21. For the growth of Boston, see Sam Bass Warner, *Street Car Suburbs: The Process of Growth in Boston, 1870–1900* (Cambridge, MA: Harvard University Press, 1978); Stephen Thernstrom, *The Other Bostonians: Poverty and Progress in the American Metropolis, 1880–1970* (Cambridge, MA: Harvard University Press, 1973); Marjorie Drake Ross, *The Book of Boston: The Victorian Period, 1837–1901* (New York: Hastings House, 1964); Andrew Burni and Alan Rogers, *Boston: City on a Hill* (Boston: Windsor Publications, 1984).

22. Horace Traubel, *With Walt Whitman in Camden*, vol. 6 (Carbondale: Southern Illinois Press, 1982), 181.

23. Martin Green, *The Problem of Boston: Some Readings in Cultural History* (New York: Norton, 1966). For a thoughtful defense of Boston's cultural elite, see Neil Harris, "The Gilded Age Revisited: Boston and the Museum Movement," *American Quarterly* 14 (Winter 1962), 545–566.

24. Horace Traubel, *With Walt Whitman in Camden*, vol. 3 (Nov. 1, 1888–Jan. 20, 1889) (New York: Rowman and Littlefield, 1961), 89.

25. The phrase is used by Mrs. Henry Ady in "Jean-François Millet," *Nineteenth Century* 137 (July 1888), 419–438. The view expressed was commonplace—see, for example, the comments of William Morris Hunt, as reported to Helen M. Knowles, *The Life of William Morris Hunt* (Boston: Little, Brown, 1899), 12; Wyatt Eaton, "Remembrances of Jean-François Millet," *Century* (May 1889), 100.

26. Susan Fleming, "The Boston Patrons of Jean-François Millet," in Alexandra R. Murphy, *Jean-François Millet* (Boston: Museum of Fine Arts, 1984), xiii. Of the fifty paintings in Shaw's possession, twenty-one pastels were exhibited in the schoolroom. After 1883, Pauline Agassiz Shaw "supported children's classes of manual arts in the public schools as well as in her North Bennet-Street Industrial School" (Dumas Malone, ed., *The Dictionary of American Biography*, vol. 17 [New York: Charles Scribner's Sons, 1935]).

27. Griselda Pollock, *Millet* (London: Oresko Books, 1977), 7.

28. Horace L. Traubel, Richard Maurice Bucke, and Thomas B. Harned, eds., *In Re Walt Whitman* (Philadelphia: David Mackay, 1893), 378–380.

29. Horace Traubel, *With Walt Whitman in Camden*, vol. 1 (New York: Rowman and Littlefield, 1961 reprint), 7, 62.

5. Fratricide and Brotherly Love

1. Edward F. Grier, ed., *Notebooks and Unpublished Prose Manuscripts*, 6 vols. (New York: New York University Press, 1994), vol. 2, p. 548.

2. Henry Steele Commager, ed., *The Blue and the Gray* (New York: Fairfax Press, 1982 edition), xxix–xxx.

3. One regrettable consequence of Whitman's figuring the Civil War as a white family "romance" was that he left "the relation of African Americans to the Civil War almost entirely unspoken, unrepresentable," because they did not "belong to the 'national' family." See George Hutchinson, "Whitman, la famiglia e la Guerra Civile," *Storia e Memoria* 9 (2000), 57–72. I am grateful to Professor Hutchinson for sight of an English version of this essay.

4. Jerome M. Loving, ed., *Civil War Letters of George Washington Whitman* (Durham, NC: Duke University Press, 1975), 80. The same author's *Whitman: The Song of Himself* (Berkeley: University of California Press, 1999), offers particularly sensitive insights into the Whitman of the Civil War period.

5. Edwin Haviland Miller, ed., *Walt Whitman: The Correspondence* (New York: New York University Press, 1961), 1, 171.

6. Floyd Stovall, ed., *Walt Whitman, Prose Works 1892, vol. 1: Specimen Days* (New York: New York University Press, 1963), 38fn.

7. An imaginative account of Whitman's relations with his mother may be found

in Vivian R. Pollock, *The Erotic Whitman* (Berkeley: University of California Press, 2000).

8. See M. Wynn Thomas, *The Lunar Light of Whitman's Poetry* (Cambridge, MA: Harvard University Press, 1987).

9. Paul Fussell, *The Great War and Modern Memory* (London: Oxford University Press, 1977), 155.

10. For hospital conditions see Robert Leigh Davis, *Whitman and the Romance of Medicine* (Berkeley: University of California Press, 1997); Gregory Eselein, *Literature and Humanitarian Reform in the Civil War Era* (Bloomington and Indianopolis: Indiana University Press, 1996).

11. The significance of the glance has been well explored by Mark Maslan, *Whitman Possessed: Poetry, Sexuality, and Popular Authority* (Baltimore: Johns Hopkins University Press, 2001).

12. As Breit Leithauser has shrewdly observed, in reviewing an anthology of Second World War poetry: "war poetry of every age characteristically employs a dynamic tension between swiftness and slowness . . . one might almost say that war is all about speed and war poetry all about mulling over the harrowing implications of that speed. . . . If death on the battlefield is often bewilderingly quick, on the page it is often elongated, as we pay the only homage we can pay—a few moments of consideration—to somebody whose life is about to be truncated" (*New York Review of Books*, Dec. 4, 2003, 41).

13. Harold Blodgett and Sculley Bradley, eds., *Leaves of Grass: Comprehensive Reader's Edition* (New York: New York University Press, 1965), 32.

6. Weathering the Storm

1. Paul Fussell, "Sunrise and Sunset," *The Great War and Modern Memory* (London: Oxford University Press, 1977), 51–63.

2. Edward F. Grier, ed., *Notebooks and Unpublished Prose Manuscripts*, 6 vols. (New York: New York University Press, 1984), 2: 534.

3. Geoffrey C. Ward, with Ric Burns and Ken Burns, *The Civil War: An Illustrated History of the War between the States* (London: The Bodley Head, 1991), 210.

4. Ward and Burns, *The Civil War*, 184.

5. Jerome M. Loving, ed., *Civil War Letters of George Washington Whitman* (Durham, NC: Duke University Press, 1975).

6. Ward and Burns, 130.

7. James Rodgers Fleming, *Metereology in America, 1800–1870* (Baltimore: Johns Hopkins University Press, 1990), xvii. I am grateful to Professor Lawrence Buell, Harvard University, for making this study available to me.

8. "Weather in War," *Atlantic Monthly* 7 (May 1862), 593.

9. Andrew Ross, "The Work of Nature in the Age of Electronic Emission," *Social Text: Theory, Culture, Ideology* 6:3 (Winter 1987–1988), 116.

10. James P. Espy, *The Philosophy of Storms* (Boston: Little, Brown, 1841), vi–vii.

11. "Meteorology: A Glance at the Science," *Atlantic Monthly* 6 (July 1860), 1.

12. For exploration of this, see M. Wynn Thomas, *The Lunar Light of Whitman's Poetry* (Cambridge, MA: Harvard University Press, 1987).

13. *Harper's Weekly* 8 (June 8, 1864), 499.

14. Eduardo Cadava, *Emerson and the Climates of History* (Stanford: Stanford University Press, 1997), 27–28.

15. See J. W. Johnson, "Of Differing Ages and Climates," *Journal of the History of Ideas* 21 (October–December 1960), 465–480.

16. Geoffrey C. Ward, *The West: An Illustrated History* (London: Weidenfeld and Nicholson, 1996), 265.

17. Harold Aspiz, *Walt Whitman and the Body Beautiful* (Urbana: University of Illinois Press, 1980), 265.

18. Frederick Van Wyck, *Recollections of an Old New Yorker* (1933: reprint, New York: Liveright, 1982), 33.

19. Nathaniel Hawthorne, *The Scarlet Letter* (New York: Norton, 1988), 106.

20. Hennig Cohen, ed., *The Battle-Pieces of Herman Melville* (New York: Thomas Yoseloff, 1964), 35.

21. *Harper's Weekly* 9 (May 6, 1865), 274.

22. *Philadelphia Inquirer*, March 6, 1965. I am indebted, and very grateful, to Dr. Dan Lewis for the materials that follow on the occasion of Lincoln's second inauguration.

23. Quoted in J. G. Randall and Richard N. Current, *Lincoln the President: Last Full Measure* (London: Dodd, Mead and Company, 1955), 344.

24. I owe this to Dr. Dan Lewis.

25. The fullest treatment of the subject remains Martin Klammer, *Whitman, Slavery and the Emergence of "Leaves of Grass"* (University Park: Pennsylvania State University Press, 1995).

26. David S. Reynolds, *Walt Whitman's America: A Cultural Biography* (New York: Knopf, 1995), 445.

27. *Wake-Robin, Writings of John Burroughs* (Boston: Houghton Mifflin, 1904), 1: 141–142. Burroughs's writings, with their emphasis both on nature and weather, had a considerable influence on Canadian poets who admired Whitman and Emerson. See D. M. R. Bentley, "American Meteorological Determinism and Post-Confederation Poetry," in Easingwoodkonrad Gross and Harmut Lutz, eds., *Informal Empire? Cultural Relations between Canada, the United States and Europe* (Kiel: Landverlag, 1998).

28. Burroughs 1: 226. Burroughs discusses Whitman's use of the hermit thrush in *Writings: Birds and Poets*, volume 3 of the Riverside Press series, 46–47.

29. "The Birds of the Pasture and Forest," *Atlantic Monthly* 2 (December 1858), 867. Burroughs admired the article, particularly the description of the hermit thrush's song, but scathingly noted that the author had confused the bird with the wood thrush (Burroughs, 1: 51–53).

30. David C. Miller, *The Dark Eden: The Swamp in Nineteenth-Century American Culture* (Cambridge: Cambridge University Press, 1989). He notes that "Walt Whitman, perhaps the most original mind in all of America, was indeed a lonely example of favorable response to the charms of the Southern swamps before the war"; and he also devotes pages 209–210 to a specific consideration of the role of the swamp in Whitman's poetry.

31. *Harper's Weekly* 7 (December 12, 1863), 796.

32. Quoted in Walter Lowenfels, *Walt Whitman's Civil War* (New York: Da Capo, 1989), 235.

7. The English Whitman

1. Entry on Edward Carpenter by Arnie Kantrowitz in J. R. LeMaster and Donald D. Kummings, *Walt Whitman: An Encyclopedia* (New York and London: Garland, 1998). For a biography of Carpenter see Chushichi Tsuzuki, *Edward Carpenter 1844–1929: Prophet of Human Fellowship* (Cambridge: Cambridge University Press, 1980).

2. Elizabeth Dell and Jay Losey, "Introduction," in Jay Losey and William D. Brewer, eds., *Mapping Male Sexuality* (London: AUP, 2000), 7.

3. William A. Pannapacker, "'The bricklayer shall lay me': Edward Carpenter, Walt Whitman, and Working-Class 'Comradeship,'" in Losey and Brewer, *Mapping Male Sexuality*, 277–298: 280–281.

4. George Chauncey, *Gay New York: Gender, Urban Culture, and the Making of the Gay Male World, 1890–1940* (New York: Harper, 1994).

5. Raymond Williams, "The little green book," *Guardian*, 20 Nov. 1980, 18.

6. Anthony Wright, *Socialisms: Theories and Practice* (Oxford: Oxford University Press, 1987), 1.

7. Editor's "Introduction," in Tony Brown, ed., *Prose Studies* 13 (1990: special Carpenter edition), 1. This provides an excellent overview of Carpenter's life, career, and thought. This important special issue of *Prose Studies* has been reprinted as Tony Brown, ed., *Edward Carpenter and Late Victorian Radicalism* (London: Frank Cass, 1990).

8. Sheila Rowbotham, "In Search of Carpenter," *History Workshop* 3 (1977), 126.

9. "In Search of Carpenter," 126.

10. Marie-Françoise Cachin, "'Non-Governmental Society': Edward Carpenter's Position in the British Socialist Movement," in Brown, *Prose Studies*, 71.

11. Stephen Yeo, "A New Life: The Religion of Socialism in Britain, 1883–1896," *History Workshop* 3 (1977), 45. This is a magisterial, definitive study of the subject.

12. Fenner Brockway, "A Memory of Edward Carpenter," *New Leader*, 5 July 1929.

13. Quoted in Stanley Pierson, "Edward Carpenter, Prophet of a Socialist Millennium," *Victorian Studies* XIII: 3 (March 1974), 313.

14. Robert Blatchford, *The New Religion*, Pass on Pamphlets No. 9, The Clarion Press, 66 Worship Street, London, 8.

15. The phrase is not Carpenter's. It comes from the title of a pamphlet by Rev. J. Stitt Wilson, *Moses: The Greatest of Labor Leaders*, No. 5 of the Social Crusade Series (Huddersfield, 1908).

16. The theme of redemption of, and through, the suppressed and brutalized classes was, of course, a commonplace of ethical socialism, as in the emphasis of Philip Snowden on a new order through "the resurrection to the New Humanity—purified by suffering, triumphant through sacrifice." Philip Snowden, *The Christ That Is to Be* (I[ndependent] L[abour] P[arty], London, n.d.), 16. Snowden also prophesies that "[t]he Christ that is to be appears. And this spirit of Christ, of love, of sacrifice, is taking possession of men's minds, and under its inspiration, old forms, old institutions, old passions will disappear, and a new and bright social order will arise. It is the promised New Jerusalem" (8).

17. Peter Washington, *Madame Blavatsky's Baboon: Theosophy and the Emergence of the Western Guru* (London: Secker and Warburg, 1993). See also Joscelyn Godwin, *The Theosophical Enlightenment* (Albany: State University of New York, 1994).

18. H. P. Blavatsky, *The Secret Doctrine* (Pasadena: Theosophical University Press, 1952: reprint of original edition of 1888), viii.

19. Edward Carpenter, *Days with Walt Whitman* (London: George Allen, 1906; reprint edition, New York: AMS Press, n.d.).

20. A note of explanation. Like *Leaves of Grass*, *Towards Democracy* was a text that grew over several editions, finally amounting to over five hundred pages, and so it represents some twenty years of writing. It includes "Towards Democracy," a poem very roughly corresponding to "Song of Myself," the founding text of Carpenter's whole enterprise. The text used throughout this chapter is the complete edition, in four parts (London: Allen and Unwin, 1905: fifth impression, 1931).

21. *Towards Democracy*, 23, 29, 32.

22. Ibid., 102, 69, 378–379, 49.

23. China is also singled out (along with Switzerland and Ireland) for favorable comments as a society with minimal government in Carpenter's *Towards Industrial Freedom* (London: George Allen and Unwin, 1917; 1924 reprint), 61ff.

24. Bryan K. Garman, "'Heroic Spiritual Grandfather': Whitman, Sexuality, and the American Left, 1890–1940," *American Quarterly* 52:1 (March 2000), 90. This outstanding essay usefully complements studies of Whitman's influence on the British Left.

25. Edward Carpenter, *Civilisation: Its Cause and Cure* (George Allen and Unwin, 1889; ninth edition, 1906), 14.

26. A. S. B. Glover, ed., *Shelley: Selected Poetry, Prose and Letters* (London: The Nonesuch Press, 1951), 1038.

27. For an interesting discussion of Carpenter's attitudes towards working-class men, both in Britain and in the United States, see Scott McCracken, "Writing the Body: Edward Carpenter, George Gissing and Late-Nineteenth-Century Realism," in *Prose Studies* 13, 178–200.

28. Edward Carpenter, *Angels' Wings* (London: Allen and Unwin, 1898: fifth edition, 1917).

29. E. P. Thompson, *The Making of the English Working Class* (Harmondsworth, Eng.: Penguin, 1974), *passim.*

30. Quoted in Pierson, "Edward Carpenter, Prophet," 304.

31. Harry Zohn, ed., Walter Benjamin, *Illuminations* (London: Fontana, 1968), 73.

32. "When he was 'on the pounce,' as [Henry] Salt called it, Carpenter was combative and teasing. In general, according to Salt, Carpenter was 'by nature autocratic' and sought 'to make everyone else's plans for them'" (Pierson, 314).

33. Anonymous reviewer, *The New Age* (May 31, 1900), 241.

8. Lawrence's Whitman

1. George Y. Traill, "Lawrence's Whitman," *D. H. Lawrence Review* 14: 2, 172–190; quotation, p. 189.

2. Richard Swigg, *Lawrence, Hardy and American Literature* (London: Oxford University Press, 1972), 351.

3. Émile Delavenay, *D. H. Lawrence and Edward Carpenter: A Study in Edwardian Transition* (London: Heinemann, 1971), 241.

4. Ezra Greenspan, Lindeth Vasey, and John Worthen, eds., *Studies in Classic American Literature* (Cambridge: Cambridge University Press, 2003). The light this edition throws on the complex development of Lawrence's responses to Whitman are explored in M. Wynn Thomas and John Turner, "'Whitman, the great poet, has meant so much to me': Lawrence's *Studies in Classic American Literature*, 1919–1923," *Walt Whitman Quarterly Review* 21:2 (Fall 2003), 41–64.

5. George J. Zytaruk and James T. Bolton, eds., *Letters of D. H. Lawrence*, vol. 11 (Cambridge: Cambridge University Press, 1981), 129–130. Lawrence's further comments are very shrewd: "Whitman is like a human document, or a wonderful treatise in self-revelation. It is neither art not religion nor truth: Just a self revelation of a man who could not live, and so had to write himself. But writing should come from a strong root of life: like a battle song after a battle. . . . He chucked his body into the fight, and stood apart saying, 'Look how I am living.' He is really false as hell—But he is fine too" (130). For the poems Lawrence is alluding to in this letter, see John Worthen, *D. H. Lawrence: The Early Years* (Cambridge: Cambridge University Press, 1991), Appendix II.

6. Wallace Martin, *The New Age Under Orage: Chapters in English Cultural History* (Manchester and New York: Manchester University Press and Barnes and Noble, 1967).

7. Lionel Trilling, *Matthew Arnold* (London: Allen and Unwin, 1939), 114.

8. "Orage deliberately attempted to make *The New Age* [what he styled] a presentative periodical, which would mediate between specialized fields of knowledge and pub-

lic understanding, and encourage a vital relationship between literary experimentation and the literary tradition" (Martin, 3).

9. E. M. Forster, "The Raison D'Être of Criticism," in *Two Cheers for Democracy* (London: Arnold, 1972), 109.

10. P. N. Furbank, *E. M. Forster: A Life*, vol. I (London: Secker and Warburg, 1977), 159n.

11. Mark Kinkead-Weekes, *D. H. Lawrence: Triumph and Exile* (Cambridge: Cambridge University Press, 1996), 190–193.

12. Vivian de Sola Pinto and Warren Roberts, eds., *The Complete Poems of D. H. Lawrence*, vol. I (London: Heinemann, 1964), 475.

13. George H. Thomson, ed., *Albergo Empedocle and Other Writings* (New York: Liveright, 1971), 170–175.

14. His self-recognition in Whitman was later to lead him to penetrating insights: "The man who says, 'Look what I'm doing!' is merely reassuring himself that he has done it. Hence the quality of empty noises in Walt Whitman" ("The Last of Abinger," *Two Cheers for Democracy*, 256).

15. Henry Bryan Binns, *The Great Companions* (London: A. C. Fifield, 1908). For information about Binns, and an assessment of him as a biographer of Whitman, see Jerome Loving, "The Binns Biography," in Ed Folsom, ed., *Walt Whitman: The Centennial Essays* (Iowa City: University of Iowa Press, 1994), 10–18.

16. "Democracy," in Michael Herbert, ed., *Reflections on the Death of a Porcupine and Other Essays* (Cambridge: Cambridge University Press, 1988), 62–83.

17. Warren Roberts and Harry T. Moore, eds., *Phoenix II* (London: Heinemann, 1968), 105.

18. For a useful survey of the history of body-imaging, see Anthony Synnott, *The Body Social: Symbolism, Self and Society* (London: Routledge, 1993).

9. "What a Welshman You Would Have Been"

1. Floyd Stovall, ed., *Prose Works 1892* (New York: New York University Press, 1964), 2: 699–700. Whitman is referring specifically to the kindness of Rossetti and his friends who supported him through subscriptions in 1875 and 1876.

2. Joann P. Krieg, *Whitman and the Irish* (Iowa City: University of Iowa Press, 2000).

3. Tom Paulin, *Minotaur: Poetry and the Nation State* (London: Faber and Faber, 1992), 282.

4. University of Edinburgh, 1962–1963.

5. Robert Crawford, *Devolving English Literature* (Oxford: Clarendon Press, 1992), 179.

6. Susan Manning, *Fragments of Union* (Basingstoke, Eng.: Palgrave, 2002), 197.

7. See, though, M. Wynn Thomas, "From Walt to Waldo: Whitman's Welsh Admir-

ers," *Walt Whitman Quarterly Review* 10: 2 (Fall 1992), 61–73; M. Wynn Thomas, "Walt Whitman's Welsh Connection: Ernest Rhys," *The Anglo-Welsh Review* 82 (1986), 77–85. Some sections of the present chapter derive from these essays.

8. For the British Isles reaction to Whitman, see Harold Blodgett, *Walt Whitman in England* [*sic*] (Ithaca, NY: Cornell University Press, 1934; reprint, New York, Russell and Russell, 1973); Douglas Grant, "Walt Whitman and his English [*sic*] Admirers," (University of Leeds inaugural lecture: University of Leeds Press, 1962); the section on Britain in Gay Wilson Allen, *The New Walt Whitman Handbook* (New York: New York University Press, 1975); the section on *Leaves of Grass* in Benjamin Lease, *Anglo-American Encounters* (Cambridge: Cambridge University Press, 1981), 229–254; and the section on Whitman in the British Isles in Gay Wilson Allen and Ed Folsom, eds., *Walt Whitman and the World* (Iowa City: University of Iowa Press, 1995), 11–70. See also Clarence Gohdes, *American Literature in Nineteenth Century England* (Carbondale: Southern Illinois University Press, 1944).

9. Sidney Morse, "My Summer with Walt Whitman," in Horace L. Traubel, R. M. Bucke, Thomas B. Harned, eds., *In Re Walt Whitman* (Boston, MA: D. McKay 1893), 370.

10. The first reference to this appears to be in H. B. Binns, *The Life of Walt Whitman* (London: Methuen, 1905). The evidence for the claim remains unclear.

11. Horace Traubel, *With Walt Whitman in Camden*, vol. 1 (New York: Rowman and Littlefield, 1961 reprint), 452.

12. See Ernest Rhys, *Everyman Remembers* (London: Dent, 1931).

13. E. H. Miller, ed., *Walt Whitman, The Correspondence*, IV (New York: New York University Press, 1965), 69.

14. Horace Traubel, *With Walt Whitman in Camden*, vol. 2 (New York: Rowman and Littlefield, 1962 reprint), 28.

15. Gertrude Traubel and William White, eds., Horace Traubel, *With Walt Whitman in Camden*, vol. 6 (Carbondale, Edwardsville: Southern Illinois University Press, 1982), 13.

16. Ernest Rhys, *Wales England Wed: An Autobiography* (London: Dent, 1940), 69.

17. The fullest examination of the sociopolitical profile of the Bolton Group is in Paul Salveson, "Loving Comrades: Lancashire's Links to Walt Whitman," *Walt Whitman Quarterly Review* 14:2/3 (Fall 1996/Winter 1997), 56–84; also relevant is Joanna Krieg's essay, "Without Walt Whitman in Camden," in the same volume (85–112).

18. Ernest Rhys, *Black Horse Pit* (London: Robert Holden & Co., 1925), 6.

19. C. J. Furness, ed., *Walt Whitman's Workshop* (New York: Russell and Russell, 1964 reprint), 164.

20. John Kelly, ed., *The Collected Letters of W. B. Yeats* (Oxford: Clarendon Press, 1986), 338–339.

21. For pan-Celticism during this period, see the important article by Daniel Williams, "Pan-Celticism and the Limits of Post-Colonialism: W. B. Yeats, Ernest Rhys

and William Sharp in the 1890s," in Tony Brown and John Russell Stephens, eds., *Nations and Relations: Writing Across the British Isles* (Cardiff: New Welsh Review, 2000), 1–29. The Yeats quotation appears on p. 19.

22. See the discussions of Cymru Fydd in K. O. Morgan, *Rebirth of a Nation: Wales, 1880–1980* (Oxford: Clarendon Press, 1981).

23. *Young Wales: A National Magazine for Wales*, vol. 1, Jan.–Dec. 1895 (Aberystwyth: Cambrian News), 4. During the course of the year, the periodical printed an essay by Hugh R. Hughes, Chicago, on "Welsh Nationalism, Viewed from America" (125–127).

24. John Davies, *Hanes Cymru* (London: Penguin Press), 384–386.

25. *Llais Llafur* (September 5, 1903), 7. I am grateful to Jasmine Donahaye for bringing this parody to my attention.

26. The portrait of cultural life in the Amman Valley that follows is indebted at many points to Huw Walters, *Canu'r Pwll a'r Pulpud* (Denbigh: Gwasg Gee on behalf of Barddas, 1987). I am also grateful to Dr. Walters for drawing additional materials relating to Whitman to my attention.

27. His younger brother, James Griffith, also began life as a miner, but his trade union activities led to his becoming a Labour MP (of very long standing) for Llanelli. He went on to a highly distinguished political career, serving in the Cabinet first as colonial secretary (overseeing, in effect, the transition from Empire to Commonwealth) and then as the first secretary of state for Wales.

28. Amanwy, *Ambell Gainc* (no publisher and no date indicated), 77 (my translation). The volume is dedicated to the memory of his brother, Gwilym.

29. What follows is drawn in part from the entry in Meic Stephens, ed., *The Oxford Companion to the Literature of Wales* (Oxford: Oxford University Press, 1986).

30. His output totaled about a dozen volumes of poetry. Some of his work is available in English, in *Prison Sonnets* (London: W. Griffiths, 1948).

31. D. Ernest Williams, ed., *Dros Eich Gwlad: Cerddi Heddwch* (Pontardawe: T. E. Nicholas, 1920), 95–128 (my translation).

32. James Nicholas, *Waldo Williams* (Cardiff: University of Wales Press, 1975); Glyn Jones and John Rowlands, *Profiles* (Llandysul: Gomer Press, 1980). Also the entry on Waldo Williams in Stephens, *Companion*.

33. I am indebted to my uncle, the late Brinley Rees, and to Professor R. M. (Bobi) Jones for parts of the discussion that follow.

34. Bobi Jones, "Ei Ewythr Gwilamus," in Robert Rhys, ed., *Waldo Williams* (Aberystwyth: Gwasg Christopher Davies, 1981), 98–102.

35. Damian Walford Davies, *Waldo Williams: Rhyddiaith* (Cardiff: University of Wales Press, 2001), 151. Waldo may well have unconsciously been recalling Edmund Gosse's famous comment: "Whitman is literature in the condition of protoplasm—an intellectual organism so simple that it takes the instant impression of whatever mood approaches it" (*Critical Kit-Kat* [New York: Dodd, Mead, 1896], 96–111).

36. His eloquent testimony, in English, before the tribunal at Carmarthen is reprinted in Davies, *Rhyddiaith*, 292–293. Tantamount to a credo, it includes the following: "I believe all men to be brothers and to be humble partakers of the Divine Imagination that brought forth the world, and that now enables us to be born again into its own richness, by doing unto others as we would others to do unto us. War to me, is the most monstrous violation of the Spirit that society can devise . . . I believe Divine Sympathy to be the full self realization of the Imagination that brought forth the world. . . . I believe that the Spirit communes not with societies as such, but directly and singly with the souls of men and women, therefore enabling us to commune fully with each other, forming societies. I believe therefore that my first duty to the community to which I belong is to maintain the integrity of my own personality" (my translation).

37. Translation by Joseph P. Clancy, *Twentieth Century Welsh Poems* (Llandysul: Gomer Press, 1982), 135–136. For fine translations of a body of Williams's poetry, including "Mewn Dau Gae," see Tony Conran, *The Peacemakers: Waldo Williams* (Llandysul: Gomer Press, 1997).

38. Ned Thomas, *Waldo* (Caernarfon: Gwasg Gwynedd, 1986). The study is in Welsh.

39. An interesting discussion in English of Waldo's millenarianism can be found in Tony Bianchi, "Waldo and Apocalypse," *Planet* 44 (August 1978).

40. Meic Stephens, ed., selections from Glyn Jones's notebooks, *New Welsh Review* 29 (1995), 18.

41. Glyn Jones, *The Water Music and Other Stories* (London: Routledge, 1944, 1945 reprint), 161. Glyn Jones's short fiction is collected in Tony Brown, ed., *Collected Stories of Glyn Jones* (Cardiff: University of Wales Press, 1998).

42. M. Wynn Thomas, "Portraits of the Artist as a Young Welshman," *Corresponding Cultures: The Two Literatures of Wales* (Cardiff: University of Wales Press, 1999), 75–110.

43. Paul Ferris, ed., *Dylan Thomas, The Collected Letters* (London: Dent, 1985), 900.

44. Dylan Thomas, *Portrait of the Artist as a Young Dog* (London: Dent, 1956: Guild Books, No. 250), 18.

45. For other detailed considerations of Whitman's influence on Thomas, see Stanley Friedman, "Whitman and Laugharne," *Anglo-Welsh Review* 18 (1969), 81; Paul J. Ferlazzo, "Dylan Thomas and Walt Whitman: Birth, Death and Time," *Walt Whitman Review* 23 (1977), 136–141.

46. "Of Monkeys, Nudes, and the Good Gray Poet," in James E. Miller, Jr., Karl Shapiro, Bernice Slote, eds., *Start with the Sun: Studies in the Whitman Tradition* (Lincoln: University of Nebraska Press, 1960), 189.

47. Chris Wigginton, "'Birth and copulation and death': Gothic Modernism and Surrealism in the Poetry of Dylan Thomas," in John Goodby and Chris Wigginton, eds., *New Casebooks: Dylan Thomas* (London: Palgrave, 2001), 102.

48. Brian Davies, "Empire and Identity: The 'Case' of Dr William Price," in David Smith, ed., *A People and a Proletariat: Essays in the History of Wales, 1780–1980* (London: Pluto Press, 1980), 72–93.

49. See John L. Sweeney, *Introduction to Selected Writings by Dylan Thomas* (New York: New Directions, 1946), x, xv, xx, xxiii.

50. Rhys Davies, *Print of a Hare's Foot: An Autobiographical Beginning* (London: Heinemann, 1969), 23.

51. Karl Shapiro, "Dylan Thomas," in E. W. Tedlock, ed., *Dylan Thomas: The Legend and the Poet* (London; Heinemann, 1960).

52. M. Wynn Thomas and Daniel Williams, "'A Sweet Union?': Dylan Thomas and Postwar American Poetry," in Gilbert Bennett, Eryl Jenkins, Eurwen Price, eds., *I Sang in My Chains: A Tribute to Dylan Thomas* (Swansea: Dylan Thomas Society of Great Britain, 2003), 68–79.

53. For the different ways in which writers from Wales have imaged the United States see "Wales's American Dreams," in M. Wynn Thomas, *Corresponding Cultures.*

54. For R. S. Thomas's developing views on this and other subjects, see Sandra Anstey, ed., *R. S. Thomas: Selected Prose* (Bridgend: Seren, third edition, 1995).

55. The original typescript of this unpublished radio talk may be consulted in the archive of the R. S. Thomas Research Center, at University of Wales, Bangor. I am grateful to Dr. Jason Walford Davies and Dr. Tony Brown for bringing it to my attention.

56. Emyr Humphreys, *Collected Poems* (Cardiff: University of Wales Press, 1999), 96. For his poetry, see M. Wynn Thomas, "The Poetry of Emyr Humphreys," *Poetry Wales* 25: 2 (Summer 1989), 10–12.

57. For Emyr Humphreys's views on these and other matters see the essays and interviews collected in M. Wynn Thomas, ed., *Emyr Humphreys: Conversations and Reflections* (Cardiff: University of Wales Press, 2002).

58. Michael Cronin, *Across the Lines: Travel, Language, Translation* (Cork: Cork University Press, 2000), 2.

Index

THE IOWA WHITMAN SERIES

Intimate with Walt: Selections from Whitman's Conversations with Horace Traubel, 1888–1892, edited by Gary Schmidgall

The Pragmatic Whitman: Reimagining American Democracy, by Stephen John Mack

Transatlantic Connections: Whitman U.S., Whitman U.K., by M. Wynn Thomas

Visiting Walt: Poems Inspired by the Life and Work of Walt Whitman, edited by Sheila Coghill and Thom Tammaro

Walt Whitman and the Earth: A Study in Ecopoetics, by M. Jimmie Killingsworth

Walt Whitman: The Correspondence, Volume VII, edited by Ted Genoways

Whitman East and West: New Contexts for Reading Walt Whitman, edited by Ed Folsom